Lineberger Memorial
Library

ODD GIRLS AND TWILIGHT LOVERS

A History of Lesbian Life in Twentieth-Century America

LILLIAN FADERMAN

Columbia University Press
New York

Columbia University Press

New York   Oxford

Copyright © 1991 Lillian Faderman

Library of Congress Cataloging-in-Publication Data

Faderman, Lillian.
Odd girls and twilight lovers : a history of lesbian life
in twentieth-century America / Lillian Faderman.
p.   cm. — (Between men—between women)
ISBN 0–231–07488–3 (CL)
1. Lesbianism—United States—History—20th century. 2. Lesbians—United States—History—20th century. I. Title. II. Series.
HQ75.6.U5F33   1991   90–26327
306.76'63'0973—dc20   CIP

Casebound editions of Columbia University Press
books are Smyth-sewn and printed on permanent and
durable acid-free paper

Printed in the United States of America

c 10 9 8 7 6 5

Between Men~Between Women
Lesbian and Gay Studies

Richard D. Mohr, General Editor
Eugene F. Rice, Columbia University Advisor

Between Men ~ Between Women is a forum for current lesbian and gay scholarship in the humanities and social sciences. The series includes both books that rest within specific traditional disciplines and are substantially about gay men or lesbians and books that are interdisciplinary in ways that reveal new insights into gay and lesbian experience, transform traditional disciplinary methods in consequence of the perspectives that experience provides, or begin to establish lesbian and gay studies as a freestanding inquiry. Established to contribute to an increased understanding of lesbians and gay men, the series also aims to provide through that understanding a wider comprehension of culture in general.

Contents

Acknowledgments

A book of this nature could not be written without the generous help of many people and institutions. For assigned time to pursue my research and writing, I wish to thank the English Department at California State University, Fresno, and the former dean of the School of Arts and Humanities, Dr. Joseph Satin. For opening their doors to me, even at hours not always convenient to them, I am grateful to the staff of the Blanche Baker Memorial Library of the One Institute, the June L. Mazer Lesbian Collection in Los Angeles and the New York Lesbian Herstory Archives. My special thanks go to Degania Golove and Joan Nestle. For invaluable photographic and computer assistance I am grateful to Phyllis Irwin and Avrom Faderman. For arranging numerous interviews for me and often providing transportation and lodging and always support and encouragement, I thank Clare Freeman, Tracy Rappaport, and Peg Cruikshank in San Francisco; Sonia and Allison in New York; Olivia Sawyers, JoAnn, Margaret, and Ann in San Antonio; the women of Bookwoman and Dede in Austin; Sharon Young, Suzanne Valery, and River Malcom in San Diego; Alice and Jacki in Los Angeles; Mary Ann and Dena in Carson City; Sari Dworkin and Nancy in Fresno; Judy Carlson in Kansas City; Marsha Pelham and Tomi in Boston; Joy Letta Alice of Commonwoman Bookstore, and Kathleen Wingard in Lincoln, Nebraska; and Muriel Rada and Rhonda in Omaha. For their wonderful support when I needed it most, I thank my agent Sandra Dijkstra and my editor at Columbia University Press, Ann Miller. I am especially grateful to the women across the country who were willing to talk to me about their lives and gave me so many hours of their time.

Introduction

In 1843 the American author William Cullen Bryant wrote an essay for the *Evening Post* in which he glowingly described a trip to Vermont, where, among nature's beauties, he had the opportunity to observe a beautiful "female friendship" between two revered "maiden ladies." Bryant was not alone in his boundless admiration for the pair and the peaceful and loving relationship they established together, as he said when he gave their history:

> In their youthful days, they took each other as companions for life, and this union, no less sacred to them than the tie of marriage, has subsisted, in uninterrupted harmony, for 40 years, during which they have shared each others' occupations and pleasures and works of charity while in health, and watched over each other tenderly in sickness . . . .They slept on the same pillow and had a common purse, and adopted each others relations, and . . . I would tell you of their dwelling, encircled with roses, . . . and I would speak of the friendly attentions which their neighbors, people of kind hearts and simple manners, seem to take pleasure in bestowing upon them.[1]

If such a description of love between two women had been published in an American newpaper a century later, surely the editor's desk would have been piled high with correspondence about immorality in Vermont (slept on the same pillow!) and the two women in question would have felt constrained to sue Bryant for defamation of character in order to clear their good names. In 1843, however, the two ladies were flattered and the newspaper's readers were charmed.

What is apparent through this example and hundreds of others that have now been well documented by social historians is that women's intimate relationships were universally encouraged in centuries outside of our own. There were, of course, some limitations placed on those relationships as far as society was concerned. For instance, if an eligible male came along, the women were not to feel that they could send him on his way in favor of their romantic friendship; they were not to hope that they could find gainful employment to support such

a same-sex love relationship permanently or that they could usurp
any other male privileges in support of that relationship; and they
were not to intimate in any way that an erotic element might possibly
exist in their love for each other. Outside of those strictures, female
same-sex love—or "romantic friendship," as it was long called—was
a respected social institution in America.

What went on in secret between two women who were passionately attached to each other, as William Cullen Bryant's friends were,
is naturally more difficult to reconstruct than their contemporaries'
attitude toward what they thought they were seeing. There were few
women before our era who would have committed confessions regarding erotic exchanges to writing. Trial records indicate that females of the lower classes who were vulnerable to harassment by the
criminal courts sometimes had sexual relations with each other, but
there is no comparable record in America for "respectable" women.
One might speculate that since they generally lived in a culture that
sought to deny the possiblitity of women's autonomous sexuality,
many of them cultivated their own asexuality, and while they might
have kissed and hugged on the same pillow, their intimate relations
never crossed the boundary to the genitally sexual. But surely for
some of them kissing and hugging led eventually to other things and
their ways of loving each other were no different from what the
twentieth century would describe with certainty as "lesbian."

However, such a description of love between two women would
have been unlikely in earlier times because the concept barely existed.
While some outrageous, lawless women might have stooped to un-
speakable activity with other females, there was no such thing as a
"lesbian" as the twentieth century recognizes the term; there was
only the rare woman who behaved immorally, who was thought to
live far outside the pale of decent womanhood. It was not until the
second half of the nineteenth century that the *category* of the lesbian—
or the female sexual invert—was formulated. Once she was widely
recognized as an entity, however, relationships such as the one Bryant
described took on an entirely different meaning—not only as viewed
by society, but also as viewed by the two women who were involved.
They now had a set of concepts and questions (which were uncomfortable to many of them) by which they had to scrutinize feelings
that would have been seen as natural and even admirable in earlier
days.

Throughout much of the twentieth century those concepts and
questions about the "true meaning" of a woman's love for other

females were inescapable and demanded responses and justifications such as would have been undreamt of before. Unlike her earlier counterparts, through most of our century a woman who found herself passionately attached to another female was usually forced to react in one of four ways:

1). She could see her own same-sex attachment as having nothing to do with attachments between "real lesbians," since the sexologists who first identified lesbianism and brought the phenomenon to public attention said that lesbians were abnormal or sick, "men trapped in women's bodies," and she knew that she was not. Whether or not her relationship was sexual was insignificant. What was significant was that she could not—or she refused to—recognize her love for another woman in the sexologists' descriptions of lesbianism.

2). She could become so fearful of her feelings toward other women, which were now seen as unnatural, that she would force herself to repress them altogether, to deny even to herself that she was capable of passionate attachment to another female. She would retrain her psyche, or society would help her do it, so that heteroaffectionality alone would be attractive to her, and even the mere notion of physical or emotional attachment between females, such as her grandmothers and their ancestors enjoyed as a matter of course, would be utterly repulsive to her.

3). She could become so fearful, not of her own emotions but of her community's reaction to them, that she would spend her whole life in hiding ("in the closet," as that state came to be described in the mid-twentieth century), leading a double life, pretending to the world —to everyone but her female friend—that she was a stranger to the feelings that in fact claimed the better part of her emotional life.

4). She could accept the definitions of love between women that had been formulated by the sexologists and define herself as a lesbian. While such definitions would set her apart from the rest of woman-kind (even apart from other females who felt no differently emotion-ally and sometimes even physically about women than she did), they would also privilege her: acceptance would mean that she could live her attachment to women for the rest of her life, without having to acknowledge that a heterosexual relationship had precedence over her same-sex love; it would mean that she could—in fact, *must*—seek ways to become an economically and socially independent human being, since she could not rely on a male to support and defend her; and it would mean that she was free to seek out other women who also accepted such an identity and to form a lesbian subculture, such as could not have existed before love between women was defined as abnormal and unusual.

For most women, who were of course socialized not to challenge their culture's ideology about acceptable behavior, with the turn of the century began not only the death knell of romantic friendship (which might have been too simple to survive in our complex times anyway), but it was also the beginning of a lengthy period of general closing off of most affectional possibilities between women. The precious intimacies that adult females had been allowed to enjoy with each other earlier—sleeping in the same bed, holding hands, exchanging vows of eternal love, writing letters in the language of romance—became increasingly self-conscious and then rare. While such possibilities have been restored, to a greater or lesser extent, by the feminist movement of the last twenty years, history does not repeat itself. Love between women in the late twentieth century can no longer hide completely behind the veil of sexual innocence that characterized other centuries. Our era, through the legacy of Freud and all his spiritual offspring, is hyper-sophisticated concerning sex; thus whether or not two women who find themselves passionately attached choose to identify themselves as lesbian today, they must at least examine the possibility of sexual attraction between them and decide whether or not to act upon it. Such sexual self-consciousness could easily have been avoided in earlier eras.

But in earlier eras a lesbian identity, which many women now find viable, appropriate, and even healthy, would have been unattainable also. That identity is peculiar to the twentieth century and owes its start at least partly to those sexologists who attempted to separate off women who continued to love other women from the rest of humankind. The sexologists were certainly the first to construct the conception of the lesbian, to call her into being as a member of a special category. As the century progressed, however, women who agreed to identify themselves as lesbian felt more and more free to alter the sexologists' definitions to suit themselves, so that for many women "lesbianism" has become something vastly broader than what the sexologists could possibly have conceived of—having to do with lifestyle, ideology, the establishment of subcultures and institutions.

In fact, for these women, lesbianism generally has scant similarity to the early definitions of the sexologists. For instance, it has little to do with gender-dysphoria: those who see themselves as men trapped in women's bodies usually consider themselves as "transsexual" rather than lesbian, and modern medical technology has even permitted them to chose to alter their sex to be consonant with their self image. Lesbianism has nothing to do with morbidity: there are enough positive public images of the lesbian now and enough diverse communities so that lesbians are assured that they are at least as healthy as the heterosexual woman. Not even a sexual interest in other women is absolutely central to the evolving definition of lesbianism: a woman who has a sexual relationship with another woman is not necessarily lesbian—she may simply be experimenting; her attraction to a particular woman may be an anomaly in a life that is otherwise exclusively heterosexual; sex with other women may be nothing more than a part of a large sexual repertoire. On the other hand, women with little sexual interest in other females may nevertheless see themelves as lesbian as long as their energies are given to women's concerns and they are critical of the institution of heterosexuality. The criterion for identifying oneself as a lesbian has come to resemble the liberal criterion for identifying oneself as a Jew: you are one only if you consider yourself one.

The changing self-definitions of lesbians have evolved in the context of a changing society in which the smug conceptions of what is normal, natural, and socially permissible have been called into question for heterosexuality as well. There has been a relative social and sexual openness in America in the last couple of decades. That factor, coupled with a strong feminist movement that was very critical not only of men's treatment of women in society but also of their treatment of women in their own homes, has meant that more and more females were willing to consider themselves lesbians. Those women have had a tremendous effect not only on many who were lesbians before this era of social upheaval, "old gays," as they have been called, but also on those who do not consider themselves lesbians but who feel now that they can give themselves permission to form more loving and more physically affectionate relationships with women friends than their counterparts might have dared to do earlier in this century.

"Lesbianism" has not yet become a term that is as neutral as "romantic friendship" once was, but love between women appears to have begun the process of being rescued from the infamous status to which it was relegated for most of this century. Many women who identify themselves as heterosexual have been far more willing in the last twenty years to see other women as kindred spirits and battle allies than such women were throughout the earlier decades of the century, when females were socialized to believe that other women were their enemies and rivals. They now have more insight into what would make some females want to identify themselves as lesbians. They have helped create a new climate in which love between women is no longer accurately described as it was in the sensational pulp novels of the 1950s and early 1960s, in titles such as *Odd Girl Out* and *Twilight Lovers*. Love between women is no longer quite as "odd," the "twilight love," the love that dares not speak its name, as it had been for so long in our century. That new climate has also permitted self-definitions that transcend the stereotypes such as were characterized by the homophobic essayist of 1942 who argued that women should not be allowed to join the military because the only woman who would be attracted to such a pursuit would be the "naked amazons and queer damozels of Lesbos."[2]

This book is a history of these metamorphoses. I am concerned with tracing the evolution of love between women as it has been experienced in twentieth-century America, beginning with the institution of romantic friendship that reached a zenith around the turn of the last century, when middle-class women in large numbers were able to support themselves independently for the first time in our history. I am also concerned with how the theories of the sexologists filtered into popular consciousness, not coincidentally at about the same time that many jobs that had earlier been closed to women were opening up. I argue that the sexologists' theories helped to erode relationships that now threatened to be permanent and thus more "serious" than earlier romantic friendships, which had to give way to marriage when women had no means of support.

My examination of the demise of romantic friendships leads to a study of how some women constructed an identity and a subculture (and how they were frequently discouraged—by psychiatrists, the law, and public and familial pressure) in which they could express their love for other women. I focus particularly on the gradual establishment of lesbian subcultures in large cities; the relationship of class to the nature of those subcultures; the effects that all-female environments such as women's colleges, the military, and women's bars have had on the development of lesbianism; the ways in which feminism and gay liberation changed the view of love between women, both for lesbians and for society in general; and the forces that have moved female same-sex loving from the status of romantic friendship to sickness to twilight loves to women-identified-women, and that are gradually destigmatizing it, so that while it is not yet viewed as positively as romantic friendship was, it is becoming far more socially neutral, as even recent opinion polls indicate.[3]

The general movement of this book is in the direction of tracing the development of lesbian subcultures. But I have tried also to provide glimpses of lesbians who have remained outside of those subcultures, both historically and in the present, those whose lives were or are lived primarily or exclusively within heterosexual communities and who may be considered lesbian only by virtue of their secret sexual identification. My goal has not been to trace the development of "the lesbian." There is, of course, no such entity outside of the absurd constructions of textbook and pulp novel writers of the first half of the twentieth century. I have been interested rather in the metamorphoses and diversity of lesbians as they related individually and/or collectively to changing eras in American life.

Through my research methodology I hoped to be inclusive of the broadest spectrum of lesbian life, past and present. For the sections of this book dealing with the previous century or the earliest decades of this century obviously I had to rely on archives, journals, and other published materials to reconstruct the history of lesbian life in America. But for the chapters for which I could locate women to tell me about their experiences (beginning with the 1920s) I was anxious to do so, not only to round out the picture of lesbian life by a conscious attempt to look at class, age, ethnic, and geographical diversity, but also to provide this study with their living voices.

I conducted 186 unstructured interviews (lasting from two to four hours) in which I asked lesbians open-ended questions and permitted them to talk as long as they would (often digressively), in the hope of establishing what seemed important to them as lesbians: how they saw themselves and their sexuality, how they related (or did not relate) to the subcultures, what lesbianism meant to them. Through contacts in various states (New York, Massachusetts, Pennsylvania, Nebraska, Missouri, Texas, and California) who assisted me in setting up interviews, I spoke to a wide diversity of women, from the ages of 17 to 86; women who are white as well as those who are Asian, African American, Latina, and Native American; women who span the socio-economic spectrum from one who milks cows for a living in central California to another who is the primary heir of her grandfather, one of the richest oil men in West Texas; women who have established their lives right in the center of a lesbian community and those who have no contact or only the most peripheral contact with such a community.

The women I interviewed are, for the most part, self-identified lesbians, in keeping with my definition of post-1920s lesbianism: you are a lesbian if you say (at least to yourself) that you are. Of course such self-definitions were rare in the late nineteenth and early twentieth century, where I begin this book, since many women did not yet have the vocabulary or even a concept of lesbianism that was broad enough to encompass them. I have included such women in my study if it is clear through what can be traced of them that their emotional lives were primarily homoaffectional.

As will be revealed in the pages of this book, in the debate between the "essentialists" (who believe that one is born a lesbian and that there have always been lesbians in the past just as there are lesbians today) and the "social constructionists" (who believe that certain social conditions were necessary before "the lesbian" could emerge as a social entity) my own research has caused me to align myself on the side of the social constructionists. While I believe that some women, statistically very few, may have been "born different," i.e., genetically or hormonally "abnormal," the most convincing research I have been able to find indicates that such an anomaly is extremely rare among lesbians. Perhaps in the future studies will emerge that present compelling support for the essentialist position with regard to lesbianism, but such work does not exist at present.[4] A small number of the women I interviewed told me they were convinced that they were born men trapped in women's bodies; however, for the most part they suspected they were not lesbians but "transsexuals" (two of them had actually had sex change operations and are living as men). Others told me they were born lesbians, but what they said in the interview suggested to me that what they saw as the earliest signs of "lesbian feeling," erotic interest in other females, in most cases may not have been particularly different from the childhood crushes that even Freudians have described as being "normal" in the young. Their early "lesbian behavior" also seemed often to have amounted only to "inappropriate" gender behavior, a phenomenon that has been convincingly called into question by feminism.

Before women could live as lesbians the society in which they lived had to evolve to accommodate, however grudgingly, the possibility of lesbianism—the conception needed to be formulated; urbanization and its relative anonymity and population abundance were important; it was necessary that institutions be established where they could meet women with similar interests; it was helpful that the country enjoyed sufficient population growth so that pressure to procreate was not overwhelming; it was also helpful that the issues of sexuality and sexual freedom became increasingly open; and it was most crucial that women have the opportunity for economic self-sufficiency that would free them from the constant surveillance of family. The possibility of a life as a lesbian had to be socially constructed in order for women to be able to choose such a life. Thus it was not until our century that such a choice became viable for significant numbers of women. This book traces the ways that happened.

1

"The Loves of Women for Each Other": "Romantic Friends" in the Twentieth Century

The loves of women for each other grow more numerous each day, and I have pondered much why these things were. That so little should be said about them surprises me, for they are everywhere. . . . In these days, when any capable and careful women can honorably earn her own support, there is no village that has not its examples of "two hearts in counsel," both of which are feminine. —Frances E. Willard,
Glimpses of Fifty Years, 1889

Ah, how I love you, it paralyzes me—It makes me heavy with emotion. . . . I tremble at the thought of you—all my whole being leans out to you. . . . I dare not think of your arms. —Rose Elizabeth Cleveland to
Evangeline Simpson Whipple, 1890

Early twentieth-century women, particluarly those of the middle class, had grown up in a society where love between young females was considered the norm, "a rehearsal in girlhood of the great drama of woman's life," where women's love for one another was thought to "constitute the richness, consolation, and joy of their lives."[1] They could still envision their relationships as romantic friendship, and if sex entered into it they may have considered it somewhat irregular, but they did not feel compelled to spend too many daytime hours analyzing its implications.

Romantic friendship in Western society can be traced back hundreds of years, at least to the Renaissance. But it was just as sexologists in the latter part of the nineteenth century were grasping their pens to suggest that women who loved other women were abnormal that romantic friendship, especially in America, truly burgeoned. Its growth was stimulated by the increasing militancy of nineteenth-century feminists who were agitating together not only for suffrage but for more opportunities in education and the professions. Its development was fostered by their shared successes. By the end of the century, ambitious women of the middle class who loved other females no longer needed to resign themselves to marriage in order to survive. They could go to college, educate themselves for a profession, earn a living in a rewarding career, and spend their lives with the women they loved. Perhaps for the first time in history they could proclaim, as Enid does to her would-be male suitor in Florence Converse's 1897 novel, *Diana Victrix:*

> I am not domestic the way some women are. I shouldn't like to keep house and sew . . . It would bore me. I should hate it! Sylvia and I share the responsibility here, and the maid works faithfully. There are only a few rooms. We have time for our real work but a wife wouldn't have. . . . Please go away! I have chosen my life and I love it![2]

Thousands of women such as Enid and Sylvia now banded together in colleges and in various professions, and they created a society of what the nineteenth century and earlier had seen as romantic friends. But there were significant differences between the relationships of these women and those of their predecessors: since they could support themselves, they were no longer economically constrained to give up their female loves in favor of matrimony, and they now had plausible excuses to resist social pressure toward marriage—they could not be adequate wives because they were engaged in pioneering in education and the professions. For the first time in American history, large numbers of women could make their lives with another woman.

Those females who enjoyed such privileges were, for the most part, of middle- and upper-middle-class backgrounds. Among the rich higher education and professional pursuits were still considered entirely inappropriate for women, and among the poor there were no such options for many decades to come. Women from wealthy families who loved other women generally remained constrained to behave much as they would have in past centuries—they still suffered under tremendous and often inescapable pressure to marry "appropriately" at a proper age. And women from poor families who loved other women also continued to be limited. It was not easy for two working-class women to set up a home together on the wages they could earn through menial labor. Economically, long-term relationships continued to be most feasible between working-class women if one of them could pass as a male and get a man's wages for a man's work, as some had managed to do in earlier eras. But for women of the middle class, these new times made a whole new lifestyle possible.

The Educated "Spinster"

More than any other phenomenon, education may be said to have been responsible for the spread among middle-class women of what eventually came to be called lesbianism. Not only did it bring them together in large numbers within the women's colleges, but it also permitted them literally to invent new careers such as settlement house work and various kinds of betterment professions in which they could be gainfully and productively employed and to create all-female societies around those professions. Although these ramifications were undreamt of when the first real college for women, Mount Holyoke, was established in 1837, those who believed in the sacredness of stringent sex role behavior or were intent on keeping females chained to domesticity were quick to sniff danger even then. As one writer observed in *The Religious Magazine* that year, the new education for women meant that all that was "most attractive in female manners" would be replaced by characteristics "expressly formed for acting a *manly* part upon the theatre of life. . . . Under such influence the female character is fast becoming masculine." Despite warnings like that, women's colleges continued to proliferate. Vassar was founded in 1865, Smith in 1872, Wellesley in 1875, Bryn Mawr in 1886. In the 1870s several universities such as Cornell and the University of Michigan also began to open their doors to females. By 1880, forty thousand women, over a third of the higher education student population in America, were enrolled in colleges and universities and there were 153 American colleges that they could attend.[3]

But conservatives continued to be unhappy about the revolution in educational opportunities for females. Most of the attacks on women's higher education centered on the ways in which it would render them unfit for the traditional roles that the writers believed vital to the proper functioning of society. Dr. Edward Clarke, for example, whose 1873 book *Sex in Education: or, A Fair Chance for Girls* continued to be printed for the next two decades, warned that study would interfere with women's fertility, cursing them with uterine disease, amenorrhea, dysmenorrhea, chronic and acute ovaritis, and prolapsed uteri. Even into the twentieth century such writers, often imbued with racist and classist theories of eugenics, feared what they called "race suicide" and prophesied that since "the best [female] blood of American stock" went off to college and probably would not marry, the mothers of America would eventually all be "from the lower orders of society" and the country would be ruined.[4]

Even worse, some writers eventually came to fear (not without cause) a problem they hardly dared to express: that higher education for females, especially in all-women colleges, not only "masculinized" women but also made men dispensable to them and rendered women more attractive to one another. One author of the 1870s, alarmed perhaps by decadent French novels such as *Mademoiselle de Maupin* (about an adventuress who has affairs with men and women indiscriminately) that were being translated into English and by the writings of the sexologists that were just beginning to emerge, hinted in the pages of *Scribner's Monthly* at the sexual possibilities that might arise if large numbers of women had unlimited access to one another. However, he obviously did not feel free to be specific in his allegations:

> It is not necessary to go into particulars . . . [but] such a system is fearfully unsafe. The facts which substantiate [this] opinion would fill the public mind with horror if they were publicly known. Men may "pooh! pooh!" these facts if they choose, but they exist. Diseases of body, diseases of imagination, vices of body and imagination—everything we would save our children from—are bred in these great institutions where life and associations are circumscribed, as weeds are forced in hot beds.[5]

Perhaps understanding the potency of romantic friendship in nineteenth-century America, such writers could imagine where that sentiment might lead in the right (or rather, wrong) circumstances. They were not far from the mark, but for many young women these effects were fortunate rather than tragic.

Statistics corroborate that those who were interested in maintaining women in the narrow prison of heterosexuality as it was experienced by females in the nineteenth century were quite right in fearing the spread of higher education. Females who attended college were far less likely to marry than their uneducated counterparts. While only 10 percent of American women in general remained single between 1880 and 1900, about 50 percent of American college women at that time remained single. Fifty-seven percent of the Smith graduating class of 1884, at the height of women's excitement over their new-found opportunities in education and the professions, never married. Marriage statistics for Vassar and Mount Holyoke were similar. Many of the most successful alumnae of that era were "spinsters."[6]

Undoubtedly some of them never married because most men in that era feared educated females and would not dare take them as wives. But others never married because they preferred to continue what they discovered in their women's colleges—relationships with "kindred spirits," other women who were interested in following the same dreams, with whom they thought it was far more possible to have a loving connection of equals than it was with a man. Many of those women paired with other female college graduates to establish same-sex households—"Boston marriages," as they were sometimes called in the East where they were so common. Whether or not those relationships were usually sexual cannot be definitively known, but they were often clearly love relationships. The nineteenth century, observing them from the outside, would have called them romantic friendships. Eventually the twentieth century would come to call such relationships lesbian. But to most of those women themselves, who were on the historical cusp in this regard, the former term would have been anachronistic and the latter unacceptable.

Such same-sex relationships were far more preferable and even practical for many women than any form of heterosexuality would have been. As middle-class women who were born into the Victorian era, they could not with ease have indulged in affairs with men outside of wedlock. While some scholars have suggested that Victorian women's "sexual restraint" existed more in ideology than fact, the evidence seems to support that position primarily with regard to sex within marriage.[7]

Outside of marriage, women were still constrained by the double standard, which denigrated females who "slipped" sexually and made them pay. Wisdom had it that women could not trust men, since the "weaker sex" would always be at a disadvantage in the battle of the sexes. The *Ladies Home Journal* advised unmarried women in 1892: "Young men soon lose respect for a girl exactly in proportion as she allows them familiarity." Such observations were not the purview of prescriptive literature alone. For example, in her book *Hands and Hearts: A History of Courtship in America*, Ellen Rothman quotes a letter from a woman of the period complaining that females are in danger if they dare even to expose their feelings to the opposite sex: "Woman should never confess her love lest the object of it . . . take advantage of [her]." And if an unmarried woman did let herself be "taken advantage of," she was lost as a social being. Frances Willard, whose encomium to love between women opens this chapter, was undoubtedly typical in her response to a college classmate who was rumored to have had male lovers:

> A young woman who was not chaste came to [college] through some misrepresentations, but was speedily dismissed. Not knowing her degraded status I was speaking to her when a schoolmate whispered a few words of explanation that crimsoned my face suddenly: and grasping my dress lest its hem should touch the garments of one so morally polluted, I fled the room.

In fantastic contrast to the situation that prevailed on American campuses in the middle of the twentieth century, in the nineteenth century it was far better socially for a woman to have been a lover of women.[8]

As pioneering females with ambition, these women understood well that marriage would most likely interfere with their self-realization. Marriage was seldom feasible for them, not only because the demands of running a home and bearing children at that time made any other pursuit all but impossible, but also because there were few husbands who could be expected to sacrifice their historically entrenched male prerogatives to revolutionary female notions. Those pioneering women who did marry generally selected very atypical men. Perhaps something of an extreme, Carrie Chapman Catt, who even married a second time after she was widowed at the age of 27, was specific about what she needed to make a heterosexual relationship palatable to her. Her second marriage lasted for fifteen years, until George Catt's death, but during their marriage they seldom lived together, since she was busy pursuing voting rights for women. She claimed that her husband, who left her a sizable income to continue her pursuits even after his death, had said to her, "I am as earnest a reformer as you are, but we must live. Therefore, I will earn the living for two and you will do reform work for both." She added, "The result was that I was able to give 365 days work each year for 50 years without a salary."

It is interesting to note that regardless of what her arrangement with her husband really was, Carrie Chapman Catt still turned to romantic friendships with women for sustenance. Her correspondence with Mary Peck, another active suffragist, suggests the intensity and sensual playfulness of their affectional relationship. For example, Mary Peck would write to her: "Goodnight, darling, beautiful, glorious, priceless, peerless, unutterably precious Pandora. . . . I love you ardently." Carrie would respond to her extravagances: "You wrote another letter concerning the charm of my lower lip! I took a day off and went cavorting from mirror to mirror and grinning like a Cheshire cat in hope of catching that 'haunting smile.' " Carrie lived with another woman, Molly Hay, for twenty years after George Catt died. It is with Molly rather than with either of her husbands that she declared she wished to be buried. One tombstone covers them both.[9]

But for the most part, these pioneering women did not marry. The observation of Harriet Hosmer, the nineteenth-century sculptor, applied not just to artists but to any women with dreams of a career:

> Even if so inclined, an artist has no business to marry. For a man it may be well enough, but for a woman, on whom matrimonial duties and cares weigh more heavily, it is a moral wrong, I think, for she must either neglect her profession or her family, becoming neither a good wife and mother nor a good artist. My ambition is to become the latter, so I wage eternal feud with the consolidating knot.

Hosmer was not, however, unwilling to tie a consolidating knot with another female, and many other professional women, into the twentieth century, shared her perspective.[10] There were few role models to show them that it was possible to combine marriage and career. It must have seemed to many of those pioneering women that a renunciation of marriage was demanded of them no less than it was of a nun. Yet such a renunciation did not preclude a relationship with another woman.

Of course many of those early professional women did not necessarily feel they were making a sacrifice in relinquishing marriage. Their choice to follow a profession may even have served as an excuse to remain heterosexually celibate. Since society generally agreed that marriage and career were incompatible for a woman, those who found marriage distasteful and preferred to live with another female realized that they would be granted social license to arrange their lives as they pleased if they pursued an education and a profession. Many of them would have well understood M. Carey Thomas (the pioneering president of Bryn Mawr) when she wrote of a male suitor: "I should, I think, have committed suicide if I had to live with him. But my choice was made easy by the fact that in my generation marriage and academic career was impossible."[11]

But even those who did not realize before they elected their revolutionary paths that they preferred to make their lives with other females often found that a "Boston marriage" had great advantages. It was not only that heterosexual marriage would have closed off possibilities for a professional life and heterosexual affairs would have been socially unacceptable. These career women's relationships with other females were not simply *faute de mieux*. At their best, same-sex "marriages" offered a communion of kindred spirits such as romantic friends of other eras had longed for. They could be not only nurturing relationships but also relationships of equals in terms of finances, responsibilities, decision-making—all areas in which the husband claimed precedence and advantage in heterosexual marriage. They potentially fostered rather than interfered with the heady and exciting new ambitions of the early generations of professional women. Coming from a tradition of romantic friendship between women that was widespread in America since the country's beginnings, being generally unaware that same-sex relationships were already being called "abnormal" and "unhealthy" among sexologists, knowing that for practical reasons they must not marry if they wanted careers, it was probably neither morally nor emotionally difficult for these women to attach themselves to each other.

The Metamorphosis of Romantic Friendship

While romantic friendship had had a long history in Western civilization, it took on particular significance in nineteenth-century America, where men's spheres and women's spheres became so divided through the task of nation building. Men saw themselves as needing the assistance of other men to realize their great material passions, and they fostered "muscle values" and "rational values," to the exclusion of women. Women, left to themselves outside of their household duties, found kindred spirits primarily in each other. They banded together and fostered "heart values." When nineteenth-century women began to engage in reform and betterment work, they were confirmed in their belief that females were morally superior to men and that their sensibilities were more refined.[12] Nevertheless, as long as the facts of economic and social life pushed them to move directly from their father's house to a husband's house, the bonds they formed with each other ultimately had to be secondary to familial concerns. But for many of them college changed that path.

Before the advent of women's colleges, there had been female seminaries in America, but their emphasis was on equipping young middle-class females only with what they needed to become admirable adornments in the home. The new women's colleges generally aimed to give them an education that went beyond domestic refinements and that challenged their minds in ways not unlike education for men. That education opened up an entirely new world, permitting some women to set their sights much higher than their predecessors could have conceived. Many women before them must have dreamed about ways to defy the usual lot of the female, yet short of passing as a man (see pp. 42–45), which could have little appeal for well-brought-up middle-class young ladies, there seemed no escape from stagnating nineteenth-century domesticity. College women found an escape.

But it was not the facts of their education alone that permitted those who wanted an alternative to domesticity to create one. Rather, it was that the young women's relationships with one another while away at college helped to make them new people. With or without the administration's or their families' blessings, college allowed them to form a peer culture unfettered by parental dictates, to create their own hierarchy of values, and to become their own heroes and leaders, since there were no male measuring sticks around to distract, define, or detract. In those ways the early women's colleges created a healthy and productive separatism such as radical lesbian-feminists of the 1970s might have envied. But unlike the 1970s radicals, the earlier women managed to fashion that separatism from institutions that were handed to them by the parent culture. They manipulated those institutions to their own needs and ends.

Perhaps the most important element in encouraging young college women in their escape from domesticity was a new form of what had been termed romantic friendship, which came to be called in college life "smashes," "crushes," and "spoons." These passions were even described in an 1873 Yale student newspaper, obviously without any awareness that relationships of that nature might have sexual undertones, or that elements of them were already being seen as "inversion" by some European sexologists (see pp. 39–40): "When a Vassar girl takes a shine to another," the Yalie observed, "she straightway enters upon a regular course of bouquet sendings, interspersed with tinted notes, mysterious packages of 'Ridley's Mixed Candies,' locks of hair perhaps, and many other tender tokens, until at last the object of her attentions is captured, the two women become inseparable, and the aggressor is considered by her circle of acquaintances as—*smashed*."[13]

Such mores and passions in women's colleges did not die with the end of the century. Romantic all-women dances were held in the early twentieth century by colleges such as Vassar and Smith, as described by the *Cosmopolitan Magazine* in a 1901 article entitled "A Girl's College Life," where the writer observed that the older student generally played "the cavalier" for the younger student:

> She sends her flowers, calls for her, fills her order of dance, . . . takes her to supper, sees her partner home. . . . And if the freshman has made the desired hit, there are dates for future meetings and jollifications and a good night over the balusters, as lingering and cordial as any the freshman has left behind.

The young women took these dances very seriously, as a veteran of such socials, Josephine Dodge Daskam, suggested in her early twentieth-century collection *Smith College Stories*. She decribes one student having delightful "visions of the pretty little freshman" whose name would fill out her dance program and another student who in disappointment over her date "cried herself to sleep for she had dreamed for nights of going with Suzanne, whom she admired to stupefaction." The writers were not disposed to speculate on the fact, but such courting often led to "lovemaking," both in the sense of the nineteenth-century sentimental usage of that term and the way we use that term today.[14]

Although romantic friendships were not yet uncommon outside of women's colleges, such passions were encouraged even more strongly in an academic setting, since females could meet each other there in large numbers and the colleges afforded them the leisure necessary to cultivate those relationships. With men living in a distant universe outside of their female world and the values of that distant universe suspended in favor of new values that emerged from their new settings, young women fell in love with each other. They became academic, athletic, and social heroes to one another; they shared a vast excitement and sense of mission about their mutual roles in creating new possibilities for women; they banded together against a world that was still largely unsympathetic to the opening of education and the professions to women. How could such excitements not lead to passionate loves at a time when there was not yet widespread stigma against intense female same-sex relationships?

Young college women also soon had role models for romantic friendships in their female professors, since the colleges often required faculty to reside on campus. Many chose to live in pairs and remained in pairs their entire lives. They pointed the direction to a new path, too, because they were self-supporting. Unlike the women in the students' previous environment, they did not have to marry in order to survive economically. Once the young women left college, however, they often felt adrift in a world that was not yet prepared to receive them. Sex solidarity became to them necessary armor against a hostile environment. They formed networks with one another, served as mentors for one another, and encouraged and applauded one another's successes, knowing that they could not trust to males (who were still jealous of what they perceived as their own territory) to be thrilled about women's achievements. But even more important than those networks, they formed intense and lifelong love relationships—"marriages"—with each other.[15]

They needed all the armor they could get, since when they entered the professions they had been trained for they frequently encountered a huge battle because of their sex. The more they succeeded the more difficulty they had. Dr. Sarah Josephine Baker, for example, a health commissioner for the city of New York in the early twentieth century (who lived in two successive Boston marriages), was told to print her name on stationery as "Dr. S. J. Baker" so the Health Department could "disguise the presence of a woman in a responsible executive post." These early professional women often felt themselves forced into dress and behavior that was also characterized as "masculine." Dr. Baker wore "man-tailored suits," shirtwaists, stiff collars and four-in-hand ties to work, not necessarily because that was her preference but rather because, as she described it: "I badly needed protective coloring . . . [so that] when a masculine colleague of mine looked around the office in a rather critical state of mind, no feminine furbelows would catch his eye and give him an excuse to become irritated by the presence of a woman where, according to him, a woman had no right to be. . . . I wore a costume—almost a uniform—because the last thing I wanted was to be conspicuously feminine when working with men."[16] "Butch drag," professional-woman style, served as armor to deflect the arrows of sexism for those early generations of career women.

Katherine Anne Porter has described such women as "a company of Amazons" that nineteenth century America produced among its many prodigies:

> Not-men, not-women, answerable to no function of either sex, whose careers were carried on, and how successfully, in whatever field they chose: They were educators, writers, editors, politicians, artists, world travellers, and international hostesses, who lived in public and by the

public and played out their self-assumed, self-created roles in such masterly freedom as only a few medieval queens had equalled. Freedom to them meant precisely freedom from men and their stuffy rules for women. They usurped with a high hand the traditional privileges of movement, choice, and the use of direct, personal power.[17]

Porter was wrong in seeing them as "not-men, not-women." They were indeed women, but not of the old mold. Out of the darkness of the nineteenth century they miraculously created a new and sadly short-lived definition of a woman who could do anything, be anything, go anywhere she pleased. Porter was half-right in seeing the importance to them in having "freedom from men and their stuffy rules for women." But writing in 1947, eons removed from the institution of romantic friendship with which those women had been intimately familiar, Porter was unable to assess how crucially important it also was to them to be tied to another like-minded soul. In giving up men they relinquished not only wifehood and motherhood, but a life of subordination and dependence. In selecting other women they chose not only a relationship of equals but one of shared frustrations, experiences, interests, and goals with which only the most saintly of nineteenth- and early twentieth-century men could have sympathized. Such private sharing was essential to these women, who often found themselves quite alone in uncharted territory. They could endure their trials as pioneers in the outside world much better knowing that their life partner understood those trials completely because she suffered them, too.

"Poets and Lovers Evermore"

In a poem of the 1890s two Englishwomen, Katharine Bradley and Edith Cooper, "romantic friends" who wrote twenty-five plays and eight books of poetry together under the pseudonym Michael Field, declared of themselves: "My love and I took hands and swore/ Against the world to be/ Poets and lovers evermore."[18] Many early professional women in America also clasped hands and swore, generally not to be poets together, but often to be doctors, professors, ministers, union organizers, social workers, or pacifist lecturers together—and "lovers evermore."

They were often barred from those careers that had long been male preserves. But fueled by the power they gave each other, they could establish their own professions in teaching and administration at women's colleges, founding and serving in settlement houses, establishing and running institutions for social and political reform, and bringing reform concerns to existing institutions. In these ways thousands of them were able to serve their own needs to be financially independent and creatively employed, as well as their social and political interests in betterment such as had concerned women of their class since the fiery mid-nineteenth-century women abolitionists saw the necessity for female participation in reform work. Perhaps they were able to play roles of prominence as professional figures despite the prevalent opinion that woman's place was in the home because what they did could often be seen as housekeeping on a large scale—teaching, nurturing, healing—domestic duties brought into the public sphere. They were eventually able to convince great portions of the country—particularly the East and Midwest—that the growing horrors perpetrated by industrialization and urbanization begged to be cured by their mass mothering skills.

But in creating jobs for themselves through their skills they achieved the economic freedom (such as their middle class counterparts in the past never could) to live as what the later twentieth century would consider lesbians, though the early twentieth century was still reluctant to attribute sexuality to such proper-seeming maiden ladies and would have preferred to describe them, as historian Judith Schwarz has pointed out, as "close friends and devoted companions." Whether or not their relationships were specifically sexual, had they lived today they would at least have been described as falling somewhere on what Adrienne Rich has called the "lesbian continuum." Their numbers included Emily Blackwell, the pioneering physician and cofounder of the Women's Medical College of the New York Infirmary, and the woman she lived with for almost thirty years until her death in 1910, Elizabeth Cushier, an eminent gynecological surgeon; renowned biographer Katharine Anthony and progressive educator Elisabeth Irwin, who developed a teaching system for the New York schools and with whom Anthony raised several adopted children in the course of a thirty year relationship; pairs of women such as Mary Dreir and Lenora O'Reilly, and Helen Marot and Caroline Pratt, who lived most of their adult lives together and organized the Women's Trade Union League, spearheading its battles to regulate women's hours in factories, fighting clothing and cigar sweatshops, forcing the appointment of women factory inspectors; Vida Scudder, who was a professor at Wellesley but fled from Back Bay Boston privilege to identify herself with the tenement population, establishing the Rivington Street Settlement House and founding the College Settlements Association to bring libraries, summer schools, trade unions, and "culture" into poor communities, and whose "devoted companion" was Florence Converse, a professor and novelist; Frances Witherspoon, head of the New York Women's Peace Party, co-founder of the New York Bureau of Legal Advice for conscientious objectors, and Tracy Mygatt, with whom she lived her entire adult life and with whom she built the War Resisters League into a large and strong pacifist organization. The list of female contributors to twentieth-century social progress and decency who constructed their personal lives around other women is endless.[19]

Some of those women were cultural feminists, fueled by their belief that male values created the tragedies connected with industrialization, war, and mindless urbanization and that it was the responsibility of women, with their superior sensibilities, to straighten the world out again. Their love of women was at least in part the result of their moral chauvinism. Others were less convinced of women's natural superiority, but they wanted to wrest from society the opportunities and training that would give women the advantages men had and thus permit them to be more whole as human beings. Their love of women was at least in part a search for allies to help wage the battle against women's social impoverishment. Jane Addams, founder of the Hull House Settlement, president of the Women's International League for Peace and Freedom, and Nobel Peace Prize winner, and M. Carey Thomas, president of Bryn Mawr, founder of the Summer School for Women in Industry to serve urban working women, and first president of the National College Women's Equal Suffrage League, represent these two different types. They are similar, however, in that they both managed to find kindred spirits, "devoted companions," who would work with them to promote the success of their endeavors.

Twentieth-century biographers have had a hard time trying to pin heterosexual interests to them. Jane Addams found her family's efforts to launch her as a debutante and marry her to her stepbrother extremely distasteful. Those attempts, Addams recalled in her autobiography, led to "the nadir of my nervous depression and sense of maladjustment," from which she was extricated by Ellen Starr, whom she met in college. Ellen appears to have been Jane's first serious attachment. For years they celebrated September 11—even when they were apart—as the anniversary of their first meeting. During their separations Jane stationed Ellen's picture, as she wrote her, "where I can see you almost every minute." It was Ellen who prodded Jane to leave her family, come to Chicago, and open Hull House together with her. On accepting the plan Jane wrote Ellen: "Let's love each other through thick and thin and work out a salvation." It was Ellen's devotion and emotional support that permitted Jane to cast off the self-doubts that had been plaguing her as a female who wanted to be both socially useful and independent during unsympathetic times and to commit herself to action: to create a settlement house in the midst of poverty where young, comfortably brought-up women who had spent years in study might now "learn of life from life itself," as Addams later wrote. Under the guidance initially of both Addams and Starr these females of the leisure class investigated sweatshops and the dangerous trades and agitated for social reforms, helped newly arrived immigrants learn to make America their home, taught skills, and promoted cultural activities. They changed the lives of the poor and were themselves changed by their confrontation with realities from which they had always been sheltered.[20]

While providing such opportunities for these young women Jane Addams also lived a personal life that most biographers have attempted to gloss over, since the facts have made them uncomfortable. For example, although it is known that Jane and wealthy philanthropist Mary Rozet Smith, who later became her "devoted companion" (as biographers must acknowledge), always slept in the same room and the same bed, and when they traveled Jane even wired ahead to be sure they would get a hotel room with a double bed, nevertheless most historians have preferred to present Addams as asexual. William O'Neill says of her:

> She gave her time, money and talents to the interests of the poor . . . and remained largely untouched by the passionate currents that swirled around her. The crowning irony of Jane Addams' life, therefore, was that she compromised her intellect for the sake of human experiences which her nature prevented her from having. Life, as she meant the term, eluded her forever.

Perhaps "Life," as O'Neill and other historians have meant the term (i.e., heterosexuality, marriage, family), eluded Addams, but love and passion did not. Similarly, Allen Davis has tried to explain away what he benightedly calls appearances of "perversion" in Jane Addams' same-sex intimacies as being instead typical of nineteenth-century "innocent" sentimental friendship. As Blanche Cook points out, Addams was a "conventional lady with pearls," and erotic passion between women has been considered perversion: the two concepts cannot be reconciled easily. But looking at the available facts, there can be no doubt that Addams was passionately involved with at least two women.[21]

Although Ellen Starr continued to work alongside Jane and to live at Hull House for many years, the early intensity of their relationship dwindled, and Mary Rozet Smith replaced Ellen in Jane's affections. Jane's relationship with Mary lasted forty years. Mary first came to Hull House in 1890 as another wealthy young lady anxious to make herself useful. In the initial correspondence between Jane and Mary, Jane always brought in Ellen, using the first person plural, writing, for example, "We will miss you." But soon Ellen dropped out of the letters, and by 1893 Mary became a traveling companion on Jane's lecture tours. Two years later Ellen went off to England alone to study bookbinding so that she could learn to construct a bookbindery at Hull House according to the plans of English socialist-aesthete William Morris and to provide artistic work for the community. The intimate side of her relationship with Jane was by then clearly over.[22]

Mary Smith and Jane Addams seem to have confided about their feelings for each other to confederates such as Florence Kelley, who wrote Mary at one separation in 1899: "The Lady [Jane] misses you more than the uninitiated would think she had time for." Letters to each other when they were separated because of Jane's busy schedule speak for themselves. Mary wrote Jane: "You can never know what it is to me to have had you and to have you now." Jane addressed her "My Ever Dear" and wrote: "I miss you dreadfully and am yours 'til death." They thought of themselves as wedded. In a 1902 letter, written during a three-week separation, Jane remarked: "You must know, dear, how I long for you all the time, and especially during the last three weeks. There is reason in the habit of married folks keeping together." In 1904 they purchased a home together near Bar Harbor, Maine. "Our house—it quite gives me a thrill to write the word," Jane told Mary. "It was our house wasn't it in a really truly ownership," and she talked about their "healing domesticity."[23]

The fact of their intimacy is confirmed no more by the knowledge that they always shared a double bed together than it is by a poem that Jane wrote Mary at the end of the century recalling their first meeting:

One day I came into Hull House,
　(No spirit whispered who was there)
And in the kindergarten room
　There sat upon a childish chair
A girl, both tall and fair to see,
　(To look at her gives one a thrill).
But all I thought was, would she be
　Best fitted to lead club, or drill?
You see, I had forgotten Love,
　And only thought of Hull House then.

That is the way with women folks
　When they attempt the things of men;
They grow intense, and love the thing
　Which they so tenderly do rear,
And think that nothing lies beyond
　Which claims from them a smile or tear.
Like mothers who work long and late
　To rear their children fittingly,
Follow them only with their eyes,
　And love them almost pityingly,
So I was blind and deaf those years
　To all save one absorbing care,
And did not guess what now I know—
　Delivering love was sitting there![4]

Despite her absorption in Hull House, Jane Addams needed personal love, and to get it from a man was impossible, not only because that would have violated her inclinations but especially because it would have made her great work unfeasible. Mary Rozet Smith fulfilled Jane's personal needs and contributed to her work through her wealth, her time and effort, and especially her supportive love.

Allen Davis tells of having spoken about the relationships between women at Hull House with Dr. Alice Hamilton, a ninety- year-old woman at the time of the interview in 1963, who had served there during the early years. As might be expected, Dr. Hamilton denied that there was any open lesbianism between Hull House residents but did agree that "the close relationship of the women involved an unconscious sexuality." She hastened to interject that because it was unconscious it was "unimportant." Davis reports: "Then she added with a smile that the very fact that I would bring the subject up was an indication of the separation between my generation and hers."[25]

But more significant differences in views toward sexuality are revealed here as well. It would seem that Jane and Mary, who became "lovers" near the turn of the century, did not fear they had much to hide—they could even allow strange hotel keepers to know that they preferred to sleep in a double bed together. They understood (regardless of the sexual nature of their realtionship) that they could rely on the protective coloring of pearls and ladylike appearance and of romantic friendship, which was not yet dead in America since the works of the sexologists were not yet widely known. Dr. Hamilton's response points up how lesbianism fared later in the century, once the public became more knowledgeable about the horrors of "perversion." She implies that if love between women were expressed erotically by those who worked at Hull House that would have been unworthy of their noble undertaking, although she grants the existence of "unconscious" sexuality for which one cannot be held responsible, a Freudian concept of the 1920s that would have perplexed the 1890s. Finally, Davis' blunt posing of the question to Dr. Hamilton in the 1960s, as compared to her veiled answer, indicates the greater freedom of more recent generations to discuss unconventional sexuality, yet Davis' tone suggests his own felt need to rescue his "American Heroine," as he calls Addams in his 1973 book, from "nasty imputation." It is only in the last few years that we can acknowledge, without the fact diminishing her stature, that Jane Addams—whether or not she knew to use the term about herself— was what our day would consider lesbian. She devoted her entire emotional life to women, she considered herself married to a woman, and she believed that she was "delivered" by their shared love.

M. Carey Thomas was a very different kind of feminist. Unlike Jane Addams, a cultural feminist, Thomas' philosophical thrust was not in demonstrating that women could redeem the world because they were different from and better than men, but rather in showing how they were like men, as good as men, and hence deserving of equal treatment. Under her leadership as president of Bryn Mawr, the school provided training for women that was a great departure from women's education in female seminaries and other colleges that still claimed as a rationale for their existence "educate women and you educate the mothers of men." Thomas was determined instead to show that "girls can learn, can reason, can compete with men in the grand fields of literature, science and conjecture."[26] She wanted to produce hard-driving professional women in her own image to invade all the worthwhile pursuits that had been closed to women before. Thanks to Carey Thomas, Bryn Mawr students, unlike those at other women's colleges, were not even expected to care for their own rooms. All was done for them so that they could spend their time being scholars, just as male students could, and the curriculum was modeled on that of the best of the men's colleges.

Carey Thomas was able to realize her childhood dreams as most women before her could not. She had written of having read Michelet's misogynist work *La Femme* as a girl and being blinded by tears: "I was beside myself with terror lest it might prove true that I myself was so vile and pathological a thing." She even begged God to kill her if she could never learn Greek and go to college. She declared early, with unshakable conviction: "I ain't going to get married and I don't want to teach school. I can't imagine anything worse than living a regular young lady's life. . . . I don't care if everybody would cut me." There must have been many young women in Victorian America who felt as she did, but it was she who was the pioneer who provided for other women a path to a real alternative to domesticity, just as she had managed to find that path herself.[27]

Even as an adolescent, Carey had written to her closest friend, Bessie King (they renamed themselves Rex and Rush because they saw that only men were permitted to do interesting things), of her dream that they would become scholars together and be together forever, surrounded by a library with "great big easy chairs where we could sit lost in books for days together," a laboratory for scientific experiments, and "a great large table covered with papers." Inextricably bound up with this vision was her fantasy of female love and mutual support, since she knew there was no way such dreams could be realized if she married a man:

> There we would live loving each other and urging each other on to every high and noble deed or action, and all who passed should say "Their example arouses me, their booksennoble me, their ideas inspire me, and behold they are women!"[28]

Her early education in the 1860s and '70s gave her no reason to believe that such an attachment that would foster both love and productivity was not possible. Her journals show that her years at a Quaker boarding school for girls and then at Cornell provided her with trial experiments on her ideas about female attachments. Nor did her society, still approving of romantic friendship, discourage her. The girls at the Quaker boarding school explained to her simply that she and a fellow student had "smashed on each other or 'made love'. . . . I only know it was elegant," she decided. At the age of twenty-three she complained to her mother, "If it were only possible for women to elect women as well as men for a life's love! . . . It *is* possible but if families would only regard it in that light." Both her Quaker mother and aunt responded to her admission of love for other females by writing her, "[We] guess thy feeling is quite natural. [We] used to have the same romantic love for our friends. It is a real pleasure."[29]

But despite her understanding female relatives, Carey Thomas had to battle her father for the right to a college education. In fact, most of her upper-class Baltimore family believed that her desire was "as shocking a choice as a life of prostitution." While middle-class girls were going to college in 1874, when Carey begged to, daughters of the wealthiest families were supposed to go on a grand tour of Europe instead, before they settled down in marriage.

After finally being allowed to attend Cornell (she spurned Vassar as an "advanced female seminary"), she attempted to get a graduate degree from Johns Hopkins but was denied entrance to the classrooms. In 1879, accompanied by Mamie Gwinn, her "devoted companion," Carey went off to Europe to study and received a Ph.D. from the University of Zurich in 1882. Both then came to Bryn Mawr to teach, and Carey was soon appointed dean. Mamie lived with her at the deanery until 1904, when Mamie mysteriously altered her powerful animosity toward males, which had surpassed that of the most militant feminists, and ran off with a philosophy professor who was a married man.[30]

But long before that, Mary Garrett, a millionaire philanthropist, had fallen in love with Carey and promised the Bryn Mawr trustees she would donate a fortune to the college if they would promote Carey Thomas to president. They did so in 1894, when Carey was 37 years old. Upon Mamie's departure Mary moved in with Carey on the Bryn Mawr campus, and the two shared a home until Mary Garrett's death in 1915.

Together, with the help of Mary's fortune, they promoted wildly controversial feminist causes such as endowing Johns Hopkins with a medical school under the stipulation that women be admitted on an equal footing with men. There can be no doubt that the relationship was what M. Carey Thomas had dreamed of as a girl: one between two women who loved each other and had great work to pursue. She acknowledged Mary as the source of her "greatest happiness" and the one who was responsible for her "ability to do work." Nor was the fleshly aspect missing, as Carey wrote to her "lover": "A word or a photo does all, and the pulses beat and heart longs in the same old way."[31]

Despite their opposite visions of female aptitudes and uses, Jane Addams and M. Carey Thomas each exemplified what turn-of-the-century women who were devoted to other women, both personally and professionally, could accomplish in the best of circumstances. Of course they had remarkable advantages: they came from wealthy families; they formed relationships with even wealthier women who used their money to aid in the pursuits Addams and Thomas held dear; during their younger years romantic friendship was not yet scoffed at and people would have been incredulous had the term "lesbian" been applied to such fine ladies. They were not targets of homophobic prejudice, since it was only later in the twentieth century that relationships such as theirs became suspect. The significance of their vision is not diminished, however, by their advantages. They saw women as productive beings who could support themselves by professional labor, and as pathbreakers they found a way to make that labor possible, to permit women not only to contribute to society but to be self-supporting so that they might pursue whatever living arrangement they wished. Both during their lives and long after, turn-of-the-century institution builders such as Addams and Thomas affected hundreds of thousands of women, but especially middle-class lesbians who needed to be career women in order to support their lesbian lifestyles.

Lesbian Sex Between
"Devoted Companions"

The psychologist Charlotte Wolff has observed: "It is not homosexuality but homoaffectionality which is at the centre and the very essence of women's love for each other. . . . The sex act is always secondary with them."[32] Many lesbians probably violently disagreed with Wolff in the 1980s, the decade after she wrote those words, when they were furiously attempting to liberate their libidos. However, Wolff's description may have been accurate enough for most lesbians of earlier eras, particularly those who were influenced by the Victorian insistence that women were not naturally sexual. But whether or not the women discussed in this chapter had sex with each other reflects less on the meaning and intensity of their involvement than on their relationship to their times. Those who did not share genital expression may have found ways more consonant with their early training to communicate the depth of their feeling—perhaps more verbal expressions of their affections, more displays of mutual nurturing, more holding.

Conditioning probably made it extremely difficult for most of these "proper" women to define themselves in terms that they learned were indecent, even if they did have sexual relationships. Since to them love for other women could still conceivably be seen as romantic friendship, any "slips" might be considered anomalous departures, not central to their relationships. Despite sexual contacts, some may have continued to see themselves as latter-day romantic friends rather than inverts or lesbians. However, it is clear that those "slips" were not entirely unusual.

Kinsey's statistics show that 12 percent of the women of his sample who were born in the nineteenth century had lesbian contacts to orgasm. While many turn-of-the-century women may have been stopped by the strictures of their times from exploring sexuality, there were a few who knew they were sexual beings regardless of the strictures and did not let themselves be affected by them. Extant letters sometimes reveal an unmistakable sexual relationship between pairs of women. One remarkable set of such letters is that of Rose Elizabeth Cleveland and Evangeline Marrs Simpson Whipple. Rose was the sister of Pres. Grover Cleveland, who was unmarried during his first two years in office. Rose lived with him in the White House at that time and took over the hostess duties of the First Lady. She later became the principal of the Collegiate Institute of Lafayette, Indiana, a writer and lecturer, and the editor of the Chicago-based magazine *Literary Life*. When she was forty-four she met a wealthy thirty-year-old widow, Evangeline Simpson. Their passionate correspondence began in 1890. For example:

> Oh, darling, come to me this night—my Clevy, my Viking, my Everything—Come!
>
> —Evangeline to Rose

> Ah, Eve, Eve, surely you cannot realize what you are to me—What you must be. Yes, I dare it now—I will no longer fear to claim you—you are mine by everything in earth and heaven—by every sign in soul

and spirit and body. . . . Give me every joy and all hope. This is yours to do.
—Rose to Evangeline

The letters became more specifically erotic as the relationship progressed. In one, Rose remembers with delight the times when

my Eve looks into my eyes with brief bright glances, with long rapturous embraces, — when her sweet life beneath and her warm enfolding arms appease my hunger, and quiet my [illegible] and carry my body to the summit of joy, the end of search, the goal of love!

These later letters even suggest that their sexual relationship included remarkable erotic fantasy and role playing. For example, Rose writes Evangeline:

Ah, my Cleopatra is a very dangerous Queen, but I will look her straight in those wide open eyes that look so imperious and will crush those Antony-seeking lips, until her arms close over (alas, for my hair with all those armlets), and she becomes my prisoner because I am her Captain. . . . How much kissing can Cleopatra stand?

The sexual relationship between the two women apparently cooled after a few years, and Evangeline, at the age of thirty-six, married the seventy-four year old Episcopal Bishop of Minnesota. When the bishop died five years later, however, the correspondence between the two women began again. In 1910 they went off together to Bagni di Lucca, Italy, where they made their home until Rose died in 1918. Before Evangeline's death in 1930 she directed her executors to bury her near Rose in Italy.[33]

Their correspondence is not unique, although not many early extant letters between women go quite so far as to talk about carrying each others' bodies "to the summit of joy." But frequently they do refer to caresses that are unmistakably erotic. Among the papers of feminist leader Anna Dickinson there is a letter signed "Ida" that recalls, "This time last evening you were sitting on my knee, nestled close to my heart and I was the happiest of mortals." The letter does not stop with such a maternal description. Ida goes on to remember Anna in bed, "tempting me to kiss her sweet mouth and to caress her until—well, poor little me, poor 'booful princess.' How can I leave thee, queen of my loving heart."[34]

Similarly, Emma Goldman kept for posterity several 1912 letters from Almeda Sperry, a woman who had been a prostitute and was so strongly affected by Goldman's lecture on white slave traffic that she became an anarchist worker alongside Goldman. The two spent a vacation in the country together, but prior to their trip Almeda wrote Emma that just before she falls asleep she imagines that "I kiss your body with biting kisses—I inhale the sweet pungent odor of you and you plead with me for relief." The letter obviously did not frighten Goldman into canceling their vacation plans. After their return Almeda wrote her again, recalling Emma taking her in her arms and "your beautiful throat that I kissed with reverent tenderness. . . . And your bosom—ah, your sweet bosom, unconfined." Their erotic relationship was apparently culminated, as still another letter from Almeda suggests:

> Dearest. . . . If I had only had courage enuf to kill myself when you reached the climax then—then I would have known happiness, for at that moment I had complete possession of you. Now you see the yearning I am possessed with—the yearning to possess you at all times and it is impossible. What greater suffering can there be—what greater heaven—what greater hell? And how the will to live sticks in me when I wish to live after possessing you. Satisfied? Ah God, no! At this moment I am listening to the rhythm of the pulse coming thru your throat. I am surg[ing] along with your life blood, coursing thru the secret places of your body.
>
> I wish to escape from you but I am harried from place to place in my thots. I cannot escape from the rhythmic spurt of your love juice.[35]

But women did not necessarily perceive themselves as lesbians simply because they lived such experiences and wrote and received such letters. Some even dismissed entirely the significance of those experiences in identifying their sexual orientation. Several years after Emma Goldman's relationship with Almeda Sperry, in 1928, the same year the famous lesbian novel *The Well of Loneliness* was published, Goldman wrote of her shock that a woman friend had run off with Djuna Barnes: "Really, the Lesbians are a crazy lot. Their antagonism to the male is almost a disease with them. I simply can't bear such narrowness." Although she had held another woman to her "unconfined bosom" and shared her "love juice" with her, Goldman did not hate men, so she felt she was not "one of them."[36]

As the century progressed, it became increasingly difficult to dismiss the new implications of such "slips." Even romantic friendship came to signify lesbianism, once women's close relationships began to appear especially threatening to the establishment of companionate marriage (see pp.90-91). The start of a transition in views is suggested in Wanda Fraiken Neff's 1928 novel about Vassar, *We Sing Diana*. In 1913 violent crushes between young women were considered "the great human experience" and it was so common for first-year students to smash on one particular professor that she was called "the Freshman disease." But when the main character returns to teach at Vassar seven years later, all has changed: everything is attributed to sex, undergraduate speech is full of Freudianisms, and "Intimacy between two girls was watched with keen distrustful eyes. Among one's classmates, one looked for the bisexual type, the masculine girl searching for a feminine counterpart, and one ridiculed their devotions." It is no wonder that M. Carey Thomas, having spent her whole life loving women, later felt compelled to express negative attitudes about homosexuality and to fear that public discussion of it would make life difficult for all women who lived together.[37]

It was to a large extent the work of the sexologists, which was disseminated slowly to the layman but finally became part of popular wisdom after World War I, that accounts for the altered views of women's intimacy with each other. It may be said that the sexologists changed the course of same-sex relationships not only because they cast suspicion on romantic friendships, but also because they helped to make possible the establishment of lesbian communities through their theories, which separated off the lesbian from the rest of womankind and presented new concepts to describe certain feelings and preferences that had before been within the spectrum of "normal" female experiences. Many early twentieth-century women who loved other women rejected those new concepts as being irrelevant to them because they could still see their feelings as "romantic friendship." But by the end of World War I the tolerance for any manifestations of what would earlier have been considered "romantic friendship" had virtually disappeared, as women were urged to forget their pioneering experiments in education and the professions and to find happiness in the new companionate marriage. Subsequent generations of women who loved other women soon came to have no choice but to consider themselves lesbians or to make herculean efforts of rationalization in order to explain to themselves how they were different from real lesbians.

Because the label "lesbian" implies *sexual* identification, historians have denied that those pioneering women for whom same-sex intimacies were so crucial had much in common with contemporary lesbians since, to the historians' relief, there is little concrete evidence

of the sexuality of "romantic friends."[38] But those early career women
who spent their lives with devoted companions share with their class
counterparts today the most crucial perceptions, values, antipathies,
and loves that shaped their existence. Professional women who are
lesbians at the end of the twentieth century are the descendants of
those pioneering women of a century ago.

2

A Worm in the Bud: The Early Sexologists and Love Between Women

Avoid girls who are too affectionate and demonstrative in their manner of talking and acting with you. . . . When sleeping in the same bed with another girl, old or young, avoid 'snuggling up' close together. . . . and, after going to bed, if you are sleeping alone or with others, just bear in mind that beds are sleeping places. When you go to bed, go to sleep just as quickly as you can. —*Irving D. Steinhardt,*
Ten Sex Talks With Girls, *1914*

Because nineteenth-century women of the working class were largely illiterate and thus have left little in the way of letters, journals, or autobiographies, it is difficult to know to what extent some form of romantic friendship may have been prevalent among them. Historians such as Marion Goldman have suggested a picture of relationships between nineteenth-century American prostitutes that appears to have commonalities with nineteenth-century middle-class romantic friends. They spent all their free time together, traveled together, protected each other, loved each other. Goldman talks about two who were so devoted that they even tried to die together. The deviance of prostitutes' roles, which set them apart and circumscribed their activities, encouraged them in a "female solidarity and bonding" that were not unlike romantic friendship. However, because their sexuality was so much more available to them than to the typical nineteenth-century middle-class woman, love between women who were prostitutes was much more likely to have manifested itself in genital relations.[1]

Women in penal institutions during the late nineteenth and early twentieth century seem also to have engaged in some form of romantic friendships. The early twentieth-century psychologist Margaret Otis described such passionate but apparently largely nonsexual relationships between black and white women in reform schools. Otis claimed that those relationships occurred only along cross-racial lines, "the difference in color . . . tak[ing] the place of difference in sex" and the black woman generally playing the "man's role." But since the black and white women were physically segregated in the institutions Otis observed, the relationships usually could have no consummation outside of romantic notes passed surreptitiously between the women and quick utterances of endearment and high sentiments— which would have rendered those affections as emotionally intense and ungenital as most romantic friendships probably were. Had the women not been segregated, however, the nature of the relationships might have been quite different.[2]

But in the era when romantic friendships between middle-class women in America were an important social institution, during the eighteenth and much of the nineteenth century, they appear not to have been common for working-class women, perhaps because the intimacy necessary for the development of such relationships required leisure and some degree of social privacy. Working-class women, who were generally employed in a domestic setting, had little of either. At the end of the nineteenth century, however, their situation began to change. American working-class women made a move into the public sphere parallel with their middle-class counterparts, taking the new jobs that were opening up with the rapid growth of American corporations and industry. There was now employment for them outside of homes, not only in factories but also in service occupations such as sales and clerical work, and the number of women in unskilled and semi-skilled occupations grew rapidly. The low-paid female wage worker figured heavily in the tripling of the female labor force between 1870 and 1900 (from 1.8 million to 5.3 million, twice the increase in the number of women in the general population).[3]

Many young working-class women left parents' or domestic employers' homes and moved to big cities where they were on their own—away from perpetual supervision and scrutiny for the first time. Such a move accounts for their changing heterosexual practices —which seem to have constituted a (hetero)sexual revolution that preceded the revolution of the 1920s by at least a couple of decades. But such a move also drew young working-class women together in ways that would have been impractical or impossible earlier. Because they lived and worked away from a domestic setting and often made less than subsistence wages, they frequently shared rooms, sometimes on a long-term basis. One historian gives several examples of women who not only lived together but moved together from city to city to find work, and she suggests that such long-term partnerships indicated "close personal bonds that existed among some lower-paid working women similar to the bonds of love and friendship [among] nineteenth century American middle-class women."[4]

But that many of those relationships were really similar to romantic friendship as middle-class women experienced it is perhaps dubious. Working-class women may have realistically felt that they did not have the luxury to engage in a connection that neither promoted survival as its chief aim nor promised starker sensual pleasures that could help them forget the bleakness of their labors. The most convincing depictions of these relationships suggest that they were far more concretely oriented—either sexually or practically—than those between romantic friends usually appear to have been. Kathy Peiss, for example, in *Cheap Amusements: Working Women and Leisure in Turn-of-the-Century New York,* observes that working-class women's same-sex friendships generally occurred in a context that permitted them to negotiate the world of heterosexual commercial amusements in order to make appropriate heterosexual contacts without being accosted by unwelcomed advances as lone women would be. Peiss contrasts this arrangement to the romantic friendships of middle-class women whose purpose was often to help them maintain their privatized same-sex world.[5]

Regardless of the extent or nature of romantic friendship and love between working-class women, when the sexologists (primarily medical men with middle-class backgrounds) who began writing about sexuality in the latter half of the nineteenth century turned their attention to homosexuality, they were more easily able to acknowledge that intimate relations between women in the classes "beneath" them could go beyond the platonic than they could with reference to women of their own class. Their early definitions of the female "sexual invert" (their term for the lesbian) were based on women of the working class. However, although they made their first observations about these women, it was not many decades before relationships between middle-class women (who were becoming entirely too independent) came to be seen by sexologists as similar to what they had observed in the "lower" classes. They were oblivious to the social and economic factors that created important differences between the women's relationships in each class.

The "scientific" classification of the lesbian in the latter half of the nineteenth century may be seen as consistent with the passion for taxonomy (the minute classification of almost everything) that had overtaken scientific circles at that time. But while they were convinced of the objectivity of their classifications, the scientists—and particularly the medical men who turned their attention to sexology —were often motivated by the moral vision of their day. Influenced by the theories of evolution, they formulated the notion that those who did not contribute to what was considered the human race's move forward—criminals and deviants and, by virtue of their socio-economic position, the "lower classes"—owed their backwardness to bad heredity. They were "degenerate" because, as the term itself suggests, their genes were defective. Their deviant or backward behavior was thought to have a physiological basis. Through this explanation of the misfit, science came to replace religion as the definer and upholder of mores. White middle-class European values and behaviors that reflected the background of the scientists came to be seen as scientifically normal and healthy. Those who did not conform were "abnormal." The sexologists thus developed a medical model to study various problems that were earlier considered social or ethical. While in previous eras a person who had a sexual relationship with an individual of the same sex would have been considered a sinner, by the late nineteenth century that person became a "congenital invert," a victim of inborn "contrary sexual feeling," a "homosexual"—all ways of looking at same-sex love that had not existed in the first part of the nineteenth century or earlier.

Much of the nineteenth-century classification was done in the name of the eugenics movement, which often attacked the poor and also marked the beginning of a long history of attempted "genocide" of those who loved the same sex. It was now claimed that sexual anomalies were congenital and would not occur without tainted heredity; thus eugenicists were determined to educate the rest of the medical community about the need to make those who were not—as an American doctor, William Lee Howard, said—in "the prime of physiological life" refrain from procreation. Masculine females and feminine males, Howard stated, were only born to parents of the degenerate class who themselves lacked the appropriate "strong sex characteristics."[6]

Sexual Inversion and "Masculine" or Transvestite Women

These medical men first observed that inappropriate sex role behavior was sometimes characteristic of women of the working class. The females that the earliest sexologists such as Karl Westphal, Richard von Krafft-Ebing and Cesare Lombroso defined as sexual inverts were often a captive population in prisons and insane asylums, daughters of the poor. Westphal, a German psychiatrist writing in 1869, was the first to describe extensively love between women in medical terms. His subject was a thirty-five-year old servant who was admitted to the Berlin Charite Hospital because of hysteria and bizarre behavior. She claimed to be profoundly disturbed by her love for a young girl. Westphal suggested that she was really a man trapped in a woman's body. As a child she had been fond of boy's games, she liked to dress in a masculine way, she had dreams in which she appeared to herself to be a man—and she apparently had sexual desires for women. To Westphal and the sexologists who came after him, the romantic interests of women like this one were inextricably linked to what the sexologists saw as their masculine behavior and their conception of themselves as male. Some historians have suggested a shift in the early sexologists' views from a concern with inappropriate gender behavior, that is, inversion of personality traits so that a female looks and behaves like a male—to a concern with inappropriate sexual object choice, or homosexuality. But such a distinction is not to be found in Westphal's work, which clearly connected the two. Nor is it to be found in the work of many sexologists well into the twentieth century or in the popular imagination, which often assumes, even today, that lesbians are necessarily masculine and that female "masculinity" is a sure sign of lesbianism.[7]

Westphal must have often witnessed passionate expression of love between women of his class since it was so prevelant in Germany during his day, but he would have regarded it as romantic friendship. In the poor servant woman he observed, who was also hysterical and not "feminine" as were refined women of his class, he could dare to see a deviant sexuality. What he could not understand about her life, however, was the reality of the perception that more feminine-looking and -acting females might have more difficulty surviving in her rough environment. He connected her "masculinity" with her "inappropriate" sexual drive, assuming a tie between the two. Despite his limited perceptions, Westphal's writing alerted other medical men to a supposed correlation between "masculinity" and female same-sex love.

There were many masculine-looking women of the working class, not only in Europe but in America as well, during Westphal's day. While women of the middle class in the latter part of the nineteenth century were enjoying a tremendous expansion of opportunities in terms of education and the slow but sure opening of various professions to them, the situation of working-class women was not to change much until the end of the century. The jobs that were open to them—usually of a domestic nature or in a factory—offered little beyond bare subsistence and no vistas of opportunity such as women from wealthier families were beginning to enjoy. It appeared to a good number of them that had they at least been men, life would have been more fair. Wages would have been higher for work that was not more difficult, and they would have been socially freer to engage in activities such as travel. There were good reasons for them to envy the privileges that males even of their class enjoyed and that were far above what was available to any female.

Most of them suffered in silence. But a few were more active in their resentment, and the most adventurous or the most desperate of them even formulated an ingenious solution to their plight. They figured out that if they moved to an area where they were not known, cut their hair, and wore men's clothes, their potential in terms of meaningful adventure and finances would increase tremendously. They often saw themselves not as men trapped in women's bodies, as the sexologists suggested they were, but rather as women in masquerade, trying to get more freedom and decent wages. Their aims were not unlike those that any feminist would applaud today.

They had few problems with detection. It was relatively easy for women to pass as men in earlier times because, unlike in the latter half of the twentieth century, women never wore pants. A person in pants would have been assumed to be male, and only the most suspicious would have scrutinized facial features or body movements to discern a woman beneath the external appearance.

Obviously there were more working-class women who were disgruntled with their limitations as females but simply eschewed feminine behavior in mild protest than who actually chose to become transvestites and try to pass as men, but the number of the latter was sizable. One researcher has estimated through Union Army doctors' accounts that at least four hundred women transvestites fought in the Civil War. Many continued as transvestites even into the twentieth century, such as "Harry Gorman," who, around the turn of the century, did heavy work as an employee of the New York Central Railway and frequented saloons and dance houses every night. Gorman was discovered to be a woman when she was hospitalized for a broken limb. She admitted that she had been passing as a man for twenty years. She also declared that she knew of "at least ten other women," also employed by the New York Central, who passed as men, appeared wholly manlike, and "were never suspected of being otherwise." Since there were at least eleven such women working for the New York Central alone and there are records of myriad other such cases, one can safely guess that transvestism and attempts to pass were not so rare and that there must have been thousands of women wandering around America in the latter part of the nineteenth century and the early twentieth century who were passing as men.[8]

Most of these working-class women appear to have begun their "masculine" careers not because they had an overwhelming passion for another woman and wanted to be a man to her, but rather because of economic necessity or a desire for adventure beyond the narrow limits that they could enjoy as women. But once the sexologists became aware of them, they often took such women or those who showed any discontent whatsoever with their sex roles for their newly conceptualized model of the invert, since they had little difficulty believing in the sexuality of women of that class, and they assumed that a masculine-looking creature must also have a masculine sex instinct.

Autobiographical accounts of transvestite women or those who assumed a masculine demeanor suggest, if they can be believed at all, that the women's primary motives were seldom sexual. Many of them were simply dramatizing vividly the frustrations that so many more women of their class felt. They sought private solutions to those frustrations, since there was no social movement of equality for them such as had emerged for middle-class women. Lucy Ann Lobdell, for example, who passed as a man for more than ten years in the mid-nineteenth century, declared in her autobiography: "I feel that I cannot submit to all the bondage with which woman is oppressed," and explained that she made up her mind to leave her home and dress as a man to seek labor because she would "work harder at housework, and only get a dollar per week, and I was capable of doing men's work and getting men's wages." "Charles Warner," an upstate New York woman who passed as a man for most of her life, explained that in the 1860s:

> When I was about twenty I decided that I was almost at the end of my rope. I had no money and a woman's wages were not enough to keep me alive. I looked around and saw men getting more money and more work, and more money for the same kind of work. I decided to become a man. It was simple. I just put on men's clothing and applied for a man's job. I got it and got good money for those times, so I stuck to it.

A transvestite woman who could actually pass as a man had male privileges and could do all manner of things other women could not: open a bank account, write checks, own property, go anywhere unaccompanied, vote in elections. The appeal was obvious. Even those passing women who denied they were "women's-righters," as did Babe Bean, had to admit, "As a man I can travel freely though unprotected and find work."[9]

Transvestism may have had a particular appeal to some minority women, who suffered doubly from the handicaps visited on women because of gender and on minorities because of racial prejudice. If they could pass as a man they obliterated at least one set of handicaps. Thus a black woman, Mary Fields, who had been born a slave in Tennessee, found remunerative and honorable employment as a stagecoach driver, even accompanying and protecting a group of nuns on a trek out West. As late as 1914 gender passing obviously provided more opportunities for a minority female than she would have had living as a woman. Ralph Kerwinieo (nee Cora Anderson), an American Indian woman who found employment for years as a man and claimed that she "legally" married another woman in order to "protect" her from the sexist world, also expressed feminist awareness for her decision to pass as a man:

> This world is made by man—for man alone. . . . In the future centuries it is probable that woman will be the owner of her own body and the custodian of her own soul. But until that time you can expect that the statutes [concerning] women will be all wrong. The well-cared for woman is a parasite, and the woman who must work is a slave. . . . Do you blame me for wanting to be a man—free to live as a man in a man-made world? Do you blame me for hating to again resume a woman's clothes?[10]

There must have been many women, with or without a sexual interest in other women, who would have answered her two questions with a resounding "no!"

It appears that an interest in sexual relations with other females came only later in the careers of many of these transvestite women (and in some cases was never of interest to them). But it is plausible that often transvestites did not become lovers with other women until they took on the persona of men and had available to them only those sexual opportunities typically open to men. As subtle as such developments may have been, the sexologists saw only the obvious when they formulated their early definitions of the lesbian. They could not recognize a woman's wish to be masculine and even to pass as a man as a desire for more economic and social freedom. In their own narrow views she acted masculine because she was a man trapped in a woman's body and all her instincts were inverted, including her sexual instinct. The sexologists conflated sex role behavior (in this case, acting in ways that have been termed masculine), gender identity (seeing oneself as male), and sexual object choice (preferring a love relationship with another woman). They believed in an inevitable coherence among the three. It was thus that transvestite women and women who behaved as men traditionally behaved, generally women of the working class whose masculinity was most apparent, came to be seen by the early sexologists as the prime example of the lesbian, whether or not those women had sexual relations with other females. And conversely, women who were passionately in love with other females but did not appear to be masculine were considered for some years more as merely romantic friends or devoted companions.

Feminists as Sexual Freaks

Masculine appearance, especially among working-class women, figured heavily in the early definitions of the female invert. A typical description was one by Krafft-Ebing in 1888: "She had coarse male features, a rough and rather deep voice, and with the exception of the bosom and female contour of the pelvis, looked more like a man in women's clothing than like a woman."[11] But as the late nineteenth-century feminist movement grew in strength and in its potential to overthrow the old sex roles, it was not too long before feminism itself was also equated with sexual inversion and many women of the middle class came to be suspected of that anomaly, since as feminists they acted in ways inappropriate to their gender, desiring to get an education, for example, or to work in a challenging, lucrative profession.

It was the European sexologists who were the first to connect sexual inversion and feminism. Havelock Ellis stated in his chapter "Sexual Inversion Among Women" in *Studies in the Psychology of Sex* that female homosexuality was increasing because of feminism, which taught women to be independent and to disdain marriage. Ellis, as a congenitalist who believed that homosexuality was hereditary, hastened to add that the women's movement could not directly cause sexual inversion unless one had the potential for it to begin with, but the movement definitely "developed the germs of it" in those who were that way inclined; and in other women it caused a "spurious imitation" of homosexuality.[12]

Like the leading English and German sexologists, the French sexologist Julien Chevalier, in his 1893 work *Inversion sexuelle,* suggested that homosexuality was congenital and that the lesbian was born with "organic elements" of the male; but despite that conviction he also observed that the number of lesbians had grown over the last decades because women were getting educations, demanding careers, emancipating themselves from male tutelage, "making men of themselves" by cultivating masculine sports, and becoming politically active. All of this "male emulation," according to him, resulted in female sexual inversion.[13]

American sexologists followed the lead of the Europeans. Frequently their goal also seemed to be to discredit both the women's movement and love between women by equating them with masculine drives and thus freakishness. They were ready to wage war on any form of women's bonding, which now, in the context of feminism, seemed threatening to the preservation of old-fashioned femininity. Dr. James Weir, in an article for the *American Naturalist* (1895), observed that the so-called New Women, and especially their foremost advocates, were really atavistic—throwbacks to the "primitive era" of matriarchy and therefore, by Weir's logic, degenerate. He managed to work the famous case of Alice Mitchell, a woman who murdered the woman she loved, into his connection between lesbianism and feminism. The modern feminist, he said, "is as much the victim of psychic atavism as was Alice Mitchell who slew Freda Ward." And just as Mitchell was recognized to be a viragint, so has "every woman who has been at all prominent in advancing the cause of equal rights . . . given evidence of masculo-femininity (viraginity), or has shown, conclusively, that she was the victim of psycho-sexual aberrancy." Weir implied that simply promoting feminist goals— agitating for "rights" that had been strictly masculine prerogatives, bonding with other women—was in itself good evidence that a woman was "abnormal," "degenerate," and a "viragint." [14]

The term "viragint" appears to have been taken from the American translation of Krafft-Ebing's *Psychopathia Sexualis,* in which "viragincy" is an advanced class of female inversion, measured according to masculinity. It served a double purpose in America, to describe both the feminist and the lesbian—and, of course, to connect the two, as the psychiatrist, William Lee Howard, did in a 1901 novel, *The Perverts,* about a degenerate Ph.D. feminist:

> The female possessed of masculine ideas of independence, the viragint who would sit in the public highways and lift up her pseudo-virile voice, proclaiming her sole right to decide questions of war or religion, or the value of celibacy and the curse of woman's impurity, and that disgusting anti-social being, the female sexual pervert, are simply different degrees of the same class—degenerates.

In his article "Effeminate Men and Masculine Women," the same author, a staunch congenitalist, explains that these feminist-viragint-lesbians—all "unsightly and abnormal beings"—are victims of poor mating. They must have had feminist mothers who neglected their maternal instincts and dainty feminine characteristics, preferred the laboratory to the nursery, and engaged in political campaigns. Thus they reproduced these mental and physical monstrosities. Howard is, however, optimistic about the future. Soon "disgusted Nature, no longer tolerant of the woman who would be a man," will allow all such types to "shrink unto death," he affirms. [15]

Howard had the assurance of the Darwinists behind him in his conviction that society and nature had evolved for the better in doing away with matriarchy and establishing patriarchy. Whatever was, at that point in time, had to be superior to what had preceded it. Nature would thus see to it that feminists and lesbians, Amazonian throwbacks in Howard's view, would go the way of the dinosaur and the dodo bird.

The early sexologists, who have been considered so brave for daring to write about sex at all in the sexually inhibited nineteenth century, were, in important ways, not much more imaginative or flexible regarding sex and sex roles than the conservative masses around them. Despite the occasional lip service to feminism such as

Ellis paid, they clearly believed that there were men's roles and women's roles, and if any woman wanted to diverge from what was appropriate it could only be because she had a congenital anomaly (a degeneracy, most sexologists believed) that made her an invert. A top item on their hidden agenda, whether they were conscious of it or not, finally came to be to discourage feminism and maintain traditional sex roles by connecting the women's movement to sexual abnormality.

The Attack on "Romantic Friendship"

It was still possible in the early twentieth century for some women to vow great love for each other, sleep together, see themselves as life mates, perhaps even make love, and yet have no idea that their relationship was what the sexologists were now considering "inverted" and "abnormal." Such naïveté was possible for women who came out of the nineteenth-century tradition of romantic friendship and were steeped in its literature.[16] Even had they been exposed to the writings of the sexologists, which were by now being slowly disseminated in America, they might have been unable to recognize themselves and their relationships in those medical descriptions. Their innocence became increasingly difficult to maintain, however, as the twentieth century progressed.

Perhaps the sexual possibilities of romantic friendship among middle-class women were overlooked by outside observers throughout much of nineteenth-century America because "illicit" sexuality in general was uncommon then (compared to earlier and later eras), judging at least from the birthrate of children born prior to the ninth month of marriage. During the Revolutionary era, for example, 33 percent of all first children were born before the ninth month of marriage. In Victorian America, between 1841 and 1880, only 12.6 percent of all first births were before the ninth month of marriage. If unmarried women, especially those of the "better classes," appeared to be by and large inactive in terms of heterosexual relations, it was probably difficult to conceive of them being homosexually active. Popular wisdom had it that decent women were uninterested in genital sexuality and merely tolerated their marriage duties. As an 1869 book, *The Physiology of Women,* observed with conviction:

> There can be no doubt that sexual feeling in the female is, in the majority of cases, in abeyance, and that it requires positive and consid-

erable excitement to be roused at all; and, even if roused (which in many instances it never can be), is very moderate compared with that of the male.

It could easily be believed that romantic friendship between two women was a "mental passion," spiritual, uplifting, and nothing more.[17]

Lesbianism became a popular topic of exotic and erotic French novels by the mid nineteenth century and a subject of great interest to later nineteenth-century European sexologists, but in America it was quite ignored almost to the end of the century. The *Index Catalogue of the Library of the Surgeon General's Office* lists only one article on lesbians between 1740 and 1895. However, soon after that point sexological writings began to fascinate American medical men tremendously. The second series of the same catalogue lists almost 100 books and 566 articles between 1896 and 1916 on women's sexual "perversions," "inversions," and "disorders."[18]

Turn-of-the-century American writers on lesbianism generally acknowledged the influence of the European sexologists while extending their observations to the American scene. For example, a 1902 article titled "Dr. Havelock Ellis on Sexual Inversion" observed that it was women's colleges that were "the great breeding ground" of lesbianism. These discussions were often very explicit about the dangers of female friendships that had hitherto seemed perfectly innocent. A medical work that appeared at the beginning of the century alerted doctors that when young girls are thrown together they manifest

> an increasing affection by the usual tokens. They kiss each other fondly on every occasion. They embrace each other with mutual satisfaction. It is most natural, in the interchange of visits, for them to sleep together. They learn the pleasure of direct contact, and in the course of their fondling they resort to cunni-linguistic practices. . . . After this the normal sex act fails to satisfy [them].

But even romantic friendship that clearly had no sexual manifestations was now coming to be classified as homosexual. Medical writers began to comment on "numerous phases of *inversion* where men are passionately attached to men, and women to women, *without the slightest desire for sexual intercourse.* [Italics are mine.]"[19]

American doctors were now genuinely disturbed that the public was still naïve about what had recently become so apparent to the medical men. Bernard Talmey, for example, in his 1904 treatise

Woman, insisted that homosexuality in females had never been made
a legal offense only because of "the ignorance of the law-making
power of the existence of this anomaly. The layman generally does
not even surmise its existence." Because of such ignorance, he concluded, women's intimate attachments with each other are considered
often erroneously as "mere friendship." They are fostered by parents
and guardians and are "praised and commended" rather than suspected of being "of a homosexual origin," as they often are. Some
doctors believed they were doing a public service in attempting to
close the gap in knowledge as quickly as possible. However, since
their writings were for the most part "scientific" it was only very
gradually that they began to filter through to popular awareness.
Early twentieth-century popular magazine fiction in America continued to treat intense love between women as innocent and often
ennobling romantic friendships."[20]

Thus lacking the concept, two women in the late nineteenth or
early twentieth century might still live in a relationship that would
certainly be defined as lesbian today and yet have no awareness of
themselves as lesbians. If their relationship was genital they could
have felt the same guilt over it that their contemporaries might have
experienced over masturbation—it was sexual pleasure without the
excuse of inescapable marital duties—but they would not necessarily
have felt themselves abnormal. In 1914 psychoanalysts were still
noting that "homosexual women are often not acquainted with their
condition."[21]

Yet there were a few indications of a change in public consciousness as early as the late nineteenth century in America. In contrast to
William Alger's 1868 view of romantic friendships bringing to women
"freshness, stimulant charm, noble truths and aspirations," an 1895
work, *Side Talks with Girls,* warns the young female that it is dangerous for her to have "a girl-sweetheart" because if she wastes her love
on another female she will not have any to give "Prince Charming
when he comes to claim his bride." A couple of decades later, advice
books of that nature were somewhat more explicit about the possibilities of sex between females, although the word "lesbian" or "invert"
was never used. In fact, a 1914 book, *Ten Sex Talks to Girls,* which
like its 1895 predecessor was aimed at adolescents and post-adoles-
cents, specifically classified sexual relations between females with
masturbation, which, the author admonished, "when practiced by
one girl is harmful enough, but when practised between girls . . . is a
most pernicious habit which should be vigorously fought against."

This author was quite explicit in his warning to girls to avoid just those manifestations of romantic friendship that were accepted and even encouraged a few decades earlier, such as hugging and exchanging intimacies. Parents were especially alerted to be suspicious of their daughters' attachments. Articles such as a 1913 piece in *Harper's Bazaar* titled "Your Daughter: What Are Her Friendships?" and signed "by a College Graduate" informed parents that most college friendships were innocent, but a tenth of them (how that figure is arrived at is never made clear) were morally degenerate and caused guilt and unhappiness because they were "not legitimate."[22]

The medical journals sometimes went much further in their imputation of wild sexual practices between females, though again their focus was generally on women of the working class. Dr. Irving Rosse, for example, discussed sex between women in sensationalistic, excessive, and bizarre terms that appear to have come right out of French novels rather than reality. In an 1892 article for the *Journal of Nervous and Mental Disease* he described one case of a prostitute who had "out of curiosity" visited various women who made a "speciality of the lesbian vice" and on submitting herself "by way of experiment to [their] lingual and oral maneuvers . . . had a violent hystero-cataleptic attack from which she was a long time in recovering." Another case he described was of a young unmarried woman who became pregnant through her married sister, "who committed the simulacrum of the male act on her just after copulating with her husband." To divine the means she used to transfer her husband's semen from her vagina to her unmarried sister's challenges the average imagination, but Dr. Rosse seemed to find nothing dubious in such a feat. In a 1906 work, August Forel, a Swiss psychiatrist and director of the Zurich Insane Asylum, wrote about lesbian sexual orgies "seasoned with alcohol" and nymphomaniacal lesbians. "The [sexual] excess of female inverts exceed those of the male," he stated. "This is their one thought, night and day, almost without interruption."[23] The literature disseminated to the lay public was considerably tamer.

Nevertheless, the new persective undoubtedly created great confusion in women who were brought up in the previous century to believe in the virtues, beauty, and idealism of romantic friendship. Suddenly they learned that what was socially condoned so recently was now considered unsalutary and dangerous. One woman remembered the shock of the new "knowledge" that came to her when she was eighteen, in 1905. She had been raised with the idea of the preciousness of intimate attachments between females, but almost overnight all changed, she suggested: "Public opinion, formed by cheap medical reprints and tabloid gossip, dubbed such contacts perverted, called such women lesbians, such affection and understanding destructive." She was, however, a tall, broad-shouldered woman with a deep voice who sold books door-to-door. Females of more "refinement," who were more feminine-looking and had a more protected social status, were apparently able to continue relationships such as earlier eras viewed as romantic friendship much longer into the twentieth century than unsheltered women who looked as though they had stepped out of the pages of Krafft-Ebing.[24]

Class may have accounted for profound differences here. The luxury of naïveté regarding lesbianism that many socially sheltered middle-class American college women were able to enjoy even into the sophisticated 1920s is illustrated in their yearbooks. The Oberlin College yearbook of 1920, for example, contains a page of thirty-two photographs of women who are identified by name under the heading "Lesbians." They were members of the Oberlin Lesbian Society, a woman's group devoted to writing poetry. The Bryn Mawr yearbook for 1921 contains an essay titled "My Heart Leaps Up," in which the writers observe ironically (but absolutely without any of the implications that psychoanalysts of that era would have felt compelled to draw):

> Crushes are bad and happen only to the very young and very foolish. Once upon a time we were very young, and the bushes on the campus were hung with our bleeding hearts. Cecil's heart bled indiscriminately. The rest of us specialized more, and the paths of Gertie Hearne, Dosia, Eleanor Marquand, Adelaide, Tip, and others would have been strewn with roses if public opinion had permitted flowers during the War.
>
> The type of person smitten was one of the striking things about the epidemic. For instance, our emotional Betty Mills spent many stolen hours gazing up at Phoebe's window. The excitable Copey was enamoured successively of all presidents of the Athletic Association, and has had a hard time this year deciding where to bestow her affections.
>
> But there were some cases that were different from these common crushes. We know they were different because the victims told us so. Only the most jaundiced mind could call by any other name than friendship Nora's tender feeling toward Gertie Steele, which led her to keep Gertie's room overflowing with flowers, fruit, candy, pictures, books, and other indispensible articles. . . .
>
> The real thing in the way of passion was the aura of emotion with

which Kash surrounded Sacred Toes. She confided her feelings to one-half the campus, and the other half was not in total ignorance, but Kash constantly worried lest it should leak out.

Of course all these things happened in our extreme youth.[25]

However, not all females of their social class remained as innocent. Although some early twentieth-century women apparently saw no need to hide their same-sex relationships (for example, Vida Scudder, discussed in chapter 4), many apparently did. Willa Cather was perhaps representative in this regard. At the beginning of her college career at the University of Nebraska in the late nineteenth century she called herself Dr. William and dressed virtually in male drag. By the end of her college years her presentation was considerably more feminine, but she continued her amorous relationships with other women—Louise Pound, Isabelle McClung, with whom she was involved for about twelve years, and later Edith Lewis, with whom she lived for forty years. Yet she cultivated the image of celibacy and pretended to reject all human ties for the sake of art. She claimed that she could not become "entangled" with anyone because to be free to work at her writing table was "all in all" to her. She seems to have felt that it was necessary to conceal the ways in which the women she loved and lived with, and was very "entangled" with, contributed to her ability to create, although the latest Cather biographers have not seen the need for such reticence.[26]

Cather became very secretive about her private life around the turn of the century because she was cognizant of the fall from grace that love between women was beginning to suffer. Other women who had same-sex relationships at about that time, when society's view of such love started to turn, adopted a much more aggressive and sadder ploy to conceal what was coming to be considered their transgressions: they bitterly denounced love between women in public. Jeannette Marks, professor at Mount Holyoke, lived for fifty-five years in a devoted relationship with Mary Woolley, president of Mount Holyoke, and yet wrote and attempted to publish an essay in 1908 on "unwise college friendships." She called such relationships "unpleasant or worse," an "abnormal condition," and a sickness requiring a "moral antiseptic." Marks appears not even to be talking about full-fledged lesbianism, since she decribes those loves only as "sentimental" friendships. But against all her own experiences and those of her closest friends, she baldly states in this essay that the only relationship that can "fulfill itself and be complete is that between a man and a woman." Later Marks even began work on a book dealing with homosexuality in literature in which she intended to show that insanity and suicide were the result of same-sex love.[27] Were those works a pathetic attempt to deny to the world that her domestic arrangement, which all Mount Holyoke knew about, was not what it seemed?

Perhaps it would be more charitable to try to understand her ostensible dishonesty through a revelation that her contemporary Mary Casal makes in her autobiography, *The Stone Wall*. Casal, writing about the turn of the century a number of years later (1930), talks frankly about her own earlier lesbian sexual relationship with Juno, which she describes as being "the very highest type of human love," but she insists on a distinction between their homosexuality and that of "the other" lesbians:

> Our lives were on a much higher plane than those of *the real inverts.* While we did indulge in *our sexual intercourse,* that was never the thought uppermost in our minds. . . . But we had seen evidences of overindulgence on the part of some of those with whom we came in contact, in loss of vitality and weakened health, ending in consumption. [Italics are mine.][28]

True lesbianism for her had nothing to do with whether or not one has sexual relations with a person of the same sex. Rather it is a matter of balance: Those who do it a lot are the real ones. She and Juno are "something else."

It is likely that many early twentieth-century women, having discovered the judgments of the sexologists, formulated similar rationalizations to make a distinction between their love and what they read about in medical books. That perception may have permitted many of them to live their lives as publicly as they did—in the presidents' houses on college campuses, the directors' apartments in settlement houses, the chiefs' offices in betterment organizations. They knew they were not men trapped in women's bodies, the inverts and perverts the sexologists were bringing to public attention. If they had to call themselves anything, they were romantic friends, devoted companions, unusual only in that they were anachronisms left over from purer times.

The Dissemination of Knowledge
Through Fiction

The readership for most of the sexologists' books and articles was long limited to the medical profession. Although lay people were

occasionally able to obtain copies of books such as *Psychopathia Sexualis* and *The Psychology of Sex,* nevertheless it took some time before
these images of the masculine female invert filtered down to the
popular imagination in America. To the extent that fiction is an
accurate reflection of social attitudes it would seem that despite the
sexologists, love between women, especially females of the middle
class, continued for many years to be seen as romantic friendship
rather than congenital inversion.

While the exotic and erotic aspects of love between women had
long been explicit themes in nineteenth-century French literature,
there was little in American literature that was comparable to *Mademoiselle de Maupin, Nana,* or *Idylle Saphique.* Occasional stories hinted
at the awareness of the sexologists' new discoveries about the dangers
of love between women. The earliest example is Constance Fenimore
Woolson's 1876 story "Felipa," which suggests that the author may
have had some familiarity with the ideas of Westphal or other sexologists who were writing at that time. The title character is a twelve-
year-old Florida girl who dresses in the clothes of the dead son of a
fisherman, which, she acknowledges, "makes me appear as a boy."
In the complicated plot Felipa falls in love with a woman and then, as
an afterthought, with the woman's fiance. When it appears that the
couple will be leaving the Florida coast where they have been vaca-
tioning, Felipa, in great anguish, wounds the woman's fiance with a
knife. The first-person narrator tries to comfort Felipa's grandfather
who is distraught over the girl's act of passion. The narrator tells
him, "It will pass; she is but a child." But the grandfather seems to
know about inversion and how it asserts itself early. It will not pass,
he insists: "She is nearly twelve. . . . Her mother was married at
thirteen." Again to the narrator's assurance: "But she loved them
both alike. It is nothing; she does not know," the grandfather replies,
"But I know. It was two loves, and the stronger thrust the knife"—
that is, Felipa's more powerful love for the woman caused her to try
to stab the man, despite her affection for him. The grandfather's main
concern is not about the child's attempt to murder, but rather that she
tried to kill a man whom she conceived to be her rival for a woman.[29]
Woolson's story, however, stands out as an almost isolated instance
of knowledge of female sexual inversion (as opposed to romantic
friendship) in nineteenth-century American literature.

There are three other examples, all dealing with violence, which,
in fact, the sexologists said often accompanied degeneracy. These
examples were influenced by the real-life 1892 murder of a seventeen-

year-old Tennessee girl, Freda Ward, by her nineteen-year-old female lover, Alice Mitchell, which brought the possibility of violent passions between women to widespread public attention, as it had never been brought before in America. The medical journals described Alice Mitchell in terms out of Krafft-Ebing's and Havelock Ellis' work: as a child she preferred playing boy's games; she liked to ride bareback on a horse "as a boy would"; her family regarded her as "a regular tomboy." Alice planned to wear men's clothes and have her hair cut like a man's so that she might marry Freda Ward and support her by working at a man's job. She killed her lover because she feared that Freda would marry a real man instead of her. Popular news coverage, such as that in the *New York Times,* was clear about Alice Mitchell's claim, which became part of her insanity plea, that "I killed Freda because I loved her and she refused to marry me." [30]

It was probably no coincidence that in 1895, only a few years after the Mitchell case received such attention, three fictional works were published that contained images of lesbians as masculine and murderous. In Mary Wilkins Freeman's "The Long Arm," Phoebe, an aggressive businesswoman with a masculine build, kills not her female love, Mary, but the man who wishes to take Mary away from her. In Mary Hatch's novel of the same year, *The Strange Disappearance of Eugene Comstock,* Rosa, alias Eugene Comstock, is not only a murderer but also manages in the guise of a man to marry another woman, just as Alice Mitchell desired. It is explained that her natural perversion was encouraged by her environment: her father had wanted a son and hence raised her as a boy until she was twelve. Like the medical descriptions of Alice Mitchell and other textbook lesbians, Rosa-Eugene disdained to sit in the parlor and do fancywork or attend to the domestic needs of a man. [31]

Dr. John Carhart's *Norma Trist; or Pure Carbon: A Story of the Inversion of the Sexes,* also brought out in 1895, most resembles the Alice Mitchell case. Norma stabs her woman love when she learns that the woman is engaged to be married to a Spanish captain and then responds to the authorities when she is questioned in terms similar to the newspaper accounts of Mitchell's response. Norma's inversion is revealed once again to have manifested itself in childhood through her masculine interest in riding "man fashion" on her pony, being good at math, and loathing perfume. Significantly, her inversion is aggravated because her father insists she be given a "good education," since she is fond, as only males presumably were, of "books and learning." [32]

Outside of these stories, however, lesbianism as the sexologists viewed the phenomenon was an infrequent theme in American fiction until the publication in the United States of *The Well of Loneliness* (1928), Radclyffe Hall's famous English novel. Surprisingly, Americans, more than Europeans, seem to have been reluctant to attribute "perversity" to women—unless, that is, the women presented a threat to the social structure by excessive feminist demands. But once the notion of female "perversity" did capture the popular imagination, love between women assumed the image of mannishness rather than the many other images it might have taken, such as exotic, orchidlike mysterious beauty suggested often in French literature, or the gentle, nurturing epitome of femaleness suggested in nineteenth- and early twentieth-century depictions of romantic friendship in American life and literature. It is not, of course, that many masculine women who loved women did not exist, but rather that lesbianism and masculinity became so closely tied in the public imagination that it was believed that only a masculine woman could be the genuine article.

Why Some Lesbians Accepted the Congenital Invert Theory

Most sexologists were not very flattering in their views of inversion. August Forel was representative in his assumption that homosexual love is pathological in nature and "nearly all inverts are in a more or less marked degree psychopaths or neurotics."[33] The new explanations for love between women made it degenerative and abnormal where earlier it was socially sanctioned. Those "explanations" eventually blew the cover of women whose sexual relationships with other women may have been hidden under the guise of romantic friendship. It would be logical to assume that women who loved other women would in a mass, categorically, reject the sexologists' theories, tainted as they were with traditionalism and stereotypes. And many women, finding the sexologists' theories disabling, did reject them. But a surprising number of women found them extremely enabling. They perceived real benefits in presenting themselves as congenital inverts.

It meant to some of them that romantic friendship would not have to give way to heterosexuality and marriage with the advent of a creditable male suitor. If they were born into the "intermediate sex,"

no family pressure or social pressure could change them. Their love
for women was mysteriously determined by God or Nature. If their
attraction to women was genital and they failed to keep that a secret,
they could not in any case be seen as moral lepers. They were simply
biological sports, as Natalie Barney, an American lesbian, wrote in
her autobiography, reflecting the sexologists' influence on her conception of her own homosexuality: "I considered myself without
shame: albinos aren't reproached for having pink eyes and whitish
hair; why should they hold it against me for being a lesbian? It's a
question of Nature. My queerness isn't a vice, isn't deliberate, and
harms no one."[34] The sexologists had provided that ready-made
defense for homosexuality.

For the woman who was caught up with notions of gender-
apppropriate behavior, the sexologists' views of the lesbian as a "man
trapped in a woman's body" could be turned in her favor sexually if
she wished: she could give herself permission to be sexual as no
"normal" woman could. In her essay "The Mythic Mannish Lesbian," Esther Newton suggests that the congenital inversion theory
must have appealed to some women because it was one of the few
ways a woman could "lay claim to her full sexuality." The "normal"
female's sexuality was supposed to be available for procreation and
her husband's conjugal pleasure only. But if a female were not a
female at all but a man trapped in a woman's body, it should not be
condemnable nor surprising that her sexuality would assert itself as
would a man's. Newton suggests that for decades the female invert
was alone among women in her privilege of being avowedly sexual.
Frances Wilder is an example of a woman who took that privilege. In
a letter she wrote in 1915 to Edward Carpenter, a leading promoter
of the congenital theory, she confessed that she harbored a "strong
desire to caress and fondle" another female. Hoping to justify her sex
drive, she explained that she experienced such a desire because she
had within her not just "a dash of the masculine" but also a "masculine mind."[35]

Such defenses, which attributed sexual difference to nature, also
meant that those who identified themselves as homosexual could, for
the first time, speak out against legal and social persecution. Lesbians
(as women) were generally seen as being beneath the law and therefore ignored, with a few rare exceptions. But homosexual men and
the lesbians who identified with their struggle through such groups
as the German Scientific Humanitiarian Committee used the congenital inversion theory to challenge legal sanctions against sodomy: the

law and society had no business persecuting homosexuals, since their behavior was normal for them. And there was no reason for social concern about homosexual seduction, since someone who was not a congenital invert could not be seduced by a person of the same sex.[36]

It was, in fact, much better to be a congenital invert than one who had the option of being heterosexual and chose homosexuality out of free will. Such a conscious choice in those unexistential times was an offense to society. As one American medical doctor, Joseph Parke, observed in 1906, "If the abnormality is congenital, clearly it cannot be a crime. If it be acquired it may be both vicious and criminal."[37] For many, to claim a birth defect was preferable to admitting to willful perversity.

The spread of the congenital theory also informed many who loved the same sex that there were others like them. That information carried with it potential political and personal benefits that would have been impossible earlier. First in Europe and later in America, it encouraged those who wished to define themselves as homosexuals to organize publicly. The sexologists virtually gave them not only an identity and vocabulary to describe themselves, but also an armor of moral innocence. Once they knew there was a sizable minority like them, they could start looking for each other.

Already by 1890 some female "inverts" had joined the sexual underworld of big cities such as New York, where, along with male "inverts" in evening gowns, they attended balls at places such as Valhalla Hall in the Bowery, wearing tuxedos and waltzing with other more feminine-looking women. The women who attended such functions were perhaps the first conscious "butches" and "femmes." There could be no such social equivalents for women who loved women before the sexologists turned their attention to them, since earlier they had had no awareness of themselves as a group. In effect, the sexologists gave many of them a concept and a descriptive vocabulary for themselves, which was as necessary in forming a lesbian subculture as the modicum of economic independence they were able to attain at about the same time in history. Historian George Chauncey points out with regard to male homosexuals that the sexologists were merely "investigating an [existing] subculture rather than creating one" through their formulations of sexual inversion. And, indeed, there is good evidence to suggest that homosexual male subcultures have been in existence at least since the beginning of the eighteenth century. But for women who loved women the situation was somewhat different, since economic depen-

dency on marriage had made it impossible for them to form such a
subculture as early as male homosexuals did. The sexologists, emerging just as women's economic position was beginning to change,
provided the crucial concept of sexual *type*—the female invert—for
women who in earlier times could have seen themselves only as
romantic friends or isolated women who passed as men.[38] If the
sexologist did not *create* a lesbian subculture, they certainly were the
midwives to it.

The usefulness of the writings of the early sexologists has been felt
even in more recent times by lesbians. Barbara Gittings recalls that in
1950 when she first realized she was homosexual she went to the
library looking for more understanding of what that meant. Although
she had to search under "Abnormal." "Perversion," and "Deviation,"
she remembers: "I did find my way to some good material. Though
I couldn't identify with the women Ellis described, at least I knew
that other female homosexuals existed. They were real-life people.
That helped." The sexologists crystallized possiblities for young women
that they would have had difficulty in conceptualizing on their own.[39]

Thus some women who loved women were happy about the
sexologists' explanations of the etiology of their "problem." Perhaps
those theories even seemed accurate to women who desired to be
active, strong, ambitious, and aggressive and to enjoy physical relationships with other women: since their society adamantly defined all
those attributes as male, they internalized that definition and did
indeed think of themselves as having been born men trapped in
women's bodies. For many of them, the image of their masculinity
was an integral part of their sexual relationships and they became
"butches" in the working class and young lesbian subcultures, especially during the 1950s. If the only cultural models they saw of lovers
of women were male, it is not unlikely that they might have pictured
themselves as male when making love to a woman, just as the sexologists suggested.

The congenital theory even enjoyed some revival in the 1980s.
While Freud's explanation of lesbianism as determined in childhood
was the dominant view from the 1920s through the 1960s and the
feminist explanation of lesbianism as a political choice held sway in
the 1970s, more recently, perhaps in response to a perceived climate
of conservatism, the congenital theory has reappeared in the guise of
essentialism. Ignoring the evidence of the 1970s, when many women
came to be lesbians through their feminist awareness, essentialists say
that biology alone explains lesbianism, which is a permanent, fixed

characteristic. One is a lesbian if one is born a lesbian, and nothing can make a lesbian a heterosexual. Heterosexuality is "natural" only to one who is born heterosexual, just as homosexuality is "natural" to the born lesbian. As an Austin, Texas, woman observed, "I'm a lesbian because of genetics. I'm sure my great-grandmother and grandmother were lesbians, even though they never came out." Her proof of their lesbianism, like many of the sexologists' "proofs," is only their feminism and their "masculinity": "They rebelled against playing the traditional roles. They smoked, hunted, did carpentry at home. And they let me know it was okay for a young girl to do things." An adherence to the congenital theory is perhaps the safest position homosexuals can take during homophobic times when they fear they might be forced to undergo "treatment" to change their sexual orientation. And it serves to get parents or detractors off one's back. Essentialism is also a political strategy. Even in conservative periods, it encourages homosexuals to build their own culture and institutions with the conviction that since they are born different from heterosexuals they must find ways to rely only on themselves and others like them.[40]

However, historically no less than today, there were other females who did not see themselves as having been born men trapped in women's bodies, despite the fact that they made their lives with other females and even had sexual relations with them. For these women, much of what the sexologists wrote was frightening or meaningless. Those who were scared by the sexologists' pronouncements perhaps ran into heterosexual marriages that would mask their feelings or lived as homosexuals but practiced furious homophobic denial to the world. But many others must have been outraged at the imputation of degeneracy and rejected the theories out of hand, believing perhaps that there were some freaks somewhere such as those the medical men wrote about, but it had nothing to do with them. They simply loved a particular female, or they preferred to make their life with another woman because it was a more viable arrangement if one were going to pursue a career, or they did not think about it at all— they lived as they pleased and saw themselves as uncategorizable individuals.

3

Lesbian Chic: Experimentation and Repression in the 1920s

In my day I was a Pioneer and a Menace. [Lesbianism] was not then as it is now, chic . . . but as daring as a Crusade; for where now it leaves a woman talkative, so that we have not a Secret among us, then it left her in Tears and Trepidation. Then one had to lure them to the Breast, and now you have to smack them, back and front, to wean them at all.
—Djuna Barnes,
Ladies Almanack, *1928*

The decade of the 1920s witnessed a permissiveness among the more sophisticated to experiment not only with heterosexuality but with bisexuality as well—with erotic relationships that were more specifically genital than the romantic relationships of the Victorian era usually appear to have been. Such sexual liberalization had been building in America since the previous decade, at least partly in response to the popularizers of the most important of the sexologists, Sigmund Freud, who began at that time to disseminate their mentor's ideas to large American audiences. Even readers of tame domestic magazines such as *Good Housekeeping* were being informed that the sex drive led one to desire various sensory gratifications and the individual had no control over its demands: "If it gets its yearning it is as contented as a nursing infant. If it does not, beware! It will never be stopped except with satisfactions."[1]

The lay public was given to understand through such oversimplifications of Freud that to fight whatever urges might make themselves felt (presumably even those that emerged out of intimate friendships between women) was counterproductive. Even those who did not subscribe to Freudianism could not escape a familiarity with it, at least in middle-class America. It permeated not only popular culture but also everyday life. The playwright Susan Glaspell, who wrote a satire on the fascination with Freud that characterized the times, *Suppressed Desires,* was probably not exaggerating completely when she said, "You could not go out to buy a bun without hearing of someone's complexes." Actions and relationships were now examined with relish for sexual meaning.[2]

The Roots of Bisexual Experimentation

By the 1920s there were already a few established communities of women who identified themselves as lesbians, in some astonishing places such as Salt Lake City as well as in more likely areas such as San Francisco. But few women, regardless of their sexual experiences, became part of the fledgling lesbian community. Even if they did not marry and had affectional relationships only with other women, they lived usually without a lesbian subculture. In small towns where heterosexuals often "never even knew that homosexuals existed," according to oral histories of those who lived in such towns through the 1920s, they passed easily for heterosexual spinsters.[3]

But although there were no huge numbers of women who suddenly identified as lesbians, statistics gathered by a 1920s sociologist, Katharine Bement Davis, indicate that many women were giving themselves permission to explore sex between women. Davis' study of 2200 females (primarily of the middle class) shows that 50.4 percent admitted to intense emotional relations with other women and half of that number said that those experiences were either "accompanied by sex or recognized as sexual in character." They frequently saw the relationship as an isolated experience (or one of several isolated experiences), and they expected eventually to marry and live as heterosexuals, though the times seemed to some of them to permit experimentation.[4]

The etiology of "lesbian chic," the bisexual experimentation of the 1920s, has been traced by some social critics to World War I. But the war, in which the United States was engaged for only two years, did not have so significant an effect in establishing a lesbian subculture in America as it seems to have had in some areas of Europe, where it was fought for five years and with much more female participation than American women were permitted. According to Radclyffe Hall's 1920s works, "Miss Ogilvy Finds Herself" and *The Well of Loneliness,* for example, in World War I many English female "sexual inverts" took jobs such as ambulance driving and had the opportunity to meet others who were attracted to the active life that war service offered. It was not until the Second World War, in which American women participated on a much larger scale, that their war effort experiences actually did stimulate an unprecedented growth of an American lesbian subculture.

But while no large lesbian subculture was established in the United States as a result of World War I, the period seems to have marked the beginning of some self-conscious sexual experimentation between women. In the midst of women's Freudian enlightenment about the putative power of sexual drives, two million men were sent overseas and many more were called away from home for the war effort. It has been speculated that women, turning to each other *faute de mieux,* found they liked sex with other women just fine. As one blues composer wag of the era suggested in his song "Boy in the Boat," it was then that women learned about cunnilingus, manipulating "the boy in the boat" (the clitoris) with each other:

> Lot of these dames had nothing to do.
> Uncle Sam thought he'd give 'em a fightin' chance,
> Packed up all the men and sent 'em on to France,
> Sent 'em over there the Germans to hunt,
> Left the women at home to try out all their new
>   stunts.[5]

Despite the composer's humorous intent, there is probably some element of truth in his explanation of the growth of sexual relations between women during those years when the relative paucity of men encouraged same-sex intimacy not only among middle-class college and professional women, who had had the freedom to enjoy each other's company for some time now, but also among a broader spectrum of females who might have married (if not out of love, then out of ordinary social pressure) had it not been for the war.

In addition to the effects of Freud and the war, bisexual experimentation was also encouraged in some circles by a new value placed on the unconventional and daring. By the 1920s, young American intellectuals, bohemians, and generic nonconformists were determined to rout with a vengeance the last vestiges of Victorianism in the country. To many of them it was clear that their parents had known nothing anyway and it was that ignorance that had not only involved the world in a fruitless war but also caused untold personal suffering in the form of harmful repression and absurd legislation. In metropolitan areas these young people often determined the temper of the times

through their preference for literature and art that challenged tradition, as well as through their resistance to laws such as Prohibition,
their adoption of new fashions such as bobbed hair and short skirts
for women, and their rejection of received notions regarding sexuality. Freud provided them with a license to explore sex openly, but
there was a particular charm in explorations that would have previously been considered especially unorthodox, that would have shocked
Babbit, flown in the face of convention, shown an ability to live
originally and dangerously. These became goals for the 1920s rebels
—and in some circles, bisexuality seemed to address all those goals.

Unlike in earlier eras, love between women was now often assumed to be sexual (perhaps even in cases where it was not), and it
was popularly described by the bald term "homo*sexuality*." With
regard to sexual awareness, much of this generation had traveled a
vast distance from their parent generation and the sophisticated would
now have been incredulous over the concept of romantic friendship.
But not only could they not believe in platonic love; they were also
voyeuristically intrigued with lesbianism. The extent to which the
subject fascinated the public is suggested by its popularity in American fiction of the era. Ernest Hemingway, for example, deals with
the subject both briefly and extensively in his fiction of the '20s: in
The Sun Also Rises (1926), with the character of the "boyish" Brett
Ashley; in *A Farewell to Arms* (1929), with Catherine Barkley's nurse
friend, Fergy, who is in love with her; in the short story "The Sea
Change," which is about a woman trying to explain to her male
companion her erotic involvement with another woman; and in his
posthumously published novel *The Garden of Eden,* set in the 1920s,
whose major focus is a triangle that includes two women who are
sexually enamoured with each other. Sherwood Anderson shows
American women "experimenting" with lesbianism in two novels of
the '20s, *Poor White* (1920) and *Dark Laughter* (1925). A bisexual
woman in *Dark Laughter* suggests that American wives played with
lesbianism with great ease since American men "knew so little" about
love and sex between women.[6] But the writers were working as hard
as they could, along with the Freudians, to inform them. Minor
novelists also, such as James Huneker (*Painted Veils,* 1920) and Wanda
Fraiken Neff (*We Sing Diana,* 1928), and playwrights such as Henry
Gribble (*March Hares,* 1921) and Thomas Dickinson (*Winter Bound,*
1929) all brought fascinated views of lesbians to literature and the
American stage. The English novel *The Well of Loneliness,* published
in the United States in 1928, became a huge *succès de scandale.*

It is difficult to assess just what that widespread interest in lesbianism meant, to American men in particular. Clearly there was ambivalence in their response. But perhaps the exoticism of the concept
captured their curiosity and sexual imagination. Or perhaps the image
of love between women aroused subconscious anxiety that was then
cathartically soothed in these fictional works, since they almost invariably ended by confirming conventional sexuality: the girl seldom
got the girl—most often a male came in and stole the booty. The
old, reassuring sexual order was restored after experimentation with
the new.

Although there was considerable interest in unconventional sexuality among sophisticates of the 1920s, the official voice was not remarkably different from that of earlier eras and lesbianism, while
discussed more openly than it had ever been before in America, was
greeted with outrage by the guardians of morality who were nowhere
near ready to accept such autonomous sexuality in women. In 1923
Theatre Magazine, an important voice of Broadway, said of Sholom
Asch's *God of Vengeance,* one of the earliest plays with a lesbian theme
to appear on Broadway: "A more foul and unpleasant spectacle has
never been seen in New York." The producer, director, and cast of
twelve were all hauled off to court on charges of obscenity. Edouard
Bourdet's play *The Captive,* about a young woman who cannot be
happy in her marriage because she is obsessed by another woman,
met a similar fate in 1926 on Broadway, as well as in San Francisco,
Los Angeles, and Detroit, when it appeared in those cities in 1927.
Another play, *Sin of Sins,* opened in Chicago in 1926 and closed after
a three-week run and a series of scandalized reviews such as that in
Variety, which described the lesbian subject matter as being "not fit
for public presentation."[7]

But despite such vestiges of suppression, public curiosity about the
subject could not be stopped. In cosmopolitan areas like New York,
the intrigue with homosexuality for the 1920s' "rebels" was manifested by drag balls where some men wore evening gowns and some
women wore tuxedos and many came to be spectators. The balls
were held in "respectable" ballrooms such as the ritzy Savoy and
Hotel Astor and in the huge Madison Square Garden. Despite the
voices of censorship such as those that occasionally emerged in response to Broadway plays, these events were officially sanctioned by
police permits and attracted large numbers, as one Broadway gossip
sheet of the 1920s announced in a headline: "6000 Crowd Huge Hall
as Queer Men and Women Dance."[8]

Although the headline hints at a clear distinction between the "queers" and the spectators, the fiction of the period (see pp. 70–71) suggests that the lines sometimes blurred as the "heterosexual" tourists made contacts that were more than social among the avowedly homosexual participants. Such balls were for many sophisticates what the '20s was all about—the ultimate in rebellion and a good laugh at the naive world that took as self-evident matters such as sex and gender.

But although the "heterosexuals" in such places may have played for a while with homosexuality, they generally did not see themselves as homosexual. Since "homosexual" was in the process of becoming an identity, one now might feel forced to chose either to accept or reject that label. But an erotic interest in another female, and even sex with another female, was not necessarily sufficient to make a woman a lesbian. She might consider her experiences simply bisexual experimentation, which was even encouraged in certain milieus. One had to *see* oneself as a lesbian to be a lesbian. But despite the apparent sexual liberalism of many in the 1920s, the era was not far removed in time from the Victorian age, and to admit to an aberrant sexual identity must not yet have been easy for any but the most brave, unconventional, committed, or desperate.

White "Slumming" in Harlem

While a lesbian identity was impossible for many women to assume during the '20s, sex with other women was the great adventure, and literature and biography suggest that many women did not hesitate to partake of it. Of course some of the women who had sex with other women did indeed accept a lesbian identity and committed themselves to a new lesbian lifestyle. By 1922, as Gertrude Stein's "Miss Furr and Miss Skeene" indicates, such women were already calling themselves "gay," as homosexual men were.[9] But whether they identified as "gay" or were "just exploring," those who wanted to experience the public manifestations of lesbianism looked for recently emerged enclaves in America. The era saw the emergence of little areas of sophistication or places where a laissez-faire "morality" was encouraged, such as Harlem and Greenwich Village, which seemed to provide an arena in which like-minded cohorts could pretend, at least, that the 1920s was a decade of true sexual rebellion and freedom.

Harlem had a particular appeal for whites who wanted to indulge in rebel sexuality. Perhaps there was a certain racism in their willingness to think of Harlem as a free-for-all party or, as *Colliers Magazine* said in the 1920s, "a synonym for naughtiness." White fascination with Harlem seems to have smacked of a "sexual colonialism," in which many whites *used* Harlem as a commodity, a stimulant to sexuality. And as in many colonized countries, Harlem itself, needing to encourage tourism for economic reasons, seemed to welcome the party atmosphere. Whites went not only to cabarets such as the Cotton Club, which presented all-black entertainment to all-white audiences, but also to speakeasies—the Drool Inn, the Clam House, the Hot Feet—that were located in dark basements, behind locked doors with peepholes. Whites snickered and leered in places that specialized in double entendre songs. They peeked into or participated in sex circuses and marijuana parlors. And they went to Harlem to experience homosexuality as the epitome of the forbidden: they watched transvestite floorshows; they rubbed shoulders with homosexuals; they were gay themselves in mixed bars that catered to black and white, heterosexual and homosexual. Made braver by bootlegged liquor, jazz, and what they saw as the primitive excitement of Africa, they acted out their enchantment with the primal and the erotic. They were fascinated with putative black naturalness and exoticism, and they romantically felt that those they regarded as the "lower class" had something to teach them about sexual expression that their middle-class milieu had kept from them. They believed Harlem gave them permission—or they simply took permission there—to explore what was forbidden in the white world. They could do in Harlem what they dared not do anywhere else.[10]

But it was not simply that whites took callous advantage of Harlem. To those who already defined themselves as homosexual, Harlem seemed a refuge, for which they were grateful. With an emerging homosexual consciousness, they began, probably for the first time in America, to see themselves as a minority that was not unlike racial minorities. They compared their social discomfort as homosexuals in the world at large with the discomfort of black people in the white world. Some sensed, as one character says in a novel about the period, *Strange Brother,* a bond between themselves and blacks because both groups flourished under heavy odds, and they believed that blacks also acknoweldged that bond: "In Harlem I found courage and joy and tolerance. I can be myself there. . . . They know all about me and I don't have to lie."[11]

In fact, however, blacks were generally as ambivalent about homosexuality as whites, but there were clubs in Harlem that did indeed welcome homosexuals, if only as one more exotic drawing card to lure tourists. Urban blacks in the 1920s did not all simply accept homosexuality as a "fact of life," as gay whites liked to think they did, but Harlem's reliance on tourism created at least the illusion of welcome.

Black novels of the 1920s show how thin that illusion really was. Claude McKay, a black writer who was himself bisexual, depicts Harlem's ambivalence about homosexuality in his novel *Home to Harlem* (1928). Raymond, an intellectual black waiter, is eloquent in his romantic characterization of lesbianism. He tells Jake, a kitchen porter, that he is reading a book by Alphonse Daudet, *Sapho:*

> "It's about a sporting woman who was beautiful like a rose. . . . Her lovers called her Sapho. . . . Sappho was a real person. A wonderful woman, a great Greek poet. . . . Her story gave two lovely words to modern language. . . . Sapphic and Lesbian—beautiful words."

But it is Jake who seems to speak for the Harlem masses when he realizes that "lesbian" is "what we calls bulldyker in Harlem," and he declares, "Them's all ugly womens." Raymond continues his liberal defense in correcting him, "Not *all*. And that's a damned ugly name." But he realistically recognizes "Harlem is too savage about some things." McKay illustrates more of Harlem's ridicule, good-natured as it may sometimes have been, when he presents in this novel a nightclub called The Congo that does cater to homosexuals along with heterosexuals, but the "wonderful drag blues" to which everyone dances suggests that the heterosexuals responded to the homosexuals around them with a gentle contempt: "And there is two things in Harlem I don't understan'/ It is a bulldyking woman and a faggoty man./ Oh, baby, how are you?/ Oh, baby, what are you?" [12]

Other novels by black writers also make it clear that while lesbians in Harlem of the 1920s went unmolested, they were seldom approved of. In Wallace Thurman's 1929 novel *The Blacker the Berry*, lesbian characters are a part of everyday Harlem, but there is always a hint of discomfort when they appear. Alva, a black bisexual who is a scoundrel, runs around with a creole lesbian, which emphasizes his unsavory character. Emma Lou, the heroine, goes hunting for a room to rent and encounters the absurd Miss Carrington, who places her hand on Emma Lou's knee, promising, "Don't worry anymore, dearie, I'll take care of you from now on," and tells her, "There are lots of nice girls living here. We call this the 'Old Maid's Home.' We have parties among ourselves and just have a grand time. Talk about fun! I know you'd be happy here." Emma Lou is frightened off by what seems to her a bizarre sexuality, although obviously there is a whole boarding-house full of lesbians who are allowed to live in Harlem undisturbed.[13] But the tone in which this phenomenon is presented, by a black writer who was himself gay, makes it clear that Harlem sees these women as "queers."

Yet most white writers who dealt with gay Harlem of the 1920s preferred the illusion of an "anything goes" atmosphere in which no one blinks an eye or expresses disapproval. In Blair Niles' *Strange Brother* when a white woman begs "to see the other Harlem" she is taken to the Lobster Pot, which vibrates with variety, both in color and sexual orientation. At the Lobster Pot,

> three white women had just taken the table next to [several Negro] dandies. One of them was a girl, rather lovely, with delicately chiseled features and short dark hair brushed severely back from a smooth low forehead. From the waist up she was dressed like a man, in a loose shirt of soft white silk and a dark tailored coat. She sat with one arm around the woman beside her.

No one makes wisecracks or exhibits disdain at such a sight. The most prominent lesbian figure in *Strange Brother* is Sybil, the black piano player at the Lobster Pot, perhaps modeled on Gladys Bentley, a lesbian transvestite Harlem entertainer. Sybil is a totally happy soul. She "filled the room with her vast vitality" and performed "as though to live was so gorgeous an experience that one must dance and sing in thanksgiving." She lives with another woman, her "wife," whom she married in a lesbian wedding, Sybil in tuxedo, the other woman in bridal veil and orange blossoms. A white character says, "They're happy and nobody they know thinks any the less of them."[14] But as black novelists suggested, such uncomplicated acceptance was less than certain.

In reality as well as in fiction, whites were reluctant to see Harlem's ambivalence toward homosexuality. Instead, they saw that Harlem appeared "wide open" sexually and, typical of many who enjoy the fruits of colonialism, they did not analyze why or even question Harlem's limits. They "slummed" in Harlem as though they were taking a trip into their id. The white women who went to Harlem to "be lesbian" were sometimes only "trying it on," taking advantage of what they assumed was the free spirit of the 1920s in Harlem to explore a variety of sexual possibilities. Some of these women considered themselves bisexual. More often they simply considered themselves adventurous, since there was not yet a pressing need to declare, even to one's self, one's "sexual orientation." They were frequently married or looking for a husband but saw that as no obstacle to their right to explore, either with the black women or with other white women they might meet in Harlem. In John Dos Passos' *The Big Money,* a novel about America after World War I, Dick Savage is implored by Patricia Doolittle (puns intended), one of the Junior League women in his group of wealthy friends, "Do take me some place low. . . . I'm the new woman. . . . I want to see life." They end up in a black, homosexual basement bar in Harlem, where Patricia dances with "a pale pretty mulatto girl in a yellow dress," while Dick dances with a "brown boy" in a tight suit who calls himself "Gloria Swanson." When Dick insists on taking Patricia home so that he can carry on without her as a witness, she screams at him, "You spoil everything. . . . You'll never go through with anything," piqued because she too had intended something further with her female partner. He later returns to the bar alone and takes "Gloria" and another young man, "Florence," home with him.[15] It is night time Harlem that unleashes inhibitions in these repressed whites. They permit themselves to live out fantasy in a world that is not quite real to them. They no longer have to "behave" as they do in white society which "matters."

Such fiction appears to have accurately reflected real life, in which wealthy whites were fascinated with "seeing life" and playing at it in various Harlem night spots that were open to displays of unconventional sexuality. Libby Holman, the celebrated singer of the '20s, who was married to a man, nevertheless came to Harlem, where she could not only act as a lesbian but even be outrageously gay. With one of her lovers, Louisa Carpenter du Pont Jenney, heiress to a great number of the du Pont millions, she visited Harlem almost nightly during one period, both dressed in identical men's dark suits and bowler hats such as they probably could not have worn with impunity in most other areas of the United States. There they were joined by other women celebrities and high-livers, most of them also married to men but out for a good time with other bisexual females: Beatrice Lillie, Tallulah Bankhead, Jeanne Eagles (who was Sadie Thompson in the first version of *Rain*), Marilyn Miller (the quintessential Ziegfeld girl), and Lucille Le Sueur (who later became Joan Crawford). Sometimes they went to the Lafayette to listen to another bisexual woman singer, Bessie Smith, or they visited Helen Valentine, the famous entrepeneur of 140th Street who staged sex circuses that featured homosexual as well as heterosexual acts.[16]

They encouraged some Harlem entertainers even to flaunt lesbianism, to make it a spectacle and an attraction to those who expected the *outre* from Harlem. Gladys Bentley, a three-hundred-pound "male impersonator" who sometimes played under the name Bobby Minton, appeared in men's suits not only onstage at the popular Clam House and the night spot she later opened, Barbara's Exclusive Club, but also on the streets of Harlem. It was said that her appearance "drew celebrities like flies." Dressed in a tuxedo, she announced her homosexuality by marrying a woman in a New Jersey civil ceremony, like her fictional counterpart Sybil in *Strange Brother*. Her blatant transvestism and homosexual behavior were part of her risqué appeal. She was the epitome of the stereotype of the lesbian that the public came to Harlem to gawk at. Gladys was in reality bisexual, but in her exceptional case it was more profitable to hide that aspect of her life from the public, which was fascinated with her outrageous image.[17]

That whites permitted themselves to act in Harlem as they probably would not elsewhere was obviously not without opportunism and a racist conviction that nothing really counted in the fantasy world of tourist Harlem. Perhaps their behavior can be attribtued to a feeling that their skin color served as armor here, making them impervious to any manner of attack or insult. But what they saw as the greater vitality of black people, "their more basic and healthier eroticism," permitted these white women to reach into those areas of their psyches (whose existence the Freudians had recently charted like a newly discovered planet) in order to discover and express desires they might have suppressed elsewhere. Many of them must have been grateful for the permission Harlem appeared to give them.

Black Lesbians in Harlem

A black lesbian subculture could be established fairly early in Harlem for several reasons. One root of that subculture might have been the demiworld. Black women who had been to jail learned there not only about lesbian sexuality but also about "mama" and "papa" sexual roles that had developed in institutionalized situations in America by the beginning of this century.[18] They sometimes established similar "butch/femme" arrangements once they were released from the institution, and perhaps they helped to bring such patterns into the fledgling subculture and to give it a clear, identifiable image.

But it was also easy for black lesbians to form a subculture in Harlem relatively early because although many Harlemites treated homosexuality with some ridicule, there was nevertheless more tolerance there than elsewhere for what the world of Babbit would have seen as outcasts and oddities, since blacks in general felt themselves to be outside the pale in white America. While homosexual men were sometimes being run out of small white towns, as Sherwood Anderson suggests in his post–World War I collection of stories *Winesburg, Ohio* ("Hands"), in Harlem tolerance extended to such a degree that black lesbians in butch/femme couples married each other in large wedding ceremonies, replete with bridesmaids and attendants. Real marriage licenses were obtained by masculinizing a first name or having a gay male surrogate apply for a license for the lesbian couple. Those licenses were actually placed on file in the New York City Marriage Bureau. The marriages were often common knowledge among Harlem heterosexuals.[19]

Such relative tolerance permitted black lesbians to socialize openly in their own communities instead of seeking out alien turf as white lesbians generally felt compelled to do. While heterosexual Harlemites often made fun of lesbians, they were willing to share bars and dance floors with them. There were thus plenty of places where black lesbians could amuse themselves and meet other lesbians in Harlem. The nightclubs that catered to gays and straights together that were described in novels such as *Home to Harlem, Strange Brother, The Big Money,* and Carl Van Vechten's *Nigger Heaven* all had counterparts in reality. The Lobster Pot, where Sybil sings and dances in *Strange Brother,* for instance, was probably the Clam House, where Gladys Bentley entertained for many years. There were numerous other bars and dance places, such as Connie's Inn, the Yeahman, the Garden of Joy, and Rockland Palace, where homosexuals and heterosexuals rubbed shoulders, although, as Van Vechten shows in *Nigger Heaven,* heterosexuals sometimes quit a club when they perceived that "too many bulldikers" were taking over.[20]

Institutions that had no counterparts in the white world also flourished in gay Harlem of the 1920s. "Buffet flats," apartments where sex circuses were staged, cafeteria style, for a paying clientele, occasionally catered to homosexual audiences. Ruby Walker Smith recalls such establishments where there were "nothing but faggots and

bulldaggers. . . . everybody that's in the life. . . . everything goes."
According to Smith, people would pay as they came in and then be
free to roam around: "They had shows in every room, two women
goin' together, a man and a man goin' together. . . . and if you
interested they do the same thing to you." While buffet flats appear
to have begun as a heterosexual institution, there were enough individuals who were interested in homosexuality to make a gay buffet
flat a profitable proposition. Equivalent buffet flats still catered to
heterosexuals as well, not only in New York, but in the ghettos of
Chicago, Detroit, Philadelphia, and Washington.[21]

While there were black lesbians in 1920s Harlem who committed
themselves to "the life" and sometimes lived with other women in
butch/femme couples, many who had affairs with other females were
married to men, either because they were bisexual, they needed to
marry for economic reasons, or front marriages permitted them to
continue functioning with less stigma in the very sexually aware and
ambivalent black community. Among Harlem women of wealth or
fame, bisexuality was not uncommon, though few would have admitted to exclusive homosexuality. Perhaps to Harlem sophisticates,
who in this respect do not appear to have been very different from
white sophisticates of the 1920s, the former seemed like adventure
while the latter seemed like disease. In any case, there is a good deal
of evidence of bisexuality among Harlem entertainers in particular.
For instance, blues singer Bessie Smith's lesbian interests were well
known among her show business intimates, although she was a married woman and took pains to cultivate that image as well. Many of
the women in Bessie's mid-1920s show, *Harlem Frolics,* were also
known to have had relationships with each other.[22]

It was popular knowledge among those in the show business world
of Harlem that Bessie was initiated into lesbianism by her old friend
and mentor Ma Rainey, another bisexual, whose "indiscreet" lesbian
behavior even got her into trouble in 1925 when she was arrested for
a lesbian orgy at her home involving the women in her chorus. A
neighbor called the police because of the noise. Reports say the women
scrambled for their clothes and ran out the back door, but Rainey's
escape was foiled when she fell down a staircase. She was accused of
running an indecent party and thrown in jail, from which Bessie
Smith bailed her out the following morning.[23]

The news of her arrest did not hurt Ma Rainey, however. Like
Gladys Bentley, she even capitalized on the shock effect that could be
produced by hints of her bisexuality. Her recording of "Prove It on

Me Blues," a blues monologue by a woman who prefers women, was advertised with a picture of a plump black woman, looking much like Ma Rainey, in a man's hat, tie, and jacket, talking to two entranced feminine flappers. In the distance, observing them, there is a policeman. The copy that accompanies the picture tries to pique the potential buyer's salacious interest by hinting at the possible autobiographical nature of the song: "What's all this? Scandal? Maybe so, but you wouldn't have thought it of 'Ma' Rainey. But look at that cop watching her! What does it all mean?"[24] The record company rightly assumed there were enough buyers in the 1920s who would not only understand the image and the implications but would be intrigued. But Ma Rainey was also sure to let the public know about her interest in young men and even to cultivate that heterosexual image of herself so that it largely undermined the other.

Similarly, Alberta Hunter, another blues singer, married in 1919 to obfuscate the conclusion she knew many people drew that she was a "bulldiker," and she apparently reasoned that although she did not live with her husband, marriage gave her a protective coloration—not of heterosexuality, which would have been going too far in favor of conservatism, but of bisexuality. She thus felt free to continue in her lesbian pursuits without excessive discretion and was known to have been the lover of Lottie Tyler (the niece of black 1920s comedian Bert Williams). She also kept company with other black show business luminaries who were not excessively careful to hide their bisexuality in Harlem, such as Ethel Waters and her lover of many years, Ethel Williams.[25] These women, who did not take great pains to pretend to exclusive heterosexuality, must have believed that in their own sophisticated circles of Harlem, bisexuality was seen as interesting and provocative. Although unalloyed homosexuality may still have connoted in 1920s Harlem the abnormality of "a man trapped in a woman's body," bisexuality seems to have suggested that a woman was super-sexy.

Among some sophisticated Harlem heterosexuals in the '20s the lesbian part of bisexuality was simply not taken very seriously. Even housewives occasionally indulged in lesbian affairs, with the open approval of their husbands. One Harlem resident of the 1920s remembers frequent lesbian parties and dinners thrown by a wealthy married woman with a big house and a lavish garden: "Her husband didn't mind her with the girls," she recalls, "but he said if he ever caught her with a man he'd cut her head off."[26] No less than among white libertines for centuries, some Harlemites believed that real sex was penetration by a penis and love between women was just fooling around.

Liberality toward bisexuality bespoke an urbanity that had special appeal for upper-class Harlemites, no less than for white worldly continentals and rebels against American Babbitry. Perhaps the tone was set for Harlem's upper class by A'Lelia Walker, who inherited a fortune from her former-washerwoman mother, inventor of a hair straightener that made millions. A majestic woman, nearly six feet tall, A'Lelia often went around with riding crop in hand and jeweled turban on her head. Though married several times, she was attended by a circle of handsome women and effete men, and as one of her contemporaries observed, "all the women were crazy about her." Some believed that her various marriages were "fronts" and her husbands were themselves homosexuals, but like many of the sophisticated bisexual Harlemites, she felt it desirable to be married, regardless of what she did in her affectional life.

A'Lelia held salons that were attended by French princesses, Russian grand dukes, men and women on New York's social register, Prohibition czars, Harlem Renaissance writers, and world-renowned intellectuals. But she threw other kinds of parties as well. Mabel Hampton, a Harlem dancer in the 1920s who attended some of Walker's less formal gatherings with a white lesbian friend, remembers them as

> funny parties—there were men and women, straight and gay. They were kinds of orgies. Some people had clothes on, some didn't. People would hug and kiss on pillows and do anything they wanted to do. You could watch if you wanted to. Some came to watch, some came to play. You had to be cute and well-dressed to get in.

A'Lelia Walker probably had much to do with the manifest acceptance of bisexuality among the upper classes in Harlem: those who had moral reservations about bisexuality or considered it strange or decadent learned to pretend a sophistication and suppress their disapproval if they desired A'Lelia's goodwill.[27] Although many were undoubtedly no less ambivalent about lesbianism than Jake, the kitchen porter in *Home to Harlem,* through Walker's example and influence they learned at least to tolerate it.

The complex attitudes with regard to female homosexual relations that were prevalent among sophisticated Harlemites in the 1920s are sometimes reflected in lyrics of the blues. Those songs, which are often satirical or funny, do not deal with bisexuality, perhaps because that affectional preference lent itself less readily to humorous caricature than did blatant lesbianism. Instead, they sometimes present extreme lesbian stereotypes (especially the mannish lesbian image that the term "bulldiker" connoted), which allowed the listener to recognize the situation without introducing subtle complications and to laugh at the in-joke. With the usual goal of titillation, the songs also satirically probed masculine uneasiness about the suspicion that women know how to "do it" better to each other than men do. And they frequently admitted to an ambivalent fascination.

In some of these songs the characterization of the lesbian combines images of freakishness with a bravado that is at once laughable and admirable. The lesbian is ridiculed for her illicit and unorthodox sexuality. But she is also an outlaw, which makes her a bit of a culture hero in an oppressed community. In Ma Rainey's "Prove It on Me Blues" the singer seems to invite jeers: she admits to wearing a collar and a tie, to being "crooked," to liking "to watch while the women pass by." But the black audience is forced to identify with her because she and they understand stigmatization. And she is also rescued from being ludicrous because she can toy with the audience. She is the jokester they must, at least grudgingly, admire. She teasingly admits that she means to follow another woman everywhere she goes and that she wants the whole world to know it. But she pretends to dangle ambiguity in front of her listeners:

> Went out last night with a crowd of my friends,
> They must've been women, 'cause I don't like no men. . . .
>
> They say I do it, ain't nobody caught me,
> They sure got to prove it on me. . . . [28]

Her message is finally that she doesn't give a damn what they think and until she is caught *in flagrante delicto* no one can prove anything about her anyway. But the audience is meant to understand that she does indeed "do it" and to simultaneously laugh at her and cheer her on for her boldness.

Teasing is recurrent in these blues songs, whose purpose seems often to be to worry the male listener just to the point of titillation. In George Hannah's "The Boy in the Boat" the singer provokingly acknowledges the superiority of lesbian sex (cunnilingus) and challenges the audience:

> You think I'm lyin', just ask Tack Ann
> Took many a broad from many a man.

Bessie Jackson's "BD [bulldyker] Women's Blues" is another provocative admonishment to heterosexual males that they are dispensable and if they will not reform women could easily do without them. She tells her male listeners that they can't understand BD women, but in her experience, bulldykers have everything a "nach'l man" has and more. They can lay their jive, they can strut their stuff, they can drink up many whiskeys, they're not too lazy to work and make their dough, and a woman misses nothing by chosing them over a man.[29]

But there is an additional dimension to Jackson's song that can also be found in a few other blues songs about lesbianism. It can be read as a subversive statement of lesbian pride in its listing of lesbian competencies, and a prefiguration of the radical feminism of a much later era in its warning that women can find other women much nicer than cruel and selfish men:

> Comin' a time, BD women, they ain't goin' to need no men.
> Oh, the way they treat us is a low down and dirty thing.

George Hannah's song, too, although it seems to be bent on provoking the male listener to both worry and laughter, contains a secret message to the female listener that lesbianism can be superior to heterosexuality. The remarkable dual message that characterizes some of these blues songs is particularly clear in one lyric that baldly states that while lesbian sex is improper, it is nevertheless terrific:

> I know women that don't like men.
> The way they do is a crying sin.
> It's dirty but good, oh yes, it's just dirty but good.[30]

The song at once urges men to worry and women to "try it." The humor is derived from the double discourse that pretends disapproval but hints at titillation in the face of sexual daring.

The listener to these 1920s blues apparently took whatever he or she wanted out of the songs. To the heterosexual male they were provocative. To the potentially bisexual female they were suggestive and encouraging. To the lesbian they could be affirming. One lesbian blues song, "BD's Dream," has been described by historians of 1920s and '30s music as one of the most frequently heard songs in the rent party repertoire. Of course lesbians sometimes attended rent parties in Harlem (parties where the guests would pay an entrance fee to help the tenant raise money for the rent), but those gatherings were generally predominantly heterosexual, which confirms that the song must have had terrific popularity with all manner of audiences.[31]

It is not surprising that sophisticated heterosexuals, both blacks and the tourists who were intrigued with black life and environs, were taken with such lyrics—they were characteristic of the era: They flaunt unorthodoxy with a vengeance, but at the same time they exhibit the vestiges of discomfort toward female nonconformity and sexual autonomy that individuals who scoffed at the conventional nevertheless maintained. That discomfort, as much as it is mitigated by laughter in these songs, suggests that even those who chose to reject the mainstream culture or who were cast outside it by virtue of their race could go no further in their own unconventionality than to be ambivalent about sexual love between women.

A Note on Working-Class Lesbian Communities Elsewhere in America

While some middle-class professional women such as those described in chapter 1 lived with other women as lesbians during the 1920s, their lesbian social lives tended to be carried on within friendship circles and away from public places. They generally would not have gone to the Harlem gay bars that emerged in the 1920s, for example. Their lifestyles did not lend themselves to the construction of a distinctive lesbian subculture that broke away from the main culture in terms of dress, language, haunts, mores, etc. But there is evidence to suggest that such a subculture was slowly being established in a number of working-class communities throughout America in the 1920s.

Recent historians have suggested that it was American working-class women of the early twentieth century who first began to enjoy a broader spectrum of public amusements and brought the concept of such diverse pastimes into the lives of middle-class women later in the century. This theory is particularly revealing with regard to the development of a visible lesbian subculture in America. For example, in the nineteenth century it would have been unthinkable for women other than prostitutes to frequent saloons. But by the second decade of this century, other working-class women began visiting saloons that offered food as well as drink. That new social custom undoubtedly made it easier for lesbians of the working class than it would have been for their middle-class counterparts to conceive of themselves in a saloon environment. Working-class lesbians could therefore become prominent in the establishment of lesbian bars, which

became the single most important public manifestation of the subculture for many decades, eventually attracting young lesbians who were
not of working-class backgrounds.[32]

A visible homosexual subculture centered on bars could be seen in
several large cities outside of New York in the course of the 1920s.
Blues singer Bertha Idaho's "Down on Pennsylvania Avenue," which
she recorded for Columbia Records in 1929, decribes one famous gay
and lesbian nightspot in Baltimore, Maryland:

> Let's take a trip down to that cabaret
> Where they turn night into day,
> Some freakish sights you'll surely see,
> You can't tell the he's from the she's,
> You'll find them every night on Pennsylvania Avenue.

Another blues song, recorded by Ma Rainey in 1924, suggests an
even earlier development of a visible black lesbian subculture on the
South Side of Chicago:

> Goin' down to spread the news
> State Street women wearing brogan shoes . . .
> There's one thing I don't understand
> Some women walkin' State Street like a man.[33]

A white working-class lesbian subculture, in which butch and
femme roles were clearly pronounced, also emerged in big cities by
the 1920s. Such a subculture, made possible by the numbers of young
women leaving their families and moving to the cities in order to find
work, began to appear in areas such as the Near North Side of
Chicago, a district of boardinghouses and furnished room rentals
where working class women without families could obtain cheap
housing. A sociologist at the end of the 1920s, researching Chicago's
Near North Side, wrote of lesbian parties that one of his female
informants had described to him that went on nightly in one set of
rooms where "some of [the women] would put on men's evening
clothes, make love to the others, and eventually carry them off in
their arms into the bedrooms." Such butch/femme dichotomies were
also manifested in the white working class lesbian bars that were
established in that city by the following decade such as the Roselle
Club and the Twelve-Thirty Club.[34]

Although the public manifestations of a working class lesbian subculture remained small throughout the 1920s, it is clear that lesbians
were everywhere in the big cities. Another sociologist at the beginning of the 1920s, Frances Donovan, who studied waitresses in Chi-

cago, suggested that lesbianism was not uncommon among them. Donovan related several stories about instances she had observed, such as catching a glimpse of two waitresses in a dressing room of a restaurant as one "passed her hands caressingly over the bare arms and breast of another." But since Donovan was an outsider looking in and frequently rendering judgment on the lives of working class women, it is difficult to tell just how accurate her other conjectures of lesbianism among waitresses really were.[35]

Unfortunately, most of the information that has survived about working-class lesbians during the 1920s has come down to us through the writings of outsiders, since the women themselves seldom committed detailed descriptions of their feelings or lifestyles to paper. Outside of the blues songs it is rare that we get to hear the voices of working-class lesbians. There is only an occasional letter that is tempting in its hints about life within the subculture but is mute about the details, such as a brief note written in 1925 and "found in the room of the writer":

> Dear Mary: I am writing a few lines to let you know that I am well and hoping you are the same . . . But kid I'd like to go out with you again the old lady throwing me out of the house because I ain't working for about a month now. why don't you call me up honey did you forget about me, did you forget my phone number . . . Good Bye, Good Luck. From Your Loving Girl Friend, Adeline J—to Mary K—.[36]

Although there is not a wealth of material that has been unearthed to give a clear picture of 1920s working-class lesbians outside of Harlem (which was influenced to some extent by its appeal to wealthier tourists), it is nevertheless apparent that lesbian life and subculture were quietly flourishing among these women by this time. Generally beyond the fear or grasp of middle-class morality, not needing a "sexual revolution" to endorse their sexual expression, and freed earlier by their class to look for amusements in public places, they were more easily able than middle-class lesbians to begin trends that were later to become the most prominent public manifestations of lesbianism.

Lesbians in Bohemia

As much as many American "rebels" in the 1920s paid lip service to the necessity of breaking with the restrictive morality of the past, they were very close in time to an era that refused to allow women a truly autonomous sexuality such as lesbianism assumes. Thus they generally had imperfect success in making the revolutionary leap to genuine acceptance of sexual love between women. If there was anywhere that a non-working-class lesbian community could flourish in the '20s, however, it should have been in an area such as Greenwich Village, where value was placed on the unconventional and the breaking of taboos. But although lesbianism was allowed to exist more openly there than it could have in most places in the United States, even in Greenwich Village sexual love between women was treated with ambivalence. On the one hand, it was an experience that the free bohemian woman should have no scruples against: it should be taken for granted as part of her liberated sexual repertoire. It was, in fact, bohemian chic for a woman to be able to admit to a touch of lesbianism, as is suggested by the panache with which Edna St. Vincent Millay is said to have answered a psychoanalyst at a Greenwich Village party who was attempting to find the cause of a headache from which she suffered. The analyst asked, with combined pride in his knowledge of the psychosomatic effects of sexual repression and trepidation at the prospect of shocking a young woman:

"I wonder if it has ever occurred to you that you might perhaps, although you are hardly conscious of it, have an occasional impulse toward a person of your own sex?"

And Millay answered with the nonchalance requisite for a true bohemian: "Oh, you mean I'm homosexual! Of course I am, and heterosexual too, but what's that got to do with my headache?"[37]

But on the other hand, among bohemian men (who controlled the mores of the Village, despite their occasional pretense to sexual egalitarianism), sexual love between women was never validated as equal to heterosexual intercourse, which was now claimed to be crucial to even a woman's good health and peak functioning.

Yet Villagers prided themselves on being "bohemian," which meant, as early as the mid-nineteenth century, being not like the creatures of society, victims of rules and customs, but free of such limitations. Narrow-mindedness would have betrayed such a lack of sophistication as to degrade the bohemian back to the position of mere worldling.[38] It was incumbent upon the Village dweller, therefore, to pretend tolerance, at least, of unconventional female sexuality. For that reason, as lesbianism started to become a lifestyle rather than a mere sexual behavior in the United States, non-working-class women who wanted to live as lesbians, as well as those who were attracted to exploring various kinds of sexuality, were drawn to Greenwich Village. It was there that some of the earliest public manifestations of a non-working-class white American lesbian subculture developed.

By the second decade of our century Greenwich Village was already well established as an offbeat community of artists and intellectuals. It was for good reason that Mabel Dodge chose to settle there on her return from Europe in 1912 and to preside over weekly salons of sophisticates and bohemians that became the center of avant-garde life. In her salons, which were attended by scruffy artists and dignified dilettantes as well as ladies with bobbed hair and "mannish-cut garments," Mabel Dodge nurtured revolutionary causes. Homosexuality was implicitly one of them. As was the case with A'Lelia Walker in Harlem, it was Mabel's own open bisexual behavior, which she wrote about voluminously in her memoirs, that helped to foster some sexual tolerance in Greenwich Village during those early years.[39]

Perhaps another reason that homosexuality became somewhat more acceptable in the Village than elsewhere was that as certain taboos began to diminish throughout America, and even people outside the largest metropolitan centers were reexamining old attitudes, the Village's exoticism required something less commonplace than mere smoking, drinking, and heterosexual experimentation. For some Village dwellers it was homosexuality that now helped to draw the line of revolt. Characteristically, that revolt was expressed in self-conscious gestures, such as a 1923 invitation to a Greenwich Village ball, illustrated by two women dancing together—one wearing pants, the other a dress. The copy read: "Come all ye Revelers! Dance the night into dawn—Come when you like, with whom you like—Wear what you like—Unconventional? Oh, to be sure . . ." Suppression of *The Captive* in 1926 and the near-suppression of *The Well of Loneliness* in 1928 also contributed to making lesbianism a *cause célèbre* for some Greenwich Village bohemians who prided themselves on being on the side of the underdog and the minority. Because of such liberality, by the end of the decade all manner of homosexual retreats flourished there, even, according to one historian who does not, unfortunately, cite his source, a brothel that catered very successfully to lesbians.[40]

There were other elements as well in Greenwich Village that helped to provide an atmosphere that was relatively sympathetic to same-sex love, such as the strong feminist bent of some of its women. A Village feminist club of middle-class professional women, Heterodoxy, brought together on a regular basis women who defined themselves as lesbians, bisexuals, and heterosexuals. About 25 percent of

Heterodoxy's membership was not heterosexual, but all of these unconventional women appear to have accepted each other's differences in sexual and affectional preferences and were mutually supportive. An anthropological spoof by one of the members referred to the organization as "the tribe of Heterodites" in which the strongest taboo is against taboo, because the imposition of restrictions is injurious to free development of the mind and spirit. "By preventing taboo," the writer observed, "the tribe has been able to preserve considerable unanimity of variety of opinion." In an unconventional women's atmosphere such as this, despite the middle-class professional affiliations of most of the members, one even received some extra points for life choices that the outside world considered eccentric. Several of the women in Heterodoxy were acknowledged couples. Although they could have hidden from the uninitiated, since their appearance was not stereotypically lesbian, in the Village their anniversary dates were celebrated by fellow Heterodites, and during times of trial they were given emotional support as couples by the heterosexuals as well as by the other homosexuals in the group.[41] Of course many of the lesbian members of this Greenwich Village club would choose to live in the Village for its ostensible laissez-faire milieu that surpassed the rest of the country, though their ties to the professional class would not permit them to participate in the formation of the more blatant lesbian bar culture that was now beginning there through the efforts of more bohemian types.

Several Village clubs that lesbians frequented were like Harlem night spots in that they also welcomed Village heterosexuals and tourists who occasionally indulged themselves in lesbian chic; others, such as the Flower Pot on Gay and Christopher Street and Paul and Joe's on 9th, catered exclusively to men and women who identified themselves as homosexual, but there were not yet enough females to support all-women's clubs. [42] Nor does there seem to have been much of a feeling of community yet, even in these clubs, between males and females who identified themselves as homosexual. They shared a sense of their differentness, but unlike in Germany, where gay men and women since the turn of the century had banded together in organizations such as the Scientific Humanitarian Committee in order to battle homophobia, the notion of homosexuals organizing for political action was still years away in America. Lesbians still had before them the major battles of defining for themselves, on an individual level, what lesbianism meant apart from the sexologists' views, fighting familial and societal opposition to the autonomous female, and staking out modest territories where they could make contact with one another. Although many of them might have called themselves "new women," they were not yet bold enough to articulate the connection between feminism and lesbianism such as women of the more radical 1970s did to fuel their militant movement. They had enough to do in merely coming into existence as lesbians, even in an environment that was quasi-tolerant of their new lifestyle.

The general ambivalence toward lesbians in Greenwich Village, despite the milieu of tolerance and a popular attitude that lesbian experimentation was chic, is suggested by a description of one retreat, Jo's, that catered to both homosexuals and heterosexuals. The presence of "oddities" such as women who called themselves lesbians was thought to bolster the artistic unconventionality of the place. When Jo's held open discussions on topics such as "What Is Sex Appeal?" the views of the lesbians present were especially called for. But there was apparently considerable discomfort about the genuine lesbian and some relief at any evidence of her bisexuality. One Village observer tells smirkingly of a young woman who was the joke of the place "because she was trying so hard to be a lesbian, but when she got drunk she forgot and let the men dance with her."[43] Despite the worship of nonconformity in the Village, lesbianism was clearly not accepted as a sexual choice as valid as heterosexuality. Bisexuality was far more easily understood here, as it was in Harlem, particularly if it ended in heterosexuality.

Perhaps the chief reason that lesbians fared at least relatively well in the Village was that bohemian men did not take them quite seriously. The men often cherished a real conviction, born of a knowledge of Freud on which they prided themselves, that lesbianism was just a phase some women went through and while it was all right to express it in order to get rid of suppressions, it must not become arrested as a way of life. They were confident it could be gotten out of a woman by a good psychoanalyst or a good man.

Edna St. Vincent Millay's experiences in the Village may be seen as a paradigm of what some women encountered if they let it be known that they considered themselves lesbian. Millay, who had been called Vincent in college, was probably the model for Lakey in Mary McCarthy's novel *The Group*. Like Lakey, she was the creative and independent leader of her fellow students at Vassar, and also, like Lakey, all her love affairs during her college career, which did not end until she was twenty-five years old, were with other women. Her strongest "smash" in that all-female environment was with

Charlotte (Charlie) Babcock, who was the model for Bianca in Millay's play *The Lamp and the Bell* (1921). The play depicts a self-sacrificing love between two women about whom others say, "I vow I never knew a pair of lovers/ More constant than these two." Millay also had a passionate attachment to Anne Lynch during those Vassar days, and even several years later she wrote Lynch: "Oh, if I could just get my arms about you!—And stay with you like that for hours. . . . I love you very much, dear Anne, and I always shall." Another Vassar classmate, Isobel Simpson, Millay called her "Dearest Little Sphinx" and "[my] own true love." From Greenwich Village she promised Isobel: "Someday I shall write a great poem to you, so great that I shall make you famous in history."[44]

But although Millay's erotic life had been exclusively with women, once out of that all-female environment and in Greenwich Village, there was pressure on her to become at least bisexual. As a good bohemian she pretended, of course, to continue to regard homosexuality in a blasé manner, as her response to the psychoanalyst who tried to cure her of a headache suggests. Yet despite her panache, Millay eventually bowed to the pressure to give up exclusive lesbianism, as many women's college graduates must have in the heterosexual 1920s, when companionate marriage was seen as the "advanced" woman's highest goal.

The unpublished memoirs of Floyd Dell, who became Millay's first male lover in Greenwich Village, give some insight into how women who came to the Village as lesbians were sometimes steered toward heterosexuality in this "progressive" atmosphere. For weeks Millay had agreed to go to bed with Dell, since she was taught in the Village that free bohemian women should have no scruples against such things; but she was obviously ambivalent, insisting they remain fully clothed and refusing to have intercourse. Finally Dell pressured her sufficiently to make her overcome her reluctance. "I know your secret," he said. "You are still a virgin. You have merely had homosexual affairs with girls in college," devaluing such relationships as a mature sexual experience. Dell claims that Millay was astonished at his deductive powers and she admitted, "No man has ever found me out before." In her chagrin she gave in to him. Dell's memoirs indicate that he was one of the early lesbian-smashers. He says he made love to her, feeling that it was his "duty to rescue her." His rescue was obviously imperfect, however, since she was still having affairs with women years later when she took up with Thelma Wood, the woman who also became Djuna Barnes' lover and her model for

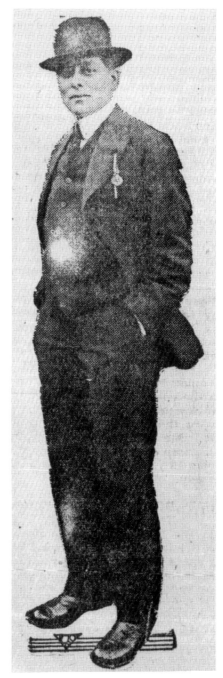

Above: Mary Fields, born a slave in 1832, often wore men's clothes as a stagecoach driver. (From *Black Lesbians* by J. R. Roberts, Naiad Press, 1981; reprinted by permission.)

Right: Ralph Kerwinieo, nee Cora Anderson, an American Indian woman: "The world is made by man—for man alone." (From *The Day Book,* 1914; courtesy of Jonathan Ned Katz.)

Right: Doctor Bernard Talmey observed in 1904 that the American public's innocence regarding lesbianism resulted in dubbing women's intimate attachments with each other "mere friendship." (Courtesy of the Found Images Collection, Lesbian Herstory Archives/ L.H.E.F., Inc.)

Above: Songwriter George Hannah observed of World War I that Uncle Sam: "Packed up all the men and sent 'em on to France, / Sent 'em over there the Germans to hunt, / Left the women at home to try out all their new stunts." (Courtesy of the Found Images Collection, Lesbian Herstory Archives/L.H.E.F., Inc.)

Top: Women Physical Education majors at the University of Texas held private "drag" proms in the 1930s. (Courtesy of Olivia Sawyers.)

Bottom: New York, 1940s. Middle-class minority lesbian styles were diverse. (© Cathy Cade, *A Lesbian Photo Album,* 1987. Reprinted by permission.)

Top: San Francisco, circa 1944. A private lesbian party. (Courtesy of the June Mazer Lesbian Collection, Los Angeles.)

Bottom: A San Francisco "gay girls" bar during World War II. (Courtesy of the June Mazer Lesbian Collection, Los Angeles.)

Left: WAC Sergeant Johnnie Phelps during World War II. General Eisenhower told her to "forget the order" to ferret out the lesbians in her battalion. (Courtesy of Johnnie Phelps.)

Above: On military bases during the 1950s informers were planted on women's softball teams, since lesbians were thought to be attracted to athletics. (Courtesy of Betty Jetter.)

Top: Beverly Shaw sang "songs tailored to your taste" at elegant lesbian bars in the 1950s. (Courtesy of the June Mazer Lesbian Collection, Los Angeles.)

Bottom: Frankie, a 1950s butch. (Courtesy of Frankie Hucklenbroich.)

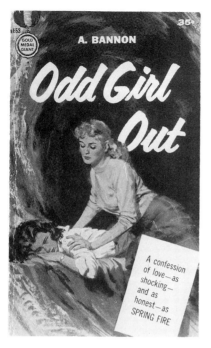

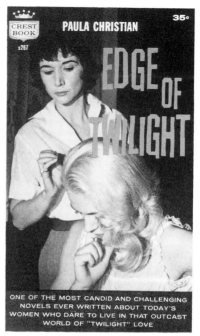

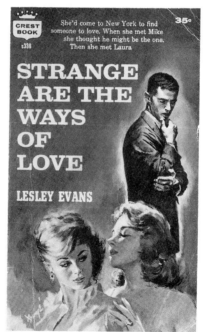

The pulps of the 1950s and '60s were full of "odd girls" and "twilight lovers." (Courtesy of Ballantine Books, Inc.)

Barbara Gittings in a pre-Stonewall lesbian and gay rights demonstration in front of Independence Hall, Philadelphia. (Courtesy of Nancy Tucker.)

Robin in *Nightwood*. Dell finally had to admit with disappointment that Millay could not be entirely rescued. Years after their relationship, he lamented in an interview, "It was impossible to understand [Millay]. . . . I've often thought she may have been fonder of women than of men." But despite his cognizance of her feelings about women he believed he had right on his side when he proselytized for heterosexuality, and he was encouraged in this conviction by the bohemians who scoffed at the technical virginity of women whose erotic lives were exclusively with other women.[45]

Dell even urged Millay to undergo psychoanalysis in order to "overcome" her interest in women, although she thought analysis silly and, with a feminist awareness developed in her all-women college environment, saw Freudian ideas as nothing but "a Teutonic attempt to lock women up in the home and restore them to cooking and baby-tending." Yet despite her various attempts to resist, she appears to have succumbed to the pressure. She married, although it was to a man who, she claimed, left her relatively free to behave as she pleased. She said of her life with her husband that they "lived like two bachelors."[46] But to have chosen to live as a lesbian, even in the world of Greenwich Village, was too problematic for her, despite her history of love for other women.

The kind of pressure that was put on Millay to give up her love for women, or at least to make it take a secondary position to heterosexuality, was probably typical of what happened to young females even in this most bohemian environment during the 1920s, when love between women such as had been so vital in earlier eras was devalued. While sex between women was acceptable and even chic in circles that were enamored with the radical or the exotic, serious love relationships between women could no longer be highly regarded since they would interfere with companionate heterosexual relationships. Of course there were some bohemian men who saw lesbianism as part of the Village's experiment with free love and they respected the women's choices, and there were others who were titillated by it, and still others who were homosexual also and happy enough that their female counterparts were enjoying themselves. However, many bohemian men, if they could take lesbianism seriously at all, resented not only the women's ties to each other but their general assertiveness, which in itself may have signified danger to some of the men.

Floyd Dell is again an example of the latter attitude. Like a good bohemian he prided himself on his radicalism, while maintaining views of women that were often quite traditional. His short stories and poems in *Love in Greenwich Village* (1926) suggest that he really believed that sexual experimentation is dangerous, women's primary concerns are, or should be, their husbands' welfare, and all women, in spite of their protest, want to be sexually conquered. Hutchins Hapgood astutely observed of the typical male in Greenwich Village at that time that he felt like a victim deprived of his property: "No matter what his advanced ideas were, his deeply complex, instinctive, and traditional nature often suffered [from woman's] full assumption of his old privileges."[47] Her most outrageous assumption was her notion that she was sexually independent. Love between women made these male bohemians uncomfortable, despite their pretended liberalism and sophistication. Even in the Village, men of the 1920s were not free of the received notions of what a woman should be. It was thus impossible for women who wanted to try to live as lesbians even in the Village to feel that they could carry on with the full approval of the "unconventional" individuals with whom they shared the turf.

However, in disregard of the discomfort of many Village men, love between women did continue to flourish there throughout the 1920s and a lesbian subculture took root, challenging the requisite tolerance of bohemia. By the early '30s there were enough like-minded women to form a real community. Its headquarters, side by side with that of homosexual men, was a block of nightclubs near the Provincetown Playhouse on MacDougal Street. Gay men converted the street into a major cruising area, and it was soon called the Auction Block, although lesbians claimed a bit of space for them-selves in the clubs that catered to them and featured lesbian enter-tainers.[48] Non-working-class lesbians were more at home in the Vil-lage than anywhere in the United States, although they were forced to recognize that even bohemians were not entirely comfortable with them.

The Heterosexual Revolution and the Lesbian in the Woodpile

Many Americans were certainly intrigued with homosexuality, but the intrigue was not without ambivalence. In some circles where sexual matters were discussed openly, lesbianism was even blamed for some women's inability to transfer their libido to their husbands and the resultant failure of marriages. Even many of the 1920s Freudians were ambivalent about homosexual experimentation between women. While some of them believed its suppression caused great damage in a patient and its expression could be very positive, others found it profoundly disturbing. And still others believed both at once, such as the doctor who stated in a 1929 article that homosexuality may represent a high stage of psychosexual development for an individual and that it is the job of the psychoanalyst working with a homosexual to study "the nature of the disorder" and ways to adjust the patient therapeutically to heterosexuality; or another doctor who reported on a diary kept by two college girls in love with each other that it expressed "the finest sentiments of sexual love I ever read" and that through proper psychiatric treatment they were "cured" and "both have lived normal lives ever since."[49]

Freud's work and distorted interpretations of it sometimes even became an excuse for various alarmists during the very sex-conscious 1920s. For example, Freud believed that all children went through a homosexual phase on their way to heterosexuality. His identification of childhood homosexuality, "normal" as Freud thought it was, alerted medical doctors to the existence of the phenomenon and then provided fuel for hysteria among some of them. A 1925 psychiatrist and psychologist team noted that during the past year a number of cases of homosexuality in children had come to their attention, and they traced the psychogenesis of those cases to an early excessive affection for the mother or the father, suggesting that parents must be wary of their children's love. The 1920s, with all its ambivalence regarding sexual revolution, ushered in a concern about childhood feelings that were previously seen as natural. Psychiatrists were now warning parents that every childhood and adolescent emotional attachment must be scrutinized in order to nip homosexuality in the bud and that reciprocal same-sex crushes, which had long been considered a normal aspect of girlhood, were truly dangerous even if no sexual activity occurred, since they might stimulate the girl's unconscious desires and fixate her on same-sex love.[50]

Romantic friendship had clearly outworn its social usefulness as a preventer of illegitimacy in America of the 1920s. By that time contraceptive devices had become widely available and birth control clinics multiplied rapidly, thanks to the efforts of Margaret Sanger, who began opening such clinics in 1916. The fear of pregnancy, which had been seen as a great danger in premarital sex, was greatly mitigated. A man could more easily demand that a woman not place limits on the degree of intimacy in which she would indulge with him. Sexual, or rather heterosexual, Puritanism became passe. Popular arguments from Freud assisted this revolution. If a woman refused to be receptive to a man, she was repressing a natural urge, she was blocking her libido, and that would cause her to be neurotic. The leaders of this sexual revolution managed to make pleasure seem like medical necessity. They argued that heterosexual intercourse cured digestive disorders and anemia, created a "salutary euphoria," and calmed the nerves even of sick people. In fact, they said, without heterosexual intercourse, nothing of value would be produced in the world, since those glands that induced the desire for intercourse also supplied the energy for work. It was intercourse, they insisted, that even helped broaden social sympathies and acted as moral inspiration. The new sexual compulsion pushed many women into heterosexual relations. As one writer in the 1920s observed, instead of living at their own tempo and inclination, "whole groups appear to fall under the suggestion that they must busy themselves with flaming bright red." The nineteenth-century excesses of heterosexual repression had been replaced in the 1920s by "the excess of [hetero]sexual expression."[51]

Such pressure to be heterosexually active brought with it in more conventional circles a concomitant pressure to eschew whatever could be characterized as homosexual, including whatever remnants were left of the old institution of romantic friendship. While such homophobia represented just one more taboo to be joyously flaunted by the adventurous and the experimental, it must have been confusing to many, especially when the popular sex reformers managed to sound modern and revolutionary while promoting antihomosexual prejudice, warning that maintenance of what they called "outworn traditions" regarding virginity was manufacturing what they called "perverts." Their advice to women, that the only true happiness lay in heterosexual fulfillment, was a far distance from the work of supposedly conservative, traditional writers of earlier centuries such as William Alger, who had advised in his 1868 book *The Friendships of Women* that unmarried females (whose numbers had increased because so many men were killed during the Civil War) would do well to form romantic friendships with other women, since those relationships bring to life "freshness, stimulant charm, noble truths and aspirations."[52]

In contrast, during the post World War I years, when for the first but not the last time in this century men came back to reclaim their jobs and their roles, it was insisted that virtues such as Alger delineated were to be found not in romantic friendships but in "companionate marriage" alone. Companionate marriage, which now became an American ideal, was supposed to rectify the most oppressive elements of Victorian wedlock; marriage would become an association of "companionship" and "cooperation," although real social equality between men and women was not a concern that its advocates addressed. As a means of achieving the goals of companionate marriage, numerous marriage manuals and other texts on how to attain happiness pressured men to perform sexually, to bring their mates to orgasm and contentment. If they were unsuccessful, the blame was attributed not only to their "performance skills" but also to the woman's "failure to transfer the libido from a love object of the same sex to one of the opposite sex."[53]

Since in earlier eras "decent" women were generally not expected to respond to men sexually, no such "explanations" for unresponsiveness had been sought and it was unlikely that lesbianism would have been suspected as a reason for heterosexual unhappiness. By the 1920s, however, the notion that love between women could stand in the way of marital happiness instead of being "a rehearsal in girlhood" for such happiness, as Henry Wadsworth Longfellow had characterized it in 1849, was so popularized that Broadway audiences flocked to see Edouard Bourdet's *The Captive,* the *succès de scandale* play devoted to that theme. Lesbianism thus became the villain in the drama of bringing men and women together through (hetero)sexual freedom and companionate marriage (in which the female companion was implored to stay put in the kitchen and the bedroom). As villain of the piece, the lesbian gradually came to be characterized by a host of nasty moral attributes that were reflected in literature and popular culture for the next half century.

The sexual revolution of the 1920s, which was felt throughout cosmopolitan areas but most particularly in offbeat centers such as bohemian Greenwich Village and tourist Harlem, had two important effects on love between women of middle-class backgrounds in particular: to some of them who were just beginning to define themselves consciously as sexual beings, an erotic relationship with another woman was one more area to investigate and one more right to demand, though quietly compared to the vociferous demands fifty years later. Unlike romantic friends of other eras, who would have happened upon lesbian genital sexuality only by chance if at all, their counterparts of the '20s *knew* all about the sexual potential that existed between females. Having been given concepts and language by the

sexologists—from Krafft-Ebing to Ellis to Freud—they could consciously choose to explore that potential in ways that were not open
to their predecessors. And the temper of the times often *seemed* to
give them permission for such exploration.

On the other hand, the times were not, after all, far removed from
the Victorian era, and despite seeming liberality, the notion of sex
between women was too shocking a departure from the past image
of womanhood to be widely tolerated. Nor could the sexual potential
of women's love for each other be ignored now by those outside the
relationship as it could be earlier. American men realized with a shock
that if they wanted the benefits of companionate heterosexuality,
which sexologists and psychologists told them was crucial to well-
being, they needed to suppress women's same-sex relationships—
which had almost always been companionate and therefore rivaled
heterosexuality. Thus, ironically, in the midst of a sexual revolution
when sex between women became an area of erotic exploration in
some circles and some women were beginning to establish a lifestyle
based on that preference, lesbians came to be regarded as pariahs.

4

Wastelands and Oases: the 1930s

Lydia to her fiancé on leaving a women's school:
These bunches of women living together, falling in love
with each other because they haven't anyone else to fall in
love with! It's obscene! Oh, take me away!
　　　　　　　　　　　　　　　—*Marion Patton,*
　　　　　　　　　　　Dance on the Tortoise, *1930*

I feel confident she is in love with me just as much as I am
with her. She is concerned about me and so thoughtful. . . .
My sex life has never caused me any regrets. I'm very much
richer by it. I feel it has stimulated me and my imagination
and increased my creative powers.
　　　　　　　　　—*32–year-old woman interviewed in 1935*
　　　　　　　　　　　　for George Henry's Sex Variants

Perhaps if the move toward greater sexual freedom that was barely
begun in the 1920s had not been interrupted by the depression, erotic
love between women might have been somewhat less stigmatized in
public opinion in the 1930s and a lesbian subculture might have
developed more rapidly. Instead, whatever fears were generated about
love between women in the 1920s were magnified in the uncertainty
of the next decade as the economic situation became dismal and
Americans were faced with problems of survival. This aborted liberality, together with the narrowing of economic possibilities, necessarily affected a woman's freedom to live and love as she chose.

While more and more women continued to be made aware of the
sexual potential in female same-sex relationships—through the great
notoriety of *The Well of Loneliness* and the many works it influenced
in the 1930s, through the continued popularity and proliferation of
psychoanalytic ideas, and through a persistently though slowly growing lesbian subculture—to live as a lesbian in the 1930s was not a
choice for the fainthearted. Not only would a woman have considerable difficulty in supporting herself, but also she would have to brave

the increasing hostility toward independent females that intensified in the midst of the depression, and the continued spread of medical opinion regarding the abnormality of love between women. On top of all that, she would need a great spirit of adventure if she hoped to seek out a still-fledgling and well-hidden subculture, or a great self-sufficiency if she could not find it. For all these reasons, few women who loved other women were willing to identify themselves as lesbian in the 1930s. They often married and were largely cut off from other women—imprisoned in their husbands' homes, where they could choose to renounce their longings or engage only in surreptitious lesbian affairs.

Kinder, Küche, Kirche and the "Bisexual" Compromise

Among middle-class women the depression was the great hindrance to a more rapid development of lesbian lifestyles, primarily because it squelched for them the possibility of permanently committing themselves to same-sex relationships. Such arrangements demanded above all that they have some degree of financial independence so that they did not have to marry in order to survive, and financial independence became more problematic for them in the 1930s. It was not that fewer women worked—in fact, the number of working women increased slightly during that decade. It was rather that in tight economic times they were discouraged from competing against men for better paying jobs and most women had to settle for low-salaried, menial jobs that demanded a second income for a modicum of comfort and made the legal permanence of marriage attractive.

Poor women who loved other women had never been led to believe that they might expect more rewarding or remunerative work. Though the depression rendered some of them jobless and homeless, they sometimes managed to make the best of a bad situation. For example, statistics gathered in 1933 estimated that about 150,000 women were wandering around the country as hoboes or "sisters of the road," as they were called by male hoboes. For young working-class lesbians without work, hobo life could be an adventure. It permitted them to wear pants, as they usually could not back home, and to indulge a passion for wanderlust and excitement that was permitted only to men in easier times. Life on the road also gave them a protective camouflage. They could hitch up with another woman, ostensibly for safety and company, but in reality because they were a lesbian couple, and they could see the world together. Depression historians have suggested that such working-class lesbian couples were not uncommon in the hobo population during the 1930s. The most detailed eyewitness account of lesbian hoboes during the depression is that of a woman who was herself a hobo, Box-Car Bertha, who reported in her autobiography that lesbians on the road usually traveled in small groups and had little difficulty getting rides or obtaining food. She attributes a surprising liberality to motorists, which seems somewhat doubtful considering the general attitudes toward lesbianism that were rampant in America by this time. Bertha claims that "the majority of automobilists" who gave lesbians a ride were not only generous with them but would not think of molesting them physically or verbally: "They sensed [the women] were queer and made very little effort to become familiar." [1]

The hobo lesbians' middle-class counterparts, who came of age hoping to enjoy the expanded opportunities the earlier decades of the century had seemed to promise, were perhaps less cavalier about the new economic developments. They must often have felt because of the depression that they had to compromise their same-sex affections through a heterosexual marriage if they found a husband who would rescue them from the ignominy of working in a shop or as a lowly office clerk. Such jobs were available to females during the 1930s, since women could be hired for a fraction of men's salaries. The "careers," however, which had been giving middle-class women the professional status that so many early feminists had fought for, were now more likely to be reserved for men who "had a family to support." [2]

That immense shift in middle-class women's expectations may account, at least in part, for the observation by a sexologist who researched lesbianism in the mid-1930s that "the bravado of talk [about lesbianism] among female college students, which was in evidence ten to fifteen years ago, seems to have measurably abated, and with this diminution, the experimentation seems to have lessened, or proved little rewarding." [3] Few middle-class women who wanted to maintain the status into which they had been born could afford to *live* as lesbians in the 1930s. Lesbian "bravado" became extremely difficult largely for economic reasons, although women who married might adjust their lives to a bisexual compromise.

Even by the end of the 1920s there had been considerable clamor from conservatives who felt that working women were eroding the American family. With the advent of the depression, the working woman had still fewer defenders. Work for wages once more came to be considered by many not a human right, such as nineteenth- and early twentieth-century feminists had fought to establish, but a privilege connected to gender. Anti-feminists wanted to turn back the clock to a simpler, prefeminist era. As one essayist for the *American Mercury* observed nostalgically in the mid-1930s: "We would all be happier if we could return to the philosophy of my grandmother's day," when a woman "took it for granted that she must content herself with the best lot provided by her husband." Working women came to be the scapegoat for the poor economy that left 25 percent of the labor force unemployed at the height of the depression. Norman Cousins' solution, rash and simplistic as it was, reflected a general view: "There are approximately ten million people out of work in the United States today," Cousins pointed out. "There are also ten million or more women, married or single, who are job holders. Simply fire the women, who shouldn't be working anyway, and hire the men. Presto! No unemployment. No relief rolls. No depression."[4]

Middle-class women who aspired to careers rather than mere subsistence came under particular attack. The dean of Barnard College told a class of the early 1930s that each woman must ask herself if it was really *necessary* for her to be employed. If not, the dean said, "perhaps the greatest service that you can render to the community . . . is to have the courage to refuse to work for gain." If patriotism could not be appealed to in order to discourage women from seeking careers, some anti-feminists determined to appeal to the womb. A 1932 article in a women's magazine mawkishly suggested that successful career women hid "a longing that hurt like a wound," especially when they saw other women's babies and bent above a crib, listening "to the heavy sleeping breath that rhythmed from rosy lips."[5] It is clear that even before the post-World War II years, society believed that women had to get out of the labor force to make way for men: the feminine mystique that Betty Friedan identified as a phenomenon of the '50s was already in effect in the '30s; World War II brought only a brief hiatus.

Of course there was little honest admission (outside of Cousins' article) that females should be bumped from jobs because it was thought that men needed the work more than women did. Instead, just as had already happened around the turn of the century and was to happen again two decades later, it was suddenly discovered that work defeminized a woman. According to their surveys, 1930s women's magazines and their readers were in agreement that if a woman held an important professional position she would lose her womanly qualities. While such a "danger" would be laughable for many women today, "well-brought-up" women of the '30s, who were too far removed from the pioneering excitement of the early twentieth century and yet not far enough removed from Victorianism, did not take such a dilemma lightly. As the title of one article subtitled "A Feminist Discovers Her Home") suggested, even those who had been active in the women's movement in the 1920s were saying, "You May Have My Job."[6] Surely many women who wavered between a lesbian lifestyle and heterosexual marriage must have chosen the latter during the 1930s, since practical considerations and the temper of the times alone would have rendered marriage infinitely more comfortable.

However, some women, who in other times, such as the economically and socially freer 1980s, might have opted to live as lesbians, arranged their lives a half century earlier so that they could have both the security of marriage and the joy of their homoaffectional inclinations. To the world, and perhaps even to their husbands, they appeared to be simply heterosexual married women. To other lesbians —and more often to only one particular woman—they were homosexual. In George Henry's extensive study (see below), begun in 1935, of "socially well-adjusted," mostly middle-class "sex variants," both black and white, the researcher found that a large number of the women he interviewed were married to men even while conducting lesbian affairs.[7] Some women who married and also had lesbian relationships were genuinely bisexual. Many others married because they could see no other viable choice in their day.

Sometimes a marriage was nothing more than a front to permit a woman to function as a lesbian and not be persecuted. M.K., who was an untenured professor at Mills College during the 1930s, tells of having contacted a distant cousin, a gay man, who lived in Washington and implored him to come to California so that she could present him as her fiancé before her tenure review came up. She even permitted colleagues to throw a wedding shower for her (although she never went through with the marriage, since she learned that the administration's suspicion of her homosexuality was irrevocable and she would not be given tenure).[8] There are no statistics that reveal the incidence of front marriages between lesbians and gay men, but it is plausible to believe they were not uncommon when homosexual life was as stigmatized and difficult as it was in the 1930s.

However, other women who loved women were in marriages that were not merely fronts—sometimes because they had no way to support themselves alone, sometimes because they could not conceive of abandoning the security and respectability of that socially condoned institution, sometimes because they were truly bisexual. The 1930s diary of Alice Dunbar-Nelson, a middle-class black woman, reveals the existence of an active black bisexual network among prominent "club women" who had husbands but managed to enjoy lesbian liaisons as well as a cameraderie with one another over their shared secrets. Dunbar-Nelson herself felt that she had to practice some discretion in front of her husband, who nevertheless knew she was bisexual. His occasional rages over her lesbian affairs did not stop her from preserving for posterity her love poems about lesbian passion and seduction with lines such as "I had not thought to ope that secret room," and "You did not need to creep into my heart/ The way you did. You could have smiled/ And knowing what you did, have kept apart/ From all my inner soul./ But you beguiled/ Deliberately."[9]

Married woman who had lesbian liaisons appeared in numerous novels and short stories of the 1930s, such as Sheila Donisthorpe's *Loveliest of Friends* (1931), William Carlos Williams' "The Knife of the Times" (1932), Dorothy Parker's "Glory in the Daytime" (1934), and Ernest Hemingway's "The Sea Change" (1938). Surviving correspondence and biographies corroborate the fiction. Not only middle-class women but some upper-class women also—even those from the "best families" in America—were married while they engaged in lesbian affairs, as had been widely revealed during the 1934 custody trial of Gloria Vanderbilt, whose mother was accused of having an affair with the Marchioness Nadeja Milford-Haven, as well as the recently published correspondence of Eleanor Roosevelt.[10]

Eleanor Roosevelt's well-documented affair with journalist Lorena Hickok was in progress when FDR was inaugurated in 1933. At the ceremony Eleanor wore a sapphire ring that Lorena had given her. It was their relationship that was uppermost in her mind during that historically momentous inauguration:

> All day I've thought of you . . . Oh! I want to put my arms around you. I ache to hold you close. Your ring is a great comfort. I look at it & think she does love me or I wouldn't be wearing it!

The affair continued through a good part of Eleanor's early years in the White House, from where she wrote endearments to Lorena during their separations, such as:

> Goodnight, dear one. I want to put my arms around you & kiss you at the corner of your mouth. And in a little more than a week now—I shall.

> Oh! dear one, it is all the little things, tones in your voice, the feel of your hair, gestures, these are the things I think about & long for.

> I wish I could lie down beside you tonight and take you in my arms.[11]

It is not known if FDR understood the nature of their relationship, but the rest of the world thought of them as good friends and little suspected that they were also lovers. Obviously women from those families did not need to worry about depression economics like some of their socially inferior sisters, but heterosexual marriage permitted them to maintain a position in their society that would have been problematic had they chosen to live openly as lesbians. The somber, worried decade of the 1930s discouraged such nonconformity on any social level, demanding that whatever explorations and small advances had been made for lesbianism as an open lifestyle in the '20s be put on ice until the times changed. For most women who loved other women, a "bisexual" compromise was the best they could manage.

The View from the Outside

Such bisexual compromises were seldom publicly acknowledged. Had their undeniable frequency (see Katharine Bement Davis' statistics, p. 46) been more widely admitted, it would have been much more difficult to stigmatize love between women to the extent that the 1930s did. But silence prevailed. That secrecy meant, among other things, that it was impossible for women who saw themselves as "lesbian" to construct their own public definitions of what that label meant, since they were intimidated into speechlessness by the prevalent notion that feelings such as theirs were "queer" and "unusual." Since they could not speak out to correct those images, the public definitions of them continued to be formulated by those on the outside.

There was some diversity in those definitions: while images of

monstrosities and decadence were often associated with lesbianism in
the 1930s, other attitudes, particularly those promulgated by "liberal"
doctors, seemed to encourage some enlightenment in the public view.
Such enlightenment, however, was largely based on a conception of
the lesbian as a pathetic creature who was cut off from the rest of
womankind by her rare abnormality and who deserved no more
punishment than was already visited on her by her unfortunate condition. Those doctors tended to argue that the notion of the homosexual as a criminal was "unscientific" and that homosexuals could be
productive human beings. But the underlying ambivalence in their
pleas for homosexuals generally bled through in statements such as
that of psychiatrist Victor Robinson, who wrote in an introductory
note to a lesbian autobiography in the 1930s: "That charming women
should be lesbians is not a crime, it is simply a pity. It is not a
question of ethics, but of endocrines." Lesbians were merely helpless
victims of nature's freakish pranks, and the best thing that could be
done for them was to finds ways to eradicate their "affliction."[12]

Not only was the extent of lesbianism and bisexuality hidden often
by heterosexual marriage and complicitously ignored on all social
levels, but also, through the prevalent view of love between women
as an affliction, it was totally forgotten that female same-sex love in
the form of romantic friendship had so recently (only a few decades
earlier) been considered normal. Since few women now were willing
to proclaim their love for other women, when medical doctors of the
1930s expressed their determination to prevent homosexuality through
"education" and treatment they went largely unchallenged. Homosexuals, the doctors said, "remained at an immature level of social
adjustment" and could not hope to achieve maturity as long as they
were homosexual. Who of the many women who had experienced
love for other women in the 1930s could dare step forward to contra-
dict them? Individually locked into their secret as most women who
loved other women were, how could they have argued against "curing" love between women by psychotherapy or doses of hormones?
How could they have responded other than with silence about their
own experiences when they read in mid-1930s newspapers that women
who were "suffering from masculine psychological states" (that is,
who loved other women) were being "cured" by removing one of
their adrenal glands and that such treatments, as a front page article
in the *New York Times* revealed in 1935, could correct "overfunction-
ing" that caused some women to have an "aversion to marriage"?[13]

The unexamined contention that the female who loved other fe-

males was someone other than the "normal" woman was thus reinforced. Her otherness was depicted sometimes as sickness, sometimes
as immorality, only very seldom as consonant with soundness and
decency—and always as a rare "condition." The contradictory notions of lesbianism as both immoral and sick were especially common
in the literature aimed at a broad reading public. With the American
publication of *The Well of Loneliness* at the end of the 1920s, there was
suddenly a great interest in the lesbian as a sexual freak, and the
floodgates opened. Each year saw the production of new novels that
were even clearer than Radclyffe Hall's book had been in their treatment of lesbian sexuality. Obviously the public had a taste for such
fare, which, unlike Hall's work, often did not even pretend to the
kind of sympathy characteristic of the medical tracts, and instead
presented lesbians as vampires and carnivorous flowers. The sensationalistic lesbian pulps of the 1950s had their forerunners in the 1930s
in books such as Sheila Donisthorpe's *Loveliest of Friends* (1931),
which described lesbians as

> crooked, twisted freaks of nature who stagnate in dark and muddy
> waters, and are so cloaked with the weeds of viciousness and selfish
> lust that, drained of all pity, they regard their victims as mere stepping
> stones to their further pleasures. With flower-sweet fingertips they
> crush the grape of evil till it is exquisite, smooth and luscious to the
> taste, stirring up subconscious responsiveness, intensifying all that has
> been, all that follows, leaving their prey gibbering, writhing, sex sod-
> den shadows of their former selves, conscious of only one desire in
> mind and body, which, ever festering, ever destroying, slowly saps
> their health and sanity.

Novels of the 1920s that were not kind to lesbians generally showed
them as more confused than vicious. The novels of the '30s often
seemed to call on French decadent writers of the nineteenth century
for their images of lesbian vampires. Perhaps the monstrous lesbian
images proliferated during the 1930s not only because they mirrored
a moralistic disapproval of lesbianism which seemed decadent during
grim times, but also because those extreme depictions afforded the
distraction of the bizarre and the exotic to a drab and gloomy decade.
In any case, the market was flooded with titles such as *Hellcat* (1934),
Love like a Shadow (1935), *Queer Patterns* (1935), and *Pity for Women*
(1937).[14]

There were, however, occasional lesbian novels written in the
1930s that were remarkably sympathetic and attest to a readership

that identified with love between women, though silently. Elisabeth Craigin's "autobiographical" *Either Is Love* (1937), for example, presents lesbian love as not only equal to heterosexuality, but "peerlessly perfect." Craigin was almost defensive in her pro-lesbian stance, writing, for example, "A so-called Lesbian alliance can be of rarified purity, and those who do not believe it are merely judging in ignorance of the facts." *Diana,* a 1939 novel that also purported to be an autobiography, even presented a kind of lesbian chauvinism. The author proclaimed that she had never seen a drab or stupid-looking lesbian:

> A stupid girl would probably never ascertain her abnormality if she were potentially homosexual . . . [and] the girl who did come to understand her inversion was likely to have character in her face. . . . No woman could adjust herself to lesbianism without developing exceptional qualities of courage.[15]

But such images were rare.

Much more common were depictions of lesbian suicide, self-loathing, hopeless passion, chicanery. Some of those novels were written by heterosexuals whose intensely angry depictions suggest that love between women posed a significant social threat in their view. However, others were written by women who had had same-sex love relationships themselves, but who were, by the 1930s, credulous of the "truths" that had been societally inculcated in them about the sickness and torment of lesbian love. Djuna Barnes' *Nightwood,* for example, has a narrator who observes that lesbianism is an "insane passion for unmitigated anguish" and a lesbian character who says of herself, "There's something evil in me that loves evil and degradation." Jan Morale, the central character of Gale Wilhelm's *We Too Are Drifting,* tells a lover, "Except for the dirty satisfaction we manage to squeeze out of our bodies, it's nothing, I hate it. When're you going to understand how much I hate it?" In response to the other woman's protestations of love, Jan replies, "Someday I'll kill you."[16]

Perhaps lesbian writers' willingness to present such images were not only signs of brainwashing but also of complicity with the demands of the publishers, who feared censorship from groups such as the National Organization for Decent Literature, established in the 1930s. If a lesbian novel showed the character's conversion to heterosexuality, publishers considered that a selling point. The American publication of Anna Weirauch's *The Scorpion* (1933) was hailed with apparent relief in the publisher's ads because the lesbian character, who had also appeared in Weirauch's earlier novel, *The Outcast,* finally "quits a circle of abnormalities, turning to her devoted men friends, apparently not lost to a normal life."[17] Editors may have reasoned that if the lesbian characters were miserable or convertible the censors would let the books slip by since the dominant "morality" was upheld.

But the would-be censors of the 1930s seemed to believe that even images of lesbians who wallowed in tragedy were dangerous. And they were right. To learn of the existence of other lesbians through the media, no matter how unfortunate those characters were, must have been reassuring to women who loved other women and feared by now, in the reticent 1930s, that they were rarities. The text offered them a double message. They could read between the lines or peek behind the agonizing theatrical depictions and know that they were not alone and that if miserable lesbians existed, happy lesbians might also exist. Perhaps it was out of such fears that the Motion Picture Producers and Directors Association of America adopted a code in 1930 that said that films must uphold the sanctity of marriage and must not ridicule "natural or human law" and filmmakers must abolish from the screen "sex perversion or any inference of it." But even that did not satisfy certain religious zealots, such as those who formed the Legion of Decency in 1934 in order to police the movies more effectively.

For that reason, when Lillian Hellman's 1934 stage play *The Children's Hour* was adapted for movies a couple of years later, any suggestion of the lesbian theme was omitted—despite the fact that Hellman's lesbian killed herself in self-hatred and despair. The movie became a story about a heterosexual triangle, and the censors demanded that even the name be changed (it was issued as *These Three*), out of fear that the public would associate it with the notorious stage play be infected by the mere thought of lesbianism. When the French film *Club de Femmes* was imported into the United States in 1937, all intimations of lesbianism were cut.[18]

Although theatrical depictions were also a view from the outside and never showed that lesbians could be anything other than neurotic, tragic, or absurd, the theater of the 1930s fared somewhat better than the movies, at least with regard to mention of lesbians. When a state senator in New York attempted to push through a bill in 1937 that would create a chief censor for Broadway—an equivalent of England's Lord Chamberlain—63,000 signatures were gathered from Broadway theater audiences to protest. The appearance of "sex var-

iants" was so common on the American stage that George Jean
Nathan even wrote a parody in 1933, *Design for Loving* (playing off
the title of Noel Coward's *Design for Living*), whose cast included not
only a hermaphrodite, an onanist, a flagellant, a transvestite, and a
male homosexual, but also a lesbian and another woman with "tri-
bade tendencies." Of course it is possible that more censorship did
not exist because theater owners and even censors could not always
understand that what they were witnessing on stage was lesbianism.
When a translation of Christa Winsloe's German play *Girls in Uniform*
appeared on Broadway in 1933 even some critics denied that it was
about lesbianism, since the characters were neither degenerate nor
decadent. The girl who falls passionately in love with her teacher,
becomes delirious with joy on being given one of the woman's
undergarments, and then decides to commit suicide because she cannot face a separation was not a lesbian. She was only experiencing an
"innocent" schoolgirl crush (as though schoolgirl "lesbians" never
had crushes and were never innocent).[19]

Those critics who recognized lesbian subject matter onstage were
often dismayed. Typical was the *New York Daily Mirror* review of
Love of Women, a short-lived play in which a woman character is
"rescued" from a productive long-term lesbian relationship by a male
suitor. The mere suggestion that the main character had been lesbian
caused the critic to exclaim, despite her "happy" conversion, "Such
matters as those with which [the play] concerns itself are best left to
the consulting rooms of psychiatrists. They do not add to the health
and well-being of the theatre."[20]

It is not surprising that some actresses who played lesbian parts on
Broadway felt uncomfortable. Ann Revere, who was Martha Dobie
(the character who commits suicide when she discovers she is a
lesbian) in the first 1934 production of *The Children's Hour,* maintained in an interview that Martha was not a lesbian, despite the
character's own admission of erotic love for another woman:

> She and the other girl were just good friends, in my mind, nothing
> more. Under the stress she cracks and thinks she is [a lesbian]. She felt
> guilty and would have thought or said anything under the circum-
> stances, done anything to take the blame on herself for what had
> happened to them.[21]

Such a blatant counterreading of Hellman's script suggests that actresses may have feared that merely playing a lesbian role placed them
under suspicion of lesbianism.

Viewed from the outside the lesbian was either sick or sinful, and no one would want to be considered one. There was little public dissent over those images of her. Lesbians were not in the position to stick up for themselves and challenge such stereotypes, since self-defense by so small a minority would have done little but expose them to hostility, disdain, or, at best, pity. The many women who had love relationships with other women but did not acknowledge themselves as lesbians were even less in the position to correct the dominant images of their affectional preferences since they needed to distance themselves, both internally and externally, from the concept of lesbianism. As would be expected, under such circumstances a lesbian subculture could not proliferate very rapidly in the light of day. It was invited into darkness and secrecy, so that the dismal popular images were more likely to become self-fulfilling prophecies than if such a subculture could have developed without fear and shame.

"In the Life"

Viewed from the inside, or "in the Life," as the bar phrase of the 1930s described it, lesbianism was of course generally quite different from the outside view of it. But because the view from the outside was so hateful, it necessarily affected the way many women in the Life thought about themselves. Females in the 1930s who did accept the label "lesbian" had to discover on their own that it was possible to live as a lesbian in America and not be driven to suicide or neurasthenia, as fictional and medical book lesbians almost always were. Many of them did find that they could forge a reasonably happy life for themselves, no thanks to the prevailing views of their day. But their problems in constructing such a life were compounded by those dominant views that scared women into hiding once they decided they wanted to live as lesbians. Their most difficult task as social beings was making contact with other lesbians in the context of a society that mandated that they be silent about their affectional preferences.

Lesbian slang of the 1930s that described various aspects of the Life provides evidence of the existence of flourishing lesbian communities, though the uninitiated would usually have been able to discover them only with difficulty. Much of the slang came originally from women's prisons, where lesbianism, which was sometimes situational and sometimes a lifetime commitment, was common. From the correctional institutions the argot seems to have filtered into working-class, and sometimes into middle-class, lesbian society. An end-of-the-decade study identified many terms used by lesbians during the 1930s, including words such as "dyke," "bulldyke," "bull dagger," "gay," and "drag," which had also been current in the '20s, as well as other terms that became current only in the 1930s such as "queer bird" and "lavender," which referred to female homosexuals; "sil"—a contraction for silly, that is, infatuated—which meant a lesbian who was currently in love with another woman; and "trapeze artist," which meant a woman who performed cunnilingus. Much of the argot described butch/femme roles in women's relationships such as "jockey," "mantee," "daddy," "poppa," "husband," and "top sergeant"—all referring to butches, and "mamma" and "wife," which referred to femmes. Those terms were probably more descriptive of institutionalized and working-class lesbian life, although they were sometimes used by middle-class women also. The author of *Diana* acknowledges a special lesbian argot even among middle-class women, in words such as "spook," which referred to a woman who strayed into lesbianism as second best but stayed because she discovered she liked it better than heterosexuality.[22]

If Box-Car Bertha can be believed, in areas such as Chicago during the depression there flourished a fairly lively lesbian subculture in which working-class women sometimes even mixed with wealthy women, a rare phenomenon in lesbian subcultures throughout this century (though common among gay men, who often class-mixed for sexual contacts). She tells of a group of lesbians who had a "magnificent apartment" where they would throw soirees called "Mickey Mouse's party." When Bertha attended she met half a dozen "wealthy women," four of whom were married. They claimed to be merely "sightseers," but she interjects, "Actually they had more than a superficial interest in these lesbian girls." Apparently Bertha continued her contact with these women after the party, despite her claim that she disliked lesbians. She reports "constant exploitation" among the women (is she hinting of blackmail or lesbian prostitution?). The working-class lesbians would get the names and addresses of these wealthy women, Bertha writes, and borrow money from them by saying, "I met you at Mickey Mouse's party."[23]

But outside of all-female institutions and rare social configurations such as Mickey Mouse's party, making contact with other lesbians for romantic or social purposes was far more complicated and problematic than it has become over the last few decades. Unless one was lucky enough to become an insider in a group, lesbian life in the 1930s could be lonely. Since there were no personal ads, no lesbian political organizations, few special-interest social groups for lesbians, none of the social abundance that exists today in many American cities, contact often depended on chance. And because silence was so widespread, it was possible that one often missed that chance. Many lesbians probably really did feel then, as Ann Aldrich's later pot boiler was titled, that "we walk alone."

A few bars congenial to lesbians still existed in the '30s. Those outside of working-class communities were like the bars of the 1920s, catering to gay men and straight gawkers as well as lesbians—such as the Bungalow, about which the *New York Evening Graphic* published a typically hostile, scandalized editorial titled "Greenwich Village Sin Dives Lay Traps for Innocent Girls":

> I doubt if there are five places like it in America. Its patronage is composed almost entirely of lisping boys and deep-voiced girls. They eat, drink, and quarrel. They display their jealousies and occasionally claw at each other with their nails. They talk loudly, scream, jibe at each other and order gin continually. Always gin.

The writer was perhaps a bit conservative in his estimate about the number of similar places in the United States, since there were several other such bars in downtown and midtown New York alone, including Tony Pastor's and Ernie's, as well as in other cities. The Barn in Cleveland, the White Horse in Oakland, and even by then a few all-women's working-class bars such as Mona's in San Francisco and the Roselle Club and the Twelve-Thirty Club in Chicago. There were even several "tea shops" that catered to lesbians on the Near North Side of Chicago. But it was not until World War II, which brought much larger populations to work in big cities, that many more lesbian bars sprang up across the United States. Many young women who would have been delighted to discover lesbian bars in the '30s undoubtedly had a difficult time locating one.[24]

Mona's, the all-women bar in San Francisco, opened first in 1936 on Union Street and in 1938 on Columbus. According to Win, one of the women I interviewed for this chapter, who frequented Mona's in the '30s, it was a hangout for young working-class women, though there are reports of middle-class women who took brief vacations in San Francisco from as far away as Salt Lake City in order to go to Mona's. Win remembers that at Mona's the butches often wore drag and the women danced together in butch/femme couples with no fear that they would be molested by the vice squad, as lesbians were in Chicago during the '30s and in later decades even in San Francisco. If a woman managed to locate such a bar, there were attempts by the other patrons, who knew it was in their interest to cherish so brave and rare a kindred spirit, to put her at ease quickly. Her problems with making contacts were at an end, at least as long as she remained a habituée. Win describes Mona's as "safe and friendly. We always used to sing 'If you're ever down a well, ring my bell.' It was just right for the atmosphere there." One would have had to go to Le Monocle in Paris or to pre-1933 Berlin to find its equal.[25]

But most lesbians never went to bars. Occasionally middle-class lesbians could make contacts with other women if they were members of a private group such as the Nucleus Club, an informal New York-based organization of the late 1930s that held weekly parties for lesbians together with gay men. But although police harassment of lesbians was not common in the 1930s, they knew, perhaps by their observation of gay male experiences, that it was a potential they had to take into account, and that awareness must have dampened the enthusiasm of many to join such a club. The Nucleus Club parties were in private homes, but the group still thought it essential to adopt the rule that each gay man would pair with a lesbian as they left the party and they would go strolling out arm in arm so that neighbors would think the couples had been to a heterosexual gathering.[26] One should not underestimate the fun in this game of "fooling the straights," but underneath the fun was genuine fear.

Middle-class women who dared perceive themselves as lesbian had some possibilities of making contacts more safely in all-women institutions such as summer camps, residence halls, or colleges and universities. Mary remembers that in the 1930s, as a teenager, she had been a counselor in the Girl Scouts and Camp Fire Girls camps, and when she decided that she was a lesbian she became aware that there were many other young women among the counselors who shared her interests and who identified themselves to each other as lesbian. University life also provided an arena for women who consciously thought of themselves as lesbians to make contact with each other. At the University of Texas in the mid-1930s women physical education majors staged a mock-prom, ostensibly making fun of the university's regular annual proms. Although heterosexual students were unaware of it, many of the physical education majors were lesbians.

The mock-prom was a great lark for them since it sanctioned them to wear drag and dance together in a hall of a hallowed institution.[27]

But such cavalier gaiety was only occasional among lesbian college women in the 1930s. Their more usual reticence suggests that they were as fearful as the members of the Nucleus Club. When Mary went to the University of Washington in the late 1930s, she and her lesbian friends had a table in the commons at which they could usually find each other any day between 8:00 and 3:00. But what Mary remembers most about the experience now is that they all felt they had to be very circumspect:

> Although several of us were in couples, no one ever talked about their love lives. We could unload with problems about families, jobs, money, but not lesbianism. If two women broke up they wouldn't discuss it with the group, though they might have a confidante who was also part of the group. It was our attitude that this sort of relationship was nobody's business. We all really knew about each other of course. But the idea was, "You don't know if someone is a lesbian unless you've slept with her." You didn't belong if you were the blabbermouth type.

Not only was it a far cry from the "outing" that has begun to take place on college campuses in 1990, but every lesbian college woman in Mary's group felt she had to be constantly guarded about herself because she was so aware of the danger of lesbian stigma. The easy intimacy that young college women often established with each other in the '30s was impossible for many college women who were lesbians. They felt compelled to assume such a protective camouflage that those outside the group would have had no idea that they were looking at a table full of lesbians. But a lesbian newcomer would not have had an easy time breaking in.[28]

Non-college women were often just as reluctant to risk betraying their lesbianism, even among women they were all but certain were also lesbians. Sandra, who worked in a Portland department store during the early '30s, tells of having been part of a group of eight women—four couples—who went skiing every winter between 1934 and '37. "I'm sure we were all gay," she remembers, "but we never said a word about it. Talking about it just wasn't the thing to do. Never once did I hear the L word in that group or any word like it— even though we always rented a cabin together and we all agreed that we only wanted four beds since we slept in pairs."[29]

Because lesbians were so frightened about divulging themselves and often had no idea where to meet other lesbians for social contact, life could be lonely even if they were lucky enough to have found a mate. May says she met her lover at the University of Texas in the late 1920s, and though they stayed together for more than twenty years, they told almost no one about the nature of their relationship. It placed such a strain on them that May often thought of leaving Virgie, especially during the '30s, because "I was tired of hiding in a corner. And there was no question of coming out. I wanted so much to be able to talk freely with people, to be like everyone else, not to feel like we loved in a wasteland, but that was impossible. I had a lot of heterosexual women friends, but I thought that as long as I was in that relationship I could never have a close friend. I knew how people would have looked down on us if they'd guessed."

Although May and Virgie had heard about homosexual men, they knew no lesbians. May claims that she did not become aware that there were other lesbians in the world until 1950, when they began going to dog shows and occasionally saw lesbian couples there, but even then they did not talk to them. At one point in the late '30s they befriended two heterosexual couples who suspected they were lovers, but those friendships did not last long: "Both the men thought all I needed was a good fuck, and they let me know it." When May left Virgie in 1953 she felt that although she was "going through a horrible time," she had to suffer in silence, because there was no one in whom she could confide. It was not until the advent of the feminist movement in the 1970s, when she was already in her late 60s, that she felt she could talk about those years of her life. But the scars remained for women of her generation, as she indicates now. She says she still feels free to talk only in "appropriate circumstances."[30]

Elisabeth Craigin also poignantly suggests the lesbian's sense of isolation in the 1930s in her putatively autobiographical novel in which, when the author and her lover, Rachel, part, she too can tell no one, since their relationship was a secret. Craigin says that shortly after the breakup she had a minor operation and her life was flooded with flowers, kind notes, and good wishes from friends, but their attention to her unimportant physical problem struck her as bitterly ironic: "I could more easily have undergone five such operations than the amputation that was going on in my soul. But sympathy was an anesthetic that that other surgical interference [her break with Rachel] never had."[31] Such difficulty, not only in making contact with others who were willing to avow their love for women, but also in sharing their dearest and most poignant emotions with friends, must have rendered the choice to live as a lesbian overwhelming and explains further why so many of those who admitted emotional and physical love for other females in George Henry's study of "sex variants" in the 1930s chose to marry men.

But life was clearly not uniformly unfortunate for lesbians of the 1930s outside of fiction. The cities were large enough and diverse enough even then to offer shelter and requisite anonymity to those who felt that they could not live an unconventional affectional life in a small town. The *New York Sun* critic who reviewed *The Children's Hour* in 1934 was right in his commonsense response to Martha's lament that because she and Karen had been accused of lesbianism, "There is not anywhere we can go": "You immediately think of half a dozen [places lesbians could go]," he said, "including the city of New York."[32] If provincial life was uncomfortable, women who identified themselves as lesbian in the 1930s could hope to find refuge and sometimes even desirable social companionship in cities such as Boston, Chicago, New York, and San Francisco. They were not geographically imprisoned as women might have been in the preceding century. Although good jobs were not easy to come by, if it were essential to them they could move and they could support themselves.

Despite society's views and restrictions, there were many compelling reasons for some women to choose lesbian relationships and remain lesbians. They found aspects of lesbian life and love far more rewarding than what heterosexuality offered. They were able to make their own lives, often without a large support group but with the help of a felicitous personal relationship that let them define themselves as they chose. While they had no notion how to go about changing the public images of lesbians, they often knew those images had little to do with them, and, as long as they remained covert, could have no effect on them. The series of interviews conducted by Dr. George Henry with lesbians in the '30s illustrates a contentment in the lives of many of these women that would have frazzled the censors had that picture been reflected in the media. Many of his interviewees were self-actualized individuals, living to their full potential in mutually productive relationships. They say things such as:

> I'm doing the work [as an editor] I always wanted to do and I'm very, very happy. I'm very much in love with the girl too. We click. . . .

She has had the most influence for good in my life.
                                                                    (29—year-old white woman)

If I were born again I would like to be just as I am. I'm perfectly satisfied being a girl and being as I am. I've never had any regrets.
                                                                    (26—year-old black woman)

Our relationship is just as sweet now [after eleven years] as in the beginning.   (29—year-old white woman)

Since we have been living together our lives are fuller and happier. We create things together and we are devoted to our [adopted] baby.
                                                                    (30—year-old white woman)

I have a great confidence in the future. I think I'm going to be a very well-known artist. . . . Homosexuality hasn't interfered with my work. It has made it what it is.   (30—year-old white woman)

Sadly and typically, all Henry was able to understand about such case histories is revealed in largely irrelevant Freudian-influenced comments that consider lesbianism as nothing more than a neurotic adjustment: for example, "Through homosexual alliances, the affection missed in childhood is obtained from women."[33] But those who were "in the Life" usually knew that their choices were far more complex and meaningful than what was understood in such simplistic little theories which were no more explanatory about lesbianism than speculations about compensation for missing a father's love would be about female heterosexuality. With or without a large group to whom they could divulge themselves, and despite their need to hide their feelings from the outside world, these women were able to find enough sexual and emotional fulfillment as lesbians to give them satisfaction with their choices such as was never reflected in the media images of their day.

Lesbian Sex in the 1930s

Women who chose to identify themselves as lesbians in the 1930s were by and large a very different group from their mothers and grandmothers who may have been involved in romantic friendships only a few decades earlier—not because the quality of their love for other women was necessarily different, but rather because the nature of their awareness (especially of genital sexual potential between women) and of society's awareness (especially of their "morbidity" and "decadence") were very different. They were totally bereft of the luxury (and frustration?) of innocence that characterized their earlier counterparts. Women's love for women was inevitably "lesbian" now—and patently sexual by definition.

Lesbian sex had long been a subject for sensationalistic and pornographic male fiction writers who aimed to shock and amuse their readers with what they considered bizarre but titillating images, and it became a focus in the work of male sexologists who considered it as bizarre as did the fiction writers, though morbid instead of titillating. However, women said almost nothing whatever about it publicly before the twentieth century. Even during the first decades of this century females who broached the subject of love between women in print were likely to write as though sexuality were definitely not a part of it.

There were rare exceptions, such as Mary MacLane, who confesses in her 1902 autobiography (whose purpose was *épater le bourgeois*) that she feels for another woman "a strange attraction of sex" and asks the reader: "Do you think a man is the only creature with whom one may fall in love?" The Anglo-American writer Renee Vivien, who wrote in French, also dealt with lesbian eroticism in the early twentieth century, but she did it under the influence of earlier male writers such as Baudelaire and Pierre Louys, who presented lesbians as unreal, exotic creatures. Vivien's lesbian lovers have more in common with those earlier fictions than real life. Her work can be placed in the context of an established genre from which she did not veer, even though she—obviously unlike her male predecessors—had actually had lesbian experiences. For the most part, however, women were silent about lesbian sex. It was not until Radclyffe Hall's 1928 novel *The Well of Loneliness* that a book written in English by a woman went as far as to say of two female lovers, "and that night they were not divided"—but it went no further. In the '30s, however, perhaps because of that one line by Hall that broke the silence, or perhaps because women who identified themselves as lesbian now saw sex as an inevitable aspect of their identity, women writers who loved other women began to treat sexuality in more vivid terms.[34]

But those lesbians of the '30s, like their straight counterparts, had a mixed and confusing legacy with regard to sex, despite their now inescapable knowledge that "lesbian" meant sex between women. On the one hand, they had been brought up by parents who were Victorians and often tried to inculcate sexual puritanism in their children. Vestiges of guilt for unorthodox sexuality must have sprouted even in many young lesbians who came out in the years after the roaring, flaming '20s. On the other hand, young women of the 1930s enjoyed, at least in the abstract, some of the vestigial benefits of the sexual revolution of the previous decade, when popular wisdom claimed that sexual inhibitions could make you sick and sexual expression led to creativity and mental health. Of course as lesbians they had to juggle the prescriptions about gender and the nature of the sex act a bit, but there were lesbians who had no trouble doing that.

The notion of sex as "good medicine" thus made some lesbian writers feel free even to explore their own form of sexuality in print. For example, Mary Casal, who was born a Victorian, in 1864, revealed in her 1930 autobiography *The Stone Wall* that she accepted not only with ease but even with relish the admonition about the unsalutary effects of repressed sexual desire. Without hesitation she announced that she and Juno, her woman lover, always "found ourselves more fit for good work after having been thus relieved."[35] Such a statement by a woman—and a self-identified lesbian woman at that—would have been inconceivable in literature of earlier decades.

Of course other lesbians of her generation were not so adaptable in their sexual adjustment, and their writing about love between women sounded much more like that of romantic friends of previous eras, except that they realized that they had to explain away the popular wisdom about the importance of sex. Vida Scudder, a retired Wellesley professor who had been a "devoted companion" of the novelist Florence Converse, waxed rhapsodic in her 1937 autobiography *On Journey* about love between women, which, she believed,

> could approach near to that absolute union, always craved, never on earth, at least, to be attained. . . . More than any sublunar forces, it initiates us into the eternal. When it has not been born of illusion, it can never die, though strange interludes may befall it. . . . Its drama normally knows no end, for death sets the seal on the union. . . . In the Ever-Living land, lover and beloved move together.

But she was certain that such passion, which combines the spiritual with the sensual, must stop short of the genital if it was to remain fine. She believed that Freud had "much to answer for" because he muddied the waters with sex. Scudder, as a displaced Victorian in a modern era, longing for the more innocent days when love between women was considered "romantic friendship," could not understand why people "pay so much attention to one type of experience in this marvelous, this varied, this exciting world." She concluded that a woman's life devoid of sex "is a life neither dull nor empty nor devoid of romance." Her own romances, she admitted, were all with other women.[36] But Scudder was a rare exception by the 1930s in her ability to avoid the sexual implications in female same-sex love.

Diana Frederics, author of the putatively autobiographical *Diana,* is a polar opposite in her focus on those sexual implications. In her view, women who loved other women in the 1930s were often sexually promiscuous, and she deals with that topic explicitly, the first female American author to do so. Frederics relates numerous incidents of lesbian sex outside of long-term commitments among women in the '30s, though sharing with Vida Scudder a sexually conservative Victorian upbringing (she claims that there is "something askew about lesbian morals"). But she also offers a credible, first of its kind, defense of casual sex between women:

> It was natural enough that the homosexual would approach intimacy more quickly than the normal person. The very lack of any kind of social recognition of their union gave it a kind of informality. Normal love, having to consider property and children, had to assume responsibilities that were of no consequence to the homosexual. Fear of conception, a deterrent to the consummation of normal love, was no problem to homosexuals.

Frederics' own vestiges of Victorian discomfort with sexuality are clearly revealed in this novel and hint at the hard time many women may have had adjusting to the sexual consciousness that had been recently foisted on them. In one scene Diana's lover, Leslie, feeling frustrated because of some emotional barrier between them and wanting to compensate, becomes very sexually demanding. Diana is worried and even admits to being uncomfortable with Leslie's sex drive. When they solve the problem and the demands abate, Diana says, "I hadn't realized how hard it had been to endure sensuality until it was over and I felt a lighthearted freedom I had not known in months. I had almost forgotten how sweet Leslie could be." Diana was too close in time to an era when sex outside of duty was disturbing to many women, too disruptive of their conception of moral decency, to be "sweet."[37]

But to other lesbians of the 1930s it was sweet, and they admitted as much in their writings. Elisabeth Craigin's autobiography, *Either Is Love,* is a post-Freudian textbook rhapsody on the beauty and salutary benefits of sex, both heterosexual and what she calls "interfeminine love." Craigin talks much of the "importance of a thorough-going sex life," and she lets the reader know that her own relationship with Rachel was filled with sexual experimentation, fantasy, and physical passion. For example, when she must go off to Europe while Rachel remains in America, Craigin observes: "The transatlantic mailbag can never have contained more incendiary matter than we put into it with all the suggestion that we could kindle at pencil-point." The sexiness of Craigin's relationship with Rachel, like Mary Casal's relationship with Juno, is indicative to them of the health of their love rather than an unfortunate distraction or a sign of trouble as it was to Vida Scudder and Diana Frederics.[38]

While there was in the 1930s a multiplicity of views about sex between females by women who loved other women, no one could pretend any longer that it did not exist. Knowledge of sexual poten-tials, which was by now virtually inescapable, necessarily had com-plex effects on female same-sex love: for example, it made love between women "lesbian"; it challenged women to explore feelings that they would have repressed in other eras; it frightened many women away from any expression of love for other women. But most of all, with regard to lesbian life in America, it was essential to the formation of a lesbian subculture, since it helped women who identified themselves as lesbians to make a conscious and firm distinc-tion between themselves and other women and thus to define them-selves as a group.

While the depression seemed to put an end to the lesbian chic that was prevalent in some areas in the 1920s, and it may have discouraged many women from living as lesbians because of economic difficulties, the momentum of the sexual revolution of the '20s had not been entirely lost on lesbians. By virtue of all the proliferation of books and plays and newspaper articles alone that dealt with lesbians, the innocence of the pre–World War I years became even more improba-ble than it was in the 1920s. In some women this new knowledge, coupled with the dreadful popular images of lesbianism, must have caused great guilt and anxiety and must have hurried them into heterosexual marriages, at the least as a disguise to the world. But others felt that their choices were expanding. Many women who would not have recognized a "lesbian" import in their own homoaf-fectional feelings twenty years earlier knew in the 1930s that lesbian-ism was not an entirely uncommon phenomenon, that there were women who even chose to construct their personal lives around that identification, and that it might have a strong sexual dimension.

Meeting lovers and making a circle of lesbian friends were not easy, and to some women lesbian life must have appeared like a virtual social wasteland, but oases were slowly proliferating. Awareness now permitted a more conscious pursuit of contacts than would formerly have been possible. And it was not much later, with the advent of World War II, that the problems of meeting other lesbians, as well as the economic problems of supporting themselves, were largely overcome for many women.

5

"Naked Amazons and Queer Damozels": World War II and Its Aftermath

World War II WAC Sergeant Johnnie Phelps, in response to a request from General Eisenhower that she ferret out the lesbians in her battalion:

Yessir. If the General pleases I will be happy to do this investigation. . . . But, sir, it would be unfair of me not to tell you, my name is going to head the list. . . . You should also be aware that you're going to have to replace all the file clerks, the section heads, most of the commanders, and the motor pool. . . . I think you should also take into consideration that there have been no illegal pregnancies, no cases of venereal disease, and the General himself has been the one to award good conduct commendations and service commendations to these members of the WAC detachment.

General Eisenhower: Forget the order.
—Bunny MacCulloch interview with Johnnie Phelps, 1982

"Now, my dear," Dr. Knox said, "your disease has gotten completely out of control. We scientists know, of course, that it's a highly pleasurable experience to take someone's penis or vagina into your mouth—it's pleasurable and enjoyable. Everyone knows that. But after you've taken a thousand pleasurable penises or vaginas into your mouth and had a thousand people take your pleasurable penis or vagina into their mouth, what have you accomplished? What do you have to show for it? Do you have a wife or children or a husband or a home or a trip to Europe? Do you have a bridge club to show for it? No! You have only a thousand pleasurable experiences to show for it. Do you see how you're missing the meaning of life? How sordid and depraved are these clandestine sexual escapades in parks and restrooms? I ask you."

"But sir, but sir," said Edward, "I'm a woman. I don't have sexual escapades in parks and restrooms. I don't have a thousand lovers. I have one lover."

"Yes, yes." Dr. Knox flicked the ashes from his cigar on to the floor. "Stick to the subject, my dear."
—Judy Grahn, "Edward the Dyke"

If there is one major point to be made in a social history such as this one, it is that perceptions of emotional or social desires, formations of sexual categories, and attitudes concerning "mental health" are constantly shifting—not through the discovery of objectively conceived truths, as we generally assume, but rather through social forces that have little to do with the *essentiality* of emotions or sex or mental health. Affectional preferences, ambitions, and even sexual experiences that are within the realm of the socially acceptable during one era may be considered sick or dangerous or antisocial during another —and in a brief space of time attitudes may shift once again, and yet again.

The period of World War II and the years immediately after illustrate such astonishingly rapid shifts. Lesbians were, as has just been seen, considered monstrosities in the 1930s—an era when America needed fewer workers and more women who would seek contentment making individual men happy, so that social anger could be personally mitigated instead of spilling over into social revolt. In this context, the lesbian (a woman who needed to work and had no interest in making a man happy) was an anti- social being. During the war years that followed, when women had to learn to do without men, who were being sent off to fight and maybe die for their country, and when female labor—in the factories, in the military, everywhere—was vital to the functioning of America, female independence and love between women were understood and undisturbed and even protected. After the war, when the surviving men returned to their jobs and the homes that women needed to make for them so that the country could return to "normalcy," love between women and female independence were suddenly nothing but manifestations of illness, and a woman who dared to proclaim herself a lesbian was considered a borderline psychotic. Nothing need have changed in the quality of the woman's desires for her to have metamorphosed socially from a monster to a hero to a sicko.

Because World War II created a need for great amounts of womanpower, popular wisdom about woman's place being in the home or the defeminizing effects of work was suddenly silenced as patriotic women took their places in the civilian and military work forces. A Fleischmann's yeast advertisement featuring an attractive woman in military uniform on a motorcycle illustrated the change in social attitude, declaring: "This is No Time to be Frail! . . . The dainty days are done for the duration."[1] Young women who might have been locked in their husbands' homes in the previous decade were now frequently thrown together in all-female worlds. Just as intense love between women often emerged in female institutions such as women's colleges and women's prisons, it was bound to emerge in factories and military units. This time, with the background of sexual sophistication that had been developing in America over the previous decades, love between women led to the establishment of a much larger, unique subculture of lesbians such as could not have occurred at any previous time in history.

Armies of Lovers

Less than a third of a million women served in the military during the war, but many of them were lovers of other women. For those who already identified themselves as lesbians, military service, with its opportunities to meet other women and to engage in work and adventure that were ordinarily denied them, was especially appealing. For many others who had not identified themselves as lesbians before the war, the all female environment of the women's branches of the armed services, offering as it did the novel emotional excitement of working with competent, independent women, made lesbianism an attractive option. The "firm public impression" during the war years that a women's corps was "the ideal breeding ground for lesbians" had considerable basis in fact.[2] And even women who were not in the military now had opportunities in civilian life (where they filled men's places in heavy industry and other occupational areas from which they had been excluded before the war) to meet other women and to form attachments that might have been unthinkable during the 1930s.

Women had served in the military and war-related industries during World War I, though on a much smaller scale than in World War II. However, the greatest reason that the First World War was not as crucial in creating a lesbian subculture as the Second was not simply that fewer women were brought together in the war effort, but rather that the consciousness of lesbianism was not as rife during 1917–1919 as it was to become in the Freudian-saturated '20s and after, and fewer women could begin to conceive of it as a lifestyle. Passionate attachments could still be "explained away" in pre-1920s America. Many women who were not devoted to careers might have assumed that once the Great War was over, their romantic friendship or devoted companionship might continue, but of course they would be obliged to marry a man, just as most women always had been. While

World War I may have clarified for some few women their option to live as lesbians, World War II brought such clarification to many more.

Those hostile to love between women in this century have not been entirely wrong in claiming that the wars encouraged lesbianism because they caused men to leave women to fend for themselves. The truth, however, is less simplistic than their analysis would suggest. As tragic as they were, both wars made women taste independence. Ironically, war permitted some of them to know for the first time the joy of being paid for their efforts. World War II in particular brought great numbers of females of all classes into a society of women where they were able not only to expand friendships but to learn to appreciate other females as serious, self-sufficient human beings. It took them away from restrictive family relations and cast them into new environments where they might redefine a narrow morality they may have accepted unquestioningly and forge for themselves a more personalized set of values.

All of this occurred not long after Freud, *The Well of Loneliness,* and the term "lesbian" became household words, in effect. For many women the coalescence of these various happenings meant that their lives were much more open to lesbian possibilities than they could have been earlier. Since World War II also brought large numbers of women to big cities, where an inchoate lesbian consciousness had been forming, finally relatively large lesbian communities could be created.[3]

For some young women, their war-related experiences helped them define amorphous feelings that they had been struggling with and for which they had no word and no concept, terms such as "romantic friendship" or "smashing" being by now nonexistent. Young females in earlier eras might have explained their attractions with just those words, but by the 1940s such feelings were clearly seen as lesbian, and many women could and did learn to apply that term to their emotions during the war. Mildred, who lived in upstate New York during World War II, remembers that the summer she was sixteen she had volunteered to harvest crops with the Women's Land Army. After she noticed two of the Land Army women acting amorously with each other, another woman told her, "It's called lesbianism. There's really nothing wrong with it." Mildred says, "For the first time I had a name for myself."[4] She was far from alone among those young females who accepted that name for themselves as an "explanation" of their emotions. Having gone into military service during the war, where they were thrown together in comradeship, day and night, with large groups of females who had varying degrees of knowledge and experience, they found not only that the war *fostered* love between women, but that such love was "lesbianism."

Critics of the proposed establishment of military service for females in the early 1940s compared women who would be interested in enlisting to "the naked Amazons . . . and the queer damozels of the isle of Lesbos," as a *Miami News* writer phrased it in 1942. In those hostile assertions there was more than a glimmer of truth.[5] Naturally women who were outside the pale of stereotypical femininity, who saw themselves as autonomous beings, and who loved the company of other females would have been most likely in the first place to volunteer; but many more women learned to love and admire women while in the military during those trying and heroic times. Although most women probably joined assuming they were heterosexual or not having thought much about their sexual orientation, once they enlisted the military was to them like a poor woman's Vassar or Bryn Mawr. Like females in the women's colleges that only the privileged few attended in earlier decades, many now found themselves in an environment where women worked together in pursuits they could consider important, and where they could become heroes to one another without the constant distraction of male measuring sticks. It is not surprising that many of them discovered through their military experiences that they wanted to be lesbians. And there was not much to discourage them.

Although females had served with distinction in military support positions during World War I, their units were disbanded and they were not allowed back into the military until World War II was well under way. In Spring 1942, the Army created the Women's Army Auxiliary Corps (WAAC; the word "Auxiliary" was dropped the following year). At the beginning of the war, in 1941, the military had concerns about homosexual males. Any man who had what were called "homosexual tendencies" was subject to court-martial. As the war progressed, however, and the need for personnel grew, not only were women taken into the military but policy toward homosexuality became more and more lenient. If homosexual behavior called attention to itself the individual might quietly be given a "blue discharge," which was neither honorable nor dishonorable; but in general, the military tried to ignore homosexuality.[6]

In 1942 and '43 when women volunteered for the Army they were routinely asked questions during the psychological exam about dating

and their attitudes toward men, but it would have taken flagrant
homosexual responses to have gotten them disqualified. And while
effeminacy in a male might have alerted military psychologists to the
possibility of his homosexuality, what was perceived of as masculinity in a female enlistee would not have rendered her undesirable,
because the military especially needed women who wanted to do
work that was traditionally masculine.[7]

The WAAC even warned officers not to set out to expose or
punish lesbian behavior. In a printed series of Sex Hygiene lectures,
officers were specifically told that the circumstances of war and a
young woman's removal from familiar surroundings could easily
promote "more consciousness of sex and more difficulties concerning
it." The lectures suggested that the officers should be sympathetic to
close friendships that might crop up between women under wartime
conditions. The officers were also alerted that such intimacies may
even "eventually take some form of sexual expression," but they
were told that they must never play games of hide-and-seek in an
attempt to discover lesbianism or indulge in witch-hunting and they
must approach the situation with an attitude of generosity and tolerance. They were to take action against lesbianism "only in so far as
its manifestations undermine the efficiency of the individual concerned and the stability of the group." Discharge was to be used only
as a last resort in cases that were universally demoralizing. The officers were specifically cautioned that "any officer bringing an unjust
or unprovable charge against a woman in this regard will be severely
reprimanded."[8] The military could not afford to lose womanpower
at the height of a war, and as WAC sergeant Johnnie Phelps pointed
out to General Eisenhower (see epigraph quotation), women who
were in love with other women did not cost the military time and
money because of venereal disease or pregnancy.

The Sex Hygiene lectures recommended to officers that if they
believed that two women who were romantically involved with each
other created a disruptive influence in a unit, they might be adminis-
tratively split, but they should not be discharged. Mary, who joined
the WAC in 1943, tells of such a case in her company. A woman
sergeant had "fallen deeply in love" with a nurse, a first lieutenant
who had quarters off base. According to Mary, "the commanding
officer was hard on the sergeant and she really restricted her. When
the sergeant was caught off base the nurse was reassigned. Then the
commanding officer succeeded in doing everything to keep the sergeant from getting reassigned." But the commanding officer had

learned to be subtle enough not to articulate any concern about lesbianism or to reveal her determination to put a stop to a lesbian affair.[9]

Officials during the war sometimes seemed to deny that lesbianism even existed in the military, since they were placed in the awkward position of either condoning what had been socially condemned so recently, or disapproving of what really worked to the military's benefit. Rita Laporte writes of being in the Army in 1943, where, for the first time in her life, she fell in love. When the other woman was transferred to a different base, Laporte decided that the only way to rejoin her was to "sacrifice all on the altar of love" by admitting she was a homosexual and thereby getting booted out of the Army. After reciting her well-rehearsed confession to the Major:

> I awaited my fate. Then the Major smiled. In a kindly voice he said, "You're kidding. I don't believe you." I was stunned. Naturally I had rehearsed all the Major's possible answers. I was ready to hang my head in deepest shame, to bear up under all insults, to weep or not weep, as might be necessary. Something was terribly wrong.
>
> At last I blurted out, "But I AM one!"
>
> We argued. I pleaded. But it was useless; I could not convince him.[10]

Such denial seems to have taken place on a much larger scale in 1944 when the Inspector General's Office sent an emergency team to investigate allegations of lesbianism at Fort Oglethorpe, a WAC basic training camp in Georgia, after the mother of a young WAC complained that her daughter was being pursued by lesbians. Although there were witnesses who testified that they had seen female "perverts" on base, "homosexual addicts" who affected "a mannish appearance by haircut, by the manner of wearing clothing, by posture, by stride, by seeking 'to date' other girls such as a man would . . . [and who] had certain signals by which they recognized each other," such as whistling the "Hawaiian War Chant" [sic], nevertheless the investigative team concluded that in all of Fort Oglethorpe they could not find any real "homosexual addicts."[11]

Of course military women during the war had been brought up in the homophobic 1930s, and they usually knew that they must not be flagrant in their lesbianism (despite the Fort Oglethorpe allegations of "flagrant behavior"). Elizabeth, who joined the Navy in 1943, says that in the Washington, D.C., hydrographic office to which she was assigned as a draftsperson there were many "butchy" women whose style suggested even the stereotype of the lesbian, "but we never talked about it. There were no problems and we wanted to keep it that way. We all knew that if we were discreet we wouldn't get caught."[12] Few women who loved other women had serious difficulty during the war, since the military needed all the women it could get who would do their jobs and not disrupt the functioning of the service, and the women understood that if they practiced a modicum of discretion they would be quite safe.

A "Government-Sponsored" Subculture

With the end of the war and the start of the 1950s the situation changed drastically, but before that was to happen a much more significant lesbian subculture developed as a result of the war years. Such development was assisted by the fact that the war and especially military life fostered some tolerance regarding lesbianism among young women who, perhaps for the first time in their lives, came in contact with sexuality between women in the close confines of the barracks. Even women who did not identify themselves as lesbians in the military tended to treat lesbianism, which became a familiar phenomenon, with a "who cares?" attitude.[13] It may be that such a relative tolerance toward homosexuality was also promoted by the social upheaval of the war, which threw off balance various areas of American life. Troubling questions of life and death confronted many young women directly for the first time, and "normality" and concepts of sexual "morality" were seen to be far more complicated than they appear during more ordinary years.

In addition to the changing attitudes about what constituted morality, the war also contributed to an easier formation and development of a distinctive lesbian "style" because it made pants acceptable garb for women. In the years before the war, the public was often scandalized if a woman appeared in pants outside her home. Even butch lesbians understood that while they might wear pants at home, they had to change to a skirt to go out on the street—unless they were able to pass as men. Not even movie stars were immune from censure, as was suggested by 1930s headlines such as "Miss [Marlene] Dietrich Defends Use of Pants" and "GARBO IN PANTS!" According to the latter article, "Innocent bystanders gasped in amazement to see . . . Greta Garbo striding swiftly along Hollywood Boulevard dressed in men's clothes."[14] But since hundreds of thousands of women who worked in war factory jobs during the early 1940s were actually obliged to wear pants, they had become a permanent part of American women's wardrobe, and they continued to be so after the war. The lesbian who loathed dresses felt much freer to wear pants out of doors than she had in the prewar years. Pants soon became a costume and a symbol that allowed women who defined themselves as lesbians to identify each other.

Perhaps because women were allowed more latitude in their dress during the war, butch and femme distinctions in style could be more pronounced, and the roles became very clear-cut for more lesbians. Rusty Brown, who was a civilian welder for the Navy, remembers that in a coffeehouse she frequented, a lesbian hangout in the early 1940s, butch and femme roles were already very strict. "You could tell when you walked in who was butch and who was femme," she recalls. Unless two women were on a date, butches would sit only with other butches and femmes would sit with femmes. Stringent codes of behavior were soon established. For example, butches could date only femmes. They must never even dance with another butch because, Rusty Brown recalls, "We were too much alike . . . If we danced, who was going to lead! We would both be dominant."[15] Such behavior codes, which seem to have received sharper definition at this time, when butches were sanctioned to appear completely masculine in their dress, became pervasive in the working-class lesbian subculture of the 1950s.

Ironically, the military also contributed to the establishment of a larger lesbian subculture when it became less lenient in its policy toward homosexuals once the war was over. Thousands of homosexual personnel were loaded on "queer ships" and sent with "undesirable" discharges to the nearest U. S. port. Many of them believed that they could not go home again. They simply stayed where they were disembarked, and their numbers helped to form the large homosexual enclaves that were beginning to develop in port cities such as New York, San Francisco, Los Angeles, and Boston. Historian Allan Bérubé wryly remarks: "The government sponsored a migration of the gay community."[16]

The military even helped to introduce lesbians who had honorable discharges to large metropolitan areas where they could meet others like themselves. Mac, who had never been out of Iowa before she joined the service, was typical. She has lived in San Francisco since the war, and explains that when she had been stationed in the Bay Area she discovered that "San Francisco felt like home. I found a lot of different sorts of attractive people there. And I knew everyone minded their own business and didn't care about what I was doing." She speculates that were it not for the war she might still be in Iowa. Many women also came to big cities in order to work in factories during the war and they, like ex-military women, stayed because they found the anonymity of a big city to be more compatible with what became their life choices.[17]

The migration to big urban centers of large numbers of women who identified themselves as lesbians during and after the war meant that for the first time in America a number of bars could survive economically if they catered exclusively to lesbians. Although military bases sometimes posted notices declaring certain bars "off limits to military personnel" and the lesbian bars near the bases were also required to display such notices, it was during the war that more all-lesbian bars were opened in big cities, such as the If Club in Los Angeles. Military lesbians on weekend passes gathered there despite the prohibitions, as did lesbians who worked in the factories and held other jobs in the cities because of the war.[18]

Bars that catered to gay men and tourists along with lesbians also proliferated during the war, such as Lucky's, a Harlem bar that opened in 1942 and attracted interracial couples as well as slumming tourists, and the 181 Club on Second Avenue in New York which opened in the mid-1940s. The 181 Club featured waiters who were butch lesbians in tuxedos and entertainers who were female impersonators. Like the bars of the 1920s, it drew many heterosexuals who came to gawk or to dabble, but many more men and women who were committed to homosexuality and who came to be with other homosexuals. Similar clubs opened during the war in smaller cities also, such as the Music Hall in Portland, Oregon, which featured male and female impersonators such as Mickey, the "master of ceremonies," a lesbian who sang in a tenor voice.[19]

While there was not yet a lot of explicit political consciousness brewing in those bars during and right after the war, they often fostered a sense of community especially among working-class and young lesbians. And in fact, the changes in women's lives that were triggered by the war—not only through experiences in the military or in factories, but also through social configurations such as the expanding bar culture—permitted those who loved other women to see their feelings in a broader context. They could now much more easily conceptualize lesbianism not simply as a secret and forbidden love but as a lifestyle shared by many other women. Perhaps some

could begin to see themselves as a "minority." This new vision
accounts for the incipient lesbian political consciousness that was now
just beginning to develop. Hints of that slowly awakening consciousness appeared even in military magazines such as *Yank,* in which one
letter to the editor written by a lesbian WAC officer at the end of the
war seemed to identify lesbians as a legitimate minority group and
appealed for social justice, consonant with the ideals of justice for
which Americans had been fighting. The writer declared:

> I have voluntarily drunk from the Lesbian cup and have tasted much of
> the bitterness contained therein as far as the attitude of society is
> concerned. I believe there is much that can and should be done in the
> near future to aid in the solution of this problem, thus enabling [ho-
> mosexuals] to take their rightful places as fellow human beings, your
> sister and brother in the brotherhood of mankind.[20]

Such emerging awareness led the way to lesbian organizing in the
next decade and can perhaps partially explain why the gay and les-
bian- feminist revolutions caught fire as quickly as they did at the end
of the 1960s.

However, while many women may have come to identify themselves as lesbians during the war years, there were some, in more
sheltered environments, far from the nascent pockets of the lesbian
subculture, who had same-sex love experiences and yet managed to
maintain something of the innocence of an earlier era. Betty, who
lived in Nebraska during the war, says that she had been a psychology
major in college, but when she fell in love with another woman in
1942 they did not call it lesbianism, any more than most of her
counterparts would have at the beginning of the century: "I didn't
think that what I'd read in an abnormal psych text applied to us in
any way." Although they had a sexual relationship, they believed
that they should both get married to compatible people so that they
could live next door to each other. When their husbands went off to
war, both women worked on a newspaper, but each moved in with
her parents: "We were earning very low salaries, and it never occurred to us to get an apartment together. We didn't even know there
were other women like us out there. We had no idea that making a
life together could be an option for us."[21] Betty's knowledge of the
medical texts that described lesbianism as a physiological or psychological problem gave her no information about her own experience,
which she knew was not sick, and did nothing to reveal to her the

growing society of women who were creating a lifestyle around their affectional preferences.

But other women, especially those in large coastal cities, became much more sophisticated during the war years. Women who identified as lesbians and who remembered the 1930s felt that lesbian life in America had changed permanently and for the better by the war. Lisa Ben, the editor of a short-lived post-war lesbian periodical, *Vice Versa* (the first of its kind in America), wrote a euphoric article in 1947 proclaiming that the day of lesbian freedom had finally come. She pointed to changes in fashion such as girls' preferences for "jeans and boys shirts [instead of] neat feminine attire," which made it easier for lesbians to dress as they wanted, and the proliferation of "night clubs featuring male and female impersonators," as well as cafés and drive-ins that may have been predominantly heterosexual but were so frequently patronized by homosexuals that they came to be known as "a likely rendezvous in which to meet those of similar inclinations." In addition, she observed, women's freedom had so escalated in the years right after the war that it was immeasurably easier to be a lesbian in 1947 than it had been at any time in the past:

> In these days of frozen foods . . . , compact apartments, modern innovations, and female independence, there is no reason why a woman should have to look to a man for food and shelter in return for raising his children and keeping his house in order unless she really wants to. Today a woman may live independently from a man if she so chooses, and carve out her own career. Never before have circumstances and conditions been so suitable for those of lesbian tendencies.[22]

Such euphoria had also been felt by many women in the early decades of this century, yet they experienced a setback in the 1930s and were about to experience another in the 1950s. But certain aspects of progress for lesbianism as a lifestyle were irreversible. Because women who loved other women were brought together in masses during the war, much larger numbers of them became aware of themselves as a group. The media acknowledgment of lesbian sexuality, which had become more explicit during the 1930s, had helped to reinforce the demarcation between romantic friends or devoted companions and lesbians. That awareness now aided the many women who fell in love with other females during the war (and who might earlier have thought of themselves in more sexually innocent terms) in becoming conscious of themselves as homo*sexual*. The mobility of the postwar years spread the word of the existence of other lesbian groups, especially in major cities. And although women were now urged back to the home, the phenomenon of the working woman had become more familiar during the war, which meant that those who were really committed to supporting themselves might once again in an improved economic environment find jobs that would let them live without a man's protection. An identifiable and widespread lesbian subculture was finally formed. Although the reactionary era that followed interfered with that subculture going public, nevertheless a consciousness had taken root that could not be deracinated.

The Heyday of the Lesbian "Sicko"

With the end of the war society took a conservative turn in all areas. Lesbians were affected particularly by the growing interest in mandating conformity through what was promoted as "mental health." It was at this time that the lesbian "sicko" became the dominant image of the woman who loved other women and curing lesbians on the couch became a big business in America.

Sigmund Freud, the guru of post-World War II psychoananlysts, had actually attempted to consider all psychological states in a value-free manner. But he was, after all, a nineteenth-century, upper-middle-class, patriarchal moralist, and he was not immune to certain assumed "truths" about the proper role of women. He was especially upset by the growing feminist sentiments that challenged those "truths" among European women in the early twentieth century, and his works frequently suggest his opposition to the women's movement. His most negative views of lesbianism are more specifically negative views of feminism. In his only protracted study of lesbianism, "The Psychogenesis of a Case of Homosexuality in a Woman" (1920), *feminism* is seen as a chief manifestation of his subject's sexual "abnormality." Even where he found no specifically *sexual* indication of lesbianism in his subjects, a woman's failure to be passive or timid, her ambition, and even her athletic interests were proof enough of a latent homosexuality, because those attributes were a failure to adjust properly to the female role as his culture knew it.[23]

For the many who shared his views, women's relative economic and social freedom during World War II must have really stimulated anxieties. Such antifeminists preferred, of course, the more traditional roles women had been forced back into during the 1930s. Their discomfort was far from tempered by the climate of the postwar years—a time when authority became king and nonconformity became close to criminality, when men were again settling back into civilian jobs and home life and women again had to be gotten out of the jobs and into the home to welcome them. Psychoanalytic attitudes served to assist those ends.

Post-World War II American psychoanalysts generally employed Freudian language and twisted Freudian theory to insist, with far greater certitude than Freud himself ever mustered and with much more vehemence than in the 1930s, on the sickness of lesbians, which they saw as being responsible for their "antisocial" behavior. Clara Thompson, for example, declared in 1949 that a person who accepts homosexuality as an overt way of life has a weak superego and is "unable to control the direction of [her] libido drives."[24] While Freud believed that a neurosis could always be traced to a disturbance in sexuality, Freudians in the postwar years came to believe that what they viewed as disturbed sexuality—same-sex love—could always be traced to neurosis, and they felt justified in attacking that sexuality since they claimed it was nothing more than a symptom of illness. A woman who loved another woman might come to analysis in the years after the war to deal with a particular problem unrelated to her affectional life, such as heterosexuals often did, or simply to know herself better, to see more clearly, to understand her motivations and choices, but she was often forced to deal with her lesbianism instead.

The consensus among the postwar professionals was that lesbians are incapable of any kind of satisfaction in life, most especially personal happiness. Even if they claim they are happy, they are deceiving themselves, a leading "lesbian expert," Frank Caprio, observed in the 1950s: theirs "is only a surface or pseudo happiness. Basically, they are lonely and unhappy and afraid to admit it." Caprio argued that women who love women are characteristically ambivalent about life situations (as though ambivalence were not a part of human nature), and he pointed to several instances of lesbian suicide in fiction (as though Western literature, from Sophocles to Shakespeare to the present, were not rife with heterosexual suicide).[25] His intent was not simply to separate off women who love women from the rest of humanity, but also to present any problems they might have not as part of the complex human condition but merely as a manifestation of their perversity.

Other psychiatrists took up his cry. "The greatest importance of homosexuality," wrote two of them in a 1958 book, "is that it causes so much unhappiness. If happiness is of any value . . . then homosexuality should be eliminated by every means in our power." They placed on women who loved women a secret and impossible burden to be happy at all times lest they admit that they deserve "genocide." Although their heterosexual counterparts in the postwar years had freedom to wallow in the miseries of the feminine mystique, women who loved women had to feel guilty if they were even briefly depressed and to attribute it to their lesbianism. But according to Edmund Bergler, another leading lesbian-smasher of the 1950s, any attempts they made to be happy would be self-defeating anyway because they had an unconscious wish to suffer that was only gratified by "self-created trouble-making" and "injustice collecting."[26] Inevitably, Bergler suggested, lesbians made not only themselves but everyone around them miserable.

According to some psychiatrists of the postwar years, same-sex love was simply a symptom of a more general character disorder. It would disappear if the disorder were resolved, and the woman would then be content to marry and stay home, raising babies and tending to hubby's needs. Other psychiatrists even declared that women who loved women were worse off than being "disordered" in their character: "not merely neurotics, but . . . actually borderline or outright psychotics." One psychiatrist, Charles Socarides, who continued to promulgate his theories of lesbian psychosis years after the American Psychiatric Association removed homosexuality from its list of mental disorders in 1973, reported that in clinical experience the connection between homosexuality and paranoid schizophrenia is "striking" in a great number of patients. He never acknowledged, of course, that the connection between paranoid schizophrenia (or depression or homocide or epilepsy) and heterosexuality is even more striking, nor that lesbians, particularly during the 1950s, often *were* persecuted and not just suffering under *delusions* of persecution.[27]

These psychiatrists disregarded the warning of their guru, Freud, who stated with surprising enlightenment in "The Sexual Aberrations" that it was not adequate to an understanding of homosexuality to consider only patients in treatment, that if doctors would "strive to comprehend a wider field of experience" they would see that homosexuality was far from being a degeneracy, and that even the concept of perversion was really a matter of cultural definition. Instead they based their definiton of lesbianism almost exclusively on records of patients who needed psychiatric care.[28] It was worse than defining heterosexuality through divorce court records.

Every aspect of same-sex love thus came to be defined as sick. Psychotherapists pointed out that within the lesbian couple there were tensions that could lead to a break in the relationship; that not only did lesbian relations serve the function of providing sexual release, but they also served a range of irrational defensive and reparative needs—ignoring the fact that similar problems were at least as probable for heterosexual coupledom.[29] In these views love between women was always implicitly contrasted to a heterosexual norm based on 1950s Hollywood movies: after boy got girl heterosexual love was supposedly without complication, conflict, eruption. Only same sex lovers had troubles in their relationships.

It is not surprising that in an era when conformity was worshiped, parents accepted such views without question and panicked if their children did not fit heterosexual norms. An adolescent crush on another female, which half a century earlier was seen as an important and welcome part of the normal course of development, made caring parents send their daughters off to psychiatrists. Parents even had daughters locked up in psychiatric hospitals for being "uncontrollable" because of their lesbianism. One woman tells of how her parents, upon discovering her crush on a physical education teacher when she was fourteen years old, first sent her to a psychologist "to find out if I was crazy." When her parents' persistent rejection of her sexual identification during her teen years caused her to be so depressed that she attempted suicide, they committed her to a hospital psychiatric ward where the nurses "tried to fix me up with boys" and the psychiatrists "made me feel I was the only one who ever felt love for someone of the same sex." When her depression continued after her release, her parents again had her hospitalized, this time in a state mental hospital. She was not alone there, she says. She met a thirty-year-old lesbian who claimed "she had been in and out of institutions all her life for being a lesbian. I thought she was the sanest person there." Similar stories were not uncommon during the mid-twentieth century.[30]

Such societal threats did terrify many females away from same-sex love. Lesbianism became a problem to be grappled with, even when parents and the psychiatrists they hired were not policing one's emotions. Intense feelings for another woman—whether physically realized or more amorphous—could cause untold hours of worry and even vast expenditures in "getting professional help." Nor was bisexuality any longer an area for exploration. It was a "condition" to be very concerned about, especially if it led to the horrors of lesbianism.

Loving another woman meant that one had to live with the realization
that almost anyone who knew would consider one a "lesbian sicko."

Curing Lesbians on the Couch

Disdain for same-sex love quickly spread in a war-exhausted country that wanted only to return to "normalcy," and American psychoanalysts felt entirely justified in their desire to cure women of
their love for each other and their independence. Modern women
who rejected what Betty Friedan has called "the feminine mystique"
were now considered "the Lost Sex," as the title of a popular 1947
book by two American Freudians suggested. According to the authors, such women were influenced in their aspirations by feminism,
which was "an expression of emotional illness, of neurosis . . . , at
its core a deep illness," foisted once again on American women
primarily by lesbians who carried the notion of independence to the
greatest extreme. Psychoanalysts of the postwar years were very
quick to pick up such a rallying cry. Not only did lesbians influence
feminism, but feminist gains in work, dress, and pastimes had "more
than likely" influenced many women to become homosexual. "This
new freedom that women are enjoying," Dr. Frank Caprio pronounced with alarm in the early 1950s, "serves as a fertile soil for the
seeds of sexual inversion."[31] A society that agreed once again that
woman's place was in the home saw feminists as a threat to the public
welfare, and lesbians, the most obvious advocates of feminism, once
more became the chief villains. The social benefits of curing lesbians,
who were all sick anyway and needed curing, were unquestionable.

In the name of science these therapists promoted heterosexuality
with religious fervor, and they were at least as intolerant as religious
zealots, despite their obligatory nod to the importance of "understanding." There was no room for debate in their view that love
between women was an illness that must be eradicated, regardless of
the individual personality or level of adjustment or productivity of
the women involved. Freud believed (and many of his early disciples
agreed with him) that the object of psychoanalysis should not be the
"cure" of homosexuality (which he thought was impossible anyway)
but rather, as he said in his letter to an American mother of a male
homosexual, to help the homosexual find harmony, peace of mind,
and full efficiency. Although in the 1920s and '30s in America there
were a few psychoanalysts who desired to cure their patients of same-

sex love, it was not until the '50s, with its worship of "normality" and its terror of female independence, that the cure of love between women became such a large-scale business.[32]

Many of the therapists of the 1950s simply ignored Freud's conservatism regarding the efficacy of treatment, claiming that lesbianism was always curable if the doctors went about it the right way. They published in books and medical journals fabulous accounts of their successes in converting homosexuals into heterosexuals and shared their formulas with their colleagues. Albert Ellis, in a 1956 article, reported that through his work with lesbian patients one-third were "distinctly improved" and two-thirds were "considerably improved" in their progress toward heterosexuality. Ellis explained that his approach was to insist on unmasking the neurotic motivations behind his patients' same-sex love and to show by his manner and verbalizations that he was himself "favorably prejudiced" toward heterosexuality. The patients were persuaded, Ellis wrote, "to engage in sex-love relationships with members of the other sex and to keep reporting to the therapist for specific discussion and possible aid with these love relationships," outrageously regardless of whether or not they had come to Ellis desiring to change their sexual orientation. Edmund Bergler actually promised his patients that same-sex love was reversible, but only through psychoanalytic treatment by a psychiatrist for one or two years, with a minimum of three appointments each week (at the cost of as much as sixty thousand dollars, calculated in present dollars).[33]

These medical doctors often promulgated a rather odd morality in their attempt to rid their patients of lesbianism. In a popular book of the 1950s, *Voyage from Lesbos: The Psychoanalysis of a Female Homosexual*, Richard Robertiello wrote of a twenty-nine year old woman who had come to him for a cure for her insomnia after the breakup of an eight-year lesbian relationship. He told her that lesbianism was fraught with difficulties and that she needed to "make a clean break" from it and go to places where she could meet men. When she reported "necking" with a married man, the doctor enthusiastically applauded her "success." By the end of her analysis she was "cured" of her lesbianism (despite the fact that she began therapy saying she had "no desire to change her sexual pattern . . . and was perfectly content to remain homosexual"). Though Robertiello was forced to admit that she continued to have insomnia (which was, of course, the problem that caused her to seek his help in the first place), he nevertheless considered his work with her a great success.[34]

As further justification of their intent to "cure," many of the leading lesbian specialists published patently sensationalistic accounts of lesbianism. Frank Caprio actually used "case histories" from true confession magazines of the 1950s such as *Life Romances* and *My Confession* in order to show how sick lesbians were. Some researchers of the early 1950s, who must have believed that the one sexual act of cunnilingus was synonymous with the entire lesbian experience, and who misunderstood even that act, suggested that homosexuality was really a manifestation of cannibalistic fantasies. References to lesbian murder, suicide, and seduction of the innocent were rife throughout the medical literature. It is no wonder, then, that popular magazines not only applauded psychiatric attempts to cure, but even adopted the language and attitudes of the medical men, further promulgating notions such as that in *Time Magazine* in 1956, that homosexuals are "generally unreliable in an essentially psychopathic way . . . regardless of [their] level of intelligence, culture, background, or education."[35]

The Freudian therapists were not alone in their promise and determination to cure lesbians. One woman tells of having gone to a Jungian therapist and discussing, among other things, her love for another woman, about which the therapist "comforted" her: "Oh, don't worry. We'll cure that in about six months." When she persisted in describing her relationship with the other woman as "the best love of my life," the Jungian replied that lesbianism was "not any worse than alcoholism, but it's on the same level."[36]

Proposals for cures were generally couched in terms that suggested the liberal sympathies of the doctors, but their ill-disguised hostility toward love between women is easily discernible. By categorizing same-sex love as a disease they pretended, perhaps even to themselves, to be moving beyond morality. But as Thomas Szasz has pointed out, the concept of disease in this respect involves a value judgment, distinguishing some states of functioning as being inferior to others. With regard to lesbianism, the judgment was clearly based not on impaired functioning such as the inability to work or love, but merely on unpopular object choice: in that judgment, homosexuality is bad (regardless of the individual's level of functioning or the quality of her love relationship) and heterosexuality is good (again, regardless of the behavior of the individual in all areas of her life or the nature of her heterosexual relationships). The doctors for the most part were blinded by their own narrow value judgments and believed they had the moral objectivity of science behind them. Typically, in his representation of the battlelines of the 1950s, Edmund Bergler bragged of his scientific stance, which he felt was embued with a humane desire to help:

> Homosexuals: We are normal and demand recognition!
> Heterosexuals: You are perverts and belong in jail!
> Psychiatrists: Homosexuals are sick people and belong in treatment.[37]

Bergler had no doubt that he was on the side of the angels.

All this is not to say that there was never complicity or ambivalence on the part of some women themselves, who sought out psychiatrists in the hope of being cured of their love for other women because they were infected with the rampant homophobia of their society. Harriet, who had been in therapy with three different Los Angeles psychiatrists during the 1950s, now explains with hindsight:

> Of course many of us were loaded with self-hate and wanted to change. How could it have been otherwise? All we heard and read about homosexuality was that crap about how we were inverts, perverts, queers—a menace to children, poison to everyone else, doomed never to be happy. And so we went humbly to the doctors, and took whatever other nastiness they wanted to spew out about homosexuality, and we paid them and said thanks.[38]

Since there were so few countering messages of support from the external world, constant exposure to antihomosexual propaganda was bound to make some women who loved women believe that salvation lay in conversion to heterosexuality. Those who sold lesbian-smashing at this time had sufficient confused and fearful buyers.

While World War II played an important role in the expansion of a lesbian subculture, the years that immediately followed determined much about its nature. The effect on lesbians of the onslaught of the psychoanalytic establishment was usually not to convince them that they were sick, though some were convinced, but rather to create cynicism toward the pronouncements of authorities because it was apparent that authorities knew nothing or lied. Since lesbians were not organized to challenge the outrageous psychoanalytic views, they also had to endure frustration born of a sense of powerlessness. There were no gay militants or lesbian-feminists to point out that, in fact, far from being sick, a woman who dared to live as an overt homosexual in such unwelcoming times might well have an ego of impressive strength and health that permitted her to know her own mind and to be true to her conception of herself.

The public image of the lesbian as sick in the years after the war confirmed the need for secrecy. A lesbian understood that if her affectional preference became known outside of her circle of lesbian friends she would be judged wholly by that preference and found mentally unhealthy. She would be discredited before any other aspect of her personality or behavior could be considered. She was virtually forced into hiding. Lesbianism, which in different societal circumstances might have signified simply affectional preference, thus became not only the basis for a covert society, but also an overwhelming aspect of one's identity, precisely because it was so necessary to live it in secret and to be constantly aware that an important part of one's life must be camouflaged at almost all times. As will be seen, the political milieu of the postwar years served to reinforce this state. In addition to the mischief wrought by the medical men who made lesbianism a sickness, the times also rendered lesbianism unpatriotic.

6

The Love That Dares Not Speak Its Name: McCarthyism and Its Legacy

*At work you completely avoided people. If you did make
friends, you had to be sure never to bring them to your home.
Never to tell them who and what you really were. We were
all terrified in those days.   Lyn on New York in the 1950s*

*When I was arrested and being thrown out
of the military, the order went out: don't anybody
speak to this woman, and for those three
long months, almost nobody did; the dayroom, when
I entered it, fell silent til I had gone; they
were afraid, they knew the wind would blow
them over the rail, the cops would come,
the water would run into their lungs.
Everything I touched
was spoiled. They were my lovers, those
women, but nobody had taught us to swim.
I drowned. I took 3 or 4 others down
When I signed the confession of what we
had done together.*

No one will ever speak to me again.
*   —Judy Grahn on the military in the 1950s,*
*   "A Woman Is Talking to Death"*

The social upheaval occasioned by the war was more than many
Americans could bear. The years after became an age of authority, in
the hope that authority would set the country back in balance. The
pronouncements of those in charge, not only in the medical profession but in government as well, were virtually sacrosanct. There was
little challenge to their notion that "extreme threats," such as the
encroachments of the Soviets, required extreme solutions to weed out
those who did not accept the reigning views. A breaking point in

American rationality, justice, and common decency ensued. If political conformity was essential to national security, sexual conformity
came to be considered, by some mystifying twist of logic by those in
authority, as no less essential. In a decade of reaction, while women
were sent back to the home, dissidents of every kind were deprived
of their livelihoods and even packed off to jail.

Twentieth-century American witch-hunts began not long after the
war. Those accused of Communism were their first target, but persecution quickly spread to other unpopular groups. Despite figures
that Alfred Kinsey gathered during these years, which showed that
50 percent of American men and 28 percent of American women had
what could be considered "homosexual tendencies" (that is, homo-
erotic interest in the same sex at some point in their adult lives), the
statistical normality of same- sex love was now denied more fiercely
than ever. The "homosexual" became a particular target of persecution in America. He or she presented an uncomfortable challenge to
the mood that longed for obedience to an illusion of uncomplicated
"morality." Even Kinsey was suspected of being a subversive, merely
because he said that so many people in his studies admitted to same-
sex attractions and experiences. Dr. Edmund Bergler angrily wrote
in the *Psychiatric Quarterly* about Kinsey's statistics on widespread
homosexuality in America that Kinsey had created a "myth of a new
national disease." That "myth" would be "politically and propagan-
distically used against the United States abroad, stigmatizing the
nation as a whole in a whisper campaign." Homosexuality was a
detriment to the country's image and standing in the world. As far as
those who spoke for mid-twentieth-century heterosexual America
were concerned, homosexuality was a love that had better not dare
speak its name. The heterosexual majority tyrannized. As one writer
expressed it in 1951, if homosexuality was condemned by most
people in a society, then loyalty to the society demanded that
good citizens support condemnation of homosexuality and the laws
against it.[1]

By commonly accepted (though statistically erroneous) definition,
the demarcation that separated "homosexual" from "heterosexual"
was now more clear than ever. Between 1947 and 1950, 4,954 men
and women were dismissed from the armed forces and civilian agencies for being homosexual. In 1950, the persecution escalated. Sen.
Joseph McCarthy, whose barbarous tactics set the mood of the era,
began by attracting attention as a Communist witch-hunter but soon
saw an opportunity to broaden his field. Ironically, McCarthy's two

aides were flamingly homosexual, even flitting about Europe as an "item," but that did not stop him from charging the State Department with knowingly harboring homosexuals and thereby placing the nation's security at risk.[2]

The Republicans decided to make political hay out of the issue. Republican National Chairman Guy George Gabrielson wrote in the official party newsletter early in 1950 that "perhaps as dangerous as the actual communists are the sexual perverts who have infiltrated our government in recent years." By April of that year ninety-one homosexuals were fired from the State Department alone. In May 1950, New York Republican Governor Dewey accused President Truman and the Democrats of tolerating not only spies and traitors in government service, but also sexual perverts. Soon after, the Senate Appropriations Subcommittee joined the attacks, recommending that homosexuals be dismissed from government jobs since they were poor security risks because of their vulnerability to blackmail.[3] Just as the number of women who dared to live as lesbians was increasing during the postwar years, their persecution was increasing as well— not just because of personal prejudices against them, but as a result of national policy.

Despite the general pretense, the concern about homosexuals in government was not primarily that they constituted a security risk because they were vulnerable to blackmail: that could have been obviated if the government simply declared that no one was to be fired on the ground of homosexuality. The concern was actually caused by discomfort with whatever was different. In fact, the Senate subcommittee admitted that there were two reasons why homosexuals should not be employed in government; that homosexuals were a security risk was only the second reason. The first was that "they are generally unsuitable," which was explained to mean that homosexuality "is so contrary to the normal accepted standards of social behavior that persons who engage in such activity are looked upon as outcasts by society in general." Official policy therefore became to persecute "outcasts." That the matter of security risk was only of secondary interest is demonstrated through the committee's recommendation that homosexuals be dismissed not only from the State Department, the military, and Congress, but also from occupations such as caretaker at the Botanical Gardens.[4]

One woman who was affected by the Senate Subcommittee recommendation recalls that she was fired in 1951 from a job that had absolutely nothing to do with "national security." She had been doing social relief work in Germany for a private agency. Like all organizations operating in occupied terrritory, the agency had to be approved by the State Department and was subject to all its regula- tions. Through a "security check" of her past, it was discovered that not only had this woman gone to a psychotherapist in the 1940s, but she had discussed lesbianism with him. Though she had had no lesbian experiences since she took the job in Germany and was even trying to live a heterosexual life, she was nevertheless found undesir- able because of her "homosexual tendencies." She had no recourse against her accusers. As she later observed of U.S. government tac- tics, "to be accused is to be guilty."[5]

The Senate also justified the government policy of harassment of homosexuals by claiming that they must be fired from government jobs because of the "lack of emotional stability which is found in most sex perverts and the weakness of their moral fiber." The cross- fertilization of ideas between government and the medical establish- ment was apparent. Both were bent on sexual conformity. and nei- ther accepted any responsibility for establishing the truth of their allegations against homosexuals. Homosexuals were condemned by the most obvious of begged questions: they were by definition per- verts, which meant that they were emotionally unstable and their moral fiber was weak.[6]

While homosexual men bore the brunt of sexual witch-hunting by the governement, women who loved women and who dared to live lesbian lifestyles became more than incidental victims. Although sta- tistically they lost fewer jobs than their male counterparts since there were fewer women than men employed by the government, lesbians realized that for the public "homosexual" was a scare-term: it was horrifying whether it referred to men or women. Lesbians believed, with plenty of justification, that whatever opprobrium was expressed for gay males would apply to them also and their livelihood and community standing would be just as endangered if their secret were known.

By 1951, federal agencies were using lie detectors in loyalty inves- tigations of men and women in supposedly "sensitive" government jobs to determine whether they were either Communists or homo- sexuals. It was clearly the intent of the Senate, whose recommenda- tions justified such measures, to include lesbians among those that were to be dismissed from government jobs, since the report on which the recommendation was based pointedly specified that 4 per- cent of the female population in the United States was lesbian. Re-

publican floor leader of the Senate Kenneth Wherry, who was the co-
author of that report, declared that he was on a "crusade to harry
every last pervert from the Federal Government services." Under the
influence of such thinking, the head of the Washington, D.C., Vice
Squad requested increased appropriations, not only to hunt down
male homosexuals but also to establish a "lesbian squad" to "rout out
the females." Senator Wherry explained, with some confusion, the
rationale for such actions to the *New York Post:*

> You can't hardly separate homosexuals from subversives. . . . Mind
> you, I don't say every homosexual is a subversive, and I don't say
> every subversive is a homosexual. But [people] of low morality are a
> menace in the government, whatever [they are], and they are all tied
> up together.[7]

Such convictions about the connections between leftists and homosexuals were apparent in the nature of the interrogation that women
who were under suspicion were forced to undergo. M.K., who held
a high ranking civil service job in Albany, New York, tells of having
been summoned to New York City by the U. S. Civil Service
Commission in 1954 and being put through a four day ordeal. For
the first three days she was confronted with "evidence" of her communist leanings, such as having danced with a (male) U.S.S.R. liaison
officer in Seoul, Korea, when she served there a few years earlier, and
having applied to visit a North Korean university. On the fourth day
she was asked directly, "Are you a homosexual?" After her denial,
she was informed that the government had unearthed evidence that
she had lived with several women in the past and had gone overseas
with one. With no better proof against her she was barred from
federal government employment "for security reasons, on the grounds
of moral turpitude."[8]

"Are You or Have You Ever Been a
Member of a Lesbian Relationship?"

The Senate Subcommittee report led finally to an Executive Order
signed by President Eisenhower as one of his first acts in office. That
Order mandated the investigation for homosexuality not only of
persons in "sensitive" positions, but of any government employee
and of all new applicants for positions. It permitted no judicial review. An employee who felt she was dismissed unfairly would have

no recourse beyond her department. She could be fired merely on the basis of anonymous accusations. Homosexuals in state and local government jobs were harassed as well. Lesbians were particularly affected. Since so few women could become doctors or lawyers or business leaders during the 1950s, because professional schools by now generally discouraged females, middle-class lesbians were forced into those professions that were more available to them as women. They made careers in teaching and social work—government jobs in which, by virtue of sexual orientation, a lesbian broke the law every day she came to work, regardless of how good an employee she was.[9]

Psychoanalysts and the government had done such a thorough job in promoting the irrational fear of homosexuality that even groups that should have seen themselves as allies because they were persecuted in the same way, and should have wanted to form a coalition to fight injustice, denounced homosexuals. Instead of banding together with homosexuals—as reactionaries accused them of doing—leftists were almost as bad in their homophobia as the government. Black lesbian poet Audre Lorde says that when in 1953 she worked on a committee to free Julius and Ethel Rosenberg she realized that the one taboo among those socially liberated people remained homosexuality:

> I could imagine these comrades, Black and white, among whom color and racial differences could be openly examined and talked about, nonetheless one day asking me accusingly, "Are you or have you ever been a member of a homosexual relationship?"

To leftists, homosexuality was reason for suspicion and shunning not only because they deemed it—through myth and prejudice equaled only by the right—"bourgeois and reactionary," but also because it made an individual more susceptible to the FBI.[10]

Not even the bravest bastion of liberalism, the American Civil Liberties Union, dared to offer a strong defense on the lesbian's behalf during those years. As astonishing as it may be in retrospect, the ACLU National Board of Directors affirmed in January 1957 that "homosexuality is a valid consideration in evaluating the security risk factor in sensitive positions" and made clear that unless it was an issue of entrapment or denial of due process, the ACLU was not going to fight battles on the side of homosexuals: "It is not within the province of the Union to evaluate the social validity of the laws aimed at the suppression or elimination of homosexuals," the Union declared. Although it took a liberal stand on all other issues, it literally advised lesbians that the best thing they could do would be to "abandon" their lesbianism and become heterosexual.[11]

Although Sen. Joseph McCarthy was censured by the Senate in 1954 for his overly zealous witch-hunting, the spirit he helped establish lived on through that decade and into the next. Homosexuals in all walks of life, not just those who worked for the government, were hunted down. Not even young college students were safe. In 1955 the dean and assistant dean of students at UCLA published an article in the journal *School and Society* lamenting the "attraction of colleges, both public and private, for overt, hardened homosexuals" and recommending that all "sexually deviate" students be routed out of colleges if they were unwilling to undergo psychiatric treatment to change their sexual orientation. Students entering state supported universities were obliged to take a battery of tests in which thinly veiled questions on sexual preference appeared over and over. What the authorities expected such tests to reveal is unimaginable, since homosexuals who were smart enough to get into those institutions were surely smart enough to realize that they must dissemble. The 1950s mandated that women learn to lead a double existence if they wanted to live as lesbians and yet maintain the advantages of middle-class American life such as pursuing higher education and the careers to which it led. As one midwestern woman recalls, "If anyone ever asked if you were a lesbian you knew that you needed to deny it to your dying breath."[12] They understood that if they could not develop the skill of hiding, if they were not wily enough to answer "no" to any form of the question "Are you or have you ever been . . . ," they would not survive as social beings.

The popular press saw nothing objectionable in the ubiquitous harassment of homosexuals. In fact, stories of lesbian conspiracies and the dangers posed by those who were sexually "abnormal" were treated with great relish. In their scandalous *Washington Confidential*, for example, Jack Lait and Lee Mortimer announced that psychologists and sociologists who had "made a study of the problem" in the D.C. area believed "there are at least twice as many Sapphic lovers as fairies" and reeled off the names of several bars where lesbians sported with homosexual men, observing "all queers are in rapport with all other queers."[13]

Mass circulation magazines presented homosexuality as a chief cause of American ills in articles with titles such as "New Moral Menace to Our Youth," in which same-sex love was said to lead to "drug addiction, burglary, sadism, and even murder." Lesbians were presented in those magazines as "preying" on innocent "victims." As *Jet,* a black magazine, characterized the lesbian in 1954, "If she so much as gets one foot into a good woman's home with the intention of seducing her, she will leave no stone unturned . . . and eventually destroy her life for good."[14]

Such sensationalism was not limited to *National Enquirer*-type trash literature. For instance, *Human Events,* a weekly Washington newsletter that purported a readership of "40,000 business and professional leaders," declared, echoing the insanity of Senator Wherry, that homosexuals must be hunted down and purged because "by the very nature of their vice they belong to a sinister, mysterious, and efficient International, [and] members of one conspiracy are prone to join another conspiracy."[15]

If a magazine attempted to present homosexuality in a better light it was subject to censorship. In 1954 when the newly established homophile magazine *One* published a short story about a woman chosing to become a lesbian, "Sappho Remembered," the Postmaster General of Los Angeles confiscated all copies of the issue that had been mailed and demanded that the publisher prove that the story was not "obscene, lewd, lascivious and filthy." With blatantly homophobic reasoning, the federal district court upheld the Postmaster General's decision, arguing about "Sappho Remembered":

> This article is nothing more than cheap pornography calculated to promote lesbianism. It falls far short of dealing with homosexuality from a scientific, historic, or critical point of view. . . . An article may be vulgar, offensive and indecent even though not regarded as such by a particular group . . . because their own social or moral standards are far below those of the general community. . . . Social standards are fixed by and for the great majority and not by and for a hardened or weakened minority.[16]

Obviously what the Court meant by "dealing with homosexuality from a scientific, historic, or critical point of view" was simply supporting the prevailing prejudice that homosexuality was diseased or sinful.

That pulp novels with lesbian subject matter should have been permitted to proliferate during this period is not as surprising as it may seem at first glance, since they were generally cautionary tales: "moral" literature that warned females that lesbianism was sick or evil and that if a woman dared to love another woman she would end up lonely and suicidal. On the surface, at least, they seemed to confirm social prejudices about homosexuality. But despite that, many lesbians read those novels avidly.

The pulps, with their lurid covers featuring two women exchanging erotic gazes or locked in an embrace, could be picked up at newsstands and corner drugstores, even in small towns, and they helped spread the word about lesbian lifestyles to women who might have been too sheltered otherwise to know that such things existed. Lesbians bought those books with relish because they learned to read between the lines and get whatever nurturance they needed from them. Where else could one find public images of women loving women? Of course the characters of the lesbian pulps almost always lived in shame and with the knowledge that, as the titles often suggested, they belonged in "twilight," "darkness," or "shadows." Self-hatred was requisite in these novels. Typically the lesbian was characterized by lines such as "A sword of self-revulsion, carefully shielded, slipped its scabbard now for one second to stab deeply to the exposed core of her lesbianism."[17] But often the books suggested that lesbianism was so powerful that a heterosexual woman only had to be exposed to a dyke and she would fall (though she was usually rescued, rather perfunctorily, by a male before the last pages—in which the real lesbian was shown to be doomed to suitable torment). Lesbians could ignore their homophobic propaganda and moralizations and peruse the pulps for their romance and charged eroticism.

Perhaps lesbians knew enough to be realistic about the limitations of the publishing industry. Just as they needed to be careful in their own lives, writers and publishers needed to be careful: novels with lesbian subject matter and even fairly explicit sexual scenes could escape censorship if they had "redeeming social value," which meant that they could not "legitimize the abnormal condition [of lesbianism]" by showing lesbians as anything other than ultimately defeated.[18]

Writers who through their personal experiences might have been able to present more honest and happier depictions of lesbians did not dare to, even if they could have gotten such a book published. For example, novelist Helen Hull (*Quest, Labyrinth*), who spent much of her adult life in a love relationship with academic Mabel Robinson, was inspired by the Kinsey report in 1953 (that showed such a high incidence of lesbian experience in America) to think about writing a novel on lesbianism. She observed in her writer's journal that such a novel could show "what I have always thought, that conduct is not in any way consistent with either social code or law." Hull reflected that most of the women she knew best had not conformed to the stated mores of their society, "even when they have been important through their work and recognized positions." She briefly considered putting some of those lesbian friends into a novel: "K. . . . had courage and serenity, had groups of followers, must have had people whom she helped; E. had courage and liveliness and capacity for work and ingeniousness about developing her school. . . . She kept her sanguineness and her invincibility." But such people, who could have been much-needed role models for young women who chose to live as lesbians, never got into a lesbian novel because Hull concluded, as would most women writers with a reputation at stake during the period, that after all, "I don't want to be connected with the subject [of lesbianism]."[19]

It was not true, of course, that lesbians during the 1950s invariably paid for their nonconformity through misery, as the pulp novelists said they did. But whatever joy they found had to be procured outside of the main social institutions, and they had to be clandestine about it in a society that withheld from them the blessings it gave freely to all heterosexuals. Front marriages with gay men were not uncommon during the 1950s, not only for the sake of passing as heterosexual at work, but also in order to hide the truth from parents who could not bear their own failure in having raised a sexual non-conformist and who might have a daughter committed to a mental hospital for lesbianism. Lesbians often felt they could not trust close acquaintances with knowledge of their personal lives, even if they suspected those acquaintances might also be lesbian. A Vermont woman remembers, "Everyone was very cagey. We pretended to ourselves that we didn't talk about it because it shouldn't matter in a friendship, just as being a Democrat or a Republican shouldn't matter between friends. But the real reason we never talked about it was that if we weren't 100 percent sure the other person was gay too, it would be awful to be wrong. We'd be revealing ourselves to someone who probably couldn't understand and that could bring all sorts of trouble."[20] It was a climate calculated to lead to paranoia, and many lesbians never overcame it, even when times improved.

It was also a climate that stripped lesbians of the possibility of self-defense by making it dangerous for them to organize effectively. The decade following the war that expanded the potential of lesbian life-styles did see the formation of the first lesbian organization in America, Daughters of Bilitis (DOB), which was originally founded as a private social group to give middle-class lesbians an alternative to the gay bar scene. That such an organization could have been started in the 1950s is testimony to the war years' effectiveness in creating something of a self-conscious lesbian community. DOB was not interested for long in remaining a social club. It soon became involved in "improving the lesbian image" and demanding lesbian rights. But an organization that valiantly attempted to be political in a time when the idea of rights for sexual minorities was inconceivable was bound to remain minuscule for a long while.[21]

Daughters of Bilitis, which was founded in the mid-1950s, understood lesbians' fears that joining the group would expose them to the danger of being harassed as perverts. Recognizing the need for lesbian anonymity, DOB tried to overcome those fears by pledging secrecy to their membership in the best of faith. At meetings a greeter would stand at the door and say, "I'm —. Who are you? You don't have to give me your real name, not even your real first name." *The Ladder,* which was DOB's official magazine, even ran articles quoting an attorney who stressed that lesbians had "nothing to fear in joining DOB," and they assured the readers: "your name is safe"—that there were no reasons to worry about the magazine's mailing list falling into the wrong hands, that the constitution guaranteed freedom of the press, and that a 1953 Supreme Court decision said a publisher did not have to reveal the names of purchasers of reading material, even to a congressional investigating committee.[22]

But such legal protection apparently did not apply to lesbians. Daughters of Bilitis could not know that informants had actually infiltrated DOB in the 1950s and were supplying the FBI and CIA with names of the organization's members. The FBI file on DOB stated, as though the mere fact in itself were evidence of the organization's subversiveness, "The purpose of [DOB] is to educate the public to accept the Lesbian homosexual into society."[23]

Nor was DOB free from local harassment. During the 1959 mayoral campaign in San Francisco, Russell Wolden challenged the incumbent, George Christopher, by saying that Christopher had made San Francisco a haven for homosexuals. Wolden's scare tactics campaign literature highlighted DOB:

> You parents of daughters—do not sit back complacently feeling that because you have no boys in your family everything is all right. . . . To enlighten you as to the existence of a Lesbian organization composed of homosexual women, make yourself acquainted with the name Daughters of Bilitis.

DOB suspected that as a result of such exposure there might be trouble, so they removed all membership and mailing lists from the San Francisco headquarters for the duration of the race. As they later discovered, they were right to be prudent, since the San Francisco police, goaded by Wolden, did search the organization's office. Lesbianism in itself was not against the law in California, but law enforcement officials ignored that detail.[24] Not by virtue of what they did, but just because of who they were, lesbians were subversive, and no such action against them by the police was considered excessive.

Obviously the time was far from ripe for any successful organizing to create a large-scale movement through which the lesbian could work to put an end to persecution. Several DOB chapters were begun around the country by the end of the '50s, but the organization remained small (though its mere existence was something of a miracle in those days). Through official intimidation, the public policy of control and containment of lesbianism was largely effective, even to the end of the next decade. The many women who loved women and were bisexual or did not wish to live a lesbian lifestyle usually felt compelled to deny that aspect of their affectional lives and thus could do nothing to challenge the view of the lesbian as "other" than the "normal" woman. Women who were part of the lesbian subculture also usually denied their lesbianism by day and even by night were afraid to join with other women politically to begin to present their own versions of what their lives were about.

War in the Cold War Years: The Military Witch-Hunts

Military life had particular appeal for working-class women who identified themselves as lesbians in the 1950s. In addition to compatible companionship, it offered them opportunities for career training and travel that females without monetary advantages would have had difficulty finding on their own. But lesbians who enlisted in the military at this time were at grave risk, regardless of their patriotism or their devotion to their tasks. Civilian life could be difficult in the 1950s, but military life was harrowing. The tolerant policy regarding lesbianism that was instituted during the war was long gone. Now love between women in the military was viewed as criminal. Military witch-hunts of lesbians were carried out relentlessly, though frequently without success: not because there were few lesbians in the military, but rather because civilian life had already trained lesbians to guard against detection and they learned in the military to polish those skills.

In contrast to the liberal Sex Hygiene lectures that military officers had been given during wartime, officers in the women's branch of the Navy (WAVE) were instructed in 1952 that "homosexuality is wrong, it is evil, . . . an offense to all decent and law abiding people, and it is not to be condoned on grounds of 'mental illness' any more than any other crime such as theft, homocide or criminal assault." The WAVE recruits in turn had to listen to set lectures which told them that sexual relations are appropriate only in marriage and that even though they were in the military they were expected to conform to the norms of femininity. Lesbians were presented in the cliche of sexual vampires who seduced innocent young women into sexual experimentation that would lead them, like a drug, into the usual litany of horrors: addiction, degeneracy, loneliness, murder and suicide. Not only were the women encouraged to inform on each other, but chaplains and psychiatrists who were naval officers were instructed to help detect and discharge lesbian personnel.[25]

Air Force policy was similar: Air Force regulation 35–66 stated that prompt separation of homosexuals from the military was mandatory, and specifically demanded that physicians and psychiatrists, as well as all other military personnel, report to administrative officials any knowledge they had of an individual's "homosexual tendencies."[26] A woman was to be considered culpable even if she had had only an isolated lesbian experience years before she joined the military, since that was evidence of her "homosexual tendencies." As Kinsey's statistics indicate, a huge number of women in the military would probably have been subject to discharge if their full histories were known, though luckily for the functioning of the female branches of the armed services, most women were willing and even anxious to lie about that aspect of their affectional lives.

But even mere association with putative lesbians was enough to get a woman discharged in the 1950s if she were caught, since this too was considered evidence of "homosexual tendencies." Annie remembers a friend who had been in WAVE officer training school with her in Virginia who had not yet even decided that she was a lesbian, but she socialized with a crowd of women who were investigated and found guilty of homosexuality. Never actually having had lesbian experiences, she nevertheless was ordered to leave the WAVES "because of the company she kept." Like all military personnel who were asked to resign, she was required to submit a statement saying she was tendering her resignation for the good of the service. If a woman refused to do so when requested she would face a trial by general court-martial. Although she had to sign such a statement incriminating herself, she had no right to know her accusers or to have access to documentary evidence against her. She had none of the protections of a civilian court.[27]

Investigations for lesbianism in the military were capricious and violated the rules of common sense and common decency. One woman who had been in the Air Force from 1950 to 1954 says that her Air Force squadron at Otis (which she estimates was about 50 percent lesbian) was required to sit through repeated lectures against homosexuality. Their personal possessions were subject to inspection at any time without notice, often at hours such as 2:00 a.m. on a Saturday, and evidence of lesbianism was especially sought by the inspectors. Official tactics defied rational explanation:

> I had my mother's wedding ring in a drawer and they took it and demanded to know who the girl was that I put *my* initials in there for —even though the date on the ring was 1930, which was before I was born. They refused to give it back to me. They said it was the property of the government and they were holding it for future investigations. They threatened me with discharge even though they couldn't prove anything. I wasn't even sexually active while I was on that base. But to this day they have my mother's ring.[28]

Entrapment was part of official policy. During the Korean War the Marines not only sent women from their Criminal Investigation Divison (CID) into lesbian bars to serve as decoys to catch other personnel, but they also planted informers on women's softball teams on military bases, assuming that an interest in athletics was practically tantamount to lesbianism. Women who looked stereotypically lesbian were sometimes kept in the service as Judas lambs, under the assumption that they would attract other women with homosexual tendencies and the military would thus be able to catch lesbians who might otherwise have gotten away.[29]

Another common lesbian-catching tactic was to identify particularly vulnerable young women who were under suspicion of lesbianism and to threaten them not only with court-martial and discharge but even with exposure to their parents. They were interrogated until they gave the names of all women from their unit they knew or even thought were lesbian—or, in at least one documented case, until they committed suicide.[30] The military's brutal methods were not much different from those of the civilian government at the time, although they must have been even more devastating to the young women who had been encouraged to see the military as one big family and a way of life. To be shamed and cast out of that family must have annihilated more than a few of them.

Since military personnel were encouraged to rid the services of lesbians, officers believed they might have a free hand in their achieving their goal. One woman, who was an Army nurse in occupied Japan in 1954, says that when she and her lover were accused of being lesbians the intelligence officer assigned to the case raped her lover "to teach her how much better a man was than a woman." When she contacted a higher officer she got his promise of protection from future harassment only in return for her agreement to leave the Army without fighting the case. Nothing was done to punish the intelligence officer.[31]

But because the military's irregular methods were sometimes incredibly heavy-handed, the most savvy lesbians were able to escape detection with ease. One former WAC estimates that of the 250 women who arrived with her at a WAC detachment, 150 were booted out, primarily on the basis of a ludicrous verbal test they were forced to take immediately upon arrival, in which investigating officers asked questions such as:

> Did you ever make love to a woman?
> Have you ever thought of making love to a woman?
> Do you envision sucking a woman's breast?

She, a lesbian, trained in hiding, of course said no to everything and survived the test. More naïve women, undoubtedly many of whom had had no lesbian experiences and knew nothing of the street wisdom that lesbians learned in the subculture, were more honest and answered as Kinsey's statistics could have helped predict they would. The next morning at the barracks the sergeant told her, "They weeded out all the Queers last night."[32]

Despite such outrageous systematic spying and demoralization, which naturally led to an atmosphere of tension and anger, many lesbians could survive precisely because they had developed such sharp skills in looking over their shoulders. As Marie remembers of her stint during the Korean War:

> You learned to always be skeptical about someone new, to always keep track of who was around before you spoke, to hang on to the friends

you knew you could trust. When I came to Camp Lejeune in North Carolina I went out for softball, but for half a year all the women on the team were really distant and quiet. I finally found out that since I was three or four years older than most of them they figured I was a CID plant. One of them had been at El Toro Air Force Base in Santa Ana where they discovered that the pitcher on the team was actually a planted informer.[33]

By refusing to acknowledge, as it had during World War II, that lesbians would be especially attracted to military life and that such a life would even encourage lesbianism, the military was denying the obvious. The military's obtuse policies encouraged lesbians to be cynical toward authority and reinforced the notion they had learned from the outside world that because enemies were everywhere, "lesbian" had to signify an "us" and "them" mentality at least as much as it signified a sexual orientation. Those lesbians who managed to get through the service in the '50s without being detected had learned that they must find ways to outwit the authorities or they would be destroyed. Usually they succeeded in manuevering. Although a secret investigative board for the Navy actually claimed in 1957 that the rate of detection for homosexual activity in the Navy was "much higher for the female than the male," lesbians who were in the military say that most of them managed to escape detection and that "for the few lesbians they got in the services, there were hundreds of us who fell through their grip." It was often a matter of luck whether or not one would get caught. But even more often it was a matter of networking. Women in the Marines, for example, were able to establish a pipeline so that they knew what was going on at all times and when crackdowns and investigations were likely to come. Friends from boot camp who had been sent to different bases kept in contact with each other. The softball teams would travel and spread the word about witch-hunts. Lesbians who worked in places such as the Filing Office would know who was under investigation and could warn other lesbians. At least partly because of such good pipelines, most lesbians who were in the service in the 1950s left with honorable discharges, although not without emotional scars.[34]

But despite networking, large numbers of lesbians were occasionally purged from some bases, such as a WAC base in Tokyo from which 500 women were sent home "under conditions other than honorable."[35] Those who were discharged from the service for homosexuality were deprived of all veteran's benefits. They were generally so upset, exhausted, and mortified by the process that they did nothing but slink off to hide and heal their wounds as best they could.

Almost never did they have the energy to protest what had been done to them, although one woman, an Air Force Reservist, Fannie Mae Clackum, actually did win a suit against the government in the U. S. Court of Claims in 1960, which suggests that in somewhat saner times an objective court could understand how outrageous the military's tactics were. Clackum demanded eight years of back pay, complaining that she was accused of homosexuality but given no trial or hearing and no opportunity to know the evidence against her or to know her accusers. From April 1951 to January 1952 she had been repeatedly questioned by an OSI officer regarding lesbianism. She was asked to resign, although she was never informed of specific charges. When she refused, she was demoted from corporal to private and ordered to take a psychiatric examination. She was finally discharged as an undesirable at the beginning of 1952. The court found that her discharge was invalid, but Clackum was an isolated instance of a woman who dared to carry out a challenge to the reigning powers in the 1950s, since everything—the psychiatric establishment, the military's demoralization tactics, the government, popular wisdom—militated against the lesbian believing that she had the human right to expect justice.[36]

A major effect that military life of the 1950s had on lesbian subculture was to confirm even further that for the outside world love between women was a love that dared not speak its name, that it would certainly not be treated with common decency and respect. But at the same time the military experience strengthened the bonds between women who chose to be part of the lesbian sisterhood; it showed them how to network and how to guard against the forces that were enemies of women who loved women. Such knowledge was also to become very useful in life outside the military.

A Sad Legacy

Although the McCarthy era has been long dead and the lot of the lesbian has improved considerably, the years of suffering took their toll and created a legacy of suspicion that has been hard to overcome, more liberal times notwithstanding. That suspicion has not been entirely groundless. Even in the last two decades, at the height of the

gay liberation movement, lesbian teachers have been fired from their
jobs, not for committing illegal acts such as having sexual relations
with a minor, but simply for being lesbian.

Wilma, who was a high school physical education teacher in Dow-
ney, a Los Angeles suburb, in the early 1970s, says that after a couple
of years at the school she decided she would tell her best friend on the
faculty that she was a lesbian because "I thought we were really close.
She was always telling me about her problems with her husband and
her children, and I was tired of living a lie with her." The other
woman went to the principal the next day, saying that in the light of
what she had learned she could no longer work with Wilma. He
immediately called Wilma into his office and demanded that she write
out a resignation on the spot. In return for her resignation he promised he would not get her credential revoked: "But he said he just
wanted me out of the school. We had been good friends. He was
priming me for a job as an administrator. I thought, 'I screwed up
my whole life for a ten-minute confession.'"

Wilma was able to get another job in the Los Angeles school
system, but she drastically changed her manner of relating to her
colleagues. She married a gay man, always brought him to faculty
parties, and made sure everyone knew to address her as "Mrs." She
came to school in dresses, hose, and high heels: "Even when I went
to the school cafeteria I'd change from my sweats into a dress."
Fifteen years later, she still feels she must constantly censor herself
with her colleagues: "I keep a low profile and I'm always on guard."[37]

Wilma's situation remains a nightmare for many lesbians. While
very few engaged in front marriages in the 1970s and '80s, some still
attempted to pass as heterosexual and even invent, or let heterosexuals assume, an imaginary heterosexual social life. Two studies of
lesbians, one in the '70s, the other in the '80s, both indicated that
two-thirds of the sample believed that they would lose their jobs if
their sociosexual orientation were known. Most of those who did not
feel threatened were self-employed or worked in the arts, where
homosexuality is equated with bohemianism.[38]

Despite the many successes of the gay liberation movement, which
has made homosexuality much more acceptable in America, middle-
class lesbians often feel that activists are a real threat to them because
they draw public attention to the phenomenon of lesbianism and thus
create suspicion about all unmarried women. The closeted lesbian's
cover could be blown. Older lesbians especially, who perfected the
techniques of hiding through most of their adult lives, still cannot

conceive of suddenly coming out into the open, even in what appear to be freer times.

They are uncomfortable not only with radicals who demand that they leave their closets, but with anyone who discusses the subject of lesbianism, as I discovered a number of times in trying to arrange interviews with "senior citizen" lesbians, women over sixty-five who were professionally employed during the McCarthy years. Despite my promise of complete anonymity, they were often fearful. As a sixty-eight year old retired teacher wrote me:

> One reason lesbians of my generation are reluctant to come out is our memory of that time; there is no guarantee that there won't again be a rush to the documents, and a resurrection of our names from somewhere, with who-knows-what-kind of repercussions. I am retired and on a pension; presumably nothing can change that. But we didn't believe the stuff McCarthy got away with, either. Can anyone promise for sure that "they" won't say to me, "You taught under false pretenses; therefore, you don't get your pension!"

They have little faith that the progress that has come about through the gay liberation movement is here to stay. There is probably nothing that would convince them that lesbians are not still surrounded by hostile regiments out to destroy them, as they were in the 1950s.[39]

Lesbians inherited a mixed legacy from the 1940s and '50s, when lesbianism came to mean, much more than it had earlier, not only a choice of sexual orientation, but a social orientation as well, though usually lived covertly. While the war and the migration afterward of masses of women, who often ended up in urban centers, meant that various lesbian subcultures could be established or expanded, these years were a most unfortunate time for such establishment and expansion. Suddenly there were large numbers of women who could become a part of a lesbian subculture, yet also suddenly there were more reasons than ever for the subculture to stay underground. The need to be covert became one of the chief manifestations of lesbian existence for an entire generation—until the 1970s and, for some women who do not trust recent changes to be permanent, until the present. The grand scale institutional insanity that characterized the Cold War also affected many lesbians profoundly by causing them to live in guilt, pain, self-hatred born of internalizing the hideous stereotypes of lesbianism, and justified suspicion as well as paranoia. The 1950s were perhaps the worst time in history for women to love women.

However, even the persecution of the 1950s aided in further establishing lesbian subcultures. It made many women feel they had to band together socially to survive, since heterosexuals could seldom be trusted. And while it made lesbianism a love that dared not speak its name very loudly, nevertheless it *gave* it a name over and over again that became known to many more thousands of American women. Were it not for the publicity that was inevitably attendant on persecution, some women, even by the 1950s, might not have realized that there were so many who shared their desires and aspirations, that various lesbian subcultures existed, that lesbianism could be a way of life. Fanatical homophobes who would have preferred a conspiracy of silence with regard to lesbianism were right in believing that silence would best serve their ends. Each time the silence was broken—even by the hateful images of homosexuality that characterized the 1950s—more women who preferred women learned labels for themselves, sought and often found others who shared those labels, and came to understand that they might probe beneath the denigrating images that society handed them to discover their own truths.

7

Butches, Femmes, and Kikis: Creating Lesbian Subcultures in the 1950s and '60s

To us it was our world, a small world, yes; but if you are starving you don't refuse a slice of bread, and we were starving —just for the feeling of having others around us: We were the Kings of the hill, we were the Moody Gardens.
    —A Lowell, Massachusetts, woman describing the Moody Gardens, a working-class gay bar in the 1950s

The bars had nothing to do with us. They were risky and rough. But we had what we needed because we had each other. All the graduate students who were lesbian in my Department found each other sooner or later. It wasn't the way we looked. It was just a feeling we got that would let us know who was and who wasn't. It was scary but wonderful —operating in a straight world, being totally undetectable by them, but knowing and trusting each other.
    —F.L., a UCLA graduate student in the early 1960s

At first glance it is surprising that it was in the 1950s, in the midst of the worst persecution of homosexuals, that the lesbian subculture grew and defined itself more clearly than ever before, but there are explanations for the phenomenon. As has been discussed in the last two chapters, not only had many women learned about love between women during the war and come together in big cities, but also powerful creators of social definitions in the 1950s such as medical men and political leaders now declared with unprecedented vehemence that those who could love others of the same sex were beings apart from the rest of humanity: They not only loved homosexually; they were homosexuals. As insistent and widespread as that view now was, many women who loved other women believed they had little option but to accept that definition of themselves. The choice of love object determined more than ever before a social identity as well as a sexual identity.

The dichotomy between homosexual and heterosexual was not only firmly drawn but, since homosexuals were of great interest to the media as sick or subversive, knowledge of homosexuality was more widely disseminated than at any previous time in history. Since one who loved the same sex was "a homosexual" and shunned in "normal" society, it became important to many who identified themselves as lesbian to establish a separate society, a subculture, both to avoid exposure such as would be risked in socializing with heterosexuals and to provide a pool of social and sexual contacts, since presumably such contacts could not be obtained in the "normal" society at large.

It is not accurate to speak of "*a* lesbian subculture," since there were various lesbian subcultures in the 1950s and '60s, dependent especially on class and age. Working-class and young lesbians (of the middle class as well as the working class) experienced a lesbian society very different from that of upper- and middle-class older lesbians. Despite heterosexuals' single stereotype of "the lesbian," lesbian subcultures based on class and age not only had little in common with each other, but their members often distrusted and even disliked one another. The conflict went beyond what was usual in class and generational antagonisms, since each subculture had a firm notion of what lesbian life should be and felt that its conception was compromised by the other group that shared the same minority status. In its virulence it was perhaps analogous to the conflict between older middle-class blacks and young and working-class blacks in the turbulent 1960s, when those groups were attempting to redefine themselves in the context of a new era.

But despite differences, what the lesbian subcultures of the 1950s and '60s shared was not only the common enemy of homophobia, but also the tremendous burden of conceptualizing themselves with very little history to use as guidelines. Unlike for American ethnic or racial minorities, for mid-century lesbians there were no centuries of customs and mores to incorporate into the patterns they established of how to live. There was less than a hundred years between them and the first definition of the homosexual which called them into being as a social entity, and there was very little history available to them about how women who loved women had constructed their lives in earlier times. There were the concepts of the "man trapped in a woman's body" and passing women, perhaps the predecessors of young and working-class butches. And there were the "romantic friends" and "devoted companions" of earlier eras who presented something of a model for middle-class lesbians. But there had been in America nothing like the politically aware homophile groups of Germany that had begun to organize in the late nineteenth century, not long after the German sexologists such as Krafft-Ebing categorized the lesbian, nor like the diverse lesbian societies of France that emerged in the late nineteenth century out of the sexually open *belle epoque*.[1] In contrast to lesbians in those countries, American lesbians after World War II had to start almost from scratch to formulate what the growing lesbian society should be like. With little help from the generations who went before them, they had to find ways to exist and be nurtured in an environment that they had to build outside of the larger world that they knew disdained them.

Working-Class and Young Lesbians: The Gay Bars

Not only were American lesbians without a history such as helped to guide other minority groups, but they were also without a geography: there were no lesbian ghettos where they could be assured of meeting others like themselves and being accepted precisely for that attribute that the outside world shunned. There was little to inherit from the past in terms of safe turf, though safe turf was crucial to lesbians as a despised minority. Young and working-class lesbians, who were even often without their own comfortable domiciles in which to receive their friends, had no choice but to frequent public places where they could make contact with other lesbians, but it was essential that those public places be clandestine enough to ensure privacy, since exposure could be dangerous. It was for that reason that the lesbian bar, called, like the male homosexual bar, a "gay" bar —dark, secret, a nighttime place, located usually in dismal areas— became an important institution in the 1950s.

There were a few attempts by working-class and young lesbians in the 1950s and '60s to build institutions other than the gay bars. The most notable was the softball team. During those years many lesbians formed teams or made up the audiences for teams all over the country. Women's softball leagues usually had at least one or two teams that were all lesbian, and most of the other predominantly heterosexual teams had a fair sprinkling of lesbians. The games did succeed in providing legends and heroes for the lesbian subculture, as well as offering both participants and viewers some possibility for making lesbian contacts outside of the bars. However, as a California woman recalls of her softball playing days, "We had no place to go after the games but the bars." The bars were often even the team sponsors, providing uniforms and travel money. And it was "an unwritten law," according to a Nebraska woman who played during the '50s, that after the game you patronized the bar that sponsored you. Young and working-class lesbians who had no homes where they could entertain and were welcome nowhere else socially were held in thrall by the bars, which became their major resort, despite attempts to escape such as the formation of athletic teams.[2]

Although the gay bars posed various dangers, many young and working-class women were thankful for their existence. They represented the one public place where those who had accepted a lesbian sociosexual identity did not have to hide who they were. They offered companionship and the possibilities of romantic contacts. They often bristled with the excitement of women together, defying their outlaw status and creating their own rules and their own worlds.

To many young and working-class lesbians the bars were a principal stage where they could act out the roles and relationships that elsewhere they had to pretend did not exist. The bars were their home turf. Once inside, if they could blur from their line of vision the policeman who might be sitting at the end of the bar, waiting for a payoff from the owner or just making his presence felt for the fun of being threatening, it seemed that it was the patrons, the lesbians there, who set the tone and made the rules. Occasional straights or "fish queens" (heterosexual men whose primary sexual interest was in cunnilingus and who hoped to find prospects in a lesbian bar) might wander in. But it was the lesbians who were the majority, and for a change they had the luxury of being themselves in public.

The bars were a particular relief for many butch working-class women because it was only there that they could dress "right," in pants, in which they felt most comfortable. There were few jobs in the 1950s for which women might wear pants, and still not many public places they could go and not be somewhat conspicuous. It was after work, at night, in the bars, that butches could look as they pleased—where it was even mandated that they should look that way.

But the most important aspect of the bars to young and working-class women was that they provided a relatively secure place where lesbians could connect with other lesbians, whether for friendship, romance, or (more rarely) casual sex. How else might a young or working-class woman meet lesbians? It was certainly not safe simply to approach a woman at work or in the neighborhood. If you suspected that another woman was gay you went through lengthy verbal games, dropping subtle hints, using the jargon of the subculture (not many straights even knew that the word "gay" meant anything other than "merry" in those days), waiting for her to pick up your clues before you dared to reveal yourself. It required great effort and some risk. In the bars there were no such difficulties.

But although the gay bars were for many young and working-class lesbians their only home as authentic social beings, they were hazardous for various reasons. They posed a particular danger because they encouraged drinking. You could not stay unless you had a drink in front of you, and bar personnel were often encouraged to "push" drinks so that the bar could remain in business. As a result, alcoholism was high among women who frequented the bars, much more prevalent, in fact, than among their heterosexual working-class counterparts. Not only did lesbians have pressure to drink while in a gay bar, and, as the cliché of the pulp novels suggested, take to drink because of the daily pain of the stigma of lesbianism, but they also had to endure the socioeconomic difficulties of their lives as self-supporting women in low-paying jobs at a time when females were not supposed to work. Donna, an American Indian woman who had lived in Los Angeles during the 1950s, remembers:

> Some gay men I knew took me to a One [homophile organization] meeting in L.A. I liked it, but it wasn't for women at my level. I was working in a plastics factory. I couldn't think about political movements. Neither could the other women I knew. We did a lot of drinking because the poorer you are, the easier it is to take if you're half-loaded. At the bar where I hung out a lot of women would come after work. We'd work all day with nothing to show for it, and we felt we might as well buy a beer where we could be around company of our own kind.[3]

Heterosexual women of their class, who were usually housewives in the 1950s, were less likely to suffer the angry conflicts of working hard to be self-supporting while realizing that one could not get far beyond subsistence and a few dimes left over for small diversions. Many working-class lesbians saw drinking in a gay bar as the one pleasure open to them. They were not very different from heterosexual males of their class in this respect.

The rebel lifestyle, in which these women as lesbians demanded some of the social privileges and customs ordinarily reserved for men, may also have encouraged heavy drinking among them. Those who challenged social orthodoxies about sexuality in the 1950s and '60s found it not only easier, but even *necessary,* to challenge other orthodoxies, such as the appropriateness of sobriety for females. They would drink if they pleased, drink "like a man." Drinking in the 1950s became another means for lesbians to refuse the confinement of femininity.[4]

However, it was not the drinking problem alone that made the gay bars a dangerous place to be. While the police frequently harassed butch-looking women on the streets, the worst police harassment took place inside the gay bars. In many cities, as long as a bar owner was willing to pay for police protection, the bars seemed relatively safe—unless it was close to an election period in which the incumbent felt compelled to "clean up" the gay bars for the sake of his record. During those times raids were frequent. The bars sometimes took precautions against raids. At the Canyon Club in Los Angeles, a membership bar patronized by both gay men and gay women, dancing would be permitted only in the upstairs room. If the police appeared at the door, a red light would be flashed upstairs and the same-sex partners on the dance floor would know to grab someone of the opposite sex quickly and continue dancing. At the Star Room, a lesbian bar on the outskirts of Los Angeles, women could dance but not too close. The manager would scrutinize the dance floor periodically with flashlight in hand. There had to be enough distance between a couple so that a beam from the flashlight could pass between them. In that way the owner hoped to avoid charges of disorderly conduct should there be any undercover agents among the patrons.

There were indeed undercover agents in the bars. Preceding the 1960 election year, the head of the Alcoholic Beverage Control in Northern California announced "a vigorous new campaign against bars catering to homosexuals," and he admitted that "a dozen undercover agents are at work gathering evidence to root out homosexual bars in the Bay Area."[5] While the prime targets were the men's bars because there were more of them, women's bars fell victim to the campaign as well.

Most street-smart lesbians who frequented the gay bars knew about undercover agents and tried to take precautions against entrapment, but there was not much that could be done. Perhaps the tyranny of "appropriate" butch and femme dress in working-class bars can be explained in part by patrons' fears: A Columbus, Ohio, woman recalls walking into a lesbian bar in the 1950s and finding that no one would speak to her. After some hours the waitress told her it was because of the way she was dressed—no one could tell what her sexual identity was, butch or femme, and they were afraid that if she did not know enough to dress right it was because she was a police-woman. L.J. remembers that the lesbians she met in Los Angeles were almost paranoid when she arrived in 1952. She was told by a stranger in the rest room of a lesbian bar that she had better be careful of "police plants" and by another woman in the bar that "sometimes they [undercover agents] would say 'I'll give you a ride home,' and they'd start talking to you in gay language. If you understood what they were saying they would just drive up in front of the police station."[6]

Whether or not the police were that capricious, it is certain that there were police spies in the women's gay bars, gathering indiscriminate bits of evidence in the hope that some of it would rile the courts. One female undercover agent was sent to stake out Mary's First and Last Chance, a San Francisco bar, for nine months. She testified in the appellate court in 1959 that "she sat at a table and that a patron dressed in mannish costume sat down and stated to her, 'you're a cute little butch' and also kissed the waitress in her presence." The patron's behavior in front of the undercover agent, as inconsequential as it may have been, became the keystone of the testimony in *Vallerga v. Munro,* in which the prosecution attempted to have the license of Mary's First and Last Chance revoked on the grounds that the existence of the bar was "contrary to public welfare and morals."[7]

Usually, however, undercover agents did not return to lesbian bars night after night to gather little bits of evidence. The police simply pounced. Perhaps it was missed payoffs that ignited their ire, or perhaps it was random chance that would make them raid one bar rather than another, but a bar raid during the 1950s or '60s could be violent. Marlene says that in San Francisco during the early 1950s the raiding police were accompanied by police dogs. In a 1956 raid at the San Francisco bar Kelly's Alamo Club, thirty-six women were hauled into the city jail and booked on the charge of "frequenting a house of ill repute." D.F. remembers a Los Angeles raid in which all the patrons' names were collected and everyone was made to strip and was searched. At raids in the Sea Colony, a Greenwich Village bar, women would be pushed up against the wall and the policemen might put their hands in the women's pants and say, "Oh, you think you're a man. Well, let's see what you've got here."[8]

In Worchester, Massachusetts, raids were so frequent, according to one woman, that it seemed the police were pulling the paddy wagon up to the door every Friday and Saturday night. "We'd make a joke of it. 'Hurry up and finish your beer,' we'd say, 'cause we're goin' for a ride.' " Not even private lesbian parties were always safe. They too might be raided and the guests' names printed in the newspaper with lurid headlines, such as that in the sensationalistic Boston paper, the *Midtown Journal:* "Butch Ball Baffles Bulls."[9]

Although young and working-class lesbians were pushed into the bars since they were welcomed nowhere else if they allowed their lesbianism to show, the raids were intended to intimidate them while there and to ruin gay bar business. Humiliation and fear were used as tactics to that end. Peg B. describes a 1964 raid at Maryangelo's, a Greenwich Village bar:

> A large man appeared at the doorway and yelled, "This is a raid."
> Everyone froze; then like a bunch of sheep we all tromped downstairs
> and into the waiting paddy wagons, about forty-three of us. We later
> learned that two women hid under a table in the back room and got
> away. In the paddy wagon a woman panicked and ate her driver's
> license.

In the search by a policewoman they were made to pull down their underpants and bend over. After the search they were transported to small cells, where they were kept all night. In the morning they were given bread and watery coffee for which they were charged a dollar each and were then taken out to court: "On the way we had to pass a line of cops on the stairs. It was like running the gauntlet because they all jeered as we went by and made crude remarks." The charges against the women were "disorderly conduct and disturbing the peace." A detective testified that some of the women were dancing together, but he could not identify them, and since there was no other evidence against the women the judge was forced to dismiss the case—but meanwhile all forty-three of the women had gone through a night of anxious misery.[10] Incredible as it seems in the context of saner times, they were forced to endure all that only because they had gone to a public place where they might meet other people with whom they could be comfortable.

Not just the possiblity of such intimidation but also the fear that if they were arrested their employers would be contacted or their names would be published in the newspapers kept some women who thought they had something to lose away from the bars. But others felt they could not afford to stay away. Since the bars alone provided a home for them, they had to risk whatever was necessary for the sake of being there. They tolerated the smallest crumbs and the shabbiest turf in their desperation for a "place." And even that was periodically taken away, whenever the majority community wanted to make a show of its high moral standards. But in their determination to establish some area, however minute, where they could be together as women and as lesbians, they were pioneers of a sort. They created a lesbian geography despite slim resources and particularly unsympathetic times.

Working-Class and Young Lesbians: Butch/ Femme Roles

Although suddenly significant numbers of women were coming together to express a lesbian social identity by the 1950s, there were few models for how to do it. The pattern they had all observed before their decision to live as homosexuals was heterosexual. While the first generations of middle class career women could see advantages in a "marriage" of equals, the world that working class women lived in never hinted at such benefits. A functioning couple for them meant dichotomous individuals, if not male and female, then butch and femme, or—as they later were called in some areas of the country—"masons and orders" or "butch and Marge." Even if they looked at their most visible counterparts, those who frequented the men's gay bars, they often observed that a heterogenderal pattern, not unlike that between straight people, was common among gay males, too: many of the men saw themselves as "nelly queens" in pursuit of "real men," those who appeared extremely masculine. The whole world, heterosexual and homosexual, seemed to be divided into masculine and feminine. As one woman who was a butch during the 1950s and '60s observed, "The problem was that the only models we had for our relationships were those of the traditional female-male [roles] and we were too busy trying to survive in a hostile world to have time to create new roles for ourselves."[11]

Yet the roles came to have an important function in the working-class and young lesbian subculture because they operated as a kind of indicator of membership. Only those who understood the roles and the rules attendant upon them really belonged. To many lesbians, the stringently mandated butch/femme dress and role behaviors that seemed to confirm the early sexologists' descriptions of "the man trapped in a woman's body" and "the mate of the invert" were a crucial part of who they were only once they discovered the subculture.

When a young woman entered the subculture in the 1950s she was immediately intitiated into the meaning and importance of the roles, since understanding them was the *sine qua non* of being a lesbian within that group. While some women saw themselves as falling naturally into one role or the other, even those who did not were urged to chose a role by other lesbians, or sometimes their own observations forced them to conclude that a choice was necessary. Being neither butch nor femme was not an option if one wanted to be part of the young or working–class lesbian subculture. Those who refused to choose learned quickly that they were unwelcome. In some areas the issue was very emotional. Shirley, who lived in Buffalo, New York, in the years after World War II, remembers being in a working–class bar and admitting to a group of lesbians there that she thought of herself as neither butch nor femme: "They argued with me for a long time and when they couldn't convince me I had to be one or the other, they threatened to take me outside and beat me up." Although the issue seldom led to violence, butches and femmes were often adamant about rejecting what they called the "confused" behavior of "kiki" women, those who would not choose a role.[12]

One New England woman remembers:

> We used to have parties and play games like charades. The butches would be on one side and the femmes would be on the other. There was one couple who'd have to flip a coin to decide who was going to be on what side, and we used to think they were the craziest people.

Another New England woman recalls that "kiki" also referred to two butches or two femmes who were lovers. They often had to "sneak it," she says, because of the hostility of those who were committed to roles. Membership in her group demanded that one select a partner who was heterogenderal, that is , who took the opposite role, at least in appearance: "If I wasn't going to choose that, I couldn't be in a gay bar. I couldn't be with gay people." In New York kiki lesbians were also called "bluffs"—the word being not only a combination of "butch" and "fluff" (another term for femme) but also an indication of how such women were regarded in that community. Even in Greenwich Village, which in the 1920s had been a melting pot of all manner of straight and gay people, the pressure to make a selection and to stick to it had become very stringent. One denizen of the

Village says that already by the 1940s one was expected to be either butch or femme. "Those who did not conform were contemptuously referred to as people who didn't know their minds." [13]

Such strict role divisions continued throughout the 1960s in much of the bar subculture, even during the era of "unisex" among heterosexuals; they are testimony to the essentially conservative nature of a minority group as it attempts to create legitimacy for itself by fabricating traditions and rules. One woman, who is 5'10" and of stocky build, remembers going to a lesbian bar in Springfield, Massachusetts, in 1967, that had two rest rooms. "I stood in line for a couple of minutes and then the girl in front of me said, 'You have to get out of here. This is the femme line.' She pointed to the signs on the rest room doors. One was marked 'butch' and the other was marked 'femme.' " [14]

Several lesbian historians, such as Joan Nestle and Judy Grahn, looking back over the 1950s and '60s, have suggested that butch and femme roles and relationships were not imitations of heterosexuality, but unique in themselves, based not on the social and sexual models all lesbians grew up with, but rather on natural drives (such as "butch sexuality" and "femme sexuality") and on lesbian-specific, lesbian-culturally developed behavior. Grahn has argued that butches were not copying males but rather they were saying "here is another way of being a woman," and that what they learned in the lesbian subculture was to "imitate dykes, not men." [15] Yet butch/femme style of dress was not much different from working-class male and female style; descriptive terms in relationships were often modeled on heterosexual language, since no other appropriate words existed to convey commitment and responsibility (for example, a butch might call the femme she was living with her "wife"); the role expectations (butches were supposed to control emotions, do the husband-type chores around the house, be the sexual aggressors; femmes were supposed to cook, be softer, more yielding, stand behind a butch as a woman stands behind a man) looked for all the world like heterosexuality.

Although the sexual dynamic between a couple who identified as butch and femme could be subtle and complex rather than a simple imitation of heterosexuality, some lesbians considered themselves "stone butches" and observed taboos similar to those that were current among working-class heterosexual males. For example, letting another woman be sexually aggressive with you if you were a stone butch was called being flipped, and it was shameful in many working-class lesbian communities because it meant that a butch had permitted another woman to take power away from her by sexually "femaliz-ing" her, making a "pussy" out of her, in the vernacular. Among black lesbians a butch who allowed herself to be "flipped" was called a pancake. In other circles also a flipped butch was greeted with ridicule if word got out, as it sometimes did if a disgruntled femme wanted to shame a former lover.[16]

The taboo against being flipped, which was probably related to the low esteem in which women were held at the time, even made some young butches try to better protect their image by refusing to undress completely when they had sexual relations. One former stone butch recalls, "The derision shown those few butches who had been flipped was enough to prevent many of us, especially those of us who were not yet secure about our sexuality, from letting our partners touch us during lovemaking." Having to hold on to power by being the only aggressor in a relationship, as some butches felt they must, was a stringent task, not too different from that of the young working-class male who had to maintain total vigilance so that no one ever made him a "punk."

Perhaps it was not so much that most butches desired to *be* men. It was rather that for many of them in an era of neat pigeonholes the apparent logic of the connection between sexual object choice and gender identification was overwhelming, and lacking the support of a history that contradicted that connection, they had no encourage-ment at that time to formulate new conceptions. If they loved women it must be because they were mannish, and vice versa. Therefore, many learned to behave as men were supposed to behave, sometimes with rough machismo, sometimes enacting the most idealized images of male behavior that they saw in their parent society—courting, protecting, lighting cigarettes, opening car doors, holding out chairs. They followed that chivalric behavior, as real men often did not outside of romance magazines and movies. It is not surprising that butch/femme was in its heyday during the 1950s, when not only were the parent-culture roles exaggerated between men and women, but the Hollywood values of dash and romance served to inspire the fancy of the young, especially those who were at a loss about where to turn for their images of self.

There were, however, factors that undercut the apparent imitation of idealized male and female gender roles. Not all butches were stone butches, and femmes were often not simply sexually and socially acquiescent women, although some butches may have preferred to see them that way. Laurajean Ermayne, writing about butches and femmes for the lesbian magazine *Vice Versa* just before the 1950s, described the femme as "of a passive nature—a fluff, a cream puff, to be devoured. . . . More intensely womanly than jam [i.e., heterosexual] girls . . . more sensitive, more high strung, more dependent." But lesbian historian Joan Nestle remembers a twenty-three-year-old femme who carried her favorite dildo in a pink satin purse to the bars every Saturday so her partner for the night would understand exactly what she wanted.[17] By the liberated 1970s some heterosexual women may have been that insistent about their own sexuality, but in the 1950s there were not many who would have made so bold a statement.

Just by virtue of being lesbians, femmes must have had a certain amount of rebellious courage that was not typical of the 1950s female. They engaged in sexual relations outside of marriage while most of their young female heterosexual counterparts did not dare. They braved the night alone to go out to gay bars to meet butches while straight women had not yet attempted to "take back the night" and wander the streets for their own pleasure and purpose. They often supported themselves as well as their butch partner if their partner was unwilling to compromise her masculine appearance and unable to find a job that would not require donning a skirt. Femmes were attracted to a rebel sexuality, and they let themselves be seen with women who made no attempt to hide their outlaw status at a time when supposedly every woman's fondest wish was to be a wife and mother and to fit in with the rest of the community. Femmes were called fluffs in some regions during the 1950s and '60s, but that term could be quite inappropriate.

The roles were also undercut by the fact that although most young lesbians went along with them, they actually had little intrinsic meaning for many of them. The roles might be merely the rules of the game that you followed if you wanted to be one of the players—or as J.C., who was a Texas "butch," phrased it, "I looked around and thought, *if that's the way you get to belong, I need to do it as good as they did*, so I made myself remember to open car doors and light cigarettes and all of that." Because they were to some only roles, they were reversible under certain circumstances. One might be a butch in one relationship and a femme in another, depending on how willing one was to accommodate a partner's preferences. The roles could even change in the course of an evening, as Ann tells it:

> Once I went to an L.A. bar to meet this butch, and I was dressed
> femme. But she wasn't there so I decided to go to another bar. On my
> way, in the car, I changed to butch. Butches had a lot more opportu-
> nities in the bars and I just wanted to meet another woman.[18]

To such women appropriate role behavior was simply a nod of
acknowledgment in the direction of subculture propriety that indicated that one knew the rules and belonged.

Sometimes there were complex factors operating in the choice of a
butch or a femme identity. Surely some women selected one or the
other not because of peer group pressure, but because that felt sexually most natural to them. To other women the choice of a butch
identity may have been motivated not at all by a "natural" or "congenital instinct" such as the nineteenth-century sexologists (and many
lesbians) preferred to believe, but rather by their desire to be free
from the awful limitations of femaleness. For some butches their sex
role identity not only preceded but even overwhelmed their sexual
interests. Lucia is representative. As a working-class Springfield,
Massachusetts, teenager in the early 1960s, she passed as a boy and
was employed at a car wash under the name of Ricky Lane. Her close
friends were six other girls who also passed. None of them was sexual
at the time. Lucia now explains:

> I have five brothers. As a girl in an Italian immigrant family I wasn't
> allowed to have a will. I envied their fucking freedom so bad. That's
> what being a boy represented—power and freedom. You could walk
> through the park at midnight or down the street at any hour. So of
> course we all wanted to pass. We even referred to each other as "he."
> We said we were butches because that's what girls like us were called,
> but we thought we were no different from any other adolescent boy.
> We did stealing. We did drugs. And we did it like a boy would.[19]

For them, it was masculine gender identity that was most important
in the assumption of a butch role. They saw that men had all the
status, and it was not easy to understand how to obtain status, even
within one's small subculture, without emulating those who had it.

Women who identified as butch during that era were often uncomfortable with their femaleness because they could not accept the
weakness, passivity, and powerlessness that were presented to them
as female. As one woman now analyzes her past identification, "Since
I refused to be 'female' as I understood it, I concluded that I had to be
a 'male.' "[20] Her confusion is understandable, since girls were indoc-

trinated with the message that only two genders were possible and the sex roles connected to them were fixed and rigid.

Without other models, many young lesbians of all classes had no choice but to accept the logic of those roles. Even those young lesbians who were not yet a part of a community often defined themselves in the roles. In lieu of real-life models, those who were desperate for images to emulate and lacked contact with other lesbians looked to Radclyffe Hall's depiction of Stephen Gordon. Hall's characterization of Stephen, "a man trapped in a woman's body," the congenital lesbian in *The Well of Loneliness*, was directly influenced by Krafft-Ebing and Havelock Ellis. As the only truly famous and widely available lesbian novel for decades, Hall's book, although it was published in the late 1920s, remained important into the '50s and '60s in providing an example of how to be a lesbian among the young who had no other guide. Stephen Gordon's butch role in relation to the totally feminine Mary in the novel could be a plausible image to any homosexual female who grew up in a heterosexual milieu.

Radclyffe Hall was, in fact, so influential among some young American lesbians that she was referred to as "Our Matron Saint" in a postwar article that suggested that the "inelegant word *butch*" be replaced by the word "Clyffe" in honor of Radclyffe Hall. One lesbian historian, Blanche Cook, has speculated that if young lesbians of her own generation of the 1950s had read the less stereotypical lesbian books that were published in the same year as *The Well,* such as Virginia Woolf's *Orlando* and Djuna Barnes' *Ladies Almanack,* "some of us might never have swaggered." But it was *The Well* that received attention as the quintessential lesbian novel and that helped to form self-concepts among the young. While literature did not have so profound an impact on all lesbians, some of those who were hungry for any discussion or information about their secret life and could find no other source were very affected by the most obvious literary model.[21]

The butch and femme roles as they continued to develop during the 1950s should also be understood in the broader context of their times. The roles may have been manifested so strongly then because of the need of postwar America to simplify by categorizing and stereotyping. (Gay men were often seduced by this need as well, and it took times more open to complexity, such as the Vietnam era, to devalorize heterogenderality for them and to encourage both members of a male couple to wear mustaches or otherwise manifest masculinity.) Roles were in a sense the path of least resistance within the communities of young and working class lesbians. They provided the subculture with a conformity and a security that answered longings that mirrored those of heterosexual America, in which all members of the subculture had been raised. Needless to say, however, the parent culture did not validate the subculture by approving those similarities. Paradoxically, it was the assumption of roles, especially the butch role, that cast lesbians even further beyond the pale of the parent culture that they seemed to be mirroring.

But the butches' adoption of male images had other kinds of usefulness. For example, it permitted them to form a community, since it identified butches more easily to each other and to femmes. In addition, the roles emulated a certain kinship structure. As with their heterosexual working-class counterparts, women who maintained butch or femme identities were often socially separated from each other, coming together only for love relationships. They were no more friends than heterosexual men and women during that era. If a butch needed consolation, defense, someone with whom to spend an evening out, it was to another butch she went. Historian John D'Emilio has offered a compelling anthropological explanation for this particular homogenderal social arrangement. He sees its function as being analogous to the incest taboo, which guarantees that parental and sibling relationships remain stable though erotic relationships may fluctuate: lovers might come and go, but friends would always remain the same as long as they were off-limits as lovers. Butches would thus always have other butches as friends, and femmes would have other femmes.[22]

But perhaps the most important function of the roles was that they created a certain sense of membership in a special group, with its own norms and values and even uniforms. The roles offered lesbians a social identity and a consciousness of shared differences from women in the heterosexual world. Through them outsiders could be insiders. And those who were not familiar with roles, rules, and uniforms were the outsiders on butch/femme turf. The adoption of roles during this authoritarian era may even have lessened the anxiety of anomie by giving what must have been a comforting illusion of structure and propriety that was meaningful and important to the group.

"Kiki" Lesbians: The Upper and Middle Classes and Subculture Clashes

Wealthy and middle class older lesbians generally rejected the roles in public and were much less likely to follow them in their love lives than were working class and young lesbians. Usually their dress and couple relationships did not readily fall into patterns of masculine and feminine. Although one woman in a couple may have been more naturally aggressive or more prone to traditionally feminine activities than the other, the development or expression of such traits was seldom as self-conscious as it was among the young and working class.

Wealthy lesbians seem sometimes to have found butch/femme roles and dress aesthetically repulsive. At Cherry Grove, a summer resort area off Long Island, New York, that was popular among rich lesbians during the 1940s and '50s, the style was "elegant" and "suave," much like that of the Paris circle of Natalie Barney. Historian Esther Newton, who interviewed several former residents of Cherry Grove, reports that by the late 1950s these women left the Grove because more obvious butch and femme types began to come in. "They were diesel dykes, big and fat and mannish," one of Newton's informants recalls. "And there was always some drama, always some femme in a fight with another femme." To them such obvious role division was strictly a manifestation of working-class lesbianism, and they had neither sympathy nor understanding for it. It was "tacky," as one informant described it.[23]

There were butch lesbians among the wealthy, but they appear to have been exceptional in their gay groups. The most notorious was Louisa Dupont Carpenter Jenny, a direct descendant and major heir of multi-millionaire Alfred Dupont. Louisa was a horse woman, a sailor of her own yacht, and an aviatrix. (She died while flying her own plane in 1976.) Her pastimes validated her predeliction for masculine dress. She preferred relationships with feminine bisexual women and had no objection to their being married. But even those in her upper-class society who were used to mixing with homosexuals were not comfortable with her. "Who *is* that person?" Helen Lynd remarked to two of her gay friends, Broadway stars Libby Holman and Clifton Webb. "She *walks* like a man, she *talks* like a man. God, she even *dresses* like a man." Her society's displeasure is suggested in Louisa having been dubbed a "he-she."[24]

Some wealthy females adopted a butch identification when young but dropped it as they grew older, often opting not only to appear more feminine but to live as a bisexual rather than a lesbian. While still a teenager, Libby Holman wrote a little jingle about herself that gave a clue to her lesbian sexuality: "I am tall and very slim./ Am I a she or am I a him?" But only a few years later she married Smith Reynolds, a tobacco millionaire, and after his death she married two more times. Since she allowed herself to be romantically linked by the media with Montgomery Clift, who was homosexual, it may be that one or two of her marriages were nothing more than fronts, although her last husband is said to have banned all her homosexual friends from their home. But during and between those marriages she had numerous affairs with women.[25]

For some wealthy women the lesbian chic that pervaded the 1920s never ceased and they did not feel compelled to hide their lesbian behavior. Some women in the entertainment world felt as free to flaunt their unorthodox romances in the '30s or the '50s as they did in the '20s. Tallulah Bankhead, for example, after passionatley kissing a young woman at a straight party, borrowed a handkerchief from an astonished male observer to wipe the smeared lipstick from the other woman's mouth. When Bankhead encountered Joan Crawford with her husband of the time, Douglas Fairbanks, Jr., on a train from New York to Hollywood, she was said to have loudly announced, "Darling, you're divine. I've had an affair with your husband. You'll be next." She could get away with any behavior because she disarmed with her stance of ultrasophistication. She presented herself as being above the laws of mere mortals and even as phenomenally bored and blasé with the shocking privileges she took for herself. "Sex?" she shouted in one group. "I'm bored with sex. What is it, after all? If you go down on a woman, you get a crick in your neck. If you go down on a man, you get lockjaw. And fucking just gives me claustrophobia."[26]

Bankhead was married from 1937 to 1941. Since her biographers do not present that marriage as anything like a love match, perhaps it is explainable by an ephemeral impulse to deceive those who had not been in earshot of her sexual confessions. However, other wealthy women who had relationships with women married not for the sake of setting up a front, but rather for male companionship. Unlike many middle- and working-class lesbians, they seemed not to be particularly desirous of establishing long-term monogamous female marriages with their lesbian lovers. The writer Jane Bowles (who self-deprecatingly alluded to her stiff knee, her Jewishness, and her predeliction for women by calling herself "Crippie, the Kike Dyke") remained married to fellow writer Paul Bowles from 1937 to her death in 1973. Paul Bowles was bisexual, though Jane seems to have had sexual relationships exclusively with other women. She and her husband agreed to lead separate sexual lives, but she relied on him for stability and continuity.[27]

There were, of course, groups of wealthy women like the Cherry Grove crowd, who were a consistent part of a lesbian subculture. But for some wealthy women who had relationships with other women such consistency seemed to have little appeal. Not only did their social position demand that they move in broader circles than a circumscribed lesbian world, but heterosexual marriage facilitated the ease of their movement. It also placated families on whom a vast inheritance might depend. Louisa Dupont Carpenter, for example, married John Jenny under pressure from her domineering father, who insisted that she make a union with a "well-situated" young man. Wealthy women who loved women generally did not seem to require an arena in which they could dress in drag, as working-class lesbians might, nor did they have the need to bond with other career women to give them courage to pursue their independent paths in a hostile world. Because they lived much of their lives outside of a lesbian subculture, free of its mores and rules, they felt less compelled to limit themselves to a lesbian identity and were more likely to behave bisexually.

Perhaps the lack of a significant subculture of wealthy lesbians in America explains why many upper-class women who saw themselves as exclusively lesbian chose to become expatriates and remained so throughout their lives. They seem to have believed that in America, close to their families and the social set into which they were born, the estabishment of such a subculture was problematic and that one needed to escape the country in order to live permanently as a lesbian. Natalie Barney's revelation of why she chose to spend almost all of her adult life in Paris undoubtedly refers to that conviction: "Paris has always seemed to me," she said, "the only city where you can live and express yourself as you please."[28] Droves of other wealthy lesbians shared that assessment.

In gay male society, wealthy men historically have often been interested in "rough trade" and class mixing was not uncommon. Among lesbians during the radical 1970s wealthier women began to pride themselves on what they perceived of as their new democratic lesbianism. But in the 1950s and '60s and earlier, such class mixing was extremely rare. Working-class lesbians tended to socialize only with other working-class lesbians. While some wealthy lesbians would occasionally have ties among middle-class lesbian groups, more often those groups tended to be made up exclusively of women who earned their livings in professions as teachers, librarians, or social work ers. The classes remained as discrete as they were in the parent culture.

The middle-class older lesbian subculture may best be understood not in juxtaposition to that of wealthy lesbians who had little in the way of a formal subculture, but rather in contrast to that of young and working-class lesbians. One reason that butch and femme role behavior may have had much less appeal to some older middle-class lesbians than to young and working-class lesbians was that it would expose them too much in times when there was good reason to stay in the closet. Whether or not they practiced role distinctions in their relationships at home, in public they had to hide any such proclivities. Working-class women and young women who had not yet entered a career could feel less fearful than those who were employed in government positions, for example, as teachers or social workers, as many middle-class lesbians were. But the private expression of the roles may also have been more important to working-class women than to those of the middle class because the latter did have other models. They could look to the tradition of romantic friends, early twentieth century professional women, or the unmarried career women of the 1920s and '30s, who may have been considered maladjusted by psychologists, but who were nevertheless valid social types—independent women who managed to live personal lives of their own choosing and to form couples that usually were not heterogenderal.

Even before the 1950s, masculine identification had less appeal to middle-class lesbians. Though some 1930s novels such as *Nightwood* and *We Too Are Drifting* feature middle-class butch lesbians (Jan Morale of *We Too Are Drifting* even models for a statue of Hermaphroditus), autobiographies suggest that middle-class women tended to reject butch/femme division. Elisabeth Craigin even talks of being repulsed by it. "The possibility of the false male was a thing I was in arms against," she says. "My lover was a girl, a particularly attractive girl, with initiative and strength and personality above most, to be sure, but a girl with all the primary feminine capacities." She describes their sexual connection as "sensuality between loving young women and not that of a loving young woman for the other gender in disguise. . . . She was my woman-mate, never a pseudo man-mate." Diana Fredricks in *Diana* says she too was repulsed by masculine women who "indulged in transvestism," and she saw them as "puerile" in their "smart-aleck unconventionality." All the lesbians who play an important part in her 1930s autobiography are femininely attractive. These writers insisted that the sexologists' observations about lesbian couples being made up of an invert and a feminine mate of the invert were totally alien to them.[29]

In the years after the war, when butch/femme roles became so intrinsic to the young and working-class lesbian subculture, a good deal of hostility developed between those who did and those who did not conform to roles. Butches and femmes laughed at middle-class "kiki" women for their "wishy-washy" self-presentation. The few lesbian publications of the era, which were middle-class in their aspirations and tone, such as *Vice Versa* and the journal of the organization Daughters of Bilitis, the *Ladder*, expressed embarrassment over butch and femme roles, which, by their obviousness, encouraged the stereotype of the lesbian among heterosexuals. Lisa Ben, for example, editor of *Vice Versa*, included in one of her issues a poem titled "Protest," which expressed her puzzlement about why young and working-class lesbians would want to "imitate men":

> What irony that many of us choose
> To ape that which by nature we despise,
> Appear ridiculous to others' eyes
> By travelling life's path in borrowed shoes.
>
> How willingly we go with tresses shorn
> And beauty masked in graceless, drab attire.
> A rose's loveliness is to admire;
> Who'd cut the bloom and thus expose the thorn? . . .
>
> Away with masquerade and vain pretension.
> 'Tis thus we bow, reversely, to Convention![30]

She, like many lesbians outside of the working class, was troubled not only because butches were aesthetically displeasing to her, but also because it seemed to her that butches acquiesced to conformity by looking stereotypically like males just because society said those who loved women were supposed to be male.

Some middle-class lesbians complained that it was butches and their femmes who made lesbians outcasts. One of the earliest issues of *The Ladder* proclaimed: "The kids in fly front pants and with butch haircuts and mannish manner are the worst publicity that we can get." Beginning in October 1957 and until the height of the civil rights movement in 1967, Daughters of Bilitis listed on the inside cover of every issue of *The Ladder* among the organization's goals "advocating [to lesbians] a mode of behavior and dress acceptable to society." The middle-class readership applauded that goal, finding it crucial to their aspirations that lesbians be tolerated in the mainstream.[31]

They believed that unpopular forms of overt self-expression such as wearing masculine garb led not only to danger for lesbians, but also to further alienation from the parent culture, which was especially painful during a time when the middle-class lesbian culture was still in a relatively inchoate form. There were not scores of organizations to join or vast numbers of friendship circles one might become a part of. Some lesbians wistfully hoped that their differences might be ignored and that they might be accepted among heterosexuals. They insisted (rather unrealistically, considering McCarthy's hunting down of covert homosexuals) that the way to achieve acceptance was to minimize differences through adopting a conventional style. As one San Leandro, California, woman said in a letter to the editor of *The Ladder*:

> I have personally proved, in more than a dozen cases, the importance of mode of behavior and acceptable dress in establishing understanding with heterosexuals. . . . [My mate of twenty years and I] have been accepted by heterosexuals and later informed by them that this acceptance, in its initial stage, was based entirely upon appearance and behavior.[32]

Many of her class counterparts would have been outraged at such heterosexual condescension by the 1970s, but in the 1950s and early '60s there was no sufficient vocabulary for such outrage nor any inclination to be militant on the part of middle-class lesbians. Like most middle-class blacks at the start of the civil rights movement in the 1960s, middle-class lesbians generally aspired to integration rather than special status based on what made them a minority. They felt most comfortable blending in, insisting that they were unlike their age and class counterparts in the parent culture only by virtue of their sexual preference, about which they would willingly be silent if they could be accepted into heterosexual society. Perhaps the conception of integration for lesbians was revolutionary enough during an era when the government and the psychiatric establishment were saying that homosexuals were outside the pale of humanity.

Statistical studies of lesbian couples during the period also concluded that middle-and upper-middle class lesbians preferred to blend
in with heterosexual society in terms of their styles. For example, a
1962 study showed that lesbians "in the upper financial brackets who
owned homes in affluent neighborhoods, generally appeared in feminine clothes and demonstrated no marked emphasis on roles." The
sociologist who conducted the study concluded that "just as in the
heterosexual group, role is more enforced [among lesbians] in the
blue collar and lower white collar classes." [33]

Such a lack of interest in stereotypical styles and roles may have
been encouraged not just by the desire to blend in with heterosexual
culture, but by the rules that were as vital to the middle-class lesbian
subculture as the rule of butch/femme was to their working-class
counterparts. "Propriety" was especially important. One could not
be part of the middle-class lesbian subculture unless one understood
the value of dressing "appropriately": A West Coast university professor remembers that she belonged to an all-gay circle of friends in
the San Francisco area—psychologists, teachers, professors, librarians
—that held salons and dinner parties regularly, to which most of the
women wore navy blue suits and pumps, almost as much a requisite
uniform as butch and femme dress in the gay bars. It was crucial in
the middle-class lesbian subculture to behave with sufficient, though
never excessive, femininity and not to call attention to oneself as a
lesbian in any way. Obvious lesbian behavior on the part of one
member might cast disgrace on the entire group. [34]

Middle-class lesbians also seem to have avoided butch/femme relationships and styles because they did violence to their often unarti-
culated but nevertheless deeply felt feminism. As a Los Angeles lesbian woman who is now a psychologist remembers of her response
to butch/femme in the '50s, "I didn't think anything could be that
simple—with the polarities of sheer masculine and sheer feminine
between two women. I didn't even like it between men and women,
but between two lesbians it really seemed strange to me." [35] The
disdain was mutual. Butches and their femmes thought these "kiki"
women were the ones who were buckling under by dressing like
conventional women. It was something of a class war.

Socializing among older middle-class lesbians was also generally
different from that among young and working-class lesbians. Part of
the difference is attributable to the fact that they were more likely to
have homes in which to entertain and money to spend on more
expensive forms of amusement outside of the bars. They were also

less likely to go to the bars because of the threat of raids. Entertainment among them often consisted of dinner parties or groups gathered around some event or ritual, such as listening to Tallulah Bankhead's weekly radio program.[36]

When middle-class lesbians did go to bars it was often with great
trepidation, as a woman who worked in a government law library
recalls. Although she lived in San Francisco, she never dared to
venture into the bars there but went instead to bars in Sacramento or
Bryte, always worrying about imaginary harrowing newspaper headlines, such as "State Law Librarian Caught in Lesbian Bar."[37] Despite
such fears, however, some did visit the bars occasionally, hoping that
the anonymity of the environment would keep them safe. The appeal
for them, no less than for working-class and young lesbians, was that
the bars were almost the only place, outside of their circle of friends,
where they could see large groups of lesbians. The bars offered them
the assurance of numbers that they could not get elsewhere.

But class wars among lesbians were especially apparent in the bars.
In small cities, which often had only one lesbian bar, such as the Cave
in Omaha, middle-class lesbians when they risked a bar visit found
they had to share the turf with butch/femme working-class lesbians,
but they drew invisible boundaries. At the Cave the middle-class
women, who dressed in conservative Saturday night finery, sat on
one side of the room, and the working class women, often in T-
shirts, "with cigarettes rolled in their sleeves" and "their overdressed
femmes with too much lipstick and too high heels," sat on the other.
"The butches would play pool and look tough," Betty, who was a
high school teacher in Omaha in the 1950s, remembers. "Some of
them were truck drivers from Council Bluffs. Some worked in factories. You would say hello, but you didn't get together at all, any
more than you did with a truck driver or a factory worker if you
should happen into a straight bar." Although the groups shared a
sexual identity and both sought places where they would feel free to
express it, that was all they shared.[38]

In large cities, where lesbians had more than one bar from which
to choose, they selected their hangout according to class, but there
were always more butch/femme bars, since middle-class women tended
to go to the bars so seldom. At the Open Door, the If Club, the
Paradise Club, and the Star Room, lesbian bars in Los Angeles in the
1950s, the customers were young women who were supermarket
clerks, waitresses, factory workers, beauty operators, prostitutes. They
were almost invariably either elaborately made up, dressed in high

heels and skirts or capris, or totally without makeup, in pegged, fly-
front pants, white cotton undershirt showing beneath a man's button-
down shirt, black penny loafers, and a ducktail haircut. A couple
would consist of one of each. Dress was the indicator regarding with
whom one might or might not flirt. But at the Club Laurel, a North
Hollywood cocktail lounge in its heyday during the same years,
which catered to older, more affluent or upwardly striving lesbians,
there was little discernible difference between two members of a
couple. The tone of the club was set by the singer-manager, Beverly
Shaw, who would entertain in the style of Marlene Dietrich, perched
atop the piano bar in impeccably tailored suits, high heels, beautifully
coiffed hair, and just the right amount of lipstick. Women in more
obvious butch-femme couples were quickly made to feel out of place
in such an environment.

Generally, however, the bar culture was alienating to middle-class
lesbians who felt they had little in common with the women who
predominated in most lesbian bars. In an article that appeared in *One*
in 1954, the lesbian writer described the gay bars as being "slightly
removed from Hell" and hoped for a public meeting place for lesbians
"who wish more from life than the nightmare of whiskey and sex,
brutality and vanity, self-pity and despair." Her pulp novel description of the bars was echoed by others who were resentful that the
most public manifestation of the subculture, the bars, often seemed
to offer only pleasures that were discomfitting to "well-brought-up"
females of the 1950s. Young women who wanted to maintain their
middle-class self-image had a particularly difficult time. Jane, who
was a USC student during those years, says that to her the bars were
degrading: "Their location in awful neighborhoods, the people who
drank too much and didn't have their lives together, just the idea of
being in a bar. I felt I had no place there." Barbara Gittings describes
her early experiences in Philadelphia gay bars in similar terms:

> Since I didn't have much money and didn't like to drink anyway, I'd
> hold a glass of ice water and pretend it was gin on the rocks. I'd get
> into conversation with other women, but I'd usually find we didn't
> really have any common interests. We just happened both to be gay. I
> just didn't run into any lesbians who shared my interests in books and
> hostel trips and baroque music. They all seemed to groove on Peggy
> Lee and Frank Sinatra and nothing older. It was only later, in other
> settings, that I found gay people I was really congenial with. In those
> days I felt there was no real place for me in the straight culture but the
> gay bar culture wasn't the place for me either.[39]

To older middle-class lesbians who had made a circle of friends, what they saw as their incompatibility with bar lesbians presented no great difficulty. But young lesbians even of their class, who did not know where else to meet other women who loved women and who were not easily welcomed into the closed, conservative and often fearful circles of the older women, could be very lonely in the 1950s and '60s.

Because middle-class lesbians were less stereotypically obvious as homosexuals, they paid less dearly in everyday life than their working-class counterparts who were more blatant in their public behaviors and in their style of dress. Women of the working-class lesbian subculture usually dressed and behaved as they did to communicate to each other, but on the streets—even going to and from their bars —they also inadvertantly communicated to heterosexuals, who were often intolerant of the implications of butch/femme style. They were harassed by any hoodlum who took it into his mind to be nasty.

Butch women who would not be covert and the femmes who let themselves be seen with them often led dangerous lives. They courted violence. Many of them were certainly courageous in their insistence on presenting themselves in ways that felt authentic, but their bravery made them victims. Heterosexuals, particularly working-class young men who were still unsure of their own sexuality, could stand neither the idea of a woman usurping male privilege in comfortable dress and autonomy of movement nor the idea of a sexuality that totally excluded them. Their outrage was sometimes limited to name-calling but often took the form of physical violence, as young males challenged butch women in the streets, saying, "You look like a man, so fight like one." The ghettos could be particularly hazardous. One researcher, who believes that in more recent times there has been a healthy integration among heterosexuals and homosexuals in ghettos such as central Harlem, says that his older black lesbian respondents informed him that from the 1930s through the 1950s lesbianism was looked on as a grave threat to working-class black males, who ascribed to lesbians a sexual prowess that exceeded their own. Butchy women were said to have been often "gang whipped by black men who were fearful of the myth of lesbian invincibility."[40]

Official hostility toward young and working-class lesbians was pervasive even outside the bars. Most middle-and upper-class lesbians who could pass for heterosexual could believe that policemen, whose salaries were paid by their tax money, were there to serve and

protect them. But butches and their partners seldom had the luxury
of that illusion. They learned to be wary, to maneuver, to move in
the other direction if they saw the law coming. Jackie, who lived in
New Orleans during the 1950s, says that she was often stopped by
the police, who just wanted to scare her, and she had to develop
"street smarts":

> They would ask if I was a man or a woman. They could arrest a
> woman for impersonating a man, so you had to be sure you were
> wearing three pieces of women's clothes. You learned to avoid the
> police by walking on the side of the street where the cars were parked,
> or in the opposite direction on the one way streets so they would have
> to back up to get to you. It was always in the backs of our minds that
> we could be arrested. Any woman wearing pants was suspect.[41]

Working-class and young lesbians often felt hunted down during the
1950s and '60s. For them, the pulp novels that presented lesbians as
outcasts carried a veracity with which they could identify.

Middle-class lesbians, on the other hand, usually had less difficulty. While they often feared that exposure would cost them their
jobs and they had to cope with preposterous images of lesbians in the
media and in psychoanalytic literature, generally their "discreet" style
permitted them to carry on quotidian existence without molestation.
As a lesbian writer for the magazine *One* proclaimed rather smugly in
1955:

> Compared to the male homosexual, the lesbian has a very easy time of
> it indeed, at least as far as persecution by a hostile society is concerned.
> Unless she chooses to deliberately advertise her anomaly by adopting a
> pattern of behavior that would be no more acceptable in a heterosexual
> than a homosexual, she is allowed to live a reasonably normal life,
> without constant fear of exposure and the ensuing ridicule, ostracism,
> and legal persecution.[42]

Surely the author's optimism was overstated. It was, for example,
perfectly acceptable for two heterosexuals to hold hands anywhere,
though two lesbians, no matter how well dressed or otherwise well
behaved, might start a near-riot if they did so in the wrong places;
and lesbians could not fail to be cognizant of the homosexual witch-
hunts of that era that affected professional women. But if they were
willing to be always covert, it is true that with a little luck the chances
of insult or violence were slim for middle-class lesbians.

Because secrecy while manuevering in the heterosexual world became almost second nature to them, it did not even seem that they were being required to pay too great a price for peace. They usually viewed the situation with pragmatic realism. Their lives were often well insulated by a circle of similarly discreet friends, which helped to mute for them the fact that in the heterosexual world they would be considered pariahs if their affectional and social preferences were known (just as to racists "respectable" middle-class blacks were "niggers"). Perhaps because they could "get by" they were less motivated to organize and protest, even during the civil rights movements of the 1960s, than they might have been otherwise; and organizations that attempted to raise political awareness in them, such as Daughters of Bilitis and Mattachine, remained small.

These lesbian subcultures that had proliferated in the 1950s continued unchanged through most of the '60s. They were, each in their own way, more conservative than heterosexual society had become during the era of flower children, unisex, sexual revolution, and the civil rights movement. The working-class lesbian subculture maintained its polarities of dress and sexual relating throughout the 1960s. Middle-class lesbians generally had no conviction during that decade that, like other minority groups, they could demand their rights. Members of both of the lesbian subcultures accepted that they were persecuted when their status was known, because society seemed always to bully minorities. After all, they had before them the fairly recent examples of Nazi Germany and of the House Un-American Activities Committee. They could not organize to protest, because they saw that the protests of victims were, anyway, not efficacious. And perhaps many of them, lesbians of all classes, internalized on some level the views of the parent culture, which deemed them outcasts and guilty. They had neither the inner conviction nor the requisite knowledge and clout to insist that they were innocent.

However, by the end of the 1960s there was some evidence of a shift in lesbian life, especially through the energies of young, college-educated women who began their lesbian careers at that time. These women, coming of age in the '60s with the reawakening of feminism and the militant civil rights movement, were not so willing to accept the style of butch/femme heterogenderality or the intimidated covertness of older lesbians outside the working-class. Because they articulately refused both the roles and the secrecy, it looked to the heterosexual world as though lesbians in general had changed: for example, a 1969 *San Francisco Chronicle* article oberved: "The notion of role-playing is considered old fashioned among an increasing number of lesbians." [43] But the older lesbian subcultures had not altered; instead, still another lesbian subculture was being created by young women who were willing to publicly proclaim their lesbianism and whose upbringing in the unisex 1960s made the polarities of masculine and feminine particularly alien to them. Because they rejected the styles and behaviors that their predecessors held sacrosanct, they came into great conflict with the older subcultures. But as more and more young women came out as lesbians in the next decade, it was their style that dominated.

8

"Not a Public Relations Movement": Lesbian Revolutions in the 1960s through 1970s

> *As homosexuals we share the dubious honor with males of being "the last of the minority groups." As Lesbians we are even lower in the sand hole; we are women (itself a majority/minority status) and we are Lesbians: the last half of the least noticed, most disadvantaged minority. There is no room here for any other cause. We have the biggest bag to carry and we need a good many strong shoulders. Get your head out of the sand hole and help with this very urgent, very needful battle.*
> —Marilyn Barrow (pseud. Barbara Grier),
> "The Least of These,"
> in The Ladder, *1968*

> *It's so strange, you know, in the early seventies, one day half the women's movement came out as lesbians. It was like we were all sitting around and the ice cream truck came, and all of a sudden I looked around and everyone ran out for ice cream.*
> —Sarah Schulman, The Sophie Horowitz Story

Because most of the nineteenth-century sexologists who first formulated the concept of homosexuality were German (Karl Westphal, Karl Ulrichs, Richard von Krafft-Ebing), their ideas were more quickly disseminated in Germany than anywhere else and permitted Germans who acknowledged they loved the same sex to identify as a group sooner than those in other countries. Men who practiced same-sex sodomy banded together at the end of the nineteenth century to form organizations such as the Scientific Humanitarian Committee in order to challenge German laws against sodomy with the "scientific" arguments that the sexologists had provided for them: legislation outlaw ing sodomy made no sense because those who practiced it were only following a congenital drive. Lesbianism was overlooked by the law since women were generally beneath the law. However, the Scientific Humanitarian Committee welcomed women who loved women into its membership because they swelled the group's numbers and because the conception of homosexuals as a "third sex" was more persuasive if the phenomenon was seen to exist among those who were ostensibly female as well as those who were ostensibly male. By the turn of the century, German lesbians were actively working with men on homosexual rights issues.[1]

There were no comparable groups in America at that time, since the sexologists' ideas were promulgated slowly among the lay public outside of Europe. Many American women who loved other women could continue to maintain the view of themselves as romantic friends or devoted companions. When a lesbian consciousness was finally established in this country, women who loved other women did not immediately band together in a political group. Lesbianism was less likely to be seen sympathetically as a "scientifically" inherent condition in the United States than it was in Germany, and the opprobrium visited on lesbianism prompted them to be silent. Numerous phenomena throughout this century—the push toward companionate marriage and the identification of same-sex attraction as a hinderance to its success, the depression, McCarthy-era persecution, the obsession with molding all women to fit the feminine mystique, and the identification of those who did not as queer or sick—also discouraged women from organizing and demanding their rights as lesbians.

The 1960s, however, altered the temper of America drastically. In the context of widespread interest in liberalization and liberation, the next decade actually saw the growth of not one but *two* strong movements for the rights of women who loved women. One included "gay" women who were "essentialists": they believed they were born gay or became so early. They identified their problems as stemming from society's attitudes about homosexuality. The other was made up of women who called themselves "lesbian-feminists" and who usually believed they "existentially" chose to be lesbians. They identified their problems as stemming from society's attitudes toward women, and lesbianism was for them an integral part of the solution to those problems.

The Gay Revolution: Quiet Beginnings

While McCarthyism persecuted homosexuals in the 1950s, it also inadvertently helped to foster self-awareness and identity among them. For a few homosexual men and women it provided a cause around which to organize, even as it pushed others further into the dark closet or into gay bars as the only place where they could feel comfortable. Although the number of organized homosexuals remained small throughout the 1950s, at the decade's end enough had joined various groups to suggest that there might be potential for more action and to tempt a writer for a lesbian magazine to wonder, although precipitously: "Is there or could there be a homosexual voting block?"[2]

Mattachine, the first homosexual organization of that era, was started in 1950 by five Los Angeles men who had been members of the Communist party. Although the organized Left was no more sympathetic to homosexuality than the Right, the men's radical origins permitted them to formulate in the midst of McCarthyism an objective that was startlingly advanced for their day (the group's rhetoric soon became more tame as its membership grew and diversified): they wished to "liberate one of our largest minorities from . . . social persecution." Like the German Scientific Humanitarian Committee at the beginning of the century, Mattachine made some attempt to attract women, and the San Francisco branch, established in 1953, actually succeeded in enrolling a number of lesbians. But the group kept such a low profile that when the first all-lesbian organization, Daughters of Bilitis, was established in San Francisco a couple of years later, the founders, Del Martin and Phyllis Lyon, did not know of the existence of Mattachine. The founders of DOB were in the beginning much less politically aware than the founders of Mattachine. Initially DOB aimed only to fill the role of a social club outside the gay bar setting. Once the organization got under way, however, it almost immediately turned its attention to the problems of lesbian persecution and their solution. DOB and Mattachine had goals that were revolutionary for the '50s, but (despite Mattachine's radical beginnings) mild by contemporary standards. Their major effort became to educate both homosexuals and the public with regard to the ways in which the homosexual was just like any other good citizen.[3]

As modest as DOB's goals were in the 1950s, its very establishment in the midst of witch-hunts and police harrassment was an act of courage, since members always had to fear that they were under attack, not because of what they did, but merely because of who they were. One early member says that even at DOB events where the group was being addressed by establishment lawyers or psychiatrists, everyone was aware that there was always the possibility of a police raid: "We were less fearful of an invasion by street toughs than by the authorities," she recalls. And such police invasions did occur. At DOB's first national convention, in 1960, San Francisco law officers came to hassle the organizers with questions about whether they advocated wearing clothing of the opposite sex, which would have been illegal. (They could have answered their own questions by looking around the auditorium, where they would have seen middle-class women clad in "appropriate" dress, as the organization demanded of its membership). It is no wonder that DOB remained small. Most middle-class lesbians, to whom DOB had tried to appeal, had no desire to expose themselves to such harassment.[4]

However, DOB has significance for lesbians not because it was able to attract large numbers or to succeed in its goal of advancing lesbian rights, but rather because of the mere fact that it existed during such dangerous times. Like the later Stonewall rebellion, DOB helped provide a history—a Warsaw ghetto-like symbol—that would suggest to lesbians in more militant times that they were not always passive collaborators in their oppression, that some fought back, even if only by refusing to deny their own existence.

It was not until the early years of the more liberal 1960s that the first lesbian and gay confrontational action was staged by a mixed homosexual group, Homophile League of New York, who picketed an induction center with signs such as "If you don't want us don't take us, but don't ruin our lives." The idea of picketing caught on quickly among the handful of homosexual activists at that time, since they were witnessing the effectiveness of such tactics by other oppressed groups. In 1964 when the news leaked that Cuba was shamefully mistreating homosexuals, conservatively dressed lesbians and gay men picketed the White House, the Pentagon, and all government installations. They carried signs that asked: "Is our government any better?" As one lesbian protestor now describes the picketing: "We knew we were on the cutting edge of an important beginning. We were tweaking the lion's tail of government to get our rights." Yet as some of the first lesbians to shed their masks and employ a bit of drama in their challenge to the establishment, they not only endured the disdain of many heterosexuals, but they were also ignored by working-class lesbians and generally treated with hostility by middle-class lesbians. Most lesbians reasoned that the less aware the public was of the existence of homosexuality, the more comfortable the homosexual's life would be. It was still too early for many lesbians to be able to have faith that confrontational tactics might improve their lot.[5]

But there were plenty of indicators that the activists were reading the new public mood correctly. By the end of 1963 the *New York Times,* which had dealt with homosexuality earlier only in critical terms, began to change its tone. It objectively reported in one article the existence of an "organized homophile movement—a minority of militant homosexuals that is openly agitating for removal of legal, social, and cultural discriminations against sexual inverts." In reaction to the dogmatic, authoritarian 1950s, the public had begun to soften toward diversity, and homosexuals were slowly reaping the benefits along with other minorities. When DOB held its 1966 annual convention in San Francisco, the *San Francisco Chronicle* ran a four-column article: "San Francisco Greets Daughters." Reporters from Metromedia News taped the program highlights, and local radio stations made on-the-hour spot announcements about convention activities. Such publicity not only was an indication of more tolerant times, but also served to spread the word to other homosexuals about an organizing community. Although according to a mid-'60s study, only 2 percent of American homosexuals were even aware of the existence of homophile organizations, such mass coverage as that of the *New York Times* and *San Francisco Chronicle* was helping to increase awareness. It made some older homosexuals ask themselves what they were doing for their own cause, and it encouraged some young homosexuals who were just coming out to develop a new perspective about the possibilities of gay rights.[6]

As the decade progressed, there was palpable evidence of change in big cities. In the mid-1960s San Francisco DOB together with Mattachine decided to tackle the most insidious persecutor of homosexuals, organized religion. With the help of a liberal Methodist minister they were able to organize a Council on Religion and the Homosexual. DOB and Mattachine held a New Year's Eve ball to raise money for the newly formed Council and invited sympathetic clergymen. The police not only infiltrated in plainclothes, but also attempted to intimidate by McCarthy-era tactics, such as having uniformed officers place floodlights at the entrance and photograph all the arriving guests. One policeman told a minister, "We'll uphold God's laws if you won't." Those ministers, witnessing firsthand the way the police harassed a minority group, became staunch defenders of that group. The Council on Religion and the Homosexual spread to other parts of America, and major Protestant denominations began to reconsider their positions on homosexuality.[7]

By the end of 1966 the New York Civil Service Commission, which had previously rejected applicants if anything in their appearance, attitude, or actions indicated they were homosexual, began approving homosexual hires. Homosexuals got bolder. In the same year, the North American Conference of Homophile Organizations took the example of the militant black movement to heart and adapted the slogan "Gay Is Good" from "Black Is Beautiful." In the spring of 1967 lesbian and gay male students at Columbia University organized the Student Homophile League, which soon spread to Cornell, NYU, and Stanford. Although as Rita Mae Brown, who was one of the organizers, recalls, "The fur flew. 'Organized Queers!' the administration gasped," Columbia approved a charter for the group. Even big city police, who had gotten used to diversity and minority protest, were becoming less belligerent toward homosexuals. In contrast to their harassment a few years earlier, by 1968 the San Francisco police were making efforts to cooperate with homosexual organizations, providing security at public events that was helpful rather than hostile and meeting with the organizations for "a mutual exchange of ideas."[8]

The older homosexual groups such as DOB realized they needed to allow themselves to be swept along with the growing militancy if they wanted to survive. Articles slowly began to appear in *The Ladder* comparing lesbians to other oppressed minorities, and the rhetoric escalated as the decade progressed. By 1968, the readership was exhorted, in the language of other militant movements, to do battle against the enemies of women in general and lesbians specifically. DOB of the mid- and late-'60s dared to be much bolder than it could have been during the McCarthy era.[9]

But the newer organizations were even more militant in their stance. Early in 1969 the Homophile Action League declared: "We are living in an age of revolution, and one of the by-words of revolution in this country is 'confrontation.' " The League insisted that the more subtle, less risky approaches of the old homophile organizations were getting homosexuals nowhere:

During the time when the black, the poor, and the student have been actively confronting the systems which deny and demean them, we have been (sometimes) writing letters to our congressmen. While others have been openly challenging discriminating statutes, we have been (sometimes) satisfied with not being persecuted. While other groups seize the initiative and therefore fight their battle on their own terms, we wait (sometimes) in dread, always in a defensive posture, never prepared.

The League advocated a more aggressive stand, more fighting on the front lines, more face-to-face challenges.[10] But there were still only a few homosexuals who would take up that program. Something dramatic needed to happen to convince more of them that despite concerted efforts for years on the part of the medical establishment, the churches, and the law to let them know that they were nothing but sick or sinful or lawbreakers, they were an aggrieved minority with as much right to demand fairness as other minorities and that if they would show themselves, others would join them.

The Gay Revolution: Explosion

On June 28, 1969, in the midst of a New York mayoral campaign —a time when the incumbent often sicced the police on homosexuals to bolster his record as a vice fighter—police officers descended on the Stonewall Inn. The Stonewall was a gay bar in Greenwich Village that called itself a private club, open to members only. The police came with a search warrant, authorizing them to investigate reports that liquor was being sold there without a license. The raid had been the third staged by police on Greenwich Village gay bars in recent nights, but this time the response was different. Instead of scampering off in relief when the police booted them out on the street after questioning them, the two hundred working-class patrons—drag queens, third world gay men, and a handful of butch lesbians— congregated in front of the Stonewall and, as blacks and other oppressed groups had done before them in the course of the decade, commenced to stage a riot. Their numbers quickly doubled, and soon —according to some sources—increased tenfold. Before the night was over four policemen were hurt as rioters bombarded them with cobblestone bricks from the Village streets, as well as bottles, garbage, pennies, and an uprooted parking meter.

The riots continued the following night. Fires were started all over the neighborhood, condemnations of the police were read aloud and graffiti appeared on the boarded up windows of the Stonewall Inn exhorting everyone to "support gay power" and to "legalize gay bars." These occurences, which came to be known as the Stonewall Rebellion, marked the first gay riots in history. While the establishment media generally missed their significance—the *New York Times* relegated the story to five inches on page 33, with the obtuse heading, "Four Policemen Hurt in Village Raid"—to many homosexuals, male and female alike, the Stonewall Rebellion was the shot heard round the world. [11]

The complaints of blacks, students, and poor people, which had been raging through much of the 1960s, had finally ignited masses of homosexuals to articulate their own complaints. It is unlikely that a gay and lesbian riot could have occurred at any previous time in history. But if by some chance it had occurred earlier, it is unlikely that it would have come to have as much significance as it did in 1969. The gay liberation movement was an idea whose time had come. The Stonewall Rebellion was crucial because it sounded the rally for that movement. It became an emblem of gay and lesbian power. By calling on the dramatic tactic of violent protest that was being used by other oppressed groups, the events at the Stonewall implied that homosexuals had as much reason to be disaffected as they. It reminded homosexuals at just the right moment, during this era of general rebellion, that now their voices might be heard among the cries for liberation.

Although violent protest had been unimaginable to the largely conservative middle-class men and women who made up the homosexual movement during the two preceding decades, a handful of activists, made militant by the general militance of the '60s, had the foresight and imagination immediately to seize upon the riots, which had been started by more flamboyant and working-class homosexuals, and present them as an event that heralded a new gay militant movement of justified fury. They understood the importance of drawing parallels between the sufferings of other minorities and those of homosexuals. As one speaker cogently remarked at a demonstration a few days after the riots, "Gay Liberation is a realization of our innocence." [12]

There were only a small number of lesbians actually present at the riots, apparently women of the working class. Along with their gay male counterparts they had had no articulated political vision when the police that summer night tried to put them out of their bar. They reacted only with the anger that had accumulated through years of raids and abuse, much like other angry minorities who had rioted in the decade that was coming to a close. But many young lesbians and gays of all classes quickly came to accept Stonewall as an icon for their own battle for justice and to formulate a gay power movement around it.

The media had been largely deaf to the polite protests of homosexual organizations in the 1950s and '60s. But once angry homosexuals stood up for themselves through violent protest, the media and institutional response was much like that toward blacks. Finally there was an attempt to understand the position of homosexuals as an aggrieved minority. While some slight liberalization of attitudes had been slowly building in the media throughout the '60s, suddenly it boomed. In astonishing contrast to a 1966 pronouncement that homosexuality should be given "no fake status as minority martyrdom," *Time* magazine announced only four months after Stonewall, in an article titled, "The Homosexual: Newly Visible, Newly Understood":

> Undue discrimination wastes talents that might be working for society. Police harassment, which still lingers in many cities and more small towns, despite the growing live-and-let-live attitude, wastes manpower and creates unnecessary suffering. The laws against homosexual acts also suggest that the nation cares more about enforcing private morality than it does about preventing violent crimes.

At the same time, the National Institute of Mental Health issued a report urging legalization of private homosexual acts between consenting adults.[13]

Frequently the new public view, at least in some cosmopolitan areas, was more than tolerant—it was truly affirming. For example, only days after Stonewall, the *San Francisco Chronicle* ran an article, "The Lesbians' Story: How Does Girl Meet Girl?," that described Bonnie, an attractive, successful young woman who showed the writer a picture of herself taken two years earlier, before she became a lesbian. In the picture she was a different personage: "drab, unflattering hairdo, matronly clothes, none of Bonnie's animation." Bonnie explained that the metamorphosis was due to her newfound lesbianism: it was a psychologist who had directed her to Daughters of Bilitis, and once she came out through that group she was able to discover "the kind of love that's encouraging rather than demanding and controlling." Such a depiction of lesbianism would probably have been inconceivable in the mass media only months earlier.[14]

But the new gay movement did not wait upon the mass media for affirmation. Within a year of Stonewall, hundreds of gay publications and organizations sprang up, many of them lesbian, and those publications and organizations helped to bring more and more lesbians into the new movement. The spread of the slogan "Gay Is Good" and later slogans that came out of the gay pride parades that commemorated the Stonewall Rebellion in the early 1970s (for example, "2, 4, 6, 8, gay is just as good as straight") also had a tremendous consciousness-raising effect. The movement spread with astonishing rapidity.

The new movement lesbians tended to be a different breed from either working-class or middle-class lesbians of the previous generation. They were often young, college-educated, and politically aware, whatever the socioeconomic background of their parents had been. For those who were born into the working class, the democratization of higher education in the 1960s meant that they might get an education (and the verbal and analytical skills that went along with it) such as only women of middle-class background might have had earlier. Many of those who were born into the middle class purposely declassed themselves in that decade that valued egalitarianism. Thus these young movement lesbians of all classes were able to come together. They were generally comfortable with language and ideas and knew how to organize as working-class lesbians of the previous generation did not, and they were confident that they should have rights no less than any other Americans, as middle-class lesbians of the previous generation were not. Their militance often outstripped the capacities and understanding of both older working-class lesbians and middle-class lesbians, and difficulties emerged between the generations.

There had been no existing groups that represented the ideals of these young activist lesbians. Despite their relatively militant rhetoric of the late 1960s, DOB and *The Ladder* could not recover from their conservative image, and they were seen as too poky for the new activists. Although some young women joined DOB for a while, honoring it as the oldest existing lesbian organization, many of them soon broke away. For example, the *Lesbian Tide,* which had been the journal of the Los Angeles branch of DOB, severed from its mother organization in 1973 because it felt the need to take a more radical stance. *The Ladder,* which had been the national DOB magazine, stopped publishing in 1972, not only because of internal difficulties with the publishing staff but also because they had failed to appeal to younger women, who were more interested in the numerous militant gay and lesbian-feminist magazines that were now available.

The young activist lesbians were not willing to accept the shabby treatment that other lesbians, regardless of class, had seen as "coming with the territory" for decades. In 1970 when Leonardo's, a woman's gay bar in Oakland, California, refused to let women post a notice of a "gay women's liberation" meeting, the young lesbians who frequented the place organized a protest and a boycott, which was costly for the bar owner. The call to boycott explained:

> The time has come today for gay people to stand up, come out of the closets, and assert their rights as citizens and human beings. We must begin to question the system that takes gay money and funnels it into the pockets of a few individuals and the police. . . . We are coming into our own, and we are thousands, and we will be heard.[15]

Such an example served to make even the older organizations somewhat more militant. When police raided a DOB dance in New York in 1971, charging that the organizers were selling liquor without a license, far from hoping to get off with a small fine as they might have in the past, a large contingent of DOB members, in coalition with Gay Activist Alliance members, staged a demonstration and met with the mayor's aides to protest harassment. The charges against DOB were dropped.[16]

This new lesbian boldness was not confined to large coastal cities. In Minneapolis in 1972 when two lesbians were evicted for dancing together in a straight bar, the gay community staged a dance-in at the bar and was able to get the commissioner of human rights to mediate in their complaints. In Milwaukee two black lesbians were married in a large wedding ceremony at an Eastern Orthodox Catholic church. When the Milwaukee county clerk refused to issue a marriage license, the women swore to continue a public battle until the license could be obtained. In Boise (where homosexual witch-hunts had been especially rampant during the 1950s), when seven women police officers were discharged because phone tapping on a police dispatch telephone designated for nonofficial use revealed they were lesbians, the women sued for $16.5 million. The chief justice district judge declared that the women had been deprived of due process and that their discharge was "an abysmal operation." He stated he could not understand a city Boise's size lowering itself to such shenanigans in the 1970s.[17]

Activist gay women were not happy to settle for tolerance: they demanded equality and full citizenship, and they were willing to be confrontational to get their rights. They were often joined in those confrontations by gay men who were, like them, young, college-educated, and politically aware, and together they became effective lobbyists. They succeeded in getting boards of education in various cities to adopt plans that allowed gay lifestyles to be a part of the family studies curriculum. They were responsible for the passage of gay rights ordinances in over fifty American cities. Their formation of organizations such as the Alice B. Toklas Democratic Club in the early 1970s, in the interest of pulling more political weight for the gay community, actually led Democratic contenders for that year's national election—Shirley Chisholm, George McGovern, and Eugene McCarthy—to make astonishing policy statements about equal rights for homosexuals. In 1976 joint efforts between lesbians and gay men resulted in the election of the coordinator of the National Gay Task Force, Jean O'Leary, as the first openly lesbian delegate to the Democratic National Convention. O'Leary declared, with perhaps more optimism than was yet warranted, "It's proven that contrary to being a liability, the appearance of an openly gay person on the ticket is an asset."[18] In the following election the Democrats actually included a gay rights plank on the party platform.

Unlike in the McCarthy era, when the more homosexuals were attacked, the more they felt compelled to hide, young radical gay men and lesbians in the 1970s understood that the temper of the times allowed support for diversity in America, so that rather than hiding they could use attacks on them to further politicize their cause and publicize their just grievances. The campaigns against Anita Bryant and the Briggs Initiative are prime examples. In 1977, entertainer and fundamentalist Anita Bryant, who established the antigay Save Our Children organization, attacked the Dade County, Florida, Gay Liberation Alliance in her book *The Anita Bryant Story: The Survival of Our Nation's Families and the Threat of Militant Homosexuality*. She succeeded in getting the citizens of Dade County to repeal a new ordinance that prohibited discrimination against homosexuals in housing and employment. At that point many lesbians pulled together with gay men in the campaign against Bryant, even boycotting orange juice until the entertainer's contract with Florida orange growers was canceled. When they heard of Bryant's intention to open counseling centers across the nation to turn homosexuals into heterosexuals, they advocated resurrecting the radical antiwar tactics of the 1960s: "Just as we helped put the brake on the war through incessant disruption and agitation, we'll employ those same methods against this new oppression," one lesbian magazine declared. They even devised plans for using overground political processes for retaliation against Bryant, such as challenging the expected tax exempt status of the counseling centers through the courts. While Bryant's chief object of attack may have been gay males, clearly many lesbians also saw themselves as embattled and chose to work with gay men against a common enemy.[19]

In the same way, lesbians pulled together with gay men in the 1978 campaign against a proposed California constitutional amendment by State congressman John Briggs, who succeeded, by riding on the hysteria of Bryant's Save Our Children campaign, in qualifying his antigay initiative for the California ballot. The initiative proposed "to fire or refuse to hire . . . any teacher, counsellor, aide, or administrator in the public school system . . . who advocates, solicits, imposes, encourages, or promotes private or public homosexual activity . . . that is likely to come to the attention of students or parents." Lesbians working with gay men in the New Alliance for Gay Equality canvased houses and raised enough money to wage an impressive battle against the initiative, which almost 60 percent of the voters rejected. As one lesbian participant described those pre-election days in 1978, "It was wonderful. The gay movement came of age through that cooperation [as] we went door to door together, saying we were gay, asking people to vote against the amendment." As a result of the campaigning against the initiative, a flourishing underground political network was established. Gay males and lesbians made similar political coalitions all over the country in the late 1970s, such as the one that led the successful 1978 fight in Seattle against an initiative sponsored by a group called Save Our Moral Ethics, which wanted to repeal a 1974 ordinance that made it illegal for Seattle employers and landlords to discriminate on the basis of sexual preference.[20]

As the successes of the gay movement multiplied, some older middle-class women who would not have dreamed of leaving their closets earlier and some working-class women who had given up on society and hidden out in gay bars now felt safe in working for gay liberation. But neither the older middle-class lesbians nor their working-class bar dyke counterparts made up the bulk of the movement. Many of them continued to live exactly as they had in the years before Stonewall. The recruits who swelled the numbers most were those young men and women who knew the McCarthy era only through history books and who had come of age listening to the demands of the oppressed on nightly television. To demand their own rights seemed entirely natural to them, as it would not have been to most of their predecessors. They were a new species of homosexual who adamantly refused the burden of guilt and fear that had once been successfully foisted on many older lesbians and gay men.

Love Between Women in a New Light

The young people's refusal was made easier by the times that were open to experimentation of all sorts, unlike those years that had shaped most older homosexuals. In this milieu of liberality and in reaction to the authoritarian years that had preceded, same-sex love was becoming far less stigmatized. Among certain radicals it even took on an aura of chic, and women whose sexual histories had been heterosexual now felt much freer to explore love between women. Not all of those who experimented with lesbianism were committed to gay rights, of course. Some saw it as simply sexual exploration, which the times seemed to encourage, and they continued to define themselves as heterosexual. But others, even among those who had earlier considered themselves exclusively heterosexual, did come to regard lesbianism in a political context, especially if they were introduced to it through militant feminism.

The decade of the '60s had ushered in an unprecedented sexual permissiveness, characterized by mini skirts, the pill, group sex, mate swapping, a skyrocketing divorce rate, and acceptance of premarital sex. The rigidity of the 1950s was turned on its head. Heterosexuality began to look somewhat like homosexuality, as nonreproductive sex and cohabitation without marriage came to be commonplace. While some women may have been pressured under the guise of sexual revolution into having sex primarily for a man's delectation, others were motivated by the desire to explore their own erotic potential and to please themselves, and they were encouraged in that pursuit by popular literature such as Helen Gurley Brown's *Sex and the Single Girl* and *Cosmopolitan* Magazine. An end-of-the-decade study by the Institute for Sex Research showed that the number of women engaging in premarital sexual intercourse had doubled in the 1960s.[21] Because nonreproductive sex outside of marriage had become more and more acceptable, it made less social sense than it had earlier to condemn lesbianism on the grounds that lesbian sexual pleasure did not lead to reproduction.

The growing liberality toward lesbian sexuality eventually infiltrated some of the most committed bastions of heterosexuality. For
example, *Vogue* Magazine, which had always appealed to women
who belonged to or aspired to belong to rich men, proclaimed in a
radical chic article, "Who's Afraid of Lesbian Sex?": "Most women
know, if they are honest with themselves, that it sometimes would
be possible for them to connect their erotic knowledge with their
early love and choose a woman partner."[22] Sexual love between
"normal" women became less unthinkable than it had been for decades, and attitudes in some circles came to resemble those of the
experimental 1920s.

The new view of sexuality coincided with the awakening of the
feminist movement, which had slept a long sleep but began to rouse
itself in the early '60s. Women witnessed the demands for rights by
other oppressed groups and concluded that it was time for their own
voices to be heard. As women had during the first wave of feminism
in the nineteenth century, the new feminists now pointed out that
females were kept second-class citizens by men who claimed all the
social, political, and personal powers for themselves, and that the
only way women would attain power was by banding together to
demand it. Eventually some feminists, taking this argument to its
radical conclusion, came to believe that banding together could be
effective only if a woman did not go home to sleep in the enemy
camp but instead devoted all her energies—not only social and political but sexual as well—to other women. While some nineteenth-
century feminists may have felt that way also, their times would not
have permitted the articulation of such an idea. The period that
followed the sexual revolution of the 1960s did. These new wave
women felt free to call themselves lesbian-feminists. To them "lesbian" meant a choice any female could make.

"Lesbian-feminism" short-circuited a hundred years of social history—all the declarations of the sexologists and the media that separated off the lesbian from the "normal" women. Lesbian-feminists
declared that the lesbian was the same as any woman and that any
women could "existentially" convert from heterosexuality to homosexuality in the name of women's liberation. Their convictions were
made credible by a new minimalist definition of mental health that
called into question older views of homosexuality as sick and abnormal. As one sociologist described it: "You don't end up in a psychiatrist's office or in the hands of the police, you stay out of jail, you
keep a job, you pay your taxes, and you don't worry people too

much. That is called mental health."[23] Such a definition was impressive after the 1950s, when mental health was tantamount to conformity to an inflexible set of prescriptions. It served to encourage women in the belief that the gender of their love objects had nothing whatever to do with whether or not they were healthy, productive human beings.

The hippie phenomenon during the 1960s—free sex, unisex haircuts and clothes, love-ins, challenge to authority and conventional morality—also served as a backdrop against which homosexuality appeared less outrageous and abnormal. For many young women who were hippies, lesbianism seemed like just one more exciting adventure, conceivable especially because hippies generally seemed to give at least lip service to the idea that if you grooved on someone, gender was not a major consideration. As Clare, who was a teenager during the '60s, recalls:

> When you start getting free in your lifestyle, it's hard to regress and go backwards. What got me into the lesbian trip is I hung out with hippie types, smoked pot, worked in the anti-war movement, rebelled in every way I could think of. I slept with most of the men in my group. Then there were two women in the group who had three-ways with men. I thought that sounded interesting. I was open to experience as a way of living.[24]

Many of the young women who experimented with lesbian sexuality in the context of the hippie milieu saw it as only an experiment and nothing more. Others took it far more seriously, sometimes through personal inclination, sometimes through sexual politics. Although hippie culture had permitted women like Clare to have their first lesbian experiences, some of them realized, once they discovered radical feminist issues (which had considerable appeal to their radical natures), that hippie culture was sexist and patriarchal. They became disgusted over incidents which demonstrated they were not considered serious members of their groups, such as when hippie males at People's Park in Berkeley demanded "Free Land, Free Dope, Free Women" and ignored their existence. The hippie milieu both liberated many women to have their first lesbian experience and pushed them into lesbianism as a way of life in order to escape hippie sexism.

To some of these radical women, lesbianism was also appealing by virtue of the fact that love between women had long suffered under an outlaw status and it appeared to them to be one more necessary slap in the face of convention. In addition, the image of the Amazon

—which had often been used as a euphemism for the lesbian—
seemed to them especially seductive in an era when wars of liberation
were being fought in Vietnam and Latin America and among ethnic
minorities in the United States. In Amazonian guise they now had
their own wars to fight.

Young females who were brought into the New Left by the antiwar movement in the 1960s had similar experiences. Like the hippie
movement, the Left was countercultural and radical on the surface,
but its attitude toward women was no more liberated than that of the
conservatives. The women of the Left who became interested in
feminism when the movement was reborn in the mid-1960s had
honed their analytical tools through New Left debate and literature.
They not only soon resented that they had been reduced to making
brown rice instead of policy, but they were also quick to recognize
sex exploitation and inequality in bed as being political. When they
tried to raise women's issues in leftist groups such as SNCC and the
National Conference for New Politics and were unsuccessful, they
were convinced that they could no longer work complacently with
males of the New Left. They would have to begin meeting separately
if they wished to focus on those issues. Some of their radical all-
women's groups eventually evolved into lesbian-feminism. In their
conviction that "the personal is political," they came to believe that
lesbian-feminism was appropriate for all women who took themselves seriously and wanted to be taken seriously instead of being
"fucked over by the patriarchy" in the secondary, auxiliary status to
which females had generally been relegated in heterosexual life.[25]
Thus the liberal sexual milieu of the era, the spread of radical behaviors, and the anger toward heterosexuality fomented by feminism all
worked to permit women who might have been fearful of the "abnormality" of same-sex love in other eras to investigate it at this time
and to scoff at the notion that it was abnormal.

The Lesbian-Feminist Revolution

The gay revolution took its steam largely from "essentialist" homosexuals who believed that homosexuality was no less involuntary
than being black or Hispanic. Like members of the early Scientific
Humanitarian Committee, they argued that because they did not
chose to be homosexual—they were born or made as they were—
discrimination against them could have no justification. Developing

alongside of that revolution of gays was the other revolution of those young women who loved other women and wished to make a political statement out of their love but denied that they were "gay." They insisted on being called lesbian-feminist.

The connection between lesbianism and feminism was not new, but in the past it had been made with unchallenged scorn. When those late nineteenth-century antifeminists who wanted to scare females away from the women's movement used the cudgel of "abnormality," warning that "Women-Righters" were "men-women," out to seduce innocent young girls and spread their taint under the guise of feminism, feminists did not dare respond to their attacks. With the start of the second wave of feminism in the 1960s, those opposed to women's rights used the same tactic, but this time, in the context of a more radical era, it backfired. Ti-Grace Atkinson, an early leader of the second wave of feminism, remembers that the first time she was called a lesbian was in the mid-'60s when she joined a group of women to picket the *New York Times* in order to desegregate the help-wanted ads. "I was so puzzled by the connection," she recalls, "that I became curious. Whenever the enemy keeps lobbing bombs into some area you consider unrelated to your defense, it's worth investigating." The investigaton brought her and many other radical feminists to the conviction that "lesbian" has always been a kind of code word for female resistance.[26]

Those late nineteenth-century enemies of the women's movement who had called feminism "a fertile breeding ground for lesbianism" were even more right than they knew—not because lesbians were vampirishly waiting to suck the blood of young innocents who had been temporarily deluded into being angry with men, but rather because feminism dissected the nature of the problems between men and women with a compelling analysis. It forced women to see ways in which they were exploited, to hear everywhere the "clicks," as *Ms.* Magazine called the sudden insights one might have when confronted with a sexist incident. In the light of women's new awareness, lesbianism seemed very attractive, and more and more radical feminists came to doubt if heterosexuality could really be consonant with their personal and political ideology. Just as heterosexuals in the past had seen their own variety of love as superior and homosexuality as a manifestaton of emotional illness, so the new lesbian-feminists, many of whom had spent all their previous adult years as exclusively heterosexual, now saw homosexuality as the highest form of love and heterosexuality as a sign of female masochism.

Lesbianism even came to be regarded as the quintessence of feminism, and in some ways the values of the lesbian-feminists of the
1970s were not unlike those of the pioneer feminists who lived together as "devoted companions" at the beginning of the century.
Lesbianism implied that a woman could live without a man if she
wanted to and still feel like a successful person. It suggested that work
might be an essential part of a woman's life and that a woman should
want to work both to support herself and change society. It emphasized the importance of women loving and respecting themselves and
other women. It had nothing to do with the sexologists' notions and
outrageous theories. Therefore, when a New York group of feminists
who called themselves the Radicalesbians explained in a 1970 paper
that as lesbian-feminists they were "women–identified–women," putting women first in their lives in all ways, including the sexual, and
that all feminists must become "women–identified," their argument
struck a chord for many. "What is a lesbian?" they asked in that
paper. Their response expanded the meaning of lesbianism so that it
applied to a far greater number of women:

> A lesbian is the rage of all women condensed to the point of explosion.
> She is a woman who . . . acts in accordance with her inner compulsion
> to be a more complete and free human being than her society . . . cares
> to allow her. . . . She has not been able to accept the limitations and
> oppressions laid on her by the most basic role of her society—the
> female role.

In one sense, the Radicalesbian group's definition came full circle,
back to the early sexologists' definition of the lesbian as a woman
whose behavior is not appropriate to "womanliness." But while the
sexologists saw such women as rare and congenitally tainted, the new
lesbian-feminists saw them as ubiquitous and heroic. Lesbianism was
to the lesbian-feminists a cure-all for the ills perpetrated by sexism.
Lesbianism was "women creating a new consciousness of and with
each other, which is at the heart of women's liberation and the basis
for cultural revolution."[27] And the best news was that any woman
could embrace it.

Lesbian-feminists thus took a revisionist approach to essentialism.
It was true, they said, that lesbians were born "that way." But
actually *all* women were born "that way," all had the capacity to be
lesbians, but male supremacy destroyed that part of most women
before they could understand what was happening. Lesbian-feminists
emphatically rejected the notion that they were part of a homosexual

minority. While the movement did not deny the existence of *primary* lesbians ("essentialists" who believed they had been lesbians for as long as they could remember), it also encouraged women to become *elective,* "existentialist" lesbians (to make a conscious political choice to leave heterosexuality and embrace lesbianism). Rita Mae Brown, one of the most articulate spokeswomen for lesbian-feminism, declared:

> I became a lesbian because the culture that I live in is violently anti-woman. How could I, a woman, participate in a culture that denies my humanity? . . . To give a man support and love before giving it to a sister is to support that culture, that power system.

To love and support women, Brown said, was lesbian. In that sense, lesbian was revolutionary, and it was imperative that all women who wanted to be feminists stop collaborating with the enemy and join that revolution.[28]

There were probably more lesbians in America during the 1970s than any other time in history, because radical feminism had helped redefine lesbianism to make it almost a categorical imperative for all women truly interested in the welfare and progress of other women. As one radical feminist, who divorced her physician husband in 1974 to become a lesbian, characterized it, lesbianism was seen to be "the only noble choice a committed feminist could make."[29] In this respect, the 1970s offer a prime example of sexuality as a social construct. It was demonstrated in that decade how the spirit of an era could influence sexual behavior in large numbers of people at least as much as those other factors that had long been regarded as determining sexuality.

Radical feminists propounded the behaviorist view of sexuality: as in a utopian socialist society where the individual could be conditioned to be nonviolent, noncompetitive, incorruptible, so too could women be conditioned to change their attitudes and desires. They would exit from the patriarchy through severing their relationships with men, which were seen as the cornerstone of the subordination of women, and they could learn not only how to make a new society with women, but also how to respond sexually to women.[30]

Unlike the era of romantic friends or devoted companions, when sexuality might have been negligible in a woman's life, in the sex conscious '70s women felt as guilty about denying themselves sexual pleasures as their predecessors would have felt guilty had they indulged. Thus when radical feminists who had previously been heterosexual experimented with love between women and discovered that it was indeed a sexual alternative for them, they were often relieved and elated. It was not that they had generally disliked sex when they were heterosexual, but rather they had come to despise all the personal and political aggravations that heterosexuality brought in its wake. They were delighted to discover in the heady early days of lesbian-feminism that they could experience sexual pleasure with other women without the inevitable subordination. As one woman who had been married before she became a lesbian-feminist in 1970 now recalls:

> We investigated the other side of humanity and it became very viable. We weren't going to give up sex, and we didn't have to. Emotionally what we had with men wasn't fulfilling. We weren't being taken care of in those relationships, and so we stepped out of them, sexually as well as in all other ways. We were bright enough to perceive that it would be decades before men were even in the ball park.

Some radical feminists were only "political lesbians," meaning that they sympathized with lesbian complaints about men and were not opposed to sexual love between women, but they chose celibacy for themselves; however, most "lesbian-feminists" did not deny themselves erotic relations with other women. Their view that men were dispensible in all ways, including the sexual, was dramatized by the logo on the T-shirts some wore and the posters that hung above their beds: "A Woman Without a Man is Like a Fish Without a Bicycle."[31]

Many 1970s feminists were encouraged in their exploration of lesbianism through consciousness-raising (CR) groups, small groups in which women met to discuss their personal lives in relation to sexual politics. In the course of those discussions women often came to believe that men were kept in power as a group because of women's nurturing, subordinate personal relations with them. It was heterosexuality that supported male supremacy. With that realization, lesbianism became for those women the rational next step. They could choose not to be heterosexual and thus not support what they saw as the power system that oppressed them. As one San Antonio woman who had been married to a Presbyterian minister for twenty-five years and had raised five children now tells it:

> I supported him while he was going to school. I walked the floor with the babies and never bothered him so he could study. And later I even did prayer meetings for him. My whole life had been devoted to doing *his* stuff. And then I went back to school and joined NOW and a CR

group, and for the first time things were crystalized for me. I realized through CR that I didn't have to be a good little girl anymore. What I wanted was an equal relationship, but I doubted it would be possible with a male—not any of the men I knew. They were trained as I had been trained, to have certain expectations about men's privileges and women's duties, and they had no reason to give it up. I did. I knew with a woman we could both just start from scratch.[32]

CR brought many feminists to such radical insights.

Through those CR groups they also became aware of the need for lesbian-feminist political goals that were far more radical than those of gay revolutionaries whose aim was equality with heterosexuals. Lesbian-feminist revolutionaries wanted a restructuring of the entire system of heterosexuality, which, they declared, was at the root of women's oppression. They wanted to provide for all women what they believed was a healthy alternative to male-female relationships. Their political work was focused not only on taking care of the problems wrought by heterosexuality, such as staffing abortion clinics and battered women's retreats, but also on creating a women's culture (see chapter 9) that would be lesbian-feminist and clearly superior to the culture that men had foisted on humanity.

Splits, Coalitions, and Resolutions

While lesbian-feminists, as homosexuals and as feminists, had natural affinities with other gay and feminist groups, their relationships were not always without ambivalences. Butch/femme women and older middle-class and wealthier lesbians generally shunned them for their radicalism. Racial and ethnic minority lesbians felt that lesbian-feminist goals were irrelevant to the major problems that minorities faced. Feminists sometimes feared that lesbian-feminists would stigmatize the whole women's movement as being made up of "nothing but a bunch of man-hating dykes." Movement gay women felt uncomfortable with the separatist program of some lesbian-feminists. Though there were occasional useful and fulfilling coalitions and mergers between lesbian-feminists and members of other groups, mistrust was frequent (just as it was between revolutionary and more conservative groups within ethnic minorities). Lesbian-feminists were especially critical of what they saw as the superficiality of the "liberal" feminist and gay demands for social change. They attempted to educate the older groups. For example, they exhorted feminists to become lesbians and lesbians were told they must become feminists in order to aid in the battle against male supremacy.

Many ignored such exhortations, but some older women who had been lesbians long before the birth of the lesbian-feminist movement found it easy to accept the movement's goals and philosophies, since they had long lived as feminists without defining themselves as such. The new lesbian chauvinism was a heady experience for them, and they were embraced by the young women in the lesbian-feminist movement with great enthusiasm. They were made to feel they had moved practically overnight from miscreants to historical role models. They remembered well the persecution and the need to hide that characterized their lives in the 1950s and throughout much of the '60s —and suddenly the world had changed. "It was like living in a time warp," one woman remembers. She had moved from the Midwest to New York in order to have more access to the blossoming new culture:

> Suddenly there was women's music, which I'd never heard before, and it was performed in front of such huge audiences of proud lesbians. There were all of these workshops. There were all-women dances at Columbia. There was a place in the Catskills where hundreds of women took over the entire hotel, running around bare, giving each other massages. And they all wanted to talk to me as a lesbian who had been around for a while. They respected me. I was forty-five years old and as delirious as a fourteen year old. It was like I'd never lived before.[33]

"Old gays" who were willing to venture out of their closets or out of their butch/femme roles (which lesbian-feminists disdained) were delighted to change their identity to lesbian-feminist. It was as though the new movement was what they had been waiting for their entire lives, but that it could come to fruition in their day was beyond their sweetest dreams.

While the lesbian-feminists welcomed older lesbians who adhered to feminist principles, they were not willing to welcome gay men into their revolution, and on this account they differed emotionally from the women who were part of the gay revolution and who insisted that even if women received all the rights they wanted, lesbians would still be pariahs by virtue of their homosexuality. "If we take up the issues of child care, wife battering, abortion rights," the "gay" women asked, "who will take up the issues of gay rights for us?" Barbara Gittings, who continued to work in the gay movement throughout the 1970s, characterized the dilemma as "It's a matter of where does it hurt the most? For me it hurts the most not in the female arena, but in the gay arena."[34] Lesbian-feminists argued in response that homophobia was due to patriarchal values and would be cured once those values were destroyed.

Although lesbian-feminists and gays occasionally worked together in the face of grave threats such as the antihomosexual Briggs Initiative in California, lesbian-feminists generally found it disruptive to be with gay males, since to them they did not constitute a special category of men: they had been socialized just as badly as straight males and had similar chauvinistic expectations of females. Lesbian-feminists most often chose to dissociate themselves from gay concerns and work on issues that were specifically feminist, because they felt that gay men wanted to use them only as mediators between gay male interests and society. They pointed out with anger that they had nothing to do with washroom sex or public solicitation, and yet those were historically the problems on which women's energies were spent in coalitions with gay men. Lesbian-feminists insisted they were not the "ladies auxiliary of the gay movement." Their slogan became: "We are angry, not gay."[35]

For many lesbian-feminists the problem stemmed from gay men's lack of a radical analysis over the questions of sex and sex roles. They accused gay men of being merely reformist—defining the issue of homosexuality as a private matter about with whom you sleep—instead of understanding the deeper political issues such as questions of domination and power. They complained that gay reformists pursued solutions that made no basic changes in the system that oppressed lesbians as women and their reforms would keep power in the hands of the oppressors.[36] As lesbian-feminists, they were not interested in promoting what they saw as trivial laws and mores that would make it possible for everyone to sleep around freely while maintaining the status quo of women's powerlessness.

They were especially repelled by gay male culture because they believed that lesbians, as women, would not naturally do as gay men did, with their dominant-submissive modes of sexual relating and their separation of sex from emotional involvement. Adrienne Rich, in a speech at the 1977 New York Lesbian Pride Rally (an event whose express purpose was to offer lesbians an alternative to the Gay Pride Rally that had commemorated Stonewall throughout the 1970s), even blamed all that she saw as wrong in old lesbian culture on the influence of gay males, including "the violent, self-destructive world of the gay bars" and "the imitation role stereotypes of 'butch' and 'femme.' " Her cry, along with that of myriads of other women, was for lesbian-feminists to create a self-defined, self-loving, woman-identified culture.[37] Because a general disenchantment with and suspicion of all males was central to lesbian-feminist doctrine, the gay man was naturally seen as being no less an enemy than any other human with a penis, and lesbian-feminists could make no lasting coalition with gay men in a gay revolution.

Although lesbian-feminists saw themselves as feminist rather than gay, they did not enjoy an unalloyed welcome in the women's movement. Betty Friedan, the founder of NOW, the largest organization of the women's movement, even went so far as to tell the *New York Times* in 1973 that lesbians were sent to infiltrate the women's movement by the CIA as a plot to discredit feminism.[38] However, despite the displeasure of NOW's founding mother and her supporters, who called lesbians the "lavender menace," when a showdown actually took place in NOW most heterosexual feminists voted on the side of lesbians. In a 1971 resolution, NOW identified lesbians as the front-line troops of the women's movement and accepted the lesbian-feminist analysis that the reason lesbians had been so harassed by society was that they were a significant threat to the system that subjugates women—the very system that heterosexual women were trying to challenge and destroy by their feminism. The 1971 resolution acknowledged the inherent feminism of lesbianism and the anti-feminism of lesbian persecution: "Because she defines herself independently of men, the lesbian is considered unnatural, incomplete, not quite a woman—as though the essence of womanhood was to be identified with men." It affirmed that the oppression of lesbians was a legitimate concern for feminism and that "a woman's right to her own person includes the right to define and express her own sexuality and to choose her own lifestyle." The resolution passed overwhelmingly and without any change in wording. That victory was a great testimony to lesbian-feminists' success in communicating their position even to more conservative feminists.

Other feminist organizations followed suit in showing support for love between women such as few would have dared to express in earlier years. In the mid-1970s the National Women's Political Caucus issued a position paper supporting nondiscrimination against lesbians in areas such as employment, housing, and education. The National Women's Agenda, which included such traditional groups as the Girl Scouts and the YWCA, supported lesbian rights in its 1975 constitution. Gloria Steinem offered the rationale for such actions in an essay titled "The Politics of Supporting Lesbianism":

> We must understand that what we are attempting is a revolution, not a public relations movement. As long as we fear the word "lesbian" we are curtailing our own strength and abandoning our sisters. As long as human sexuality is politically controlled, we will all be losing a basic human freedom.[39]

But while many gay women were shouting "Out of the closets and into the streets" at Gay Pride parades and lesbian-feminists were openly demonstrating their contempt for heterosexual institutions, most older lesbians still felt that their best chance was in continued silence. They left confrontation and admission to younger women who had been brought up in more liberal times and who had often even declassed themselves in the push toward downward mobility in the radical '60s and the aftermath of that decade. Older lesbians explained to themselves that the younger women had less to lose.

An uncomfortable split sometimes developed between those who felt free to come out and those who remained in the closet. As an Albuquerque, New Mexico, woman who worked as an administrator in education wrote defensively:

> Radical feminist politics would be ill at ease among the company I keep, which often includes some very conservative, yes, "straight" people. . . . My words would be dismissed, my credibility destroyed if it were known that I was a lesbian. I *choose* the closet. That is surely my right. . . . More power to those who open a collective or a women's service of some kind, but would everyone please get off my case for doing what I know and like best?[40]

They had been practicing all their adult lives to live in hiding and to maneuver despite that handicap, just as the times that formed them had demanded, and they now resented what seemed like the cavalier exhortation of the younger women not only that they risk everything they had built but that they change the very *modus operandi* that had become second nature to them.

Nevertheless, those who were fearful of coming out were often honest enough with themselves to realize that they owed the activists a debt. It was through the revolutionary efforts of gays and lesbian-feminists that the lives of many of the more cautious women were made easier. They were able to feel, albeit in secret, that they were socially or professionally a little safer and a little more comfortable. Not only had the activists pushed for policies and legislation on various levels that often meant that those covert lesbians no longer needed to fear they would be discriminated against in a job or in school or with regard to housing, even should their sexual orientation become known, but the activists had also succeeded in remaking the lesbian self-image so that shame about love between women could feel anachronistic.

The benefits even covert lesbians enjoyed came from the work of both revolutionary movements, as basically different as they were. Gay revolutionaries of the 1970s saw lesbians as unlike most women, an aggrieved minority who were justified in demanding rights that had been denied them ever since the sexologists first identified them in the previous century. In contrast, lesbian-feminist revolutionaries of the '70s saw themselves as being just like other women, except that they were more astute in their sociopolitical analysis and they believed that once other women saw the light they too would become lesbian-feminists. But unlike many lesbians who had been indoctrinated with guilt and self-hatred in earlier decades, lesbian-feminist and gay women revolutionaries were similar in refusing to accept the premise that love between women was inherently flawed. And they battled that notion openly. They agreed that society was at fault for its policies of persecution and its dissemination of misinformation about same-sex love. Homophobia, and not homosexuality, needed curing. It was not lesbians, they agreed, but society that was sick.

Top: 1970s dyke style. Although butch-and-femme were "politically incorrect" in the lesbian-feminist community, everyone looked butch. (© Cathy Cade, 1972. From *Lesbians Speak Out* by Cathy Cade, 1974. Reprinted by permission.)

Bottom: Lesbian Nation required that women learn new skills so that they might be independent of "the man" in all ways. (© JEB [Joan E. Biren], 1979. From *Eye to Eye* by JEB, 1979. Reprinted by permission.)

Above: Artist/designer Wendy Cadden of Women's Press Collective at the printing press. Lesbian-feminists learned to print so they could communicate their own vision of lesbianism in the 1970s. (Courtesy of the June Mazer Lesbian Collection, Los Angeles.)

Right: Country Women in the 1970s. Lesbian separatists who went off to the country wanted to escape the man-made world that drained their energies. (© JEB [Joan E. Biren], 1979. From *Eye to Eye* by JEB, 1979. Reprinted by permission.)

Above: Third World lesbians of the 1970s did not always trust white lesbian-feminists to be sensitive to their special problems. (© JEB [Joan E. Biren], 1979. From *Eye to Eye* by JEB, 1979. Reprinted by permission.)

Left: Older Latina lesbians of the 1980s. The visible lesbian community became increasingly diverse. (© Cathy Cade, 1982. From *A Lesbian Photo Album* by Cathy Cade, 1987. Reprinted by permission.)

Top: In the 1980s the increasing number of visible Asian American lesbians permitted them for the first time to establish a separate group within some communities. (© Cathy Cade, 1981. From *A Lesbian Photo Album,* 1987. Reprinted by permission.)

Bottom: Betty Shoemaker and Sylvia Dobson at the first old lesbians convention in 1987. "To walk in and see 200 white-haired dykes, all ready to stand up and assert themselves, was mind-boggling." (© Ruth Mountaingrove, 1987. Reprinted by permission.)

Above: The 1980s saw a baby boom in the lesbian community. (© Cathy Cade, 1981. From *A Lesbian Photo Album* by Cathy Cade, 1987. Reprinted by permission.)

Left: S/M lesbians believe that feminists have much to learn from sexual outlaws. (Courtesy of Jesse Merril.)

Right: Lesbian sexual radicals of the 1980s wanted to escape from "politically correct" sex and expand lesbians' sexual horizons. (Courtesy of National Entertainment Network; photograph by Jill Posner.)

Above: Lesbian punk styles, 1980s. (© Isa Massu, 1987. Reprinted by permission.)

THEY'RE CALLED "PUMPS" NOT "TOOLS OF THE PATRIARCHY" & HOW MUCH TOFU HAD TO DIE FOR YOUR OUTFIT?

Left: Lesbian style wars in the 1980s. (© Kris Kovic. Reprinted by permission.)

Above: Lipstick lesbians of the 1980s at a lesbian wedding. (Courtesy of the June Mazer Lesbian Collection, Los Angeles.)

Top: "Softball is the only consistent thing in this community. Political groups and social groups come and go, but softball will always be around," Rhonda in Omaha. (Courtesy of JEB [Joan E. Biren]. Reprinted by permission.)

Bottom: The 1990s?—"The thing that's important to me about Queer Nation is that we're ready to act. . . . Sometimes you have to take to the streets." (Courtesy of Robert Fox/Impact Visuals.)

9

Lesbian Nation: Creating a Women-Identified-Women Community in the 1970s

Sweet Betsy the Dyke
(to be sung to the tune of "Sweet Betsy from Pike")

Oh do you remember Sweet Betsy the Dyke
Who came from New Jersey on her motorbike,
And riding beside her was her lover Anne,
A sister, a friend, and a far out woman.

(CHORUS) *Singing "Dykes, come together, we can change*
this land!"
Singing, "Dykes come together, we can change
this land!"

They rode across the country, Sweet Betsy and Anne,
And said to all women, "YOU KNOW THAT YOU
CAN!
So leave all your men folk and come on with us.
If you don't have a cycle, we'll charter a bus . . .
—Les B. Friends, 1973

The two things we are trying to do—set up a counterculture
and make a revolution—It's hard to do both things at the
same time. *—June Arnold,*
The Cook and the Carpenter, *1973*

Despite the strong movements of the 1970s that attracted multitudes
of lesbians, others remained untouched. Many middle-class white
lesbians who did not declass themselves in the radical 1970s continued
to be completely closeted outside of their circle of lesbian friends.
Those women saw movements based on sexual politics as being
superfluous to their lives. They were joined in that view by lesbians
who had come out in the gay bar culture of butch and femme and

had no desire to adapt to a new set of standards. Their view was also shared by lesbians who belonged to racial and ethnic minorities and felt they had to place the needs of those communities first. To all of them, as to Jane Rule's character in her novel of the 1970s, *Contract with the World,* "loving another woman [was] nothing but that, with no redeeming politics or transforming art."[1] But lesbian-feminists often built their entire existence around politics based on their feminism and lesbianism.

Many lesbian-feminists had discovered lesbianism through the radical feminist movement. They were often women in their twenties who had grown up in the era of the flower child and had learned to approach life with passion and idealism. Their decision to become lesbian-feminists stemmed from their disillusionment with the male-created world and their hope of curing its ills. The fruitless war in Vietnam, the proliferaton of ecological problems, the high unemployment rate even among the educated, the general unrest that was left over from the 1960s, all contributed to their radical lesbian-feminist vision that American culture was in deep trouble and drastic measures were required to reverse its unwise course. Since they were convinced through feminism that the root of the problem was male —caused by the greed, egocentrism, and violence that came along with testosterone or male socialization—they believed that only a "woman's culture," built on superior female values and women's love for each other, could rectify all that had gone wrong in male hands. Thus not only was love between women—"lesbianism"— destigmatized among them: it was "aristocraticized."[2] Although women before the 1970s often became lesbians because of their discontent with the way men behaved, the lesbian-feminists were the first to articulate such motivation and to create a coherent philosophy out of it.

In their idealism they resembled the cultural feminists of the beginning of the century, such as Jane Addams, but instead of hoping to transform patriarchal institutions as the earlier women often did, they wanted to create entirely new institutions and to shape a women's culture that would embody all the best values that were not male. It would be nonhierarchical, spiritual, and without the jealousy that comes of wanting to possess other human beings, as in monogamy and imperialism. It would be nonracist, nonageist, nonclassist, and nonexploitative—economically or sexually. It would be pro-women and pro-children. These women believed that such a culture could only be formed if women stepped away from the hopelessly corrupt

patriarchy and established their own self-sufficient, "women-identified-women" communities into which male values could not infiltrate. Those communities would eventually be built into a strong
Lesbian Nation that would exist not necessarily as a geographical
entity but as a state of mind and that might even be powerful enough,
through its example, to divert the country and the world from their
dangerous course. Their visions were utopian. Lesbian-feminists were
true believers and destined, as true believers often are, for fanaticism
and eventual disappointment.

They found themselves in conflict with working-class butch/ femme
lesbians whose roles they considered an imitation of heterosexuality
and hence heterosexist. But they were in even greater conflict with
lesbians who maintained what the lesbian-feminists scoffed at as
bourgeois lifestyles, and those women often returned their disdain.
By the 1970s a number of middle-class lesbians felt that they had
made a sort of peace with the establishment world, which had many
rewards to offer if one were willing to practice a modicum of discretion. They deplored the radicals' funky and flamboyant style. Although some middle-class lesbians worked within the feminist movement, they would never refer to themselves as lesbian-feminist. They
found the radical lesbian-feminist philosophy naive and thought that
the radicals were giving lesbianism a bad name. Although middle-
class lesbians usually did not feel free to represent lesbianism to
heterosexual society, they unrealistically hoped that someone who
was more in their own (idealized) image would represent them. As
one woman observed:

> The public is still not seeing that there are good and bad in this life,
> too. And, unfortunately, the ones they've seen aren't the ones I'd run
> around with either, at least some of the ones I've seen on television.
> Why, they're not the caliber that I would associate with—you get a lot
> of mouthy women up there, who go hollering around and they're
> obnoxious. . . . I guess they are out there fighting the battles for us,
> but I'd rather see some women up there who look like women, presi-
> dents of companies that had responsible jobs saying their piece, on a
> little higher plane.[3]

In their turn, lesbian-feminists criticized middle-class lesbians for
benighted behavior, believing that if they saw the light, they would
come to understand that their bourgeois capitalism and all its social
manifestations were corrupt. Most frequently lesbian-feminists tried
to ignore the existence of both working-class and middle-class lesbi-

ans, appropriating the term "lesbian" for themselves as being synonymous with "lesbian-feminism" and thereby excluding all lesbians who were not a part of the movement. The split that developed between lesbian-feminists and lesbians who just loved other women could be as virulent as the split between the classes and generations in the 1950s. But despite detractors and the philosophical obstacles they represented, the radical lesbian-feminists forged ahead to create a unique community and culture. While their community encompassed only a fraction of American women who loved women, it was their image of lesbianism that dominated the 1970s, since they felt freer than the other women to present themselves through the media.

Blueprints for a Lesbian-Feminist Culture

The utopian world that lesbian-feminists envisioned was based largely on socialist ideals and reflected the background many of them had had in the New Left. But those ideals were filtered through lesbian-feminist doctrine, which sometimes led to extreme convictions such as the importance of separatism to attain their goals: some lesbian-feminists thought it necessary to exclude all heterosexual and homosexual males as well as heterosexual females from their personal and political lives, just as militant blacks had urged separatism from whites. Not all lesbian-feminists agreed on that issue, or on any other issue, for that matter. But though varying from the start with regard to the extent of their radicalism, lesbian-feminists believed in the beginning of their movement that the commonality of committed lesbianism would be sufficient to help them build a unified lesbian community. Such unity seemed easy to attain, since there appeared to be a consensus among them about what the broad configuration of the Lesbian Nation would finally look like: a utopia for women, an Amazon dream.

Lesbian-feminists sometimes called the culture they were building "women's" rather than "lesbian" culture, perhaps because they felt that it was the nurturing, loving values associated with women that they wanted to emphasize in their communities. They also chauvinistically believed that all the women who were producing anything worthwhile—books, music, women's centers, abortion clinics, women's garages, women's restaurants—were lesbians and hence "women's culture" and "lesbian culture" were synonymous. So "women's books," for example, meant books by, for, and about lesbians.

Language became important to them as an indication of political awareness and as a tool to raise consciousness. Sometimes lesbian-feminists changed the spelling of "woman" and "women" to "wo-myn," "wimmin," or "womben" in order to obliterate the root "man." "History" became "herstory"; "hurricane" became "hisi-cane"; "country" became "cuntry." Lesbian-feminists wanted espe-cially to reclaim the word "lesbian" from the psychiatric and moral morass into which it had fallen, and they exhorted each other to use that previously taboo word and even the word "dyke," understand-ing, as African-Americans had about "black," that it was possible to take a word used by the enemy to hurt and reclaim it by giving it proud associations. The vocabulary of the old lesbian subculture was usually rejected as being counter to their politics. "Butch" and "femme" disappeared as far as lesbian-feminists were concerned, as did "gay," which they saw as belonging to homosexual men. "'Gay' doesn't include lesbians any more than 'mankind' includes love and sister-hood," they wrote.[4]

Their initial euphoria brought a great blast of energy and industry. By the early 1970s there were active lesbian-feminist groups in most states, scores of newspapers and journals that were predominantly or exclusively lesbian-feminist, and numerous bookstores that sold only women's culture books. Even women who were not in the big city lesbian-feminist communities could take part in that culture through the written word.[5]

The creation of economic institutions that would lead to financial independence was considered particularly crucial to the blueprint for a lesbian-feminist community. Such independence was necessary so that lesbian-feminists would not have to fear that they would lose their livelihood because they "came out." They also felt that they should not waste effort that ought to go to the lesbian-feminist community in working for heterosexuals. As one writer phrased it, "Hopefully, we will soon be able to integrate the pieces of our lives and stop this schizophrenic existence of a straight job by day and lesbian political work at night. It keeps us in a state of permanent culture shock and drains our energies."[6]

They attempted to create economic cooperatives, child care cen-ters, food co-ops, health clinics, halfway houses, and skills centers, and they dreamt grandiously about multiplying their institutions all over the country so that their values would eventually predominate.

Borrowing from *Daily Worker* rhetoric, they declared: "Ultimately, women must be prepared to take over the power of the State and reorganize society. As long as power remains in the hands of men, we are at their whims and our lives will not be free." They wanted to bring their ideals about integrity, nurturing the needy, self-determination, and equality of labor and rewards into all aspects of institution building and economics. For example, they recommended that priority in hiring be arranged according to need, lower-class women and Third World women coming first. They were opposed to the concept of bosses and workers. All the "shit work" must be shared, they said. Everyone must be given the choice of learning new skills and holding different jobs in the company for which they work. Workers would not have to give up control over the quality and the politics of what they produced. Whatever they did would be nonoppressive and non-sexist.[7]

But it was in the working out of the details and the day-to-day living that the blueprint broke down. It became apparent in the course of the decade that lesbian-feminists were as diverse a group as one might find in the heterosexual world. And those who were brought together by their general radical views were not immune to the factionalism that has beset most minority groups after the initial euphoria of discovering commonalities.

Culture Building: The Media

Lesbian Nation was doomed finally to failure because of youthful inexperience and inability to compromise unbridled enthusiasms, but nevertheless it helped to change the meaning and the image of lesbianism by giving love between women greater visibility and by presenting visions of self-affirmation through lesbian-feminist music and literature. In its success in reaching large numbers of lesbians, women's music was perhaps the most effective of all the enterprises undertaken by the lesbian-feminist community in the 1970s. Women's music attracted huge crowds at concerts and women's festivals around the country and came into the homes of vast numbers of lesbian-feminists with self-affirming lyrics about lesbian politics, lesbian love, lesbian unity. The music, which was generally inspired by a folk art tradition, not only helped to create community by bringing women together, but it also proselytized for the cause. As one lesbian singer, Willie Tyson, observed in 1974, "We know about ten women who were straight before they came to the concert and were [lesbian-feminist] about two weeks later. The concert just blew their minds."[8]

Although in the gay bars of the 1940s, '50s, and '60s lesbian singers like Lisa Ben and Beverly Shaw had performed songs "tailored to [the lesbian] taste," as Beverly Shaw's publicity blurbs touted, they were generally popular ballads that incorporated lesbian-specific words into heterosexual lyrics. For example, in "Hello, Young Lovers," instead of "I've had a love like you," the singer would substitute the line "I've had a butch like you." During most of the 1960s, when, led by Bob Dylan, popular lyrics often expressed political consciousness, there was no attempt by lesbian singers to raise awareness of lesbian social and political difficulties through music. Under the influence of lesbian-feminism this changed. The first musician to perform publicly as a lesbian-feminist was Maxine Feldman, whose 1969 song, "Angry Atthis," was about wanting to hold her lover's hand in public. In 1971 Alix Dobkin began writing the lyrics that were finally collected on her album *Lavender Jane Loves Women*, which was heavily political in terms of lesbian-feminist consciousness. Songs such as "Talking Lesbian," for example, warned that men cannot relate to a woman's mind or a woman's state and offered the "women-identified-women" solution of constructing a woman's culture, which would be made possible only through lesbian love:

> If you want high consciousness, I'll tell you what to do,
> You got to talk to a woman, let her talk to you.
> You got to build you a union and make it strong,
> And if we all stick together, girls, it won't be long. . . .
> Of course, it ain't that simple, so I'd better explain.
> You got to ride on the lesbian train. . . .
> Women lovin' women is where it's at . . . [9]

It was soon clear that there was a wide audience for such entertainment.

Olivia Records was established in 1973 by ten women who had already been members of lesbian-feminist living and working collectives. The company ultimately became the leader in women's music, with albums that sold in the hundreds of thousands and nationwide tours that attracted huge audiences. As a result of the taste Olivia helped to create, large annual women's music festivals proliferated all over the country. The festivals were modelled on the hippie be-ins of the 1960s, in which counter-culture crowds, in various stages of undress, would dance, get high on LSD or pot, and listen to music.

The women's festivals, however, always had political overtones. Workshops were held that attempted to raise and solve lesbian-feminist problems; movement literature and paraphernalia were widely available; and the organizers attempted to be sensitive to all the issues: they provided day care, easy access for the disabled, vegetarian meals, sign interpreters for the deaf, "chemical free" areas for women who disapproved of substance use, sliding scale entrance fees so that the poor would not be excluded. Nothing was allowed at the festivals that was not "politically correct," a label that was to become a benchmark of all judgments in the community, even judgments passed on lesbian-feminist entertainers. At the first National Women's Music Festival in Champagne, Illinois, in 1974, singers who appeared too professional, too much like stars, got a cold reception. The audience wanted to see their own declassed, unslick image on the stage. Making a mistake, being "human," was better than being perfect. As Meg Christian, one of Olivia's most successful singers, observed, "There was a big difference [in audience reaction to] performers who related to the audience as if they were there and women who got up and pulled a shell around them to perform, which is essentially your male performing trip." To be in any way like a male professional was to be politically incorrect. In fact, "professionalism" of any kind was considered undesirable hierarchical behavior: it represented artificial and destructive categories, barriers set up by the patriarchy that limited the possibilities of women "creating a vision together." Professionals were as suspect in the 1970s as they had been venerated in the 1950s.[10]

Women's music companies also proliferated after the success of Olivia. By the mid-1970s they were scattered throughout America and women's distribution networks were often able to get even establishment stores to set up women's music sections and FM stations to play women's music. The effect of women's music in rousing and consciousness-raising was tremendous, both in private homes and in public settings. At the end of many concerts in the 1970s the all-women audiences stood up spontaneously, locked arms, and sang the refrain, which they had learned through records, from the entertainer's finale—usually a number that was meant to inspire politically, such as Margie Adam's "We shall go forth,/ We shall not fail,/ Bringing together all we know." Through the self-affirming lyrics women were made to feel good about love between women. The music reached out even to lesbians who were not a part of the radical community, communicating to them that they were not alone and that lesbianism was a noble choice. As one woman who became a lesbian before the lesbian-feminist movement and was a teacher throughout the '70s in a conservative Central California community now recalls:

> When I first came out I used to think that a lot of lesbians were misfits, and my lover and I were just exceptions. But the music changed my perception—like Cris Williamson. Her songs talked about serious issues. I knew for the first time that lesbians didn't have to be flaky. And it drew me to concerts, which were a thrill. To be in Zellerbach Hall and know that everyone in that room would be spending the night with her female lover! And the variety of people! There was no way you could stereotype who lesbians were. It made me really feel for the first time that there were millions of us in this world. It was powerful.[11]

But despite all these successes, difficulties emerged quickly in lesbian-feminist music, just as they did throughout the utopian-seeking lesbian-feminist world. Olivia Records' problems were characteristic in the way their ideals could not finally withstand the crunch of reality. Olivia was conceived as one of the alternative economic institutions that would both produce a product that women would buy and employ women in a "nonoppressive situation." The women who established the company believed they could operate collectively because, as Ginny Berson, a key founder, observed simply, "We trust each other politically. . . . We are all lesbian-feminists who see our present and future intimately connected with the future of all women." They determined to pay women in their company "on the basis of need, instead of on the basis of male societal values, so that a book-keeper with six children to support will be paid more than a soloist musician who has just inherited six million dollars."[12] There were to be no stars and no flunkies, only "cultural workers."

Because lesbian-feminists were encouraged to believe that the singers were "cultural workers" and that Olivia itself belonged to "the people"—the lesbian-feminists who supported it—they felt that the company must always be sensitive to them in making policy. However, the community was diverse enough so that Olivia's policies were always bound to offend someone. When Olivia sponsored women-only events, they were attacked by some for excluding male children; when they opened their concerts to everyone, they were attacked for offending lesbian separatists. As Judy Dlugacz, a founding member and the present director recalls, "We couldn't win." The company found itself under the greatest attack in 1976 when it unwittingly hired a recording engineer who was a male-to-female transsexual "lesbian" and refused to fire her once her chromosomal sex was discovered. "A man is a man," the lesbian-feminist community cried, accusing Olivia of trying to put one over on them, since the news had leaked only by chance. Olivia so constantly felt the brunt of anger, Dlugacz recalls, that the company rethought many of its earlier idealistic policies: "It forced us to back away; we had to become more defended because we were getting crucified."[13] Olivia's original idealism and the hard lessons it eventually learned were repeated often in the lesbian-feminist community and caused a blurring of the community's utopian vision.

The women's presses that emerged in the early 1970s had a function similar to the music, speaking not only to women in organized lesbian-feminist communities in big cities, but also to women isolated in the hinterlands. The periodicals they produced were often modeled on the hippie underground newspapers of the 1960s, but the focus was almost exclusively on lesbian and feminist issues. The papers proliferated because lesbian-feminists believed they must control the words written about them, since they could not trust the establishment press. The periodicals, which were usually put together by a collective of women who had learned to print just so that they could contribute to the movement, were touchingly marked by their youth, energy, innocence, and good faith. Throughout the 1970s the publishers made every attempt to keep costs down so that poor women could buy their newspapers or magazines. *Lesbian Connections,* which began in 1974, was even circulated for free, until the mailing list surpassed five thousand and the publisher was forced to request a small payment "from those who can." Other periodicals also stated (under a usually very modest asking price of fifty cents or a dollar), "More if you can, less if you can't." Such idealism often meant that a periodical went under after a year or two of publication, though others soon sprang up to take its place.

Like the newspapers and magazines, lesbian-feminist book publishing houses were often run collectively, with decision making not in the power of a hierarchical head, but rather of a group of women. Their growth and distribution was aided by the formation of businesses such as Bookpeople, a distributor specializing in women's books, and women's bookstores that featured such work. Lesbian-feminist readers were wildly enthusiastic about the new literature.

What made those books so appealing was that the authors portrayed becoming a lesbian as connecting a woman with power. In exhilarating contrast to the 1950s novels where love between women led to defeat, in the novels of the 1970s it led to freedom. Many of them echoed the major interests of women's music: the characters not only created themselves anew through their love; they also created a woman's community and a woman's culture that mirrored the ideal images that lesbian-feminists were trying to construct in their own lives, a world where, as Elana Nachman described it in *Riverfinger Woman* (1974), "all women are strong and beautiful . . . [and] unafraid to give to each other, one to one, in specific ways, and more than one to one, in groups, in the new ways we are learning." [14] Also like the music, women's novels in the 1970s were crucial in promulgating the new values and in helping to affirm the lesbian-feminist in her conviction of good sense in having chosen to love women.

Although lesbian-feminist publishers aimed their work at a committed lesbian-feminist readership, their books and lesbian-feminism itself presented such an interesting new phenomenon that the attention of the establishment press was attracted. The *New York Times,* for example, ran a major feature article on lesbian-feminist publishing, "Creating a Woman's World," and the staid *Library Journal* presented a full-cover portrait of Jill Johnston with the title of her new book, *Lesbian Nation,* blazoned across the cover in 1973. Establishment publishers were now bidding for books that dealt with lesbianism, and they provided insurmountable competition for most of the small lesbian-feminist houses, which were plagued by financial and management inexpertise and could not hope to match the big commercial houses in terms of advances, advertising, and distribution. [15]

Because of such difficulties, most of the women's houses of the 1970s eventually failed. There were more lesbian novels published by women's publishers in the mid-'70s than at the end of the decade. Nevertheless, although most of the lesbian-feminist publishers did not have the business savvy to make sufficient profit from their enterprises, they were instrumental in encouraging lesbian-feminist authors to depict their lives as happy or hopeful and in pointing the way to commercial publishers, who saw that there was a market for literature about love between women that did not present the lovers in perpetual despair, speaking only in whispers and dwelling only in twilight. Because of the breakthoughs by the lesbian-feminist houses, by the end of the 1970s virtually every major New York house had

published at least one novel or nonfiction book that presented love
between women in a sympathetic and informed light. The counterculture publishers had contributed to a genuine metamorphosis among
mainstream publishers with regard to the lesbian image in print.

Taking Care of Our Own: The Body and the Soul

Many lesbian-feminists envisioned a rebirth of the great matriarchies that they were certain held sway in the eras of prehistory.
Toward a realization of the new day they insisted on the necessity of
bonding with other women to create not only a material society that
would function according to what they set forth as matriarchal ideals,
but especially a spiritual society. Their vision was of a totally self-
sufficient community where lesbian-feminists would be able to take
care of their own.

Their goal of self-sufficiency included all aspects of life, from food
co-ops, such as the New York Lesbian Food Conspiracy where food
was sold at cost, to women's credit unions, which were run by
members for members. Lesbian health care, especially good gynecological care, became available in various parts of the country through
free lesbian clinics. Since they felt they could not hope to get the
establishment courts to understand them and take their relationships
seriously, lesbian-feminists even explored the possibility of creating
their own quasi-legal system, like the independent Jewish courts of
the *shtetl* in pre-World War II Eastern Europe. One proposal suggested that they should make contracts and accept arbitration by a
"Lesbian Fairbody" made up of peers from the lesbian community
agreed upon by the litigants. "In this way," they said, "we legitima-
tize ourselves . . . [and] we elevate our own capabilities to determine
justice for ourselves above those of a male, patriarchal court system."[16]

In many lesbian-feminist communities, resource centers were established to provide programs in "self-development," job placement
services, twenty-four hour hotlines, and places for women to meet
one another and discuss political and personal problems in groups.
Lesbian archives were established in several big cities to preserve a
record of what was happening then and to try to gather a record of
what had happened in the past. Although most women in the lesbian-
feminist community were young, some had the imagination to envision themselves and their friends old, and they began to draw blue-

prints for lesbian old age homes, such as a 1975 proposal that suggested that lesbian-feminists start incorporated nonprofit organizations in their communities in which dues would be invested to buy and run large houses as retirement homes for those who had no money or no one to take care of them. Wealthier lesbian-feminists would be encouraged to leave their money to the organization in their wills. The blueprint even suggested the establishment of nationally coordinated pension plans for lesbian-feminists.[17]

To many, the care of the lesbian-feminist soul was as important as the care of the body. But lesbian-feminist spirituality had to have a political base as well as a mystical base. Lesbian-feminists were concerned that their spirituality not be simply inner-directed and a mere palliative, a revision of Christianity—from God the Father to God the Mother, with all the attendant problems intact. Their idealized models were those ancient cultures, whether in myth or reality, in which women held secular power along with religious power. Lesbian-feminist spirituality was to resurrect the matriarchy, which would eliminate all of the destructive institutions of patriarchy—economic, political, sexual, educational—and return society to the maternal principle in which life is nurtured. But how was women's spirituality to be translated into political action? Workshops at spirituality gatherings often struggled with the philosophy and logistics of reconstruction. Conferences were held with names such as Building the Lesbian Nation, which, the organizers hoped, would "contribute to the rebirth of the matriarchy." However, plans for the implementation of reconstruction were more vague than the conception. Some suggested that spirituality would automatically spark a mystical special fire such as had always smoldered quietly within women, which would work to help them transform themselves and society. More extreme elements wanted more concrete magic, believing that since women lacked both muscle and money, they would have to develop their psychic abilities in order to accomplish the task of obliterating the patriarchy through spells and curses.[18]

Lesbian-feminists who were involved in women's spirituality in the 1970s were enamored with the theories of Elizabeth Gould Davis, author of *The First Sex* (1971). Davis' work was a call to arms for the new matriarchy. She exhorted women to remember a glorious past and create an equally glorious future, and she gave them fuel for their ambitions and fantasies:

> So long has the myth of feminine inferiority prevailed that women themselves find it hard to believe that their own sex was once and for a

very long time the superior and dominant sex. In order to restore
women to their ancient dignity and pride, they must be taught their
own history, as the American blacks are being taught theirs.

   Recorded history starts with the patriarchal revolution. Let it continue with the matriarchal counterrevolution that is the only hope for
the survival of the human race.

Matriarchal religion, Davis insisted, had succeeded for ten thousand
years in keeping men's bellicosity and superior physical strength in
check and in giving women the peace and power to develop agricul-
ture, weaving, architecture, science, and art. Its resurrection would
restore such happy benefits. Davis' matriarchies became a dream
model for the woman-identified societies that spiritual lesbian-feminists wanted to have a hand in recreating.[19]

Matriarchal mythmaking, drawing on various cultures (American
Indians, witch religions, Greek depictions of Amazons) for images to
ignite the imagination, became a popular subject even in lesbian-
feminist comic books. Small groups sprang up, such as the Matriarchists, a New York organization that was committed to "working for a society which would be fashioned after the ancient matriarchies." They believed that their nurturing powers would eventually
transform society, ridding it of racism, classism, and imperialism.
When Merlin Stone, author of another influential 1970s work, *When
God Was a Woman,* suggested that in 8000 B.C. women were still
powerful and goddess worship was the reigning religion, many spiritual lesbian-feminists adopted a new system of calculating time,
rejecting the Christian calander and instead counting forward from
8000 B.C. (for example, 1978 became 9978).[20]

In contrast to the matriarchal longings of lesbian-feminists, lesbians who were part of the gay movement and felt the need for spiritual
sustenance helped to organize mixed gay groups within established
churches, such as Dignity in the Catholic Church, Integrity in the
Episcopal Church, and various small groups within Judaism; or they
joined the newly formed gay Metropolitan Community Church,
which was established by Troy Perry, a homosexual fundamentalist
minister. But lesbian-feminists felt that no matter what reforms were
attempted in traditional organized religions, the churches and syn-
agogues still perpetrated patriarchy. One lesbian-feminist tells of visiting a Metropolitan Community Church and feeling compelled to
walk out when a man shouted, "Let Jesus come into you!" She
remembers: "I stood up and said, 'How can you lesbians listen to
this?' "[21] The Metropolitan Community Church did nothing to sat-

isfy the "womanspirit" of radical lesbian-feminists who, craving the occult, the unconscious, the intuitive, employed tools such as tarot cards, astrology, I Ching, numerology, laying on of hands, herbalism, dreams and visions, and women-identified rituals.

The witch had particular appeal for lesbian-feminists as a spiritual-political model. As Jane Chambers suggested in her novel *Burning* (1978), the lesbian-feminist equivalent of former times was the witch who defied men, and lesbian-feminists of the 1970s identified with, and sometimes really believed they were, witches. Witches, lesbian-feminists said, had nothing to do with the evil that patriarchs attributed to them through fear of "wicce," which meant "women's wisdom." Witches stood for life-oriented, women-oriented values. In lesbian-feminist vision and mythmaking, the coven, a group of women who considered themselves witches, came to be associated with "the great peaceful matriarchies of the past" and with goddess worship, which was the core of paganism. Z. Budapest, the founder in 1971 of the first feminist coven (Susan B. Anthony Coven #1), explains of the rebirth of witches: "Women lost their power through religion. We were determined to gain it back again through a religion that had always belonged to women." They believed that witches of the past knew how to unlock the secrets of health and love, how to fight and how to live, and as lesbian-feminist witches of the 1970s, they sought to reclaim those powers through psychic experiences in the safety of feminist witch covens.[22]

Many lesbian-feminists sought a women's religion simply for spiritual sustenance, but others had more complex needs. A Syracuse, New York, woman explains that when she became a lesbian through her feminist interest in womanbonding, she felt she had to find some legitimacy for lesbianism in terms of a history that went back more than a few decades or a century. She was able to do this, she believes, through her romance with witches, Amazons, matriarchies, and the Mother Goddess. "I desperately needed to validate my roots," she says, "and that was the only extended history I could find." Lesbian-feminist spirituality served those multiple purposes of nurturing, providing a history, and furthering the cause of cultural feminism by proclaiming women's innate spiritual superiority.[23]

By constructing material and spiritual institutions to take care of their own, lesbian-feminists were convinced they could eradicate from their lives all the social corruption they attributed to patriarchy. Their ambitions were tremendous. Not only did they charge themselves with simultaneously creating a revolution and a counterculture, as

June Arnold observed in her lesbian-feminist novel *The Cook and the Carpenter,* but many of them, who had previously lived as heterosexuals, had to learn at the same time how to be personally independent as well as how to trust and love other women, both emotionally and sexually. They had given themselves a huge task that required of them nothing less than constant effort and vigilance.

Being "Politically Correct"

For many women the desire for a Lesbian Nation was founded on so intense an idealism and required such heroic measures that fanaticism became all but inevitable. In their youthful enthusiasm, lesbian-feminists believed that they had discovered not just a path but the only path. Thus despite the movement rhetoric about love for all women, those who, by some infraction of the code, were judged "politically incorrect" were given cold treatment by the community. Being politically correct ("p.c.") meant that one adhered to the various dogmas regarding dress; money; sexual behavior; language usage; class, race, food, and ecology consciousness; political activity; and so forth. The values, once again, were not unlike those of the hippie counterculture and the New Left, but filtered always through a radical feminist awareness.

The concept of nonhierarchy became an inflexible dogma. Collective decision making was encouraged, as was communal living, in which privileges and responsibilities were to be shared equally. There were to be no leaders. When the mass media focused attention on one woman, the group often became concerned about "star tripping" and support for her sometimes fell away; this happened to Rita Mae Brown, who had been a great hero in the lesbian-feminist community before her popular success, but became the target of strong criticism after. It was even speculated that star tripping was the reason for the failure of ancient matriarchies, in which the queens eventually took too much power for themselves. The modern Lesbian Nation was determined not to repeat such a mistake.[24]

There were rules for everything, even acceptable dress. Makeup, skirts, high heels, or any other vestiges of the "female slave mentality" would arouse suspicion in the community and were shunned. The uniform was usually jeans and natural fiber shirts. Expensive clothing suggested conspicuous consumption and was inappropriate in a community where downward mobility was "p.c." "Fancy threads" meant thrift shop elegance: vests, ties, fedoras or berets, pinstripes and baggy flannels.[25] Although butch-and-femme were "p.i.," in the lesbian-feminist community everyone looked butch. But the goal was to appear strong and self-sufficient, rather than masculine: no matriarchy could function if its inhabitants had to run or fight in high heels and tight skirts.

There was eventually some bitter skepticism and rebellion against p.c. dogma in the lesbian-feminist community, particularly among women who were stung by its carping criticism. Nan, who lived in a lesbian-feminist community in upstate New York, remembers that aspects of radical life were very healthy for her: "I really felt I was developing and experiencing myself for the first time as an adult—picking up on the bold, independent personality I'd dropped when I was twelve years old." But she came finally to reject the regimentation and constant demands:

> You had to live in a certain kind of place, have certain bumper stickers, be anti-male and a separatist. I liked to throw dinner parties with the accoutrements I'd had left over from my marriage—linens, dishes, nice pieces of art and collectible items. The women in my community made me know it didn't fit with a classless society. And I was too feminine for them because I liked to wear period clothes, Victorian and 1920s outfits—go out in drag and have a lot of fun with it—instead of jeans all the time. They decided I was an enemy of the people. I decided they were "lavnecks" [lavender rednecks].[26]

She chose to drop out of the movement rather than tolerate perpetual scrutiny.

Even sex was scrutinized for political correctness. Lesbian-feminists pointed out that men ruined heterosexual sex by objectifying women and being goal-oriented. As one writer complained in a 1975 essay, "Nobody Needs to Get Fucked," she, like most lesbians-feminists, had learned her sexuality from "The Man" and thus thought in terms of couples and of orgasms as the main goal of sex. But lesbian-feminists had to unlearn such values, she proclaimed, and construct their own way of loving that would be different:

> Lesbianism is, among other things, touching other women—through dancing, playing soccer, hugging, holding hands, kissing. . . . [Lesbians need to] free the libido from the tyranny of orgasm-seeking. Sometimes hugging is nicer.
>
> If we are to learn our own sexual natures we have to get rid of the male-model of penetration and orgasm as the culmination of love-making.

> Holding hands is love-making.
> Touching lips is love-making.
> Rubbing breasts is love-making.
> Locking souls with women by looking deep in their eyes is love-making.

Mutual sensuality became more politically correct than genital sexuality, which might too easily imitate the exploitative aspects of heterosexual sex.[27] For some lesbian-feminists, love between women was not very different, despite the space of a hundred years and at least two "sexual revolutions," from that of their "romantic friend" predecessors.

Because butches seemed to imitate men, they and their sexuality were considered politically incorrect. Lesbian-feminists protested that the butch image was created by males so that "the female homosexual was groomed to appear as a burlesque of licentious, slightly cretinous, ersatz men" and that some lesbians had accepted that image because they had been saturated with it and believed it was the only way to feel authentic. But lesbian-feminism would rectify that delusion. Both partners in a sexual relationship would take turns being soft and strong, since both qualities were female. There were to be no more " 'male-female' shit-games. It's all feminine because we are," they insisted.[28]

Lesbian-feminists were sometimes revolted at signs of what they regarded as excessive sexuality among a few lesbians, and they took a moralistic, Carrie Nation-like stance. When *Albatross,* a lesbian satire magazine, dared to print some explicitly sexual words, the lesbian-feminist editor of another publication wrote *Albatross* an outraged letter canceling their exchange subscription agreement:

> Terms such as "cunt" and "pussy" degrade and devalue women's sexuality; I can't imagine why use them. Likewise, phrases such as "love at first lick" are not only repulsive aesthetically but also carry an implication that lesbian sexuality is psychiatric, rather than the warm, close, emotional, spiritual expression we know it to be.[29]

They would tolerate nothing that resembled the raw sexuality of male eroticism.

The lesbian-feminists' rejection of monogamy (a permanent commitment to only one woman) was in seeming opposition to their deemphasis on sex. But the contradiction was more apparent than real. The idealization of nonmonogamy did not originate with the lesbian-feminist community. Early utopias, such as John Noyes' Oneida

Community, which began in the 1840s, encouraged nonmonogamy in the belief that the "one love" concept was born of selfishness and jealousy. Noyes' followers practiced "complex marriage," in which everyone in the community had sexual access to everyone else. Hippie communal life in the 1960s was frequently modeled on that ideal. In the 1970s other progressive heterosexuals were questioning too close an adherence to monogamy, preferring "open marriage," in which two people in a primary relationship gave permission to each other to be free to explore the various and separate paths down which their feelings led them. The wisdom of the day was not only that it was unhealthy for two people to own each other, but also that in a quickly evolving world, where personalities evolved quickly as well, it was unrealistic and unloving to force two people to be everything to each other. To sanction monogamy, the lesbian-feminists believed, could only bring grief to them as it had to heterosexuals.

Lesbian-feminists were also convinced that monogamy was bad not because it inhibited wild sexual exploration, but rather because it smacked too much of patriarchal capitalism and imperialism. It was men's way of keeping women enslaved. People are not things to own, lesbian-feminists said. No lesbian should want to have the right to imprison another human being emotionally or sexually. The most popular lesbian-feminist novels, such as Rita Mae Brown's *Rubyfruit Jungle* (1973) and June Arnold's *Sister Gin* (1975), reflected the community's distrust of monogamy, which the authors presented as inhibiting a free exploration of self and detracting from one's commitment to the lesbian-feminist community, since it led to nesting rather than involvement in political work. Some lesbian-feminists (particularly those in the larger cities) even believed it a duty to "Smash Monogamy," as their buttons proclaimed, sporting a triple woman's symbol (♀ ♀ ♀), and rejecting the notion of the lesbian couple (♀ ♀).

Although most lesbians had been conditioned to monogamy by the parent culture and had sought it in their own lives with varying degrees of success, the big city radical lesbian-feminist community and the precedence of heterosexual rebels now provided support to explore new ways. "What could be more natural," they asked, "than surrounding oneself with a group of loving individuals, carefully chosen for their congeniality?" or "Why can't one of the dyad bring in another person, add this person to the couple, and love this person as well as the other partner? Why can't the other person do the same if she is so inclined?" "Forever" and "only you," the staple words of lovers' talk, came to be seen as limiting and even corrupt terms that

needed to be excised from the lesbian-feminist vocabulary. "Monogamy" came to be jeeringly called "monotony." [30]

Some radical communities even put pressure on lesbians to break
out of the dyad pattern of relationships. Those who were not at ease
with changing became convinced that it was their own "hang-up,"
which they had to get over. As one woman confessed in the 1970s,
"It's hard for me to think of Sheila relating to other people, but that's
a distress born of my insecurities that I can counsel on to get rid of,
and I do." Another woman now wrily remembers the pressure she
felt to be nonmonogamous because monogamy was "part of the male
power structure we didn't want to buy into." But she says it led to
confusion and hard feelings and was eventually responsible for destroying a long-term relationship. Her lover, Marsha, would sleep
with another woman on Sundays and Thursdays. Once she and
Marsha had sex with two other couples. "It was like our political
duty to do this," she says. "We wanted to create a new society, to
carve out a niche in history, though I don't think anybody was very
comfortable with it—and it just didn't work." [31] The efforts required
to adjust to nonmonogamy were heroic, since even radical lesbian-
feminists had been socialized by a monogamous parent culture. Although their belief was born of idealism, few women could endure it
for long, and by the 1980s nonmonogamy became passé in most
lesbian-feminist communities.

But the sexual issue that tyrannized the most over lesbian-feminists
who wanted to be politically correct in the 1970s was bisexuality.
Ironically, at a time when bisexuality became quite acceptable to
liberals, it became unacceptable among lesbian-feminists. Jill Johnston
called it a "fearful compromise" because half the bisexual woman's
actions were "a continued service to the oppressor." Women who
were bisexual were accused of "ripping off" lesbians—getting energy
from them so that they could "take it back to a man." Bisexual
women were the worst traitors to the cause, lesbian-feminists believed, because they knew they were capable of loving women and
yet they allowed themselves to become involved with men and neglected their duty to help build the Lesbian Nation. Bisexuals were
especially suspect because they received all the heterosexual privileges
—such as financial and social benefits—whenever they chose to act
heterosexually. Although lesbian-feminists recognized that human
nature was indeed bisexual, they pointed out that the revolution had
not yet reached its goals and women who practiced bisexuality were
"simply leading highly privileged lives that . . . undermine the fem-

inist struggle." It was suggested that, at the very least, those bisexuals who could not ignore their heterosexual drives should put the bulk of their energies into the political and social struggles around lesbian-feminism and keep secret from the outside world their straight side so that they would not be tempted to fall back on their heterosexual privileges.[32]

Lesbian Nation of the 1970s was far-flung across the country, yet the abundant literature that reached everywhere and the influence of hippie and Left values guaranteed a certain amount of conformity in doctrine, whether among lesbian-feminists in Georgia, Boston, Idaho, or California. But the list of what was politically correct and politically incorrect grew as the decade progressed. The most committed lesbian-feminists preferred to believe that there was nationwide unity and general consensus with regard to their principles. That belief seemed to mandate an inflexible dogma that was often violated by human diversity among them and necessarily led to frequent unhappy conflicts.

Factions and Battles

The uncompromising stance and rhetoric of rage that many women adopted in the movement was bound to bring about bitter feelings and factionalism. Perhaps rage was an inextricable part of lesbian-feminism, because once these women analyzed the female's position in society they realized they had much to be furious about. But their anger was sometimes manifested as a horizontal hostility in which members of the community were constantly attacking other members, either because they had strayed from some politically correct behavior or because the diversity within the growing groups was not sufficiently recognized to appease everyone. As the decade progressed, the core groups tended to get smaller as factions multiplied and splintered and become more and more insistent in their demand to be heard or in their conviction that they alone were the true lesbian-feminists. Attacks were often brutal, combining what one victim described as "the language of the revolution [with] the procedure of the inquisition."[33]

Like the Left, lesbian-feminists believed that the revolution meant change—women changing themselves as well as changing the world. Criticism and self-criticism were thus crucial in order to perfect themselves in their quest for utopia. It was to the credit of lesbian-feminists that they wanted to provide a platform for criticism in the name of improvement, but criticism often became vituperation. This was particularly true when the community opened itself to criticism from all minority voices. Old lesbian-feminists as well as teenage lesbian-feminists complained that they were being patronized; lesbian separatists as well as lesbians of color complained that they were being compromised; radical socialist lesbian-feminists complained that they were being co-opted; fat lesbian-feminists, working class lesbian-feminists, disabled lesbian-feminists, all complained that they were being oppressed by their sister lesbian-feminists.

Women felt freer to complain within the lesbian-feminist community than in the more oppressive heterosexual world, where their mistreatment was by far worse. Not only did community doctrine mandate listening to criticism by all members, but also they felt the community was or should be family and they were claiming their rightful place in their family. But the word "oppression" was then tossed around so loosely as an accusation that it came to be devalued. Criticism too often became crippling. It seemed that every move one made was sure to be found politically incorrect by a dozen others. While there were frequent attempts to reconcile differences—such as the establishment in Los Angeles of an Intergroup Council of lesbian-feminists after a pitched battle took place among various factions—vast amounts of energy were wasted on conflicts.[34]

Although most lesbian-feminists were middle class by virtue of their education, which tended to be much higher than that of women in the general populace, class became a major divisive issue among them. As radicals, lesbian-feminists generally shared the intellectual Left's romance with the working class. Women who had the skills to make a living at nontraditional jobs—carpenters, house painters, welders—were far more politically correct than professionals, who were seen as having to compromise themselves in the system in order to advance. A mystique developed that could be used as a guilt-inducing bludgeon on those who had been raised in the middle class.

Class was determined not by the usual American indicators such as schooling or even present salary. "You can have a college education, but you don't stop being working class," "working-class" women (many of whom had been to college) attested with pride. They observed that women who tried to stop being working class and sought upward mobility risked oppressing women who could not be anything other than working class. As one lesbian-feminist writer lamented about her earlier behavior when she left the working class into which she was born, "The most oppressive attitude I had accepted was that because I had become middle class, worked my way 'up,' I was better than other working-class women who were still down there." The working class was seen as superior to the middle class, at least partly by virtue of its poverty, which attested to its moral innocence in a corrupt society. Lesbian-feminists who had been raised in the middle class and had been willing or unwilling beneficiaries of their fathers' corruption were regarded among "working-class" lesbian-feminists in the same way that light-skinned blacks were during the era of black militancy: their past was not quite honorable.[35]

Middle-class lesbian-feminists were thus constantly on the defensive. "You are an enemy of lower-class women," they were reminded early in the movement, "if you continue destructive behavior based on your sense of middle-class superiority." "Destructive behavior" might even consist of using big words that would show off a superior education. When one lesbian-feminist writer admitted her pleasure in "the art of conversation," she felt she must hasten to add, "Lest you think I'm suspect, my father was a barber, my mother a housewife, and I only pay $1.00 for my food stamps."[36] Since they generally adhered to radical ideas about the corruption of hierarchy, many "middle-class" lesbian-feminists acquiesced to the burden of guilt and felt they had to drop out of the middle class. They became *nouveau pauvre* or at least downwardly mobile.

Another major source of conflict within the movement came from those who wanted to push radicalism even further than other lesbian-feminists were prepared to go. Lesbian separatists were at the forefront of this battle. Borrowing from the example of black separatists who believed that blacks were impeded by any relationship with whites—even the most liberal and beneficent-seeming—lesbian separatists argued that Lesbian Nation would never be established unless lesbian-feminists broke away not only from men but from all heterosexual women as well. They believed that now, while they awaited the millennium when a true Lesbian Nation would be born, they must establish outposts to the future, tribal groupings of a fugitive Lesbian Nation, and not vitiate their energies. in trying to reform the present hopeless structure of patriarchy. They put out a call to all lesbian-feminists to "explore with fact and imagination our dyke/amazon culture of the past, before there were parasitic male mutants, and to work toward our dyke/amazon culture of the future, when only xx's exist." They had blind faith that their withdrawal from heterosexuals in itself would hasten the dissolution of the patriarchy and the advent of a utopian dyke/amazon world.[37]

Although many lesbian separatists had come to lesbianism through feminism, they quickly dissociated themselves from the feminist movement, which was involved in issues the separatists believed to be irrelevant, such as abortion, child care, and shelters for battered wives. In impassioned rhetoric they exhorted other lesbians:

> Quit begging our straight sisters to let us be their niggers in the movement, and stop taking all the insults and shit work the pussy cats and their toms can heap on us. If we can step forward, we should do so with the intention of working for *our own cause*. Either way, we Lesbians are going to get it right between the legs in a sex war unless we realize soon the folly of our Pollyanna relations with straight sisters and gay brothers and especially Big Brothers.

The separatists felt they had to be perpetually alert to other lesbian-feminists' confused priorities and commitments, which would vitiate their program. They wanted to impose a purity of vision on the community by refusing energy not only to straight women, but even to lesbians who befriended straight women. Lesbians' needs had to come first, they insisted, even if it meant giving up relations with heterosexual relatives that one might love. To avoid psychic contamination the separatists demanded women–only spaces, both at home and when they went into the community for social or political events.[38]

Some lesbian separatists formed living and working collectives in the cities. But since it was harder to be purist in their practices if they lived in a city, many separatists established communal farms and became, as one of their 1970s journals called them, country women. The country was, anyway, preferable to city living, they said, because the city was a man-made world where lesbians' energy was diverted in a struggle to survive and live true to their principles. There were even attempts to establish land trusts that would be available to all women "at all times, forever," and there was a "women's land circuit," which consisted of individual women-owned farms where lesbians could drop by to work and stay for days or months or even years.

Their utopian quests were reflected in women's science fiction novels written in the 1970s in which the characters usually took refuge in distant countrysides, away from the evils wrought by men, who had mucked up most of the world so it could not be lived in anymore. In Sally Gearhart's *The Wanderground,* women are able to wander the grounds in the country under the protection of nature, unlike in the city, where they are men's prey. In Rochelle Singer's *The Demeter Flower,* nature obliges the women by wiping out the civilization of men "because it threatened her and her children" and women can start from scratch.[39]

But starting from scratch in real life was not easy. Most of the separatists had been city women without even the basic country survival skills such as splitting wood, plumbing, or planting. They had to learn quickly, often with no help. Their problems could be intensified by the isolation of their chosen situation. They had no outside input to aid them in mediating conflicts that arose within the commune. Rough spots in relationships were not smoothed over by consanguinity or legal ties as in a heterosexual family, and a bad quarrel could easily break up a collective. Although the women often made noble efforts, most of the country communes that were established in the 1970s died before the next decade.[40]

Perhaps some lesbian separatist communes did not enjoy longevity for the same reasons that the many hippie communes which preceded them were not long-lived: in an isolated situation, where none of the measuring sticks and brakes of the outside world had relevance, listlessness and anomie set in. As they awaited the birth of Lesbian Nation, the members found themselves becoming diverted from their high purpose, and the realization that utopia was not within easy grasp became disillusioning and frightening. As Suzanne remembers her experience on a commune outside of Plymouth, Massachusetts, in the mid-1970s:

> Some women got a hundred acres in the country with a house and some small buildings, and about twelve of us started living on the land. It was great in the beginning, but after a while I felt I was getting too far out. We were all doing hallucinogens and coke. I had no idea where people got the money, but the drugs were always there. No one had jobs. We just did odd jobs once in a while. We just worked to get by. We were doing vision quests (spiritual seeking), being in touch with nature. My cat was a psychic traveller. We grew fat. I finally got a dog just to keep me grounded. Then I left.[41]

But although like Suzanne many women left the communes and separatism with some disillusionment, they often recognized that they had gained from the experience. Separatism allowed them to immerse themselves in women's culture in a way that for many of them resulted in "an overwhelming positive sense of congruency" that was "a powerful healing force," as one 1970s separatist describes it. They were not forced to feel split and disoriented by working in the heterosexual world by day and the lesbian-feminist world by night, as many women were. Separatism had value, too, in that it sent a dramatic message to heterosexual feminists and homosexual men who cared to listen that lesbians believed that their interests were being overlooked in the feminist and gay movements and that they had some grievances that needed heeding before they were willing to become political allies. For some women, separatism became a political tool, a dynamic strategy that they could move in and out of whenever they felt their interests were being ignored in the larger movement or they needed more space to develop their insights.[42] Separatism as a permanent way of life, however, as most of the separatists discovered, was easier in science fiction than in reality.

The grievances lesbian separatists had toward the larger movements were analogous to the grievances lesbians of color had toward white lesbian-feminists. Although radical doctrine enthusiastically encouraged the inclusion of lesbians of color in the lesbian-feminist movement, few participated. They too felt that their interests had been overlooked and it would not be to their advantage to try to integrate into a predominantly white movement.

Racial and ethnic minority homosexuals saw that lesbians and gay men were scorned in their parent communities, because at the height of civil rights movements it seemed that suddenly homosexuals had popped up and were trying to steal the minorities' thunder by calling themselves a "minority." But even before that source of conflict, homosexuals were generally more outcast in those communities than in many white communities, because the minority racial and ethnic communities tended to be working class and particularly rigid about machismo and sexuality. One black writer attributes homophobia among blacks to the black movement's attempt to offset the myth of the black matriarchy by enhancing the image of black manhood. She observes, "Naturally the woman-identified-woman, the black lesbian, was a threat not only to the projection of black male macho, but a sexual threat, too—the utmost danger to the black man's institutionally designated role as 'King of Lovers.' " While black women on the whole may have found more freedom than white women to participate in sex, such freedom was limited to heterosexual sex.[43] The black lesbian was safest in the closet. Other racial and ethnic minorities shared that antipathy toward lesbianism. Perhaps lesbianism was in such disfavor among minorities because on American ground they had often fought to preserve their own culture, which might dictate that women be unquestioningly obedient, and lesbianism is the epitome of sexual and social disobedience.

To compound the problem, socially aware racial and ethnic minority lesbians frequently felt that at a time when their people were finally organizing to demand rights, it was their inescapable duty to give their allegiance to their parent culture. They believed they needed to fight side by side with heterosexual men and women of their group in order to alleviate the kind of discrimination and oppression they had experienced even before they became lesbians. To them their parent culture seemed to have the greater need, and they felt they could not fight in two armies. Many believed that compared with the problems of their ethnic and racial groups, lesbians' and women's problems were insignificant. "We are fighting for survival—jobs, housing, education, and most importantly struggling for a sense of dignity in a country dominated by whites," one Puerto Rican woman wrote after resigning her brief membership in a group called Lesbian Feminist Liberation: "Our problems are immediate, not long range. We as women in the [ethnic] community in order to be effective must accept their priorities as our own. We must put aside our lesbian-feminist perspectives and work within the framework that exists." As minority members in a racist society, they also believed that there was a danger in attributing patriarchal corruption to biological maleness. Any kind of argument based on biological determinism was bad, they recognized, since it had often been used by racists to "prove" the inferiority of minorities. They felt greater solidarity with "progressive" minority men than with white lesbian-feminists who, it seemed to them, were denying that race could be as much a source of women's oppression as sex.[44]

Although the lesbian-feminist community tried to welcome them, even those minority lesbians who were not involved in civil rights struggles often felt alienated from lesbian-feminism. They believed that in a pinch it was their parent community that they would have to rely on for survival. They continued to live lives not significantly different from those of lesbians in earlier eras, frequently in butch/femme role relationships or without social contacts among other women who loved women. For them there was nothing relevant or comfortable in lesbian-feminist life. Leslie, a Native American woman who had had an eighteen-year relationship with a black woman, a mother of two children, explains that throughout the 1970s: "Because of the children we didn't have any lesbian friends. We didn't want the kids to have to suffer in school. And we didn't have anything in common with the lesbian community around here anyway. I didn't want to go in the street and hold up signs and march in parades." They socialized with other minority people who were heterosexual. Lesbian-feminism seemed like a strange and distant world to them.[45]

The few minority women who became part of visible lesbian-feminist life in the 1970s were usually able to do so only at the cost of alienation from their ethnic communities. Often they were women who had a love relationship with a white woman and maintained few ties back in the ghetto. But the discomfort of some minority women who tried to work in the predominantly white lesbian-feminist movement of the early 1970s is captured in black lesbian writer Pat Parker's poem "Have You Ever Tried to Hide?," in which she observes that a white lesbian may have a smaller foot than a white man, "but it's still on my neck."[46] Maintaining the rhetoric and militancy of the ethnic movements of the preceding years, it was not easy for minority lesbians to be convinced that white lesbian-feminists really could reverse the racism implanted in them by their parent culture. Midway through the 1970s, when more minority women began to identify themselves as lesbian-feminists, they aligned themselves with those who shared their backgrounds, not trusting white lesbian-feminists to be sensitive to the special problems of what came to be called in the 1970s Third World lesbians.

Black lesbians were the first to organize as lesbians and feminists along racial lines. They were active in the formation of the National Black Feminist Organization in 1974, and in 1978 they formed a National Coalition of Black Lesbians and Gay Men. They also established in 1978 *Azalea: A Magazine by Third World Lesbians,* which had in its beginning little political awareness but recognized that it was important to create unity with other women who were both lesbian and Third World. Out of similar convictions some Hispanic, Native American, and Asian lesbians eventually formed lesbians of color organizations, published their own journals such as *Vagina,* and even established their own Third World softball teams such as Oakland's Gente. Multicultural alliances that excluded whites seemed beneficial because the various Third World lesbians felt they all shared the experiences of racism in a white society and white women needed to deal with their racism on their own. As a Latina Gente member expressed it:

> There's gotta be some separation some place to really get our own shit together. A white woman can sit down and talk to a white woman more than I can about what it feels like to be a white woman and have racist feelings about black people or Asian people or Indian people. I don't have the time or the inclination to discuss these sorts of things with a white woman, but I can sit down and talk to somebody black about what it feels like to be oppressed. Some positive things can come out of that. [47]

Minorities were critical of white lesbian-feminists especially because they felt that while denying their racism those women acted on racist assumptions. As Chicana author Cherrie Moraga wrote, Third World lesbians became fed up with white lesbian-feminist organizations that would claim: "Well, we're open to *all* women. Why don't [lesbians of color] come?" but would refuse to examine how the very nature and structure of the group took for granted race and class. The criticism was puzzling to white lesbian-feminists who had been lamenting that the great majority of the movement was composed of white, educated women of middle-class backgrounds. They really did want to broaden the base of their group by attracting lower-income and Third World women, but they sincerely did not know how, outside of welcomes and appearing receptive. As radical as they were, they suffered from the liberal's basic ineptness in dealing with other classes and races. In their frustration they sometimes came to suspect that they were being emotionally blackmailed by lesbians of color:

> All the women were white on the commune where I lived except for Cara. She could be very violent and schizo. Sometimes she would beat the women up. We wanted to include her, but we didn't know how to deal with the race issue. We just weren't experienced enough to separate her violence out from her color. And she would use that against us, accusing us of racism—like when she stole one of our cars and drove it into the river and said we were racist just because we were angry at her. [48]

Needless to say, such paralyzing guilt, confusion, and ambivalence did little to patch the rifts between white lesbian-feminists and lesbians of color.

The women-identified-women who hoped to create Lesbian Nation in the 1970s failed in their main goal. But it was a goal born of excessive idealism as well as excessive youth and was probably un-realizable without the help of a cataclysmic disaster that would some-how render the earth all xx, as the seeker after the dyke/amazon world of the future had prayed. Their failure was inevitable not only because of their unrealistic notions, but also because, like most true believers, they had little capacity to compromise their individual visions. Whenever one set of visions clashed with another in their communities, tremendous and exhausting upheavals occurred.

But despite those clashes, the successes of the lesbian-feminists of the 1970s must not be ignored. They were able to take messages from both the women's movement and the gay movement and weave them into a coherent theory of lesbian-feminism. They identified the wom-en's movement as homophobic and the gay movement as sexist, and they fought against both. In the process they not only forced those movements to open up to lesbian and feminist ideas, but they also established their own movement that created a unique "women's culture" in music, spirituality, and literature that made at least a small dent in mainstream culture.

However, their accomplishment was less in realizing their vision than in raising consciousness, particularly among more moderate lesbians who sometimes used them as a measuring stick. If the radical lesbian-feminists could go so far, be so bold and outrageous, then surely the moderates could be a little braver than they had been. As one California woman now remembers:

> I was not a conscious participant in the lesbian-feminist community, but I was eventually a grateful beneficiary. I'm still not an activist, though I acknowledge a debt to women who spoke out for and to people like me, and reminded us that there is no reason to go on fearing ourselves because other people fear us out of ignorance. . . . Would I have even "come out" without all their clamor? Hard to say. But I believe I owe a lot to those loud-mouthed lesbian-feminists who re-fused to swallow all the crap I swallowed about us.[49]

The lesbian-feminist contribution to lessening lesbian guilt and kin-dling self-acceptance—even among women who perceived them-selves as in no way radical—was considerable.

Radical lesbian-feminists had one other function as well. They played a kind of "bad cop" in a social drama, which then permitted more moderate activist lesbians to play the "good cop." It became hardly threatening for lesbians who were willing to work within society to be asking for rights such as institutional policies of nondiscrimination on the basis of sexual orientation. Such requests could be seen as entirely reasonable compared to radical lesbian-feminist demands for a separate society. Functioning as foils, lesbian-feminists made agitation for simple justice (which was considered outrageously radical in other times) seem tame. Through their very extremism— which allowed other homosexual activists to appear far less extreme —they made a vital contribution to the spread of gay and lesbian rights.

10

Lesbian Sex Wars in the 1980s

I do not know any feminist worthy of that name who, if
forced to choose between freedom and sex, would choose sex.
                                                    —*Ti-Grace Atkinson,*
                                    "Why I Am Against S/M Liberation," 1982

Could it be that the real fear of those who want to use sexual
repression to fuel the Women's Movement is that we might
actually make so much progress that (gasp!) we would not go
to meetings at all? I guess some people would just be happier
in a world where there's never any time for romantic picnics
or week-long orgies. They'd rather caucus than copulate or
cunnilingicise. Un-fuck them, I say. They've already wished
that on themselves anyway.
                    —*Pat Califia, introduction to* The Leading Edge:
                    An Anthology of Lesbian Sexual Fiction, *1987*

The French author Colette, who wrote about lesbianism from her
firsthand experiences, observed about love between women:

> In living amorously together, two women may eventually discover
> that their mutual attraction is not basically sensual. . . . What woman
> would not blush to seek out her *amie* only for sensual pleasure? In no
> way is it passion that fosters the devotion of two women, but rather a
> feeling of kinship.[1]

The sense of her 1930 observation was generally not contradicted by
women who lived as lesbians in the 1970s. This is at first glance
curious, since America was in the throes of sexual exploration during
that decade. Thousands of X-rated movie houses and "adult" bookstores emerged across the country. Gay men were graphically describing in newspaper personal ads what they wanted in a sex partner.
Heterosexual females were in hot pursuit of the multiple orgasm.
Heterosexual men and women were avidly reading books such as

Alex Comfort's *The Joy of Sex* (1972) that would make them sexual gourmets, or Helen Kaplan's *The New Sex Therapy* (1974) that would help them overcome whatever obstacles stood in the way of their becoming sexual gourmets. As historians John D'Emilio and Estelle Freedman observe, America in the 1970s had become "the Sexualized Society."[2]

But such "sexualization" passed most lesbians by. Despite the relish of pornographers in depicting lesbianism as merely a sexual phenomenon, it has seldom been just that, and lesbian-feminism, which dominated the visible lesbian community in the '70s, rendered it less so than ever. Because most lesbians had been socialized first and foremost as female, they were no more able than most heterosexual women in the past to form relationships primarily on the basis of sexual lust. And unlike heterosexual women in the 1970s, lesbians generally did not have partners who would prod them on to greater sexual looseness. Thus, in the midst of rampant sexuality among heterosexuals and homosexual men, lesbians in the 1970s either felt the new "sexualization" to be irrelevant to their old life styles or—as lesbian-feminists—were too busy designing the Lesbian Nation to turn their attention to what they generally regarded as the triviality of sex.

Not only were lesbians outside of committed relationships far less sexual than gay male and heterosexual singles, but even within long-term relationships they tended to be much less sexual, as statistics gathered during the 1970s for a major study of both heterosexual and homosexual American couples confirmed. For example, only one-third of the lesbian couples in relationships of at least two years had sex once a week or more (compared to two-thirds of their heterosexual counterparts), and almost half the lesbians in long-term relationships (ten years +) had sex less than once a month (compared to only 15 percent of their heterosexual counterparts).[3]

One explanation for the relative infrequency of lesbian sex may simply be physiological. Because there is no visible erection that must be dealt with between two women, affectionate holding or petting is easily substituted for more demanding sexual performance once the first heat of passion has subsided. But the relative paucity of sex between lesbians is certainly aggravated by socialization. Since both individuals in the couple have been raised as female, there is no trained sexual initiator who will *automatically* make the first move over a period of time. Often each woman waits upon the other to initiate. Female sexuality has been socially constructed around reacting rather than acting, and lesbians as women have generally not been able to transcend with ease what they have been taught.

Lesbian sexuality within committed relationships is further complicated because, according to various psychological studies, relationships between women are stronger when background, status, and commitment are approximately equal between them. When one partner feels that her lover holds more power, her capacity for intimacy is diminished. Yet sexual desire requires some kind of "barrier"— some taboo, tension, thrill of conquest, or disequilibrium. A difficulty is created because two women who are "well suited" to each other tend to merge in an intimate relationship; barriers that are often present between men and women break down between two women. While such fusion promotes affection, it diminishes sexual excitement. It leads to what came to be called in the 1980s "lesbian bed death"—the oft-observed phenomenon of the disappearance of sex in ongoing lesbian relationships.[4]

Not all lesbians have been disturbed by the fact that lesbians tend to have less sex than heterosexuals or gay men. Lesbians who are cultural feminists and believe that women's culture and values are different from and better than those of males usually minimize the importance of sex in their realtionships with the conviction that men have exaggerated its importance. Their views are not unlike those of romantic friends of bygone eras. Pam, who has been a lesbian for twenty-three years, says "sex doesn't have much to do with it." She explains that "the emphasis in lesbianism is being in a mutually nurturing relationship that permits both of you to be the best you can be, functioning comfortably, accepting success." Its advantage over heterosexuality is that a woman can work up to her potential as a human being instead of concerning herself only with her husband's potential and success. "I have a good sexual relationship with Joan," she says, "but it's definitely not the glue that keeps it together."[5]

Cultural feminists insist that women's capacity for shared intimacy is preferable to the disequilibrium that men contribute to relationships, which may perhaps stimulate sexual excitement but also brings intolerable problems in its wake. Lesbians who are cultural feminists may be saddened by the quicker diminution of passion in their intimacies, but they would be leary of any sexual exploration that seemed to emulate male sexuality, even if its putative goal were to improve lesbian relationships. In the lesbian community, the 1970s was dominated by cultural feminists—especially lesbian-feminists and middle-class lesbians—who generally shared a mistrust of masculine/feminine roles, sexual "violence" (whether real or in play), and pornography, which they saw as a manifestation of the misguided male sex drive.

But by the 1980s the views of these cultural feminists were being called into question by a small group of women—some who emerged out of lesbian-feminism, others who had kept apart from the movement because they felt it denigrated the sexual expressions that were important to them. They believed that it was time that lesbians took up arms to fight the most neglected battle for equality. They were determined to overcome the sexual repression suffered by lesbians, who had been left out of the socially sanctioned pursuit of sexual pleasure in the 1970s. They wanted to find ways for lesbians to claim their sexual selves, just as heterosexuals and gay men had been doing. To that end they were willing to borrow those groups' time-tested techniques such as the use of pornography and sexual role playing to stimulate sexual appetite.

Their goals were twofold, addressing lesbian sexuality in terms of both long-term and more casual relationships. They wanted to increase the duration and intensity of lesbian sexual pleasure, and they wanted to liberate lesbians from the sexual limitations that had been imposed on them as females. Such limitations, they felt, hindered women from asserting a boldness that was necessary for true social equality. The battle lines were thus drawn between lesbian cultural feminists, who believed it necessary to fight against what they saw as the harmful objectification of women through male sexual habits, and lesbian sexual radicals, who believed that such "habits" had too long been a male prerogative and needed to be adopted by lesbians for their own personal and social welfare. These tremendously divergent views led to still another internecine war within the lesbian community.

Lesbian Sex and the Cultural Feminists

Lesbians who were cultural feminists were very uncomfortable with the "sexualization" of America in the 1970s, because they believed that it served men's cruder appetites and put pressure on women to behave in ways that were not intrinsic to them. When the Supreme Court declared in 1970 that not only was pornography not harmful and not a factor in the cause of crime but was actually beneficial because it served to educate and release inhibitions, cultural feminists drew the first of their battle lines. They maintained that the "liberalism" of supporters of pornography was only a mask for sexism that permitted even those who were supposedly sympathetic to women's rights to consider women's exploitation and suffering as "titillating." They formed groups such as Women Against Violence in Pornography and the Media, and Women Against Violence Against Women, which staged Take Back the Night marches and conducted angry tours of places such as New York's Times Square to expose the thriving pornography industry and ignite women to fight against it. Their efforts led to the drafting of a model law that was adopted first by Minneapolis and then by other cities (though later it was found unconstitutional), declaring pornography a form of sex discrimination and making traffickers in pornography legally liable.[6]

And so, when some lesbians at the end of the decade began encouraging lesbian interest in pornography and even strip shows and certain forms of violent (albeit consensual) sex, cultural feminists felt betrayed and furious. It was to them as though the enemy—male-identified perverts in dyke clothing—had all the while been living in their own camp and were now attempting to weaken the ranks by disseminating propaganda in support of everything the cultural feminists most despised: pornography, sexual role playing (including s/m "violence" and butch/femme relationships), and even public sex.

The cultural feminists were unimpressed by the argument of lesbian sexual radicals that until women are free to explore their own sexuality any way they wish, they will never be truly free. Such freedom came at too great a cost, cultural feminists said. They believed the sexual radicals' pursuit of ways to "spice up" lesbian sexuality, such as pornography and the sexual role playing of s/m or butch/femme, validated the system of patriarchy, in which one person has power over another or objectifies her. They insisted that such pursuits were counter to the vision of the world that feminists had been striving to create and that it was the responsibility of lesbians to help build the new world upon a model of equal power such as is, anyway, the most "natural" to lesbian relationships.[7]

Cultural feminists believed that lesbian sex must be consistent with the best of lesbian ethics. They acknowledged that images of domination, control, and violence, which have been men's sexual stimuli, have become a part of everyone's cultural environment and thus have shaped women's sexual fantasies and desires. But they also insisted that lesbians should permit themselves only those sexual interests that reflect superior female ideals. They wished to deconstruct harmful desires that were socially constructed, instead of giving in to them by wanting to "explore" them. They feared that the lesbian sexual radicals were not only making a big deal out of sexuality, which should be incidental to lesbianism, but were also deluding themselves and other women into believing that male images, fantasies, and habits were desirable for women, too.[8]

The cultural feminists were particularly annoyed at the sexual radicals' argument that their sexual pursuits were feminist because they encouraged women to fight repression by examining sexual feelings that had been taboo for women. Feminism must be about more than exploration of feelings, they declared: feminist thought stresses analysis of the political significance of feelings, which the sexual radicals had failed to do in their enthusiasm for "improving" lesbian sex lives. They accused the sexual radicals of refusing to consider where those feelings originated and the ways in which they perpetuated the values of the patriarchal ruling class.[9]

These issues became so heated in the 1980s that they even led to public confrontations and protests such as the one at a Barnard College conference, The Scholar and the Feminist, in which cultural feminists handed out leaflets objecting to the lesbian sexual radicals because they constituted a "backlash against feminism." Cultural feminists declared that sexual radicals had internalized the messages of the enemy by advocating those very sexual practices that were the psychological foundations of patriarchy.[10]

Under presssure from the cultural feminists, some of the women's music festivals adopted what they called a "pro-healing policy," forbidding the sale of sexual paraphernalia and public displays of s/m techniques because, as the organizers of the New England Women's Music Retreat claimed, a number of women had "experienced psychic damage" as a result of such exposure. The Michigan Womyn's Music Festival exploded with ugly confrontations when two Chicago women attempted to organize a group interested in publishing a lesbian porno magazine. Cultural feminists demanded that the festival producers draft a "code of feminist ethics and morality " that would put an end to such activities. The issue continued to tear the festivals apart throughout the 1980s. At the 1987 Midwest Women's Festival, s/m was the hottest topic on the agenda. Seminars were disrupted as some women wanted to run off to s/m talks and scenes while cultural feminists wanted to keep them focused on "serious business." Violent debates erupted that further splintered the community, and the following year festival attendance was cut in half because many cultural feminists refused to go when it was advertised that s/m was to be a topic of discussion.[11]

The cultural feminists were able to get the massive power of the National Organization of Women behind them when NOW passed a resolution reaffirming its advocacy of lesbian rights but condemning other issues such as pornography, public sex, and sadomasochism, "which have mistakenly been correlated with Lesbian/Gay rights by some gay organizations." Those are issues of exploitation and violence, NOW wrote, and NOW must oppose them not only because they have nothing to do with lesbian rights, but also because they violate feminist principles. The cultural feminists who were behind that resolution and in the forefront of other attacks on lesbian sexual radicals simply could not take seriously the assertion that more and better sex would help in the fight for liberation. They saw the sexual radicals as provocateurs who threw out the red herring of wild sexuality during a conservative, repressive era—or worse, as idiots who were removing their attention from truly pressing issues that affected women in general and lesbians in particular, in order to waste their energies on the triviality of sex.

The Struggle To Be Sexually Adventurous

In response to what they considered the antisexual censoriousness of the cultural feminists, the lesbian sexual radicals were happy to create a public debate around the issue of lesbian sex. They criticized the cultural feminists for reinforcing traditional concepts of gender instead of encouraging women to try to gain access to what has historically been a main bastion of male privilege—freewheeling sexuality. They compared the cultural feminists to the nineteenth- and early-twentieth century puritanical females who had vitiated the first feminist movement by misdirecting their energies—axing saloons and making the lives of prostitutes more miserable, instead of attending to the business of wresting more freedom for women. Those earlier women also had prudishly tried to depict the world in simplistic terms of male vice and female virtue, the sexual radicals said. Feminism should by its very nature be a radical movement, they insisted, scoffing at the contemporary feminists who were attempting to turn it conservative by promoting the old notion of universal differences between men and women.

The lesbian sexual radicals of the 1980s believed that too many women who loved women had been deluded by the movement into suffering boring, "politically correct" sex. They sought to create an alternative to the tame sexuality of lesbian-feminism, which denied lesbians those experiences that heterosexuals and homosexual men had claimed as their right. Politically correct sex they characterized as being obsessively concerned with not "objectifying" women and with promoting humdrum "equal time" touching and cunnilingus; they found absurd the "politically correct" notion that any kind of penetration was heterosexist. Such dogmas produced "vanilla sex," the sexual radicals said. They insisted that there neither is nor should be any automatic correspondence between lesbian-feminist political beliefs and lesbian sexual practices and that it was time that lesbians freed themselves to enjoy sexuality without any of the restraints inculcated in them as women or imposed on them by the movement.

However, they met with only mixed success in the 1980s. Many lesbians were curious about their ideas and briefly excited about the novelty of the notion that they had a right to the same kind of carefree sexuality that men have always claimed for themselves and were at least pretending to let heterosexual women claim in more recent times. But those lesbians were seldom able to maintain an interest in constructing a sexuality that departed too much from their socialization. The lesbian sexual radicals who could do so over a period of time remained a small minority within a minority. And by the end of the 1980s the AIDS scare had discouraged many women from attempting greater sexual experimentation that would challenge their socialization.

The sexual radicals considered themselves revolutionaries and contrasted their own sexual revolution to that of the 1970s. That earlier revolution they saw as a "rip-off of women," since it did little other than make women more available to men, whether through counterculture gang bangs and groupie sex or pressure to "put out" in more conventional heterosexual relationships. They wished their own sexual revolution to be by and truly for women. They wanted to convince lesbians of the importance of enjoying the most imaginative and exciting sex their minds and bodies could construct. In their conviction that lesbians have a personal right to complete fulfillment of sexual desires and that women's sexual liberation is a crucial component of women's freedom, they created a panoply of new lesbian sexual institutions: pornographic videos and magazines, clubs de-

voted to sexual practices such as lesbian sado-masochism, stores that
specialized in products intended to promote female sexual enjoyment.
They saw lust as a positive virtue, an appreciation of one's own and
others' sexual dynamism.[12]

Their success was limited primarily because lesbians are raised like
other women in this culture. They are taught that what is most crucial
about sexuality is that it leads to settling down in marriage. Not
having the official heterosexual landmarks of engagement and wedding, lesbians create their own, often telescoping those events in time
toward the goal of establishing a home. Joann Loulan, a lesbian
sexologist, jokes: "The lesbian date is like an engagement . . . [and]
once you have sex with her you get married." Despite the 1970s'
ideological push toward nonmonogamy in the lesbian-feminist community, most lesbians continued to idealize monogamy, although the
pattern tended to be serial monogamy—that is, relationships last for
a number of years, break up, and both women get involved in a new
monogamous relationship. In their approach to sexuality they have
been much more like heterosexual women than homosexual men,
who historically and statistically have many more brief sexual encounters. When both parties in a couple are female, it appears that the
effects of female socialization are usually doubled, lesbianism notwithstanding. While a few lesbians have been able to overcome that
socialization, most have not yet been able to.

Typically, in a 1987 survey among lesbians in Boulder, Colorado
—a liberal, trendy university community—fewer than 10 percent
had ever experimented with sexual activities such as s/m or bondage,
75 percent said they had never been involved in sexual role playing,
and only 1 percent thought casual sex was ideal for them.[13] Clearly,
in the midst of such sexual conservatism, lesbian sex radicals could
not have an easy time promoting their theories about the path to
equality and happiness.

In the late 1970s, when a handful of lesbians who wanted a more
radical sexuality first began to surface, they found their best allies
among gay men. Before the impact of AIDS became known, the
sexual explorations of gay men, which surpassed even those of heterosexuals in the "sexualized" '70s, seemed very enviable to those
lesbians who had managed to (or wished they could) transcend the
sexual constrictions that had been imposed upon them as women. In
big cities such as New York, Los Angeles, and San Francisco, they
had been witnessing gay male sexual freedom, as exemplified through
public cruising, sexually explicit ads in gay newspapers, and flamboy-

ant styles in dress that advertised sexual tastes. Those were exciting concepts, especially to lesbians who remained outside the constraints of cultural feminism, and the gay male example allowed them to feel more self-permissive about their own sexuality. They observed that while many women were busy in the 1970s building lesbian-feminist alternative institutions such as women-only living places and women's music, their male counterparts were exploring revolutionary sex; and they were convinced that it was an area that the lesbian subcultures, especially lesbian-feminism, had neglected to their own detriment. The women who saw themselves as lesbian sexual radicals thus went about the business of modifying gay male sexual customs and institutions—which represented the essence of liberation to them—for a female community.

Some behaviors were adopted by them without modification. For example, s/m lesbians copied the handkerchief code developed by gay men who enjoyed s/m sexual practices: a handkerchief worn in the left hip pocket meant that one was dominant; in the right hip pocket, that one was submissive; a black handkerchief in the right hip pocket meant one desired to be whipped, and so forth. Leather, which had long represented to gay men machismo and a preference for s/m sex, was also imported into the lesbian community. Kathy Andrew, the proprietor of Stormy Leather, a San Francisco wholesale-retail establishment that caters especially to lesbians of the s/m community, explains that she got her initial inspiration working in a homosexual male leather store in the gay Castro district. Throughout the 1980s she made and sold leather specifically for lesbian s/m: leather corsets, leather bras with cut-out nipples, leather-and-lace maid's aprons, leather garter belts, dildo harnesses in black or lavender leather. There was for a time such a growing interest in those products that her volume of business doubled each year during the mid-1980s.[14]

There was some interest, too, in promoting more casual sex between lesbians, toward the goals of pleasure and liberation. Street cruising—making "quickie" sexual contact with strangers, which gay men had always enjoyed—has never been a lesbian practice, not only because of the way women have been socialized, but also because of the physiology of female sexuality. But that is not to say that lesbians have never envied men the ease with which they obtain sexual relief with a partner. Writing at the height of lesbian-feminism, in a 1975 essay titled "Queen for a Day: A Stranger in Paradise," Rita Mae Brown expressed her disappointment in the lesbian's lack of opportunity for casual sex. She described dressing in male drag and

invading Xanadu, a gay male bathhouse in New York. Women had
built no Xanadus where they could make casual contacts, Brown
pointed out, not only because they lacked the money but also because
they lacked the concept. They had been too well taught that sex for
the sake of sex is wrong, that it must at least be connected with
romance. She suggested that such a rigid equation of sex with romance and/or commitment had limited lesbians' choices. Brown voiced
a cry in that essay that was enthusiastically echoed by lesbian sexual
radicals a decade later:

> I do want a Xanadu [Brown said]. I want the option of random sex
> with no emotional commitment when I need sheer physical relief. . . .
> It is in our interest to build places where we have relief, refuge, release.
> Xanadu is not a lurid dream; it's the desire of a woman to have options.
> Like men we should have choices: deep, long-term relationships, the
> baths, short-term affairs.

Brown's avant-garde conviction was that women could not hope to
be truly equal unless they were sexually equal and shared men's
prerogatives even in the area of casual sex.[15]

But apparently because of socialization, from which lesbians often
had as much difficulty escaping as heterosexual women, the realization of such prerogatives was not achievable in the 1980s despite
militant efforts. Serial monogamy continued throughout the decade
to be the predominant pattern of lesbian sexuality. The institutions
that lesbian sexual radicals devised to expand avenues of lesbian sexual expression were either short-lived or greatly modified to reflect
values that are, ironically, not very different from those promoted by
the cultural feminists. For example, in the early 1980s lesbian Xanadus became a reality, but their success was limited. JoAnna remembers attending the Sutro Baths, a San Francisco swingers' bathhouse
that had opened its doors exclusively to lesbians one night a week:
"Six or seven women walked into this large group room a few
minutes after I arrived. One of them shouted, 'Let's get down!' and
everybody started doing everything. Everywhere you looked there
were women doing it, either in couples or in large groups." Such a
scene was precisely what Brown and the sexual radicals who followed
her had envisioned, but this initial enthusiasm for casual sex was not
long maintained among lesbians. Clare, who attended the Sutro a few
months later, shortly before it discontinued its lesbian nights, says
that she found only eight or ten women in the orgy room, sitting
around in their towels, talking. "Nobody was even kissing. We

ended up playing a nude game of pool." There were apparently not enough lesbians who felt comfortable about public sex and would attend often enough to make the venture economically feasible for the Sutro and the few other bathhouses that attempted lesbian nights, and the AIDS scare soon militated against further endeavors by the baths.[16]

Another attempt to expand the possibilities of lesbian sexuality— lesbian strip shows—illustrates how female values that reflect the ways women have been socialized can infiltrate even the baldest of male sexual institutions when adopted by lesbians. The first shows were staged in the early 1980s in lesbian bars in San Francisco and drew large crowds, with women reportedly "hanging from the rafters," although by the late '80s the novelty had worn off and sheer lust alone could not sustain the institution. But clearly sheer lust was never the point of those shows, though on the surface they seemed to resemble heterosexual burlesque where nude women danced and men ogled. Lesbian strip shows, which began as a determined attempt to claim male prerogatives and increase women's choices, were generally overlaid with women's consciousness. The strippers who did lesbian burlesque sometimes had an almost spiritual zeal for their work that is not found among those who do burlesque for men.

One stripper, Rainbeau, who also managed several other dancers in a group called Rainbeau Productions, explained that she used a diversity of women in her company, including black women, fat women, and older women, because it made the diverse groups in the audience feel good about themselves. "I pray to the goddess before I go out on stage," she remarked, "to help me do it right." Rainbeau's analysis of her work as a lesbian stripper was patently political, a product of lesbian-feminist consciousness of the '70s, though expressed through the '80s' sexual radicals' desire for more freedom of sexual exploration: "Women's eroticism is a main source of female power. It's taken away from us by men because it's tied in with bearing their children. But we try to help women understand that it's important for them to reclaim their power and love their bodies." Tatoo Blue, who also did burlesque exclusively for lesbians, had similar ideas about her work being more significant than mere lustful entertainment. Stripping for other women was "a way of expressing myself or touching people without ever knowing them. . . . What I do is make people stop and think about a lot more than just a body taking her clothes off."[17] Lesbian strippers in front of lesbian audiences transformed the heterosexual institution of burlesque, bringing to it traditional female values—nurturing, relating, emotionally touching—that had been totally outside the concerns of such entertainment.

Several lesbian movie companies devoted to making lesbian sex films also emerged in the 1980s, such as Blush Productions, which released a cinematic trilogy, *Private Pleasures,* in 1985 that laughed at the notion of "politically correct" sexuality and gave women permission to explore butch/femme role playing, s/m, leather, the use of dildos, and "fist fucking" (a technique that spread among the gay male community in the 1970s, in which one man gradually inserts his entire fist into another man's anus. Among lesbians who adopted the technique in the 1980s the act was often accomplished vaginally). But like in lesbian burlesque, and unlike in similar heterosexual institutions, sheer sleaze was less an express value in lesbian porno films than promoting lesbian sexual freedom to explore.

Generally the lesbian film companies emphasized the erotic rather than the pornographic. Lavender Blue Productions, for example, produced *Where There's Smoke* in 1986, in which the sex is even politically correct: two women drink tea and have gentle conversation before they make love orally, with soft guitar music in the background. In the same vein, Tigress Productions made the film *Erotic in Nature,* which, although advertised in lesbian pornographic magazines, promised the reader to go beyond pornography: not only does it "steam with pleasure," according to the producers, but it also "exults in beauty and displays a tenderness which we feel will warm your hearts." The film aimed at the graphic sexuality that lesbian sex radicals encouraged, but maintained traditional female moods and images.

Like lesbian burlesque shows and films, lesbian-centered pornographic books and magazines in the 1980s were also concerned with more than titillation. The lesbian sex magazine *On Our Backs* announced in its first issue, in 1984, that its goals were beyond entertainment: the staff wanted to encourage "sexual freedom, respect and empowerment for lesbians." Susie Bright, *On Our Backs'* editor, said of the magazine's purpose, "I think women should be pissed that sex is a good old boys' club and they weren't allowed in. We're letting them in." *Bad Attitude,* another lesbian sex magazine that began in 1984, claimed: "We call our magazine *Bad Attitude* because that's what women who take control of our sexuality are told we have." The magazine was published by a collective of lesbians who were committed to "a radical politics of female sexuality." Although both magazines featured stories and articles that advocated casual and even sometimes violent sex, often in fantasies that mirrored what has more commonly been gay male sexual behavior, the editorial emphasis was invariably on responsibility such as consensuality and safety, as well as freedom.[18]

The biggest ad feature in lesbian porno magazines was the personals, in which women described themselves and the partners they desired. Personals have had some history among lesbians since the mid-1970s, when the *Wishing Well,* a quarterly devoted to personal ads, presented itself as "an alternative to *The Well of Loneliness.*" The *Wishing Well* personals provided a vivid contrast to gay male personal ads at that time, since the lesbian emphasis was on seeking romance, while the gay male emphasis was generally on seeking sex partners. But some ads even in the lesbian porno magazines of the 1980s continued to call wistfully for a partner with whom to share moonlit walks: "Let me prove to you romance is not dead," one implored. Others forthrightly admitted, again in language first used by gay men during their 1970s sexual revolution, to wanting "fuck buddies" and rejected romance and "marriage." One woman confessed in a personal ad: "I'm tired of pretending love when I want sex." However, the ads often began with the boldness advocated by lesbian sexual radicals, listing, for example, interests in "bare bottom spankings, immobilizing bondage, enemas, colonic irrigations, vaginal and rectal exams, dildos, vibrators," but ended on a more conventional female note: "After I've endured what was bestowed upon me, comfort me in your loving arms. Long term relationship possible."[19]

It seems that to this point, female upbringing, which inculcates in most women a certain passivity and reticence, has made it difficult for many lesbians to admit or encourage within themselves an unalloyed aggressive interest in sex outside of love and commitment. It is not surprising that as women they have problems even admitting such interests. Kinsey reported that 77 percent of the males he interviewed acknowledged being aroused by depictions of explicit sex, but only 22 percent of the females admitted to such arousal. A more recent study gives a possible insight into this discrepancy between male and female response to pornography. Both men and women were exposed to explicitly erotic audiotapes while they were connected to instruments that measured their physical arousal. The instruments actually recorded no difference in arousal rate between men and women, but while all the male subjects who were aroused admitted arousal, only half the aroused female subjects admitted arousal.[20]

Of course it is much more difficult for a man to deny the physical, very visual evidence of his arousal than it is for a woman, who has only to turn a mental page in her mind and say—and perhaps even believe—the arousal never happened. Females have been socially encouraged in such internal and external denial.

Even some of those who prided themselves on aspects of their sexual liberation in the 1980s still had to admit to their difficulty in overcoming their well-inculcated sexual timidity. One woman who made a living manufacturing sex items and spoke unabashedly of having attended sex orgies nevertheless admitted:

> It's still not easy to pick someone up at a bar. What do you do and say? With gay men, they have it down pat. They don't worry if the other man's lover is there. With women you worry, and you feel guilty. And you always have this frantic look about you. Everyone I've spoken to says it takes ages and ages before you do such things with ease. Maybe never. [22]

The lesbian sexual radicals thus found that their struggle to encourage a more adventurous sexuality among lesbians was not easily won. While some few lesbians were successful in constructing a new sexuality for themselves, changing old attitudes among lesbians on a large scale proved to be virtually impossible in the course of one decade.

The Attraction of "Opposites"

Another way the sexual radicals hoped to enliven sexuality (even for those engaged in long-term lesbian relationships) was in attempting to avoid lesbian merging by encouraging polarities such as "top" and "bottom" or butch and femme. While some lesbians who engaged in sexual polarities felt that those roles were *natural* to them and had no superimposed meaning, others in the 1980s deliberately experimented in the hope that games of opposites would help them escape from the tedium of egalitarian vanilla sex. They also believed that the boldness of the roles made a blatant statement of their desire to overturn those conventional female sexual attitudes that lesbians shared with heterosexual women.

The group that worked the hardest to break down conventional female sexual attitudes was those lesbians who rallied around the label of sadomasochists, not merely as an expression of private sexual taste but as a public stance. Their purpose, in addition to enjoying their own sexual preferences, was consciousness-raising: it was their goal to get women to understand that they have a right to their sexual desires, no matter how unconventional or "perverted." In fact, they referred to themselves as "perverts," both to parody public conceptions of them and to insist that it is all right, even admirable and beneficial, to be what society has dubbed "perverted."

Perhaps because they had to battle so much with the cultural feminists, lesbians who were involved in s/m and other radical forms of sexual expression often made pleasure seem like medical prescription. The clubs devoted to lesbian s/m during the 1980s such as Samois and the Outcasts in San Francisco, Leather and Lace in Los Angeles, the Lesbian Sex Mafia in New York, and SHELIX in Northampton, Massachusetts, were careful to explain that s/m sex has nothing to do with real-life violence or oppression of women. Instead, it is a cathartic sexual game based on fantasy, an important kind of sexual psychodrama in which the partners agree upon the limits, establish "safe words" that permit the bottom to stop the action whenever she wishes, and help each other return to everyday consciousness when the scene is concluded. They argued that it gave healthy release both to the top, who could deal in a controlled setting with her human perplexities about power and aggression, and to the bottom, who could surrender to her sexual pleasures and lose control safely. They insisted that it in no way affected a woman's real-life personage, as a lesbian limerick about s/m bondage from a bottom's perspective suggested:

> Jane rode around on a Harley-bike.
> To strangers she looked just like a bull dyke.
> But at home in bed,
> To her lover she pled:
> "Get the ribbons. You know what I like." [22]

Many of them saw s/m not simply as a bold sexual adventure, but also as a solution to "lesbian bed death" within long-term lesbian relationships. It was a way of creating a "barrier" that is necessary for continued sexual interest by constructing sexual polarities in bed such as mistress and slave, dominant and submissive, top and bottom. It could be a useful aid to monogamy if a couple wished to utilize it that way.

Women who were involved in lesbian s/m in the '80s also generally maintained that there is nothing about s/m that is inconsistent with the principles of feminism, since it is opposed to all hierarchies based on gender. The early founders of Samois, in fact, had their roots in the feminist movement and were among the first to insist that women must claim their sexual birthright, which was no different from that of men and only appeared different because society's emphasis on exclusive gender identity suppressed natural similarities. Women who joined such organizations were usually s/m enthusiasts, but many felt they had joined not so much for s/m itself as for their perception that those groups presented the ultimate in female sexual liberation. The meetings were erotically affirming, conveying the idea that "sex is o.k. It's o.k. to be sexual, to feel sexual, to act sexual."[23] Members believed that they were modeling an important concept of sexual freedom for all women, since women could not be free unless they owned their own bodies and had unrestricted right to pursue their erotic pleasures.

S/m leaders specifically articulated connections between unfettered sexuality and the success of feminism. They claimed that examination of their s/m interests was a "feminist inquiry." Corona, a professional s/m dominatrix, who did counseling for s/m lesbians and staged "Erotic Power Play" workshops as well as s/m orgies, asserted that feminists must not be afraid of power nor of looking at themselves to understand how their psyches operate and s/m helps them achieve such fearlessness. Other s/m activists emphasized that feminism that runs from sexual exploration is "femininism"; it is restrictive and contributes to women's difficulty in breaking out of their hindering socialization as "good girls." Feminists had much to learn from sexual outlaws, they said.[24]

Several lesbian psychologists of the 1980s helped to promote s/m by agreeing that it could be a healthy working out of traumas rather than a giving in to them and that as an exploration of sexual variety it could add richness to lesbian sexual lives. They pointed out that dominance and submission, as well as pleasure and pain, are deep and troubling issues in society and in the individual psyche and that there is real value in exploring and experimenting with feelings about them. The realms of sexual fantasy and erotic play, they suggested, were enormously fruitful for examining these issues. The lesbian psychologists gave support to women who wanted to experiment by their hypothesis that s/m—where mind and body, ideas and sensations interplay—was much too promising for opportunities in self-knowledge to remain hidden behind the curtains of taboo.[25]

Because the sexual play of s/m seemed both to produce catharsis and to create stimulating polarities, its appeal among lesbians spread for a period of time. Even those outside of cosmopolitan cities were instructed in the techniques in workshops at the huge annual women's music festivals all over the country, and they imported what they had learned into their communities. Lesbians in Austin, for example, recall that several of the leaders in the Austin lesbian-feminist community were introduced to the ideas of s/m at the workshops of the Michigan Womyn's Music Festival at the beginning of the 1980s and brought those ideas back to Austin. Consciousness-raising groups met to talk about it. Support groups were formed. It felt almost "religious," the Austin women say. Those who didn't do it were considered inhibited. It went on for about five years. But none of those groups exists anymore.[26]

However, while not many women chose finally to make s/m a major part of their sexual repertoire, it has fostered changes among some by demanding that they understand that sexuality, even for lesbians, may be far more complex than loving sisterhood and that it is sometimes connected with deep, dark aspects of the psyche that are not always "politically correct." The publicity of the debate around s/m served to liberate sexuality somewhat for lesbians who were not tied to the dogmas of cultural feminism; it made them want to experiment with their sexual repertoire, as one woman enthusiastically observed:

> I'm not really into S and M, but what I read about it was a wonderful opening for me. The theory gave me the right to practice things I'd thought about, play out fantasy roles I couldn't before, do penetration. It led me to explore sexual things like being in control and not being in control, to sometimes be a top and sometimes be a bottom. Those aren't ways to live; they're not social roles. They're just sexual. But they're a part of me and I like to look at them.

One San Diego psychologist who sees many lesbians in her practice believes that bondage and related light s/m acts have become common even among women "who could think no further than vanilla sex in the 1970s." She attributes the change to a freeing up of sexuality for which the lesbian sexual radicals have been responsible: "It's curiosity, innovation, playfulness—a desire to know oneself in different ways. And it's more socially acceptable now." To the extent that she is right the sexual radicals have been at least modestly successful in their goal of liberating lesbians.[27]

The resurgence of butch and femme roles in the 1980s can be seen in part as another conscious attempt to create sexual polarities in order to enhance erotic relationships between women and break away from the limiting orthodoxies of lesbian-feminism and middle-class

lesbianism. Many young women who claimed butch or femme identities in the 1980s saw themselves as taboo-smashers and iconoclasts.
They were no longer primarily working-class women who chose
those roles because they were their only models, as happened in the
'50s and '60s; butches and femmes in the '80s were just as likely to be
intellectuals whose roots were in the middle class and who had carefully thought out the statements they wanted those roles to make.
They had been fed up with the "proprieties" of lesbian-feminists,
cultural feminism, and conservative middle-class lesbians—all of which
seemed to them aimed at molding lesbians into a single image and
standard of behavior. In their view, lesbian "propriety," which even
swept into women's bedrooms, was detrimental to the lesbian pursuit
of happiness and an absurd contradiction of their conception of the
lesbian as bold and original. In reaction to that propriety they now
flaunted the tabooed roles: "I like being a butch," they said. "I like
being with other butches with our nicknames and ballgames—women
with muscles and pretty faces." The newly proclaimed femmes expressed resentment that they had had to "trade in our pretty clothes
for the non-descript lesbian uniform of the 1970s." "Let's face it,"
they said disdainfully of the '70s style, "feminism is not sexy." [28]

Working-class lesbians and some lesbian essentialists tended to
identify as butch or femme in the 1980s with the same deadly seriousness that characterized many women of the '50s. They sought to
discover the sexual role most "natural" to them and to stick to it. But
some neo-butches and -femmes chose their identities out of a sense of
adventure, a longing to push at the limits, a desire to be more
blatantly sexual than the doctrinaire lesbians of the '70s had allowed.
They found themselves in conflict with lesbian-feminists and cultural
feminism, but even for them neo-butch/femme roles and relationships maintained the lessons of feminism that lesbians had learned
from the 1970s.

There were, for example, few butches in the '80s who would
entertain the notion that they were men trapped in women's bodies,
as butches in the 1950s sometimes did. For many of the neo-butches
or -femmes the roles actually had little connection with the idealized
butch and femme behaviors of their predecessors. While some lesbian
historians have convincingly argued that even in the '50s butch/
femme roles could be very complex, in the '80s they could be even
more so, because they reflected the new complexity of sexual roles in
the parent culture. Just as heterosexual roles, through the influence of
feminism, ceased to be universally two-dimensional and could legiti-
mately take on all manner of androgynous nuances, so lesbians who

wanted to identify as butch or femme in the 1980s could choose to express themselves in a larger variety of images. While distinctions in dress in 1980s butch/femme couples were not unusual, it was also common for both women in the couple to dress in a unisex style or to combine styles. For example, one woman who said she identified herself as a butch admitted that she also liked to wear long dresses occasionally. Her sartorial flexibility was dramatized by her dress at a function in the lesbian community: "a tuxedo with a matching shade of eye shadow, and a necklace along with a bow tie." "Butch" and "femme" in the 1980s, much more than in the restrictive 1950s, came to mean whatever one wanted those terms to mean. A woman was a butch or a femme simply because she said she was and that self-conception helped her to enhance her sexual self-image. The *Random House Dictionary of the English Language* definition of "butch" as "the one who takes the part of a man" in a lesbian relationship lost whatever inevitable truth it may have once had.[29]

The more egalitarian day-to-day living arrangements that feminism brought to the parent culture were also reflected in butch/femme relationships. By design (and not simply by chance, as may have happened in the 1950s), in most aspects of their lives, such as household responsibility or decision making, there were few clear divisions along traditional lines between neo-butches and -femmes. Neo-butch/femme often boiled down merely to who made the first move sexually, and for many women that was its primary value. To other women it meant not even that once they began exploring roles such as "butch bottom" or "femme top."[30] Too much had happened for history simply to repeat itself. The male hippies of the 1960s had challenged the old concept of masculine: a man could wear his hair to his shoulders and be opposed to violence and wear jewelry. The feminists of the 1970s had challenged the old concept of feminine: a woman could be efficient and forceful and demand a place in the world. Except to the most recalcitrant, there was little that remained of the simplistic ideas of gender-appropriate appearance and behavior. And lesbians, who have historically been at the forefront of feminism (in their choice to lead independent lives, if nothing else), could not easily accept the old fashions in images and behaviors. Most would have had a hard time taking those notions seriously. For that reason, butch and femme existed best in the '80s in the sexual arena, which invites fantasy and the tension of polarities.

One woman who identified herself as a femme in the 1980s explained that being a femme sexually meant playing off of feminine stereotypes—the little girl, the bitch, the queen, the sex pot—and

making those images into your sexual language. For her it was primarily camp and fantasy and did not necessarily have to do with
other aspects of her personality. Nor were those roles limited in
themselves, she pointed out. In the '80s one could, for example, be a
femme who was the sexual dominator and "ran the fuck" or a butch
who submissively acted out the femme's desires.[31]

Lesbian fiction of the 1980s reinforced the notion that while butch/
femme roles were useful to lesbians, it was important not to take
them literally. The stone butch, for example, who was so popular in
the lesbian novels of the 1950s and '60s such as Ann Bannon's Beebo
Brinker series, was passé as a figure in the 1980s lesbian novel. In
Ellen Frye's *Look Under the Hawthorne* (1987) a stone butch is told by
a character who functions as a spokeswoman for the author, "You've
got to let other people love you, too. Loving's got to be both ways.
It won't last long if it's always one way." While butch/femme roles
were seen to be sexually healthy, to be rigidly fixed in those roles was
unhealthy. Lee Lynch's *The Swashbuckler* (1985) offered a model for
flexibility. Frenchy and Mercedes, two butches, fall in love with each
other. Mercedes observes, without the shame that was requisite for a
"flipped" butch in the 1950s, "I see all of a sudden that every butch is
a femme; every femme is a butch. I know the lips of my friend could
get me hotter than the lips of any femme in the room."[32]

Autobiographical writing generally reflected the same view. Authors suggested that when the roles were taken with great seriousness
—for example, when butches felt that the entire weight of being the
sexual aggressor was invariably placed on them—the butch/femme
dichotomy could become counterproductive. As Cherríe Moraga,
who called herself a "post-feminist butch," observed in a 1980s article:

> It might feel very sexy to imagine "taking" a woman, but it has
> sometimes occurred at the expense of my feeling, sexually, like I can
> surrender myself to a woman; that is, always needing to be the one in
> control, calling the shots. It's a very butch trip and I feel like this can
> keep me private and protected and can prevent me from fully being
> able to express myself.[33]

"Post-feminist butches" were free to accept the notion that female
sexuality was more complicated than the 1950s butches openly admitted and that they sacrificed something important to their own emotional and sexual pleasure if they maintained a "stone" role.

The concepts of butch and femme became so flexible that, unlike the '50s when women who chose the roles were enjoined by the subculture to adhere to a certain code of behavior, their meaning was totally subjective in the 1980s. The terms were often used as catchwords to describe relationships that were far more complex than "butch" or "femme" would seem to denote. One lesbian writer, for example, who called herself an '80s femme, claimed that her sexual life was "entirely involved in a butch/femme exchange. . . . I never come together with a woman sexually outside of those roles. I'm saying to my partner, 'Love me enough to let me go where I need to go and take me there. . . . You map it out. You are in control.' " She admitted, however, that her interest in such a dynamic came from "much richer territory" than simply that of roles, but the terms "butch" and "femme" had come to connote in the '80s all manner of complex dynamics.[34]

The most important aspect of butch/femme in the 1980s was that it created roles that were sexually charged in a way that would have been unthinkable in the sexually tame '70s, when erotic seduction was considered a corrupt imitation of heterosexuality; but the actors who indulged in these roles in the '80s, femme as well as butch, were frequently cognizant of the feminist ideal of the strong woman, even in the context of sexuality. The femme fantasy image could be a lesbian Carmen rather than a Camille, as one woman suggested; in her favorite sexual fantasy she would appear at a lesbian dance in a "sleazy" black silk low cut dress with hot pink flowers on it:

> I would come in, not, I repeat, *not* like a helpless femme-bot [cf. robot], but like a bad-ass-no-games-knows-her-own-mind-and-will-tell-you-too femme. First I would stand there and let my lover wonder. Maybe I would just stand there altogether and let her come to me. Or maybe, while all the heads were turning . . . I would stride across the dance floor in a bee-line for that green-eyed womon [sic] I love, so that everyone could see who the one in the black dress was going to fuck tonight.[35]

As expressed in the 1980s, the roles became both a reflection of and a feminist expansion of the socialization lesbians had undergone in the parent culture. But the goal was for women to use those roles for their own pleasurable ends, to demand freedom and sexual excitement as lesbians seldom dared before.

The roles, styles, and relationships of butch/femme in the '80s often appeared to be conducted with a sense of lightness. As Phyllis Lyon, co-founder of Daughters of Bilitis, who has been active in the lesbian community since the early 1950s, characterized neo-butch/ femme, "women 'play at it' rather than 'being it.' " Other lesbians testified to that sense of play. One writer said that she, a butch, and her femme lover complemented each other in the roles they played, but they recognized it as play, as a pleasurable game: "She really can find a spark plug, she just prefers not to. Feeling that I have to protect her is an illusion that I enjoy. She allows me my illusion for she enjoys being taken care of like this." [36]

The resurgence of butch/femme was also a reaction to the "drab stylelessness" of the lesbian-feminist community in the 1970s that was "anaphrodisiac," as one woman described it. Her friends in the '70s, she recalled, were philosophically appealing, but they created "the most unerotic environment. . . . No make-up, denim overalls, flannel shirts. I compared it to Mao's China. Plain and sexless." [37] In contrast, butch/femme roles in the '80s opened to lesbians who wanted to explore that avenue the possibility of fashions that were signals for the erotic in the heterosexual Western world in which they grew up. Though such fashions would have been disdained by lesbian-feminists in the 1970s, neo-butches and -femmes felt free to deck themselves out in high heels, leather, lace, delicate underwear—whatever emblematized sexuality to them.

All of this erotic play that was at the center of neo-butch/femme mirrored Michael Bronski's definition of "gay lib" as it related to gay men: "At its most basic, [it] offers the possibility of freedom of pleasure for its own sake." [38] During the 1970s when lesbian-feminists, who dominated the visible lesbian community, were busy defining the very serious tenets of their movement and living by them, the idea of pleasure for its own sake was alien. In fact, it had never been a comfortable concept among lesbians, since they had had to battle so hard against the stereotype of homosexuals that saw them as nothing but selfishly pleasure-oriented. While the AIDS crisis in the gay male community made Bronski's definition problematic for homosexual men, the lesbian sexual radicals in the 1980s (when AIDS was still considered largely a gay male disease) decided that it was time for them to compensate for the seriousness of the past. The openly erotic statement made by their butch/femme styles was one signal of their determination.

The lesbian sex wars of the 1980s between those lesbians who were cultural feminists and those who were sexual radicals reflected the conflicting perceptions of the basic meaning of femaleness and lesbianism with which women have long struggled. The arguments centered on such related questions as: Are there natural differences between males and females, or are the apparent differences simply induced through socialization? Does women's "moral superiority" create in them a disinterest in certain pursuits, or has their negligence of those pursuits been to their social and personal detriment? Can women will themselves to be a particular way sexually, or is their sexual makeup involuntary and inescapable?

Such philosophical splits between cultural feminists and radicals were apparent from the beginning of the century among women who loved women, although they did not lead to the same kinds of confrontations that have been so prevalent in recent times. For example, Jane Addams' view that women were better than men and thus had the responsibility to behave better fueled her efforts to establish institutions that reflected women's morally superior nature (see pp. 24–28). M. Carey Thomas' view that women had been kept socially inferior by accepting the notion that they were different from men, and that they would become equal only by claiming male prerogatives, fueled her visionary academic leadership in female higher education (see pp. 28-31). Behind Addams' position was a philosophical stance similar to that of the cultural feminist lesbians of the 1980s who said that the male pursuit of sexuality was corrupt and beneath women; Thomas' stance was similar to that of the more radical lesbians of the 1980s who said that until women were as free as men to pursue anything they wished, including sexuality, they would never be really free.

The century-old debate between lesbian essentialists and lesbian existentialists may also be seen in this conflict of the 1980s. In a sense, the cultural feminists were essentialists, believing not only that by essence women were different from and better than men, but also that lesbian culture, which was made up of nothing but women, must be doubly different and doubly better. The sexual radicals were existentialists, at least in their beliefs that not only was sexuality morally neutral but also that lesbians could consciously create for themselves any kind of sexuality they found desirable.

On the surface it appears at this time that the cultural feminists were more accurate than the sexual radicals in their conviction that female sexuality is very different from male sexuality. The sexual radicals' attempts to convince lesbians that they must wrest for themselves male sexual freedoms have to date failed to alter much of the lesbian community. Although they have managed, as the San Diego psychologist suggests, to free up sexuality to some extent for lesbians

who do not feel they must be guided by the tenets of political correctness, nevertheless lesbian pornography and sex ads could not escape
from the influence of interpersonal values that have been considered
characteristically feminine; lesbians quickly lost interest in strip shows
and bathhouse impersonal sex once the novelty wore off; and serial
monogamy remains the dominant pattern of lesbian sexual relating.
The encouragement of the sexual radicals was not sufficient to counter
the greater forces of their female socialization. Thus lesbian sexual
radicals have remained a tiny minority within a minority.

But so short a period, particularly one in which a sexually related
epidemic is raging, is not enough time to prove or disprove the
possibility of altering female sexual habits. Therefore, the facts must
be treated with caution. They do not demonstrate that lesbians in
general will never be as baldly sexual as men because it is not "natural" to them as women; rather, they may be seen to reaffirm to what
extent sexuality is a social construct. Lesbians obviously have different object choices from heterosexual women but they were raised as
female no less than heterosexual women, and they cannot easily
overcome the effects of what has been so basic to their upbringing.

Their ability (or inability) to do so still remains to be seen. It is
impossible to generalize at this point about what can or cannot be
consciously created with regard to sexual appetites. Nor will the
remainder of the twentieth century render any definitive answers,
since the recent increase of AIDS outside the gay male community
has already begun to put a damper on free sexual experimentation
among lesbians. What is predictable, however, is that lesbians' sexual
freedom will be closely tied to the ethos of the parent culture in
which they have been socialized. If the parent culture becomes less
sexualized or the women's liberation movement loses its momentum
—as has happened in other eras—the push toward more aggressive
sexual expression by those lesbians who have been in the forefront of
sexual radicalism will be halted. If, after the AIDS epidemic, the
parent culture becomes more intensely sexualized (as it may in response to the relative aridity of the present) and females continue on
their course toward greater social equality, more lesbians, along with
more heterosexual women, will alter their sexual habits to resemble
those of men—to the dismay of the cultural feminists and the delight
of the sexual radicals.

From Tower of Babel to Community: Lesbian Life in the 1980s

This was not the 1940s with the isolation and lack of support that existed then for lesbians. . . . There is a women's newspaper to which I can turn to find the groups where I belong. I can purchase that newspaper at a women's bookstore, or subscribe to it, openly. There are disabled rap groups, groups for aging lesbians. There are places where we can network, to help each other. We fight together for our place in the sunshine. —June Patterson, disabled lesbian, age 62,
in Long Time Passing, 1986

I was thinking of how far lesbians and gay men have come in this terrible decade, regardless of the concern or indifference of the rest of the world: how we are capable of forming, affirming, validating our own partnerships, raising our own children, mourning our own dead. —Jennifer Levin
at the Seventh Annual Gay Pride Run,
New York, 1988

While the 1970s rode on the steam of the social revolution that had been set in motion by the flower children of the '60s, the momentum appeared to have been lost in the '80s as mainstream America returned to more conservative times. Although the effects of the sexual revolution of the previous decade could not be totally eradicated and the sexual ethos of the 1980s was light-years away from times such as the McCarthy era, the "New Right" became vociferous in its desire to turn back the clock. The New Right, which had long been around but received little audience earlier, became increasingly effective in its techniques of fund-raising and proselytizing. It was partly responsible for the landslide 1984 defeat of the Democrats, whose presidential delegates had included activist lesbians and gay men. The Democrats' platform had contained a plank for gay rights that they erroneously believed, in the context of the liberality of the past years, would be

popular. Ronald Reagan, who understood far better than the Democrats that moods were shifting, played to the New Right with promises such as his intention to squelch hopes for gay rights by resisting
"all efforts to obtain government endorsement of homosexuality."[1]

The years that followed the election seemed to confirm the shift
towards sexual conservatism. For example, in the mid-'80s a commission was formed, headed by Attorney General Edwin Meese, that
reexamined the 1970 Supreme Court deliberations on pornography.
The commission concluded, totally counter to the earlier findings,
that pornography did indeed lead to violence. The conservatism of
the Supreme Court also made itself felt in those years when it issued
a decision (*Bowers v. Hardwick*) upholding the constitutionality of
laws against homosexual sodomy.

The liberalism that opened the way for the radicalism of movements such as lesbian–feminism had slowed to a shuffle. The temper
of the times seemed to demand if not retreat at least moderation. Had
the questers after the Lesbian Nation not exhausted themselves by
fanaticism, the new conservative mood would have checked the extremism of their visions anyway. That is not to say that lesbians were
silenced in the 1980s, but rather that the community became increasingly moderate in its demeanor.

The change was a great shock to more radical lesbians who had
not yet awakened from their dream of a lesbian-feminist utopia. They
panicked at what seemed like mass defection and the breakup of their
movement. As a character in Jean Swallow's *Leave a Light On for Me*
(1986) laments:

> I thought I was home. But I wasn't. And now, there's no more
> movement. We're all scattered and all hell's breaking loose all over the
> world. . . . I couldn't find me anymore. . . . Everything's changing
> and I'm frightened.[2]

But while it may have appeared that nothing much was left by the
mid-'80s of the lesbian-feminist movement as it existed in the '70s, in
fact it had reconstituted itself. Women who identified themselves as
lesbians were exploring new ways to build personal and social lives
and a community.

Many young lesbians who now entered the lesbian subcultures not
only took for granted their feminist rights, but also made light of the
high seriousness associated with being a politically correct lesbian-
feminist. The young women demanded freedom to be as they pleased.
They described themselves in terms, such as "girls," that would have

infuriated lesbian-feminists in the '70s. Some of them reintroduced makeup and sexy clothes into the most visible part of the lesbian community. They were far less distinguishable from heterosexual women than their 1970s counterparts had been. The new young lesbians created images such as that of the "glamour dyke" or "lipstick lesbian," and their frequently glamorous self-presentation may have been responsible for the beginning of a new "lesbian chic" that seems to be making bisexuality as provocative in some sophisticated circles as it had been in the 1920s.

Through those images lesbianism could once again be associated with a kind of super-sexy rebelliousness and allure. As in the 1920s, female entertainers by the end of the '80s began to tantalize their audiences with hints of bisexuality. Madonna and Sandra Bernhard, for example, let it be known on network television that they were "an item" at the Cubby Hole, a New York lesbian bar. They even incorporated lesbian material into their shows. Sandra Bernhard reinterpreted the song "Me and Mrs. Jones" to be a story of a surreptitious lesbian affair and ended with the outrageously gleeful exclamation, "The women are doin' it for themselves!" Lily Tomlin and her longtime companion and writer Jane Wagner made lesbians the heroes of half Tomlin's skits in her virtuoso one-woman performances. Rock singer Melissa Etheridge skyrocketed to fame with her totally androgenous performance style and dress. Country-western singer K.D. Lang proudly declared of her own bisexual appeal, "Yeah, sure, the boys can be attracted to me, the girls can be attracted to me, your mother . . . your uncle, sure. It doesn't really matter to me."[3]

Of course small enclaves of older lesbian lifestyles continued to exist as new ones were being formed. But the most visible lesbian community changed its character so that in the '80s it was made up in good part of women who were far less separated from the mainstream in their appearance and outlook than had been the butches and femmes of the 1950s and '60s and the lesbian-feminists of the 1970s. Perhaps many women who made up the dominant visible community of the '80s intuited that less militance was appropriate to conservative times, and they were reinforced by the inclusion in their community of more and more lesbians whose economic status, lifestyles, and philosophy rendered them much more moderate than their lesbian-feminist predecessors. But together with the growing moderation of the most visible lesbian community, it grew in other ways as well: it came to include many more lesbians of color, women who "did not look lesbian" (i.e., "politically correct"), old people, gay men, and children of lesbian mothers. Despite this greater diversity, and some very polarizing issues such as the lesbian sex wars, the community was considerably more successful in fostering unity in the 1980s than was the visible community that had been dominated by lesbian-feminists in the '70s. It generally understood that during conservative times, when many would rather see them disappear, lesbians would not survive as a community and they would be forced to return to the isolation of earlier years unless they became less doctrinaire about how to be a lesbian. They needed to discover areas where they might come together and work together despite differences.

The Shift to Moderation

Although the conservative swing in America was undeniable in the 1980s, women who loved women did not retreat en masse to the closets of pre-Stonewall and prelesbian-feminism. In fact, women who had been reluctant to become a part of the visible community that was dominated by radical lesbian-feminists in the '70s mustered the courage to show themselves in the '80s as the mood of the visible community shifted. Middle-class women and older women now dared to participate in public events they would have avoided in the '70s (and run from in the reactionary McCarthy era) and even to stage their own public events. They were not ignorant of the conservative swing in the country, but they were also aware that the '70s had wrought some positive changes. Those changes, such as the passage of gay rights bills in many cities and policies of "non-discrimination on the basis of sexual orientation" in many institutions, had not been eradicated even by the new conservatism. Lesbians could be fairly confident that America was still sensitive to issues of civil rights, and the shift to the Right, as annoying as it might be, was a far cry from the reactionary '50s. They believed they were safe in venturing further into the visible lesbian community as long as they avoided extremism.

As more moderate women claimed a place in the community, they succeeded in shifting its values toward moderation even further, but the shift in values did not mean that all the "politically correct" issues of the 1970s were relegated to the history bin as being no longer relevant in the 1980s. Rather, some aspects of "political correctness" were taken for granted as the only way to proceed when reaching out to the lesbian community. For example, there were few public events for lesbians in the '80s that did not promise child care, wheelchair accessibility, and interpretation for the hearing impaired. Radical lesbian-feminist theory had promoted a concern with human connections that went beyond simply enhancing the personal goals of career or self-gratification, and that concern was adopted even by less radical women as they joined the community.

But many of the issues that had plagued the lesbian- feminists were now seen as jejune, both by sophisticated young women who were coming into the community for the first time and by older women who were veterans. It no longer felt crucial, or even sensible, to shun whatever was valued in the heterosexual world for fear that it would sully lesbian aspirations for a non- hierarchical, egalitarian society. For example, 1970s lesbian performers had been given a cold reception by lesbian audiences if they appeared too polished, too much like professional male performers (see p. 222). The 1980s change in attitude was dramatized by Robin Tyler, the producer of what had been since the 1970s the very politically correct, huge West Coast and Southern Women's Music and Comedy Festivals. Tyler proclaimed:

> We're at the point now where I think we should be professional about what we do, where professional is a good word. I think we need to start examining our attitude toward success and power. I'm not talking about parroting the patriarchy. I'm talking about wanting people to stand up and achieve a level of quality.[4]

Success, power, professionalism, which had been tools of the enemy in the eyes of the radicals, became signs of accomplishment to the more moderate community of the '80s. Striving to "achieve a level of quality" ceased to be feared as divisive and inegalitarian. The greater acceptance of "professionalism" was connected with attitudes toward class, which were also defused in the more moderate '80s. Middle-class lesbians became more prominent in the visible community, young women of middle-class background no longer felt they must declass themselves to join the community, and many of the women who had been young, declassed radicals in the '70s changed their socio-economic status. Olivia record company has served as a revealing barometer of these changes. This company that had started business in the '70s, enchanted with the classless ideals of lesbian-feminism (see p. 223), by the end of the '80s was sponsoring luxury cruises to the Caribbean for lesbians.

Having gotten older, former lesbian-feminists, like the counterculture heterosexuals of the 1970s, often took the jobs in the '80s for

which their educations had equipped them. Their new status sometimes sat heavily upon them, and they tried to retain at least the
symbolic signs of their earlier affiliations, as Frederika, a Kansas City
woman, observed of her friends who were formerly radical lesbian-
feminists and had now entered the professions. They went to work
in skirts and high heels, but many of them could not wait to put on
their "lesbian clothes" when they got home or when they went out
for amusement: "Not just something comfortable, but ragged Salvation Army type clothes, and they shop at thrift stores." They continued to "live poor," although their socioeconomic positions had
changed. They were embarrassed by their apparent compromise with
middle-class values in "moving up on the status-financial ladder,"
according to Frederika.[5] However, by all American indicators of class
they had become part of the middle class that they had "trashed" in
the '70s, their social lifestyle notwithstanding.

But as many lesbians of the '70s got older in the '80s they tended
to become less radical and less critical of society in general, perhaps
because they found a not-uncomfortable niche in the mainstream
world. It was not atypical for them to say, as one Omaha woman did
of the women in her social circle who were in their forties:

> I think the whole picture has changed. The women in our group have
> it all together. They're happy with what they're doing. They all have
> good jobs. They're career women who chose to be career women.
> They have nice homes. They have the money to take the kinds of
> vacations they want to. They don't wish for anything to be different.
> Our group is happy.[6]

The visible lesbian community in the past often lacked older women
as role models. If one knew only the bar culture or the softball teams,
it would have appeared that there were no lesbians over thirty in the
world. But many of the lesbians whom the Omaha woman described
came up through lesbian-feminism, and they continued to go to
lesbian events. Their more moderate demeanor could create for young
women a new role model of how to be a lesbian. But the younger
women's broader version of ways to be a lesbian also gave the older
women permission to revise the images of the 1970s.

The 1970s glamour related to jobs in which one worked with one's
hands had largely worn off in the next decade. Nora, who became an
electrician in the '70s, felt by the end of the '80s that she wanted to
find a "more respected profession." She complained that while at the
height of the lesbian-feminist movement blue collar workers were

really valued, in the '80s "those same dykes say classist things, even though I'm making twice the money they are. I just want to get out of it." Class membership affiliations had shifted dramatically for many older lesbians.[7]

Some lesbians accepted what has been called "the politics of accommodation." They believed that lesbians can, after all, carve safe niches for themselves in a world that is less threatening to the well situated, while not feeling compelled either to hide or to reveal themselves. Unlike their counterparts of the '50s, they were generally not fearful about their sexual orientation being known. They had no reluctance, for example, about appearing at public lesbian events. But unlike their counterparts of the '70s, their shift in the direction of moderation gave them little interest in confronting the heterosexual world with personal facts. Like Sandy, who called herself a radical in the '70s and had since become a social work director, they said:

> I don't think it's necessary to be out professionally. It's irrelevant in terms of what I do in the day to day world. I think it's even hostile: "I dare you to get heavy with me because I'm a lesbian." I'm not primarily a lesbian in terms of how I identify myself. If you have to put all your chips in the dyke pile, you're not very comfortable about who you are. I would never deny it, but I wouldn't bring it up as a topic for discussion.[8]

The middle class in the visible lesbian community expanded not only through former radicals who joined the mainstream economically and professionally, but also through women who had never been part of the radical movement but felt in the '80s that there existed enough social and civil protections so that no harm would come to them if they ventured out with some discretion. Although there were career women who loved women throughout the century, their number was greatly multiplied as the economic opportunities of all women with middle-class educations improved in the '80s. Such increased numbers permitted the establishment of organizations all over the country devoted to lesbian career women, such as the Professional Women's Network in New York, the San Diego Career Women, and the Kansas City, Missouri, Network. Their purpose was to bring together lesbians with shared professional and cultural interests. Their goals, as the San Francisco Bay Area Career Women stated, were typically "to empower lesbians to achieve their full promise and potential." That full promise and potential, they believed, was facilitated by such middle-class, mainstream interests as

forums on estate planning, buying real estate, (lesbian) parenting, and
traveling for business and pleasure. Although groups made up of
lesbian professionals were usually shunned by the radical community
when such groups first started in the early '80s, by the end of the
decade, as the founder of the Bay Area Career Women observed,
"many of those who called us classist are coming to our dances,"
which often attracted two thousand women and more.[9]

All of these women were part of a growing class of what Phyllis
Lyon has described as "luppies" (lesbian yuppies). The phenomenon
was even reflected in lesbian fiction of the '80s. Numerous novels
presented characters who were less concerned with exiting from the
patriarchy, as they were in the '70s, than with buying Gucci luggage
and French calf boots, furnishing their living rooms to look like those
in *Architectural Digest,* driving Mercedes 450SLs or Buick Rivieras
that "shine like a polished panther," going to "snooty French restaurants," and sporting twenty-four karat gold cigarette lighters. Some
of those novels created fantasies and dream images of wealth merely
to amuse the reader, comparable to heterosexual Harlequin novels,
rather than to set up a model for reality. But in the '70s they would
have been trashed for being politically incorrect; in the '80s there was
little criticism of their characters' penchant for conspicuous consumption.[10]

There were even a number of very wealthy women who identifed
fairly openly with the lesbian community and helped to support it in
the '80s, further bridging class gaps and bringing in the money that
was requisite to making the community more substantial. Wealthy
lesbians helped form organizations such as Women With Inherited
Wealth and sponsored monthly meetings in which philanthropy toward
lesbian and women's causes was encouraged. They donated money
for the purchase of the Women's Building in San Francisco; they
bailed lesbian publishing houses out of the red; they even provided
meeting spaces for lesbian groups by throwing open their own resi-
dences. Coming from largely conservative backgrounds, those women
may have been fearful of identifying themselves as lesbian in earlier
eras. But despite the signs of social conservatism that reemerged in
the '80s, the battles of the preceding decade had helped more of them
to feel free to live as they pleased and let it be known that they had
ties to the lesbian community. The increased wealth and professional
status of women in the visible community altered its face in spite of
the sentimental attachment some women retained to more radical
times.[11]

Those who remembered the earlier years sometimes feared that all had been in vain. They bitterly regretted the demise of their dreams for an Amazon world. Looking superficially at the new face of the community, what they saw was a disappearance of the old concerns and institutions and an interest among lesbians in resembling mainstream society. They despaired, for example, that in Austin, Texas, where women's music had been such a living force in the '70s, concerts were losing money in the '80s, and young lesbians were buying mainstream music. Kasey, who was in her '40s, lamented:

> Someone's got to replace me for the Cris Williamson concerts. I've heard her twenty times. Where are the young lesbians? They don't know how hard we all struggled to get such things going in the '70s. The young people think no matter what happens it will continue to exist, and they can go once in a while if they feel like it. All they really want to do is make money and have a good time.

Kasey also despaired that in Kansas City, where she had lived during part of the '70s, the Women's Liberation Union was defunct and the Women's House where they met was sold; a radical Austin women's radio program that was started in the '70s was off the air; young women had gone back to the bars—more than five hundred of them, all under thirty, usually gathered to dance at an Austin lesbian bar called Nexus on weekend nights in the late '80s—instead of going to women's events.

But while the quest for a Lesbian Nation had surely been lost by the '80s, lesbianism as a lifestyle and the lesbian community were far from dead. Kasey also had to admit that despite the losses, there were some significant gains: Kansas City no longer had a Women's Liberation Union, but lesbians were openly welcomed in Kansas City NOW and a new young lesbian and gay group emerged out of the 1987 Lesbian and Gay March on Washington. Austin lesbians who wanted to go dancing on Saturday nights were not limited to Nexus; they could even dance at the Unitarian Church, which made a place for them in the '80s. If they wanted to go to a concert they had a choice not just of "women's music" but music by "crossover" entertainers such as K. D. Lang and Melissa Etheridge, and they felt no need to be shy about holding hands with their women lovers in the theater lobby, despite the fact that half the audience was heterosexual. Lesbians in Austin were no longer doing a radical radio program, but young lesbians were joining the Austin Blood Sisters in order to give blood to people with AIDS; they were part of the Austin Lesbian-Gay Political Caucus, from whom candidates for local offices sought endorsements; and they succeeded in pushing through an Austin antidiscrimination ordinance for lesbians and gay men.[12] To the extent that Austin and Kansas City were representative of fairly large lesbian communities in the 1980s, radicalism was defunct, but in its place there was a new lesbian and gay male unity, an increased acceptance of homosexuality in liberal circles, and even some manifestation of a growing political clout in that part of the mainstream that was not insensitive to the civil rights of homosexuals.

The goals of lesbian-feminism and the tenor of the community it established had come to seem too narrow and unrealistic. In the 1980s lesbians often sought ways to engage themselves politically that would not compromise their ideals but would be less parochial than what lesbian-feminism had permitted. Some of them maintained the utopian vision they had developed as lesbian-feminists but brought it to bear on larger issues. Others rejected utopian visions and wanted to find realistic ways to improve the world. In her novel *Valley of the Amazons* (1984), Noretta Koertge dramatizes the disillusionment with lesbian-feminism and the new yearning for action that might bring some results. Tretona, the lesbian hero, wanders from one lesbian group to another, discussing lesbian identity, non-monogamy, witchcraft as a religion. But she comes to believe about those "utopian" and visionary lesbian-feminist groups that

> All [they ever do] is trash what there is and dream about perfect little doll houses in the big separatist sky. I think it's time we started with the here and now and started thinking about alliances and working to really change things instead of trying to define perfection.

Like many women who left lesbian-feminism, Tretona rejects the segregated lesbian-feminist community and works to create a unified gay and lesbian political community.[13]

Such interest in working to solve the problems of the here and now that were often broader than the lesbian community was reflected in many of the novels of the 1980s. In Maureen Brady's *Folly* (1982), the lesbian characters are concerned with fighting corrupt factory owners. In Barbara Wilson's *Ambitious Women* (1982), the lesbians battle urban terrorism. In Chris South's *Clenched Fists, Burning Crosses* (1984), they fight the Ku Klux Klan.[14] The novels mirrored real life.

"There is nowhere to run from nuclear ruin or chemical waste," lesbians said in the '80s. Those older women who maintained their gender chauvinism remained cultural feminists. They had been convinced by lesbian-feminism in the 1970s of women's superior moral perceptions, and through that conviction they now developed the confidence to lead movements whose base is a utopian social vision. They often became the backbone in "direct action" peace and environmental movements: for example, they helped organize the Seneca Encampment to protest the army depot in Seneca Falls, from which cruise missiles were being sent to Europe; they were central in the Women's Pentagon Action, in which the protesters wove shut the doors of the Pentagon with brightly colored thread.[15] Their radicalism of the '70s was thus modified and diverted to different uses. Though the vision of a separate Lesbian Nation disappeared, some lesbians began to attempt in the '80s to bring their own values and presence to the broader nation.

Other manifestations of the shift in mood during the '80s were less global and had more to do with lifestyles in the dominant lesbian community, which came to reflect mainstream lifestyles much more than they had in the past. The '80s saw a certain sobriety settle over the dominant lesbian community with regard to issues that had been treated more lightly in the '70s, such as non-monogamy (the efforts of the sexual radicals notwithstanding) and drug and alcohol use. "Marriage" and "clean and sober" lifestyles became "in" among lesbians, just as they did among heterosexuals in the '80s.

To the more radical women who remained in the community it was not necessarily a positive sign to see lesbians who had once proclaimed the virtues of non-monogamy and the excitement or enlightenment they got from highs suddenly become "conventional." Some were fearful that the current war on drugs, sex, and other modern "evils" was really a hypocritical effort to rub out the culture changes of the past two decades by "masquerading as a caring crusade" about lesbian health. But many lesbians felt they had legitimate reasons to be concerned about their health. Lesbians as a group have the lowest incidence of AIDS in America; nevertheless, it is more frightening to them than to most heterosexuals because many of them have seen it up close among their gay male friends. Because of their concern, monogamy came to look attractive even to women who had been personally and ideologically against it in the past. Some of those who admitted to having been "promiscuous" said their patterns changed in the late '80s. A San Diego woman reflected:

> I really enjoy sex and would like to sleep around. I used to do it with
> women I didn't care anything about—after a few beers. But I haven't

been to bed with anyone since the AIDS virus became heavy here—
it's been years. I'm not infected with anything now. For a one night
stand, if I get AIDS it just wouldn't be worth it.

Casual sex was never widely popular among lesbians, but AIDS made
it even less so in the '80s. According to one mid-1980s survey of
lesbians, almost 80 percent viewed monogamy as "the ideal relationship." Because of this renewed commitment to monogamy it is
probable that the '90s will see more "holy unions" or "relationship
ceremonies" between lesbians such as those that were conducted in
the '80s by various liberal churches.[16]

But it was not AIDS alone that made the lesbian community much
more sober than it was in the 1970s. The "clean and sober" movement operated to help stem the party frenzy that many lesbians said
they experienced in the 1970s. One study by Jean Swallow (*Out from
Under: Sober Dykes and Our Friends,* 1983) said that 38 percent of all
lesbians are alcoholics and another 30 percent are problem drinkers.
Swallow concluded: "For a lesbian, those statistics mean you either
are one or you love one." While other studies suggest that Swallow's
statistics are inflated, there is no question that alcoholism as well as
drug abuse were common in the lesbian community in the '70s just
as they were among heterosexuals. That the incidence should be
somewhat higher among a segment of the lesbian community is not
surprising, since historically so much of lesbian life was lived in the
bars. As Diane, a Boston woman, recalls of the late 1960s when she
first came out:

> Learning to drink played a big role. The whole culture revolved around
> the bars. It would be the main social event during the summers. We
> would just bar hop from one place to another—in Boston, Province-
> town, Providence. It was just what everyone did.[17]

The campaign to "just say no" and live "clean and sober" that was
waged in the mainstream throughout the '80s caught fire in the
lesbian community. Alcoholics Anonymous, the 12 Step Program,
and Living Sober groups quickly adapted themselves to the needs of
homosexuals. For example, the patriarchal, Christian emphasis of AA
literature was modified when presented to the all-lesbian AA and Al-
Anon (partners of alcoholics) groups that cropped up around the
country. Boston alone had eighty weekly AA meetings for lesbians
in the late '80s. San Francisco had ninety such weekly meetings.
Living Sober conventions that targeted the lesbian and gay commu-

nity attracted large, rapidly growing numbers. The Living Sober contingents were the biggest in the Gay Pride parades at the end of the decade. There were even all-lesbian and -gay residential programs for the treatment of alcohol and drug dependency, such as the Pride Institute in Minnesota, where patients were encouraged not just to deal with drug and alcohol abuse but also to think affirmatively about homosexuality as an alternative lifestyle.[18]

Lesbians who participated in "clean and sober" programs were often euphoric in their enthusiasm. Janet said unabashedly:

> AA saved my life. I'm so different than I was a few years ago. I was going to die. I was spiritually bankrupt. I had no hope. I got to the point where the coke and the alcohol weren't fun anymore. And then Living Sober AA came along and gave me a whole support group—a peer group. Ten years ago there weren't such things as lesbian AA. I wouldn't have gone in with all those hets who probably hate queers anyway. There was no place for me to go. Now there are even sober lesbian dances.[19]

A whole culture of sobriety developed to replace the bar culture that had been so pivotal to the lives of many lesbians in the past. Women who, outside of the lesbian community, might not have identified themselves as being in need of "recovery" found support for such identification within the community, and "clean and sober" became a social movement for lesbians.

All these phenomena illustrate the shift to moderation that overtook a community whose dominant tone in other eras had been far more extreme. While the general relative conservatism of the '80s had an influence on the shift, there were additional factors that explain it, such as the influx of young, postfeminist women who saw no need for serious militance, the disillusionment of lesbians who had been around in the '70s with the older lesbian lifestyles, and the realistic fears about health. But it appears to be warranted to conclude that the demeanor of the visible community changed primarily because of economic reasons. There were in the '80s more women in the American work force who were pursuing careers than ever before, and more opportunities were opening up to them. Since lesbians have generally attained higher levels of education than heterosexual women because they knew they had to be self-supporting and they seldom have multiple children who could interfere with career advancement, they are more likely to be successful professionally. There was a significant increase in the number of lesbians who reached middle-

class status through their work and who would have difficulty denying their middle-class socioeconomic position and values in the 1980s.
Those women had fewer fears than their middle-class lesbian predecessors about becoming a part of the visible lesbian community. Thus
their values gave a tenor to that community that connected it to the
mainstream much more closely than it had been connected since
lesbianism first became a subculture in America.

Of course not all middle-class lesbians became part of the visible
community. Some were still no more comfortable with being lesbian
than their 1950s counterparts may have been. They saw their lesbianism as a problem for their careers and believed that exposure would
do them great professional damage. A central California woman told
of having regular "fire drills" with her lover, who was employed in
the same public institution where she worked: "We made up a complete story. Like if anyone would accuse us we would absolutely deny
it. We practiced answers about why we weren't married, why we had
gone somewhere together (just in case anyone saw us), why we have
to share a home. We know how we would answer everything." [20]

In the 1980s some lesbians still went to such lengths as to ask gay
men to "front" for them at work-related social functions, or they
constructed a second bedroom so that they would not be suspected of
sleeping together if heterosexuals came to visit. As one San Antonio
lawyer said, "We don't exactly live in a gay ghetto here. Texas is
twenty years behind the rest of the country unless you're in Austin.
So we even have to hide our Lezzie library. You just don't display it
here. Our housecleaner would faint, and I have clients coming over."
But thanks to the sexual and social liberation of the '70s, the need to
hide was not a foremost consideration for many women who loved
other women in the 1980s. While they tended to be closeted in some
situations, they did not feel that they must disguise their affections at
all times, as their counterparts did in more conservative eras. On the
whole they were free to be—as psychologist Barbara Sang described
a group of lesbian career women she studied—"self-actualized," "self-
confident," "self-accepting." [21]

Validation of Diversity

The San Francisco Gay Pride Parade of 1987, which commemorated the 1969 Stonewall Rebellion, ended in front of the City Hall
area, where three stages were set up in order to accommodate a

variety of speeches and entertainment, all going on simultaneously. Three separate stages had been erected not only because the organizers despaired of being able to communicate anything to an audience of a third of a million people with only one stage, but also because after almost two decades of parades and "Gay Pride" they realized that there is no such entity as "the gay" or "the lesbian" and speeches or entertainment that would be welcomed by one segment of the community would be irrelevant to another. The parade organizers' strategy was, as the lesbian president of the parade board of directors announced, "to offer diversity to a diverse community."[22]

The sexologists who first described lesbians seemed to believe they were mostly all alike, and the heterosexual world allowed itself to be cognizant only of the most obvious stereotypes. Even many lesbians themselves have preferred to see all women who loved women as being from the same mold, such as the butches and femmes in the 1950s and '60s and the dykes of Lesbian Nation in the 1970s. But lesbians have always comprised a diverse community or, more specifically, diverse subcultures. As more women in the 1980s dared to join the visible lesbian community and to demand a place within the definition of the lesbian, the extent of the diversity became clearer. Paradoxically, the community's shift toward moderation actually encouraged that diversity. It muted the passion for conformity that had characterized lesbian communities, and the peripheries felt more able to make themselves visible, since the dominant community was generally not as violently critical of all who did not fit its mold. Although significant conflicts still erupted in the '80s such as the sex wars, the end of the decade seemed to promise more acceptance of diversity within the larger lesbian community than at any other time in the past. Peripheral groups and the dominant community sought ways to coexist and to merge whenever it was mutually helpful.

The visible lesbian community became more racially and ethnically diverse in the 1980s, succeeding to some extent where radical lesbian-feminists had reaped mostly frustration (though it was the radicals who had helped to foster awareness in minority lesbians, who now began to see themselves as a group with lesbian and feminist political interests). "Integration," however, has been complicated because minorities who were very sensitized to issues of injustice were often quick to see prejudice among white lesbians. White lesbians, hoping to ameliorate such distrust, helped to place minorities in leadership positions in the dominant lesbian movement—which sometimes backfired, resulting in accusations of tokenism and then more distrust.[23] By the end of the '80s minority lesbians usually felt most comfortable working and socializing with each other when possible; however, they were also willing to offer their input to the larger lesbian community on issues they felt were pertinent. Although the arrangement was not ideal as far as activist white lesbians were concerned, it was consonant with their desire to nurture diversity and be able to rely on unity when it was crucial to the circumstances.

Minority women had been slower to organize as lesbians because they often witnessed acute homophobia in their parent communities. It was difficult for them to risk the animosity to which lesbian activism could subject them. But the growing feminist sentiments in America during the 1970s eventually encouraged many minority women also to choose to be lesbians and finally to dare to organize as lesbians. Most refused, however, to call themselves lesbian-feminists because they were alienated by certain tenets of lesbian-feminism such as lesbian separatism, which, they believed, shared many of the components of racism. Minority lesbians preferred to call themsleves "lesbians of color" in the '80s, rejecting the 1970s term "Third World," which they now felt to imply that the "First" and "Second" worlds are better. As their numbers grew in the visible community, especially in the largest cities, it was not uncommon by the end of the '80s for there to be not only "lesbians of color" groups but also organized groups of Latina lesbians, Chicana lesbians, Asian lesbians, South Asian lesbians, Japanese lesbians, black lesbians, fat black lesbians, etc.

Their splintering reflects a ubiquitous desire to discover common roots and experiences, a desire that had been prevalent in the parent culture as well over the last two decades. But it was intensified for lesbians. While in earlier eras accepting a lesbian identity was in itself so overwhelming that it was important just to find other lesbians with whom to share that identity, the loosening of social strictures in the '70s made the choice to be lesbian somewhat less overwhelming. By the '80s many lesbians required something more than just a shared sexual identification with other lesbians. The larger the lesbian community grew, the deeper became the realization that a shared sexual orientation alone does not guarantee that its members will have much in common. A great longing emerged to have all aspects of self validated by the group, not just the sexual aspect.

While the white lesbian community saw itself as being welcoming, many lesbians of color believed that their deeper selves were left untouched in that community. They needed to combat the sense of alienation that comes from perceiving an insufficient commonality. But because their parent communities were usually intolerant of homosexuality, there was nowhere that they could feel that their entire self was recognized. Abby, a Native American, characterized that sense of frustration:

> When I went to Eureka, to my Yoruk tribe, I felt as though I was somewhat accepted but they were not always ready for me as a queer, so I had to keep that part hidden a little. It felt easier for me to live in San Francisco than at home. But when I was in San Francisco, in a lesbian group, I felt they couldn't understand the Indian part of me. They're different from what I'm used to: different values, different approaches, a different sense of humor. They didn't know about those families back home I grew up with, the disputes, the importance of questions like "How's the fishing?" There was no place where all of me was validated.

Other lesbians of color such as Mariana Romo-Carmona, a Latina lesbian from New York, described such frustration as feeling "kind of like you're in exile wherever you go." She explained that it was to combat that sense of exile that she helped to form the Latina lesbian group Las Buenas Amigas (the Good Friends—a Spanish euphemism for women in lesbian relationships). She believed that such groups were vital because, try as they might, white lesbians had no way of understanding the alienation of lesbians of color or of accepting their unique perceptions.[24]

The last minority to become part of the lesbians of color groups in the '80s were Asians. Although there were isolated Asian lesbians within the community during the '70s and earlier, it was not until the next decade, as more Asians became Americanized and broke out of the confinement of immigrant values and deeply entrenched traditionalism, that their numbers became sufficient to permit them to establish a separate group within some lesbian communities. The largest Asian lesbian group was in San Francisco, which has the oldest and therefore most acculturated Asian population. But Asian lesbian organizations were also started in other areas, such as the Chicago Asian Lesbians Moving (CALM), the New York based Asian Lesbians of the East Coast, Houston's Gay Asians and Friends, and Philadelphia's Lesbian/Gay Asian Network.[25]

At the 1987 Gay and Lesbian March on Washington, Asian lesbians gathered as a group, chanting, "Say it clear,/Say it loud,/We are Asian, gay and proud." After the march they declared in *Phoenix Rising,* an "Asian/Pacific Lesbian Newsletter":

We are not going to let ourselves be forgotten. . . . We are so mar-
ginal, so out of view, a secret our own people won't dare admit. To
mainstream America we are unheard of, unthought of, impossible. A
contradiction in terms. Seeing our faces and hearing our names on
national news was one step closer to where we can be.

While in the past they may have been relieved by their lesbian invisi-
bility, in the late '80s it became a source of irritation to many Asian
lesbians. They wanted to claim a place in what they saw as a flourishing community that represented women's strength and an effective
protest against the coercions into feminine weakness they often associated with their parent culture. They became anxious to dispel the
myth that lesbianism is a Western phenomenon and, in doing so,
legitimize their own choices.[26]

Lesbians of color in the 1980s were sometimes as critical of the
white lesbian community as their "Third World" counterparts were
in the '70s. They pointed to instances of racism that they believed
were rampant even in the lesbian bars. "At Billie Jean's Bar in Kansas
City," a Missouri lesbian insisted, "there was an unspoken policy
that we all knew about. If you were white you could get by with a
driver's licence. If you were black you needed three pieces of i.d. and
suddenly there was a cover charge." But unlike earlier years, when
Third World lesbians suffered such discrimination by themselves, in
the '80s they were able to make coalitions with white lesbians to
protest. At Private Eyes, a woman's club in New York, when word
got out that the manager "had instructions from headquarters to not
let too many blacks in," lesbians of color joined together with predominantly white lesbian groups for a victorious protest. The incident itself confirmed the conviction of many lesbians of color that
racism is far from eradicated among lesbians and that they have
reason to look primarily to each other for comfort and unity. But the
interracial picketing helped to dispel the impression that racism was
ubiquitous in the larger lesbian community.[27]

Other minorities, such as disabled lesbians and fat lesbians, continued the battle that they began in the 1970s for recognition and regard
in the lesbian community. They organized groups such as Fat Dykes
and published magazines such as *Dykes, Disability, and Stuff.* They
adapted the psychology and rhetoric of the gay liberation movement,
calling themselves "differently abled;" referring to "fat liberation;"
and proclaiming, "The space I take up is the space I deserve." Because
the basis of lesbianism as a lifestyle is a challenge to accepted notions
about what is normal, they felt that the lesbian community, more

than any other group, was obliged to understand and help them fight their own battles against stale perceptions of "normal" regarding appearance or abilities. They demanded that the community continually renew its commitment to pluralism and non-discrimination and that it invent new and better ways of treating one another, lest it mirror the injustices of the outside world. For example, when a fat lesbian was fired from a counterculture food collective in 1988, she not only brought the case to the Fair Employment Commission but also called on the lesbian community to boycott the collective and write letters of protest against "fat phobia." Throughout the '80s splinterings continued among lesbians with special interests. However, they invariably grappled for acknowledgment as organized parts of the lesbian community, and they demanded support that would prove the community's devotion to the principle of diversity-within-unity.[28]

The visible lesbian community also became more diverse in the '80s with regard to age. While in earlier decades it often seemed like a youth culture because as lesbians got older they would drop out of the visible community, in the '80s new resources and particularly encouragement of diversity caused older lesbians and even old lesbians to remain and take an active part. Like other lesbians with differences, by the end of the 1980s they began to organize on their own, often clarifying their position to themselves and others with angry rhetoric. But the larger community took some care to assure them of a place despite differences, consciously opening up to include not only middle-aged lesbians, but old lesbians as well.

In the 1980s old lesbians undertook for the first time to organize. They held gatherings such as the West Coast Conference and Celebration by and for Old Lesbians. The conference participants militantly preferred the term "old" for the same reason that other minorities have preferred to call themselves "black" or "dyke"—to defuse its power to sting and to reject trivializing euphemisms. The keynote speaker at the first conference set the tone with an angry volley charging her audience to confront ageism in lesbian and feminist groups, which, she said, is covered up as respect for older women. As one conference participant observed, "This was the birth of the angry old woman [cf. the "angry young man" of the 1950s]. . . . To walk in and see two hundred white haired dykes, all ready to stand up and assert themselves, was mind-boggling." Like other minority lesbians, they looked to each other for a sense of solidarity, but at the same time they demanded visibility within the larger lesbian community. At the 1988 San Francisco Gay Pride March a contingent of old lesbians chanted as they marched, "2, 4, 6, 8, how do you know your grandma's straight?"[29]

Younger lesbians took seriously old lesbians' criticism which was being voiced in books such as Barbara McDonald's *Look Me in the Eye* and Baba Copper's *Over the Hill*.[30] Some of the younger women who were social workers (a time-honored profession among lesbians) focused their interest on lesbian gerontology. They helped start groups such as Gay and Lesbian Outreach to Elders (GLOE) and Senior Action in a Gay Environment (SAGE), which attempted to encourage old lesbians to be a part of the visible lesbian community, offering services such as visiting homebound or isolated seniors, organizing lesbian senior citizen dances, and providing information regarding housing, health, and legal matters. The presence of old lesbians in the community served to remind younger lesbians that they could not simply sit and dream about the Lesbian Nation of the future. They had some responsibility to deal with those who were here now.

The increased presence of children served a similar purpose. There had always been mothers within the lesbian community, but they usually became mothers through marriages that antedated their lives as lesbians, and they sometimes made other lesbians uncomfortable, since children were seen as antithetical to an all-women environment. In the '80s, however, a growing number of women chose to have children after they established themselves as lesbians. One study of lesbians at the beginning of the 1980s indicated that 49 percent had considered motherhood since they became homosexual. The community generally supported such a choice by the 1980s. There was even a spate of books and films aimed specifically at lesbians that discussed getting pregnant outside of heterosexuality and being a lesbian parent.[31]

Thus not only had the visible community become chronologically older, but many more lesbians opted to raise families, further challenging the public image of lesbianism as a youth culture that was carefree and without lasting ties. It was also another indication of the growing acceptance of diversity within the community that lesbian motherhood was no longer seen as a contradiction in terms and women were not so quick to claim, as they had been in the past, "I became a lesbian because I didn't want children in my life."

While in earlier eras the choice to get pregnant and raise children outside of heterosexual marriage was unthinkable for most women, including lesbians, the 1970s had taken the sting out of single parenting. For lesbians, who had seen examples in their community of women who had had children in marriage and then were forced into traumatic, disheartening court battles over custody, it was especially important to find ways to have children without men. Those ways were not so difficult to envision in the '80s when heterosexual women were taking for granted the fact that intercourse did not necessarily lead to having a child; lesbians felt the right to assume that having a child was not necessarily the consequence of intercourse. Since working mothers also became more acceptable in the larger culture during the 1970s, lesbians by the '80s were more easily able to envision undertaking the responsibility of having children and working to support them without the help of a man. Some chose to adopt or become foster parents in the states where they could do so; there have even been court-approved joint adoptions by openly lesbian couples in recent years. But most of those who felt the need for motherhood chose donor insemination (often self-administered with the help of a turkey baster). That choice was made easier during the 1980s not only by the numerous sperm banks set up originally to service heterosexuals, but also by the establishment in some large cities of sperm banks for the primary use of lesbians, which promoted a minor baby boom in the lesbian community.[32]

The community generally encouraged women who wanted to be mothers. For example, in 1987 the San Francisco Lyon-Martin Women's Health Service and the Lesbian Rights Project co-sponsored a well-attended "Parenting Faire." There were not only numerous lesbian mother support groups in big cities such as Latina Lesbian Mothers, Lesbian Couples With Children, Lesbian Moms of Young Children, Lesbians Parenting Adolescents, Gay/Lesbian Parenting Group, Lesbian Mothers Problem Solving Group, and Lesbian Parent Counselling, but even play groups for children of lesbian mothers. Lesbian newspapers ran articles that would have been found only in *Family Circle*-type magazines a decade earlier, exhorting prospective lesbian mothers: "Well, if you're trying right now, take heart. It almost always happens. . . . Honor yourself and keep on!" Lesbian mothers marching in the 1988 Gay Pride parades chanted, "We're here and we're gay and we're in the PTA."[33] The 1980s saw the birth of the first generation of openly gay parents. Against considerable odds, the lesbian community became one that included many children. Not only was more tolerance demanded from the childless, but also a more moderate approach to life (which parenthood demands) had to be developed by lesbians who chose to become mothers.

In accepting into their fold a wide range of people, the most visible lesbian community demonstrated for the first time that unity was possible even though it had become much too large to hope for uniformity. The extent of lesbian diversity was really dramatized when a conservative institution such as Yale University, which had not one *admitted* lesbian twenty years earlier (when it first began admitting women), had in the late 1980s what the *Wall Street Journal* described as "a growing number of special-interest [lesbian] factions," including the "lipsticks" (Yale's "radical chic lesbians"), the "crunchies" ("granola dykes who have old-fashioned utopian ideas about feminism"), a "Chicana lesbian group," and the assimilationists ("who don't want to draw attention to their sexuality").[34] Such diversity was multiplied myriad times over in the lesbian communities across America.

The lesbian-feminists of the 1970s attempted to create a transcendent lesbian identity in which all lesbians looked alike, ate alike, thought alike, loved alike. Since lesbians had never been uniform, lesbian-feminism's ideological rigidity generally doomed it to failure. But lesbian-feminists were successful in that they drew a good deal of public attention to lesbianism, usually without disastrous results, since the liberal '70s permitted differences. This meant that less radical lesbians began to feel that it was safer to come out than it had been in the past, and it also meant that the visible lesbian community could become much more diverse than ever before. By the end of the '70s the proliferation of small groups fraught with mistrust for other groups seemed to signify the death of any hopes for a strong lesbian community. But as the '80s progressed, because moderation replaced ideological rigidity, it began to seem that the community could learn to deal with diversity and that a politics of coalition was possible when desirable, as symbolized through the tremendous numbers of diverse lesbians who appeared for the many Gay Pride parades and the National March on Washington for Lesbian and Gay Rights.

Unity

Coalitions within the lesbian community were more than symbolic. Obviously not all the issues that divided the community and made a unified Lesbian Nation impossible to attain in the 1970s disappeared entirely in the '80s, but they were usually met with less passion. Although the very real splits between groups such as the cultural feminists and the sexual radicals cannot be discounted, the '80s brought significant truces which suggested a healthy semblance of unity in the visible community.

Separatism, for instance, ceased to be the burning topic it once was. There still existed in the late '80s some enclaves of separatists who insisted that in rejecting separatism the rest of the lesbian world had "lost its vision." However, most of the lesbian community felt by the end of the decade that while separatism may be effective for a specific struggle at a certain time, as a lifestyle it attests to a "failure of global vision." They now insisted that it is simply not possible for lesbians to separate themselves from the problems of the world. In growing numbers, they proclaimed in lesbian publications that a lesbian is also a complex human being, with attachments often to fathers, sons, male friends, and straight women, and separatism had failed to speak to all of the lesbian's complexity. Separatism came to be identified with bigotry by some lesbians because it "judged people by gender and class rather than as individuals." The greatest contact most lesbians had with separatism by the late '80s was a temporary one, at the huge all-women's music festivals around the country. For them it became a fantasy world of how life may once have been in an Amazon nation but no longer a model for how life could or should be in America as it approaches the end of the century.[35]

Separatism would probably have died in the lesbian community just by virtue of its dogmatism, which choked off the possibilities of all relationships and interests outside of a narrow circle. But the AIDS crisis, which profoundly affected gay men in the 1980s, demanded soul-searching on the part of lesbians that not only led for many to a reconciliation with the men but also brought about a political and social unity on a scale much larger than ever before. Many lesbians felt called upon to take in active role in dealing with the crisis. As a blood drive advertisement sponsored by a lesbian group put it (in language reminiscent of World War II patriotic drives), "Our boys need our blood. . . . . Stand by our brothers in fighting the AIDS epidemic."[36] In the face of such an overwhelming threat to a segment of the population that has ties with lesbians, in terms of common enemies if nothing else, many lesbians felt they had no choice but to put aside the luxury of separatism.

There were lesbians who believed that gay men brought AIDS on themselves because of their promiscuous lifestyle. Some proclaimed that if a fatal disease had threatened to wipe out the lesbian community, gay men would not be putting their resources and energy into helping lesbians as many lesbians felt obliged to help gay men. "I feel resentful," one said, "because this crisis already overshadows many others, and because men's issues always take precedence over women's. . . . What about women's health? What about lesbian health services?[37] But such a response did not reflect many in the visible lesbian community who put a vast effort into raising money, giving blood, and serving as volunteers for projects that assigned them to make dinner, walk dogs, or go shopping for people with AIDS. Lesbians provided such remarkable support that a gay moviemaker, David Stuart, felt moved to produce a film of thanks called *Family Values,* a "salute from us gay men to you lesbians," spotlighting women who brought gay men into their homes so that they could die surrounded by peace and love.

The film's name, with its ironic thrust at homophobes who claim that homosexuality is antifamily, was apt. The crisis did create a sense of family among many lesbians and gay men that was missing during the 1970s. As one woman explained the metamorphosis in lesbian-gay relationships, "When a whole community is dying you drop a lot of the in-fighting."[38] For many lesbians, losing acquaintances through AIDS made them reexamine how they wanted to live the rest of their lives and to conclude that the antagonism between the two linked communities was counterproductive and tragic. They undertook the battle against AIDS as though they were fighting for members of their very own family.

Although AIDS was not the anticipated next step in their march toward liberation, many lesbians were convinced in the '80s that the strength of the contemporary lesbian and gay movement would be judged by its response to AIDS. They believed that the right wing, which used AIDS as an excuse to attack all homosexuals, aimed to wipe out lesbians along with gay men, even if only as an afterthought. They quoted from homophobic literature such as a pamphlet issued by a group called Dallas Doctors Against AIDS: "Such a severe public health concern must cause the citizenry of this country to do everything in their power to smash the homosexual movement in this country to make sure these kinds of acts are criminalized." Lesbians could have responded to statements by such hate groups, which claim that AIDS is God's judgment on homosexuality, by saying that lesbians must then be God's elect, since the incidence of AIDS among them is far lower than among heterosexuals. But they generally chose to make common cause with gay men rather than distinguishing themselves.[39] The right wing's poisonous attack on homosexuality because of AIDS reminded lesbians that there really were enemies out there they had forgotten about and they could not afford the complacency of turning their backs on their battle allies. Despite the loss of many gay male leaders through AIDS, the united homosexual community took the crisis as a rallying point and proved itself to be at an apex of strength in terms of its ability to mobilize and fight back.

While compassion was instrumental in bringing about the reconciliation between lesbians and gay men, the growing realization that collectively they had greater power with which to fight their common enemies also led to their making common cause. Their potential for collective power was dramatized nowhere so much as at the 1987 National March on Washington for Lesbian and Gay Rights. The march far exceeded the expected quarter of a million participants, drawing 650,000, which made it the largest civil rights march in American history, far surpassing the 1963 Civil Rights March and the 1969 Vietnam Moratorium demonstration. The mood of reconciliation was symbolized by the chants and the placards of the March that suggested the irrelevance of separatism, such as "Gay power is people power" and "We're one country, one people—We're part of the fabric of life in our country."[40]

Lesbian fiction in the 1980s sometimes reflected such reconciliation between lesbians and gay men, in dramatic contrast to the lesbian novels of the '70s in which gay men were practically nonexistent. Vicki McConnell's *The Burnton Widows* (1984), for example, shows a new unification coming about when heterosexuals throw lesbians and gay men together through homophobia and they are forced to create a "gay family." As one character proclaims, "Even when a lot of places we live in won't claim us or include us in any real sense, don't think we don't have our own network. . . . People with no civil rights have a historic bonding."[41]

Where lesbians and gay men pulled together in the '80s they were able to affect startling and wonderful changes. Obviously their successes were most apparent in large cities, but what happens in large cities is often a harbinger of the future for the rest of the country. New York, for example, established a liaison out of the mayor's office to the gay and lesbian community. Its lesbian head, Lee Hudson, believes, "I may have to initiate things with public officials, but once I do there's always a lot of sympathy. I've never had a battle

from them. They admit there have been problems in the past, and
they haven't known what to do or how to do it. But now they're
very interested in helping in whatever way they can." [42]

Other elected officials such as the Manhattan district attorney, the
City Council president, and the Controller, all had similar liaisons to
the gay and lesbian community in the 1980s. The chancellor of the
Board of Education had appointed a multicultural task force to re-
write areas of the curriculum that were insensitive to various populations, including lesbians and gay men. An open lesbian was placed on
the advisory committee for the sex equity task force of the Board of
Education. The New York Police Department staged a major recruit-
ing campaign to hire lesbian and gay police officers. Groups that
discriminated against homosexuals lost city funding. A comprehensive gay rights bill was passed in New York in 1986 (New York was
the fifty-sixth city to pass such a bill). Public officials in New York
saw homosexuals in the 1980s as a vital constituency. Progress, such
as could only come about through a sense of community at the
necessary times, was undeniable.

Lesbians and gay men also joined forces in national organizations
to exercise political influence. Unlike co-ed homosexual organizations
of the 1950s and '60s, those national organizations often made a
special point to represent lesbian concerns as much as those of gay
males. The Gay and Lesbian Democratic Clubs, for example, promulgated their support of equal rights and reproductive choice for
women no less than their support of the abolition of all sodomy laws.
Activist gay men appear to have taken to heart lesbians' complaints
in the '70s that they were insensitive to women's issues. Many lesbians thus came to see a coalition between homosexual men and women
as being to everyone's benefit. "We need to be a political force with
gay men," they said, "because unless we hang together and lobby to
get the things we want, we'll hang separately. We'll remain invisible
and be stepped on. We need more numbers and the way to get it is to
join forces." Lesbians' concerns of the '70s largely vanished as they
proclaimed in the '80s, "We don't fear being subsumed. Wilting
flowers are not common in the lesbian community." [43]

The increased tolerance among lesbians also had much to do with
their disillusionment with "political correctness" and their shift to
perceiving the world with more subtlety and complexity than the
doctrinaire '70s allowed. The issue of bisexuality presented a particular challenge to the tolerance of the visible lesbian community. Lesbians with a commitment to the lifestyle had feared and been suspi-

cious of women who seemed to be merely "experimenting." Not only could bisexual women break hearts when they returned to men, but also they might betray the secretiveness that was requisite for the community. When lesbians became political the suspicion was intensified because committed lesbians wanted all women in the lesbian community to be battle allies, and they were discomfitted by those who might fall back on bisexuality when the going got tough.

As militancy decreased, some women became more willing to leave open questions of their own sexuality and that of other women. As a Texas woman characterized it, "I feel now there are more options open to me. Maybe one of the things that's come out of the '80s is that we all have more options. You don't have to rigidly define yourself as one thing or another. If you can live with indefiniteness there's a lot more potential."[44]

Though some continued to have reservations about bisexuality, they opposed it not because it was considered politically incorrect as it was in the '70s, but rather because they were cognizant of the dangers of a bisexual contracting the AIDS virus heterosexually and bringing it into the lesbian community. However, philosophically there was far more openness to bisexuality. By the end of the decade there were about two dozen bisexual support groups in the United States, and lesbian newspapers gave significant space to reports of their concerns and activities. There was more willingness to recognize, as a character observes in a late 1980s lesbian novel set in a lesbian woman's clinic, that not only do "straight women come to dyke bars to get picked up," but also, although they may deny it even to themselves, sometimes "lesbians get swept away" and have sex with men.[45] Such an admission was a tacit recognition of the accuracy of Kinsey's finding that few people rank as a pure 0 (completely heterosexual) or a pure 6 (completely homosexual) on the Kinsey scale. While movement lesbians were very uncomfortable with that fact in the '70s, it was not so politically disturbing to them in the less rigid '80s, and bisexuals were no longer categorically shunned. Such a leap in tolerance made unity possible with one more group that was seen in less moderate times as pariahs by the lesbian community.

While the radical vision of the '70s was nowhere near realized in the 1980s, strong lesbian or lesbian/gay communities flourished. In some areas lesbians were able to live their whole lives in a homosexual context if they wished. Kriss, a 21 year old San Francisco restaurant worker, said, "My landlord is gay, my boss is gay, everyone I associate with is either gay or is used to dealing with gay people. I can walk down the street for miles holding hands with my lover. Nobody would say 'dyke' who wasn't one around here." [46] Some gay and lesbian ghettos were so self-contained and populous in the 1980s that if one did not have to leave in order to make a living it might well seem that homosexuality was the norm and straights were "queer." Although most lesbians lived outside of such ghettos, knowledge of them was psychologically beneficial. They represented a mecca to which one might retreat, even if only in fantasy, should one's own milieu become difficult.

Of course, for some lesbians those meccas may as well have been on another planet. Despite the gay and lesbian ghettos, the spread of civil rights, the successful challenges that had been made to the popular media images of lesbians as "odd girls" and "twilight lovers," they remained as closeted as they or their predecessors had been during the McCarthy era. Their lifestyles were not very different from what lesbian life had been thirty or forty years earlier, as the San Antonio and central California women suggested (p. 284). As far as they were concerned, homophobia had been so ingrained in America for so long that they did not trust to the changes, and they continued to be fearful that they would lose their jobs, be kicked out of their homes, or be disowned by their famiilies should their lesbianism become known. But there were far fewer objective reasons to harbor such fears in the 1980s.

And most lesbians, even outside of the ghettos, did indeed feel that their lives had changed. There were more numbers, more choices, more possibilities of meeting other women who loved women. The proliferation of visible community members was not only reassuring; it also provided support systems that did not exist earlier. In a 1980s study of older lesbians (ages fifty to seventy-three) more than half the women said that in earlier decades, during the traumatic events of their lives such as a breakup of a relationship, they received little or no comforting since they did not belong to a lesbian community and they could not tell their heterosexual friends why they were suffering. But most of those women in the 1980s stated that "things were different for them now." They perceived themselves as having more lesbian friends to turn to since the community had grown so much, not only because more women were becoming lesbians, but especially because fewer lesbians were in the closet to the degree they had once been. [47] Of course there were still many women in the '80s who found themselves isolated and alone in their lesbianism, but if they were willing to seek out a community, it was there for them. The phrase "the well of loneliness" as a description of lesbian life lost any aptness it many once have had.

By the end of the '80s, as some lesbian communities grew older together, a sense of security within their friendship circles was even further reinforced. As one thirty-six-year-old woman observed:

> I'm much closer to my lesbian friends than I am to my family. We're really there for each other. If I never had a lover again it wouldn't matter because I have so much love in my life. Most of my friends I've known for ten or twelve years. We're really family.[48]

The sense of family and the larger sense of community had not been easy to come by. It required not only that women acknowledge their love for women as they did at the beginning of the century, but that they accept the definition of themselves as "lesbian" and part of a sexual minority. It required not only that they commit themselves to lesbianism as a lifestyle as they did in the 1950s, but that they see themselves as having distinct political needs because they are homosexuals in a heterosexual world. It required not only that they temper their views about how lesbianism should be lived as they did after the radical '70s, but that they learn to create coalitions with those who do not live it as they do. There was insufficient consciousness, moderation, and savvy to do all of that in the past, and the hostility of heterosexuals seemed too forbidding to permit lesbians to think creatively. In the course of the 1980s, however, lesbians who sought it were able to find all that was requisite to create among themselves both family and community.

A Note on the '90s: Queer Nation?

As the last decade of the twentieth century begins there is evidence that yet another change may be evolving in the most visible segment of the lesbian community. The shift to moderation that characterized much of the 1980s seems to have brought about a reaction among some young lesbians, particularly those who are now in their early twenties. There are hints that they are demanding more drama and intensity, not only in their personal style, which is often far more colorful than that of older lesbians, but especially in their emerging political stance. An incipient movement seems to be gathering momentum. In its angry militance this new movement promises to have something in common with lesbian-feminism of the 1970s. It is different, however, in that gay men were its first organizers and it is presently dependent on coalitions with gay men.

The new militance actually began near the end of the 1980s and owes its start to impatience felt by gay men and concerned lesbians with the heterosexual world's slow response to the AIDS crisis. ACT-UP (AIDS Coalition to Unleash Power) was formed by a group of gay men and some lesbians who were activists in the fight against AIDS and felt that more confrontational action was required to bring attention to their cause. For example, to dramatize the reality of AIDS deaths, the gay men and lesbians of New York ACT-UP staged a huge mock New Orleans-style funeral procession in front of the Waldorf-Astoria hotel where President Bush was speaking at a Republican fund-raising dinner. By the beginning of 1990 several members of ACT-UP had also begun the tactic of "outing," exposing public figures who were closeted homosexuals. One argument they used in favor of outing was that if the heterosexual world understood that "we are everywhere," even in the most respected and admired positions, it could not pretend that AIDS should be ignored because it struck only the most despised and insignificant.[49]

In April 1990 a group of New York ACT-UP lesbians and gay men who were interested in doing direct action around broader lesbian and gay issues formed Queer Nation, which almost immediately spread to other coastal cities such as Boston and San Francisco. Although gay men were the most active in establishing Queer Nation they clearly wanted the participation of lesbians, and hence carefully selected the word "queer" to serve as an umbrella term—a synonym not only for "faggots" and "fairies," but also for "lezzies" and "dykes." At writing, only approximately twenty percent of Queer Nation is lesbian, but press coverage of the group's activities often focuses on the women in Queer Nation who seem very committed to its principles.

The rhetoric and tactics of Queer Nation hark back to those of earlier black militants and lesbian feminists. The name Queer Nation itself is reminiscent, of course, of Lesbian Nation. "Straight" is their code word for oppressive mainstream culture equal to "white" or "patriarchal" in the earlier groups. The language of angry separatism is also familiar. For example, one member of Queer Nation is quoted in Boston's *Gay Community News* as saying:

For fifteen years as an activist I have tried to explain the gay and lesbian lifestyle to the straight community, and I don't have time . . . [to educate them] anymore. If straights can get it together on their own, fine. But I don't have time for them.[50]

The New York group has issued a broadside entitled "I Hate Straights," decorated by a pink fist, exhorting the "queers" to whom it is addressed:

How can I convince you, brother, sister, that your life is in danger. That everyday you wake up alive, relatively happy, and a functioning human being, you are committing a rebellious act. . . . Until I can enjoy the same freedom of movement and sexuality as straights, their privilege must stop and it must be given over to me and my queer sisters and brothers. Straight people will not do this voluntarily and so they must be forced into it.

Thus far "force" has consisted primarily of lesbian and gay kiss-ins in straight bars, lesbian and gay marches through straight neighborhoods, and the wearing of confrontational T-shirts, such as one that reads, "Queer Nation—Get Used To It." But more militant tactics are in the planning stage. For example, Queer Nation is in the process of organizing "Pink Panther" (cf. Black Panther) vigilante groups that could respond physically and immediately to gay- and lesbian-bashing. "Queers Bash Back" is their slogan. They are also exploring ways to express economic power such as a campaign to ask businesses to sign an antidiscrimination statement of principles, which would then entitle those businesses to display a pink triangle or a rainbow flag sticker so lesbians and gay men could shop selectively.

Although Queer Nation realizes that it is to the organization's benefit to involve women and people of color, they have already been accused by members of both groups as having too narrow a focus, one that appeals primarily to white, middle class gay men and is oblivious to the special problems of lesbians, the working class, and racial and ethnic minorities. In the east, women's caucuses of Queer Nation have already been formed. The divisiveness that plagued militant groups in the preceding decades may be repeated in the 1990s. It is too soon to predict whether Queer Nation will be able to transcend those earlier problems, or even whether it will really appeal to large numbers of lesbians, who may still be wary of being sucked into concerns that are peculiar to gay men. But one female member of Queer Nation may be voicing the feelings of many other young lesbians who are not fully cognizant of the achievements of the lesbian movement since the 1970s and who are impatient with the "tame" community they inherited in the 1980s:

> The thing that's important to me about Queer Nation is that we're ready to act. People are frustrated with endless talking about issues around lesbian and gay concerns. We don't want to sit around and strategize anymore. . . . I want to do something provocative. Sometimes you have to take to the streets.[51]

Epilogue: Social Constructions and the Metamorphoses of Love Between Women

> *Jeradine: Aliciane! I've just had a vision—of the future!* . . .
> *In a thousand years or so, why, the population will be*
> *tremendous, don't you imagine? I mean, everybody living to*
> *two hundred and eighty-five and so on? Well, now picture it:*
> *every place just like China, say. Or India. Stacks of people*
> *and not enough food and not enough places to live. So—the*
> *psychologists, et cetera, will all begin telling everybody it's a*
> *sign of a definite inferiority complex to want to be having*
> *children all the time . . . that no really well balanced individ-*
> *ual would be so unhappy with [herself] and [her] kind any-*
> *way that [she'd] so much as think of falling for anybody of*
> *the opposite sex! . . . Can you imagine it? All the poor*
> *heteros slinking about furtively? Pretending they were only*
> *friends and all that? Why, why, y'know, in time there might*
> *be* laws *against it!*   *—N.M. Kramer,*
>   The Hearth and the Strangeness, *1956*

I have tried to illustrate through this history of lesbian life in twentieth-century America the extent to which sexuality, and especially
sexual categories, can be dependent upon a broad range of factors that
are extraneous to the "sexual drive." For example, love between
women, especially those of the middle class, was dramatically metamorphosed from romantic friendship over the last century: it became
"lesbianism" once the sexologists formulated the concept, economic
factors made it possible for large numbers of women to live independent of men, and mobility allowed many women to travel to places
where they might meet others who accepted the label "lesbian."

Another metamorphosis that has come about in the twentieth
century through factors extraneous to the "sexual drive" is in the
meaning of lesbianism itself, which has been transformed from a state
from which most women who loved women dissociated themselves,

to a secret and often lonely acknowledgment that one fell into that "category," to groups of women who formed a subculture around the concept, to a sociopolitical statement and a civil rights movement that claimed its own minority status and even formed its own ghettos.

And just as "lesbianism" as a phenomenon barely existed a hundred years ago, lesbians now have little similarity to their counterparts that the sexologists first described into being. There are, for instance, not many lesbians today who would see themselves as men trapped in a women's bodies; yet in the earlier decades of this century that seemed a perfectly plausible explanation to a woman who had no interest in the pursuits that were permitted to females or who let herself be convinced that she must have a "masculine soul" because only men would want to arrange their affectional lives around women. Today a female who feels she is a man trapped in a woman's body might more likely consider herself a victim of "gender dysphoria," a transsexual—another sexual category that is a social construct of our century—rather than a lesbian. Modern medicine and technology have even made it possible in the twentieth century for such a woman to rid herself of "gender dysphoria" through "sex reassignment surgery" that would metamorphose her into a man.

But there are few women who see themselves as men trapped in women's bodies today because feminism has helped bring about another metamorphosis by calling the idea of appropriate gender behavior and even appearance into question. Body image has become far less rigid. It is not just that women can now wear pants almost as often as men; in recent years strength and even muscle have become acceptable for women. And of course sex roles have become much more flexible. At this point in time in America there are few areas that are considered by great consensus totally inappropriate for a female. A woman today who is unhappy with whatever is left of sex role restrictions would more likely think of herself as a feminist (whether or not she also considered herself a lesbian) rather than a man trapped in a woman's body.

The metamorphosis of love between women has been accompanied by a metamorphosis in public attitudes, from the sentimental admiration suggested by the William Cullen Bryant quotation that begins this book, to a view of it as a rare medical phenomenon, to public fear, disdain, and condemnation, and slowly, in more recent years, to a view of same-sex love as an individual right. One aspect of this metamorphosis was dramatized for me vividly in the course of my research for this book: In Omaha, Nebraska, there is a bright yellow building on a main street. It is across from a police station and a parking lot filled with scores of police cars. Having come out as a working-class lesbian in the 1950s, when McCarthyism was still giving its tenor to American life and lesbians were outlaws, I cannot see so many police cars at once without an almost unconscious sharp intake of breath. Police cars always meant trouble for us in those days, and there is something inside that does not forget. But it was almost the 1990s and I was here with Rhonda, a twenty-six-year-old woman, a college graduate who wears lipstick and eye shadow and restores cars for a living. She chauffeured me from interview to interview around the lesbian community in Omaha during my visit and brought me to the Max, a huge lesbian and gay bar that is housed in the big yellow building.

She told me that on weekend nights the place is so crowded with homosexual men and women that their sociability often pours out onto the street. "But what about all those police?" I asked. She did not seem even to understand the import of my question at first. Then she explained, "But we're happy they're there. There's a strip joint not too far away, and those guys sometimes try to cause trouble. The police come to help us. It's a real comfort to have them so close." I understood for the hundredth time since I began my research on lesbian life in twentieth-century America that there are no constants with regard to lesbianism, neither in the meaning of love between women nor in the social and political life that is created through it.

These metamorphoses in meaning and attitudes developed because of factors that have been peculiar to our century. For example, more than any other era in history, the twentieth century has been one of sexual awareness. It has been virtually impossible to escape "knowledge" of the existence of sexual repression, expression, sublimation, symbolism, perversion, inversion, and so forth. Ironically, that awareness meant for a while a lessening of affectional possibilities. Romantic friendship had to breathe its last shortly after the century began, since intense love between women was coming to be seen as sexual. It became so incredible to our century that passionate love could occur without genital sexual expression that the term "romantic friendship" dropped out of the language. Such a relationship between women was either lesbian, that is, genital, or it did not exist. Whatever wide spectrum of subtleties, gradations, or varieties that were once possible in women's love relationships with each other became much more circumscribed. Even if two twentieth-century women

might have thought that their intense feeling for each other was more
like what some women experienced in other centuries—perhaps more
spiritual than erotic, more amorphous than concretely definable—
they would undoubtedly have been disabused of their ideas by any
outside observer who could tell them it was lesbianism, whether
repressed, suppressed, or secretly expressed.

But while one form of female same-sex relationships became impossible in this century, myriad ways to live a lesbian identity were
invented for the first time in history. What was most vital before such
a variety of lifestyles could be developed was the proliferation of
possibilities that would enable women to support themselves without
relying on fathers or husbands. Without women's economic independence, lesbians, as they emerged in the twentieth century, could not
have existed, regardless of the nature of their love for other women,
since they would have had to obey papa or to lock themselves in
heterosexual marriage for the sake of survival alone. While a few
working-class women might have managed, might even have exer-
cised the option of passing as men, for middle-class women who
were tied to their class status (as most "well-brought-up" females
were before the radical 1960s and '70s), unless they could have found
a way to be decently employed lesbian life would have been impossible for them. It was only the twentieth century that offered such ways
to large numbers of women.

Lesbian life has also been made possible in the twentieth century
by the formation of institutions that did not exist at any other time:
not only women's colleges, which began in the latter half of the
nineteenth century, but also women's military units, women's athletic organizations such as softball teams, and bars for women. Without those institutions not only would large numbers of women have
been unable to make contact with other women in order to form
lesbian relationships, but also it would have been impossible to create
lesbian communities. Even if the concept of lesbianism had been
available to women in earlier centuries, they would have had difficulty establishing lesbian communities because historically females—
other than prostitutes—were permitted little mobility, nor did they
have many meeting places where they might feel free of restrictions
by family or church. Women had been virtual prisoners in the home,
whether as ladies of leisure or as houseworkers. The twentieth century saw their release as well as the creation of meeting places for
them.

But while this century has allowed women who love women the

consciousness, the space, and the wherewithal to create communities
and lifestyles such as never before existed, the rapid and continual
flux in values and mores in the parent culture, which inevitably affects
the lesbian subculture, has helped to guarantee constant metamorphoses in the conception of lesbianism and the nature of lesbian
communities and lifestyles. Circumstances and events that once seemed
inextricably a part of lesbian culture and even of the definition of
lesbianism itself have constantly come and gone throughout this century. It is hard now to remember that around the turn of the century
those few who knew about the existence of the lesbian believed that
she was a man trapped in a woman's body; or that at the same period
of time two women could have loved each other, slept in the same
bed, held and petted each other, and yet thought of themselves as
romantic friends rather than lesbians; or that even as late as 1919 a
magazine such as *Ladies Home Journal* would publish a story in which
one woman is described gazing on another "as if a goddess, high-
enshrined and touched by the sun, stood revealed. She gave a gasp of
pleasure." It is also hard now, near the end of the twentieth century,
to remember that in the 1950s lesbians were frightened by the sight
of a police car or that in the 1970s many lesbians thought the birth of
a Lesbian Nation was imminent. The lesbian community and lesbians' relationship to society in the twentieth century have defied any
pat definition; they have been in perpetual metamorphosis.

Most of all, lesbians themselves have defied definition. In 1964,
Donald Webster Cory, a gay man who was, according to his publisher, a "widely acknowledged spokesman for the homosexual community in the United States," wrote a book titled *The Lesbian in
America*. Lesbians were still so afraid to identify themselves that no
woman dared to undertake a book on that subject because it might
cast suspicion on her. Although few people remarked on the pre-
sumption of Cory's endeavors then, it is obvious now. The problem
was not simply in his daring to speak for lesbians though he was a
man. It was, even more, in his conception, implicit in his title, that
there was such a being as "The Lesbian" who was representative of
all lesbians in America.

Even in 1964 lesbians and lesbian communities were extremely
diverse. They have metamorphosed to be even more so as more
women have dared in a relatively liberal society to accept a lesbian
identity and a broader spectrum of women has publicly claimed a
place in the community. More than ever they challenge the notion
that lesbians can be described as a whole, as writers have tried to do

since the sexologists first formulated the concept. Not only are lesbians as diverse proportionally as the female heterosexual population, but if any generalization can be made about large numbers of them at any given time, it is bound soon to change anyway, just as it has throughout the course of the century. The only constant truth about The Lesbian in America has been that she prefers women.

The twentieth century inherited a penchant for classification from the nineteenth century, with its delirious enthusiasm for the new science and its conviction that everything—even affection and sexual feeling—was unquestionably categorizable. Love between women was classified as "sexual inversion," a category that encompassed women who were uncomfortable as women, women who had sexual relations with women, women who thought women's socioeconomic opportunities needed to be expanded, and even women who were romantic friends. Paradoxically, such rigid and simplistic categorization opened new possibilities to some women by permitting them to begin to create subcultures of "inverts"—lesbians—such as had never before existed. However, once they became a part of the category the nineteenth-century sexologists had established, they altered it continually by their own lived experiences of love between women. And they thereby helped to demonstrate the large extent to which sexuality is often a social construct—a product of the times and of other factors that are entirely external to the "sexual drive."

Notes

Introduction

1. William Cullen Bryant to the *Evening Post,* July 13, 1843, in *Letters of William Cullen Bryant,* vol. 2, eds. William Cullen Bryant II and Thomas G. Voss (New York: Fordham University Press, 1977), pp. 238–39.

2. *Miami News,* May 20, 1942, quoted in John Costello, *Virtue Under Fire: How World War II Changed Our Social and Sexual Attitudes* (Boston: Little, Brown, 1985), p. 43.

3. The latest Gallup Poll seems to suggest that homophobia in general is quickly receding. In 1987 only 33 percent of those polled believed that "homosexual relations between consenting adults should be legal." By Fall 1989 the number had risen to 47 percent. Similarly, in 1987 only 59 percent of those polled believed that "gays should have equal job opportunities." In Fall 1989, 71 percent of the respondents were in favor of such equality. Reported in "The Future of Gay America," *Newsweek,* March 12, 1990, p. 21.

4. Since the 1930s there have been a number of studies that have argued that male and female homosexuals are hormonally or genetically different, but many other studies have been unable to replicate such findings, and frequently those studies that have announced hormonal or genetic differences appear to be questionable in their methods. For example, in an article in the *American Journal of Psychiatry* (October 1977), 134(10): 1117–18, "Plasma Testosterone in Homosexual and Heterosexual Women," Nanette Gartrell et al. found that testosterone was 38 percent higher in the plasma of lesbians than in heterosexual women. But the researchers accepted subjects as homosexual or heterosexual by determining only that their sexual practices "during the preceding year had involved only individuals of the same sex (for homosexuals) or the opposite sex (for heterosexuals)." But what if a woman had had exclusively heterosexual relations all her life and then formed a relationship with another woman in the preceding year, as often happened during the lesbian chic era of the 1920s or the radical-feminist 1970s? Or what if a woman who had long been a lesbian decided that she wanted to experiment with heterosexuality, as many lesbians do for significant periods of time? Would their testosterone levels rise or fall depending on with whom they had been sleeping? Such studies generally classify sexuality simply into homo and

hetero, refusing to acknowledge (or paying only lip service to) the continuum that Kinsey observed in his massive research or the changes in sexual behavior that many individuals experience in the course of their lives. For studies that fail to replicate previous findings that show a physiological base for homosexuality see, e.g., J. D. Rainer et al., "Homosexuality and Heterosexuality in Identical Twins," *Psychosomatic Medicine,* (1960), 22: 51–58; G. K. Klintworth, "A Pair of Male Monozygotic Twins Discordant for Homosexuality," *Journal of Nervous and Mental Disease,* (1962), 135: 113–25; K. Davison et al., "A Male Monozygotic Twinship Discordant for Homosexuality," *British Journal of Psychiatry,* (1971), 118: 675–82; Bernard Zuger, "Monozygotic Twins Discordant for Homosexuality: Report of a Pair and Significance of the Phenomenon," *Comprehensive Psychiatry,* (Sept./ Oct., 1976), 17(5): 661–69; N. McConaghy and A. Blaszczynski, "A Pair of Monzygotic Twins Discordant for Homosexuality," *Archives of Sexual Behavior* (1980), 9: 123–31; Elke D. Eckert et al., "Homosexuality in Monozygotic Twins Reared Apart," *British Journal of Psychiatry* (April 1986), 148: 421–25; David Barlow, et al., "Plasma Testosterone Levels in Male Homosexuality: A Failure to Replicate," *Archives of Sexual Behavior* (1974), 3(6): 571–75; Susan Baker, "Biological Influence on Human Sex and Gender," *Signs* (1980), 6: 80–96; H. F. L. Meyer-Bahlburg, "Sex Hormones and Female Homosexuality: A Critical Examination," *Archives of Sexual Behavior* (1979), 8: 101–19; P. D. Griffiths et al. "Homosexual Women: An Endocrinological and Psychological Study," *Journal of Endocrinology* (Dec. 1974), 63(3): 549–56; Ruth G. Doell and Helen Longino, "Sex Hormones in Human Behavior: A Critique of the Linear Model," *Journal of Homosexuality* (1988), 15(3–4): 55–78.

1. *"The Loves of Women for Each Other"*

1. Henry Wadsworth Longfellow, *Kavanagh* (Boston: Ticknor, Reed and Fields, 1849); William Alger, *The Friendships of Women* (Boston: Roberts, 1868), pp. 346–58. Ellen Rothman's study, *Hands and Hearts: A History of Courtship in America* (New York: Basic Books, 1984) suggests that for many young women in the nineteenth century it was not romantic friendship but their "relationships with lovers and future husbands [that] provided their first experiences with closeness," but Rothman too admits that there were others "who found openness and intimacy only with female friends," p. 114.

2. Florence Converse, *Diana Victrix* (Boston: Houghton Mifflin, 1897).

3. E. A. Andrews, quoted in Helen Lefkowitz Horowitz, *Alma Mater: Design and Experience in the Women's Colleges from their Nineteenth Century Beginnings to the 1930s* (Boston: Beacon Press, 1986), p. 58. Statistics from Duncan Crow, *The Victorian Woman* (London: Allen and Unwin, 1971), p. 326, and Arthur Mann, *Yankeee Reformers in the Urban Age* (Cambridge: Harvard University Press, 1954), p. 202.

4. Edward Hammond Clarke, *Sex in Education; or A Fair Chance for Girls* (Boston: J. R. Osgood, 1873). Robert J. Sprague, "Education and Race

Suicide," *Journal of Heredity* (May 1915), 6: 158–62. See also Roswell H. Johnson and Bertha Stutzman, "Wellesley's Birth Rate," ibid., pp. 231–32.

5. "A New Women's College," *Scribner's Monthly* (Oct. 1873), 6: 748–49. Writers in the twentieth century were much more explicit in their accusations that women's colleges were responsible for promoting homosexuality; see, e.g., Floyd Dell, *Love in the Machine Age: A Psychological Study of the Transition from Patriarchal Society* (1930; reprint, New York: Farrar, Straus and Giroux, 1973), p. 308. Notions of the danger of female education were not peculiar to the United States. European writers went even further. Cesare Lombroso, for example, presented in his 1893 book *The Female Offender* a chapter titled "Education—The Bad Results of It," in which he argued that education drew moral women into crime: "Many women of intelligence find themselves with nothing to show in return for much expense and labour. They are reduced to want while conscious of not deserving it, and being debarred from the probability of matrimony owing to the ordinary man's dislike of a well instructed woman, they have no resource but in suicide, crime, or prostitution. The chaster ones kill themselves; the others sell themselves or commit thefts" (1893; reprint, London: T. Fisher Unwin, 1895), pp. 204–205. Similar absurd views regarding female education continued well into the twentieth century in Europe also: see, e.g., Walter Heape, *Sex Antagonism* (London: Constable, 1913), pp. 212–13.

6. Statistics in William G. Shade, "A Mental Passion: Female Sexuality in Victorian America," *International Journal of Women's Studies* (1978), 1(1): 16; Miriam Slater and Penina M. Glazer, "Female Friendships and the Emergence of Professionalism," unpublished paper, New York Lesbian Herstory Archives, p. 31; Mabel Newcomer, *A Century of Higher Education for Women* (New York: Harper and Row, 1959), p. 212.

7. Carl Degler, "What Ought to be and What Was: Women's Sexuality in the Nineteenth Century," *American Historical Review* (1974), 79: 1469–77 and Peter Gay, *Education of the Senses,* vol. 1, *The Bourgeois Experience* (New York: Oxford University Press, 1984) argue that sexual behavior often violated ideology. Clelia D. Mosher, *The Mosher Survey: Sexual Attitudes of Forty-Five Victorian Women,* eds. James MacHood and Kristine Wanburg (New York: Ayer, 1980) shows that a large percentage of those forty- five women believed that coitus in marriage was for mutual pleasure as well as reproduction. This was far from the "official" view of the period: cf. Dr. Alice Stockham (*Tokology: A Book for Every Woman* [Chicago, 1887], pp. 151–52), who observed that most women believed "that sexual intercourse is a 'physical necessity' to man but not to woman." In *Hands and Hearts* Ellen Rothman demonstrates that kissing and embracing were often acceptable for engaged couples in the nineteenth century, but genital sexual exchanges were forbidden, op. cit.

8. "At Home with the Editor," *Ladies Home Journal,* April 1892, p. 12. Rothman, p. 112. Frances E. Willard, *Glimpses of Fifty Years: The Autobiography of an American Woman* (Chicago: H.J. Smith, 1889).

9. Catt quotations from Robert Booth Fowler, *Carrie Catt: Feminist Politician* (Boston: Northeastern University Press, 1986), pp. 16, 53–56.

10. Letter to Wayman Crow, August 1854, in Cornelia Carr, *Harriet Hosmer: Letters and Memories* (London: Bodley Head, 1913), p. 35. Her letters as well as biographies of her friends such as Charlotte Cushman (see, for example, Joseph Leach, *Bright Particular Star: The Life and Times of Charlotte Cushman* [New Haven: Yale University Press, 1970]) suggest intimate relationships with Annie Dundas, Matilda Hays, Charlotte Cushman, and a Mrs. Sartoris.

11. Quoted in Marjorie H. Dobkin, *The Making of a Feminist: Early Journals and Letters of M. Carey Thomas* (Kent, Ohio: Kent State University Press, 1979), p. xv. See also James R. McGovern, "Anna Howard Shaw: New Approaches to Feminism," *Journal of Social History,* Winter 1969, pp. 135–53. Shaw, a minister and renowned suffragist, wrote to a friend who was contemplating marriage in 1902: "Just think of the men along your street . . . .If a human being or a god could conceive of a worse hell than being the wife of any one of them I would like to know what it could be . . . .I have seen nothing so far which does not make me say every night of my life, 'I thank Thee for all good but for nothing more than I have been saved from the misery of marriage."

12. For discussion of the male-female division in nineteenth- century America see Barbara Welter, "The Cult of True Womanhood, 1820–1860," *Dimity Convictions: The American Woman in the Nineteenth Century* (Athens, Ohio: Ohio University Press, 1976), pp. 21–41; G. J. Barker-Benfield, *The Horrors of the Half-Known Life: Male Attitudes Toward Women and Sexuality in Nineteenth Century America* (New York: Harper and Row, 1976); Ann Douglas, *The Feminization of American Culture* (New York: Alfred A. Knopf, 1977); and my discussion in *Surpassing the Love of Men: Romantic Friendship and Love Between Women from the Renaissance to the Present* (New York: William Morrow, 1981), ch.2, 2: "Kindred Spirits." For a discussion of women's views of their superiority in the second half of the nineteenth century see Judith Becker Ranlett, "Sorority and Community: Women's Answer to a Changing Massachusetts, 1865–1895," Ph.D. diss., Brandeis University, 1974, esp. pp. 41–42, 120–21.

13. Yale quotation in Nancy Salhi, "Smashing: Women's Relationships Before the Fall," *Chrysalis* (1979), 8: 21.

14. Lavinia Hart, "A Girl's College Life," *Cosmopolitan* (June 1901), 31: 192. Josephine Dodge Daskam, "The Evolution of Evangeline," *Smith College Stories* (New York: Scribner's, 1900). For some working-class females of that period women's prisons fostered the same kinds of romantic relationships that were found in women's colleges. Margaret Otis in 1913 described relationships between white and black women prisoners that were much like those between freshman and sophomore students. Typically, a black woman would send a white woman a lock of hair and a note asking for her love. The romance that ensued was described by Otis as being often "very

real . . . .almost ennobling." But, writing with an awareness of the sexologists who preceded her, Otis calls such relationships "perversions": "A Perversion Not Commonly Noted," *Journal of Abnormal Psychology* (June/ July 1913), 8 (2): 113–16. There is, unfortunately, no large statistical study of sexuality between college women in the nineteenth century, but Robert Latou Dickinson's casual study of women he encountered in his gynecological practice beginning in 1890 identifies twenty-eight cases that he inferred were lesbian. Almost half of those women were college graduates; Robert Latou Dickinson and Lura Beam, *The Single Woman: A Medical Study in Sex Education* (New York: Reynal and Hitchcock, 1934), p. 207. Katharine Davis' broader 1929 survey offers some revealing figures. Davis discovered that more than 50 percent of the 2200 women she studied had experienced "intense emotional relations with other women" and more than 25 percent said those experiences were either specifically sexual or "recognized as sexual in character." About 88 percent of the latter had been college women, and 78 percent of the former had been college women. Many said their relationships began in women's colleges and typically characterized them as "an expression of love [which has] made my life inexpressibly richer and deeper"; Katharine Bement Davis, *Factors in the Sex Life of Twenty-Two Hundred Women* (New York: Harper and Row, 1929), p. 308.

15. Blanche Weisen Cook discusses networks in "Female Support Networks and Poltical Activism," *Chrysalis* (Autumn 1977), 3: 43–61. For descriptions of female "marriages" see, e.g., Anna Mary Wells, *Miss Marks and Miss Woolley* (Boston: Houghton Mifflin, 1978); Mary Gray Peck, *Carrie Chapman Catt* (New York: H. W. Wilson, 1944); Nancy Manahan, "Future Old Maids and Pacifist Agitators," paper given on panel "Lesbian Survival Strategies: 1850–1950," National Women's Studies Association, 1981; McGovern, "Anna Howard Shaw," op. cit.; Judith Schwarz, *Radical Feminists of Heterodoxy: Greenwich Village, 1912–1950* (Norwich, Vt.) New Victorian Publishers, 1986); Judith Schwarz, "Yellow Clover: Katharine Lee Bates and Katharine Coman,"*Frontiers* (Spring 1979), 6(1): 59–67; Leila J. Rupp, "Imagine My Surprise: Women's Relationships in Historical Perspective," *Frontiers* (Fall 1980), 5(3): 63–64.

16. S. Josephine Baker, M.D., *Fighting for Life* (New York: Macmillan, 1939), p. 64.

17. Katherine Anne Porter, "Gertrude Stein: A Self-Portrait," *Harpers* (December 1947), 195: 519–27.

18. Michael Field, *Underneath the Bow* (1893; 3rd ed., Portland, ME: Thomas B. Mosher, 1898), p. 50.

19. Emily Blackwell obituary in *Vigilance* (New York) (October 1910), 23:13 describes Cushier as her "devoted friend" who was "with her when she passed away." Irwin and Anthony are discussed in Matthew Josephson, *Infidel in the Temple* (New York: Knopf, 1967), p. 38, where he describes them as "life long friends." They were also known as "the gay ladies of Gaylordsville [Connecticut]." The lesbianism of the leaders of the Women's

Trade Union League is discussed in Sarah Schulman, "When We Were Very Young: A Walking Tour Through Radical Jewish Women's History on the Lower East Side, 1879–1919," *Sinister Wisdom* (1986), 29/30:232–53. Vida Scudder and Florence Converse are discussed in Mann, op. cit. Frances Witherspoon and Tracy Mygatt are discussed in Manahan, op. cit.

20. Jane Addams, *Twenty Years at Hull House, with Autobiographical Notes* (New York: Macmillan, 1910), p. 77. Addams' relationship with Starr is discussed in Allen F. Davis, *American Heroine: The Life and Legend of Jane Addams* (New York: Oxford University Press, 1973).

21. Willam O'Neill, *Everyone Was Brave: The Rise and Fall of Feminism in America* (Chicago, 1969), p. 120. Davis, p. 46. Cook, p. 47.

22. Regarding Starr's reflections on her personal break with Addams see Davis, p. 85. Mary Rozet Smith is described in Alice Hamilton, *Exploring the Dangerous Trades: The Autobiography of Alice Hamilton, M.D.* (Boston: Little, Brown, 1943), p. 67, as "one supremely lovely figure . . . the most universally beloved person."

23. Davis, pp. 85–89.

24. Poem quoted in James Weber Linn, *Jane Addams: A Biography* (New York: Appleton Century, 1935), pp. 289–90.

25. Davis, p. 306n.

26. M. Carey Thomas, quoted in Elaine Kendall, *"Peculiar Institutions": An Informal History of the Seven Sister Colleges* (New York: G. P. Putnam's Sons, 1975), p. 132.

27. Thomas' girlhood is discussed in Edith Finch, *Carey Thomas of Bryn Mawr* (New York: Harper and Row, 1947).

28. Dobkin, pp. 69–70.

29. For Thomas' early romantic attachments to other females see, e.g., Dobkin, pp. 90, 118. Letter to mother in Dobkin, p. 229. Mother and aunt quoted in Salhi, p. 22.

30. Gertrude Stein's treatment of the Thomas-Gwinn-Hodder triangle in *Fernhurst* (1904–5?) leaves much to be desired. Stein presents Gwinn as a passive creature and Thomas as a controlling bitch, closer to images in nineteenth-century French decadent novels than the reality. But perhaps this portrayal is not surprising since Stein got the story from Bertrand Russell, who was not very sympathetic to women's relationships, his friendship with Stein notwithstanding. The Mamie character returns to Carey's clutches at the end of *Fernhurst* instead of running off with Hodder.

31. Quoted in Horowitz, p. 193.

32. Charlotte Wolff, *Love Between Women* (New York: Harper and Row, 1971), p. 86.

33. Alfred Kinsey et al., *Sexual Behavior in the Human Female* (Philadelphia: Saunders, 1953), p. 495. Robert Latou Dickinson, whose gynecological practice began in the 1890s, observed a number of "known or inferred homosexual cases," but while some of those women were "in relationships

of companionship, chief interest and so on with women friends over periods of years . . . [though] very fond of each other [there] had never been anything of physical consumation in their relationship." Dickinson and his co-author found that credible because "these accounts of love between women follow the pattern of Victorian ideals and perfectionism." However, it is certainly possible that Dickinson's lesbian patients simply lied to him: Dickinson and Beam, pp. 426, 211. See also Havelock Ellis, *Studies in the Psychology of Sex,* vol. I (1897; reprint, New York: Random House, 1936), pp. 219, 222–28. Rose Elizabeth Cleveland to Evangeline Marrs Simpson Whipple, 1890, quoted in Paula Petrik, "Into the Open: Lesbianism at the Turn of the Century," unpublished paper, New York Lesbian Herstory Archives; original letters in Minnesota Historical Society, St. Paul, Minn.

34. Ida to Anna Dickinson, quoted in Lisa Duggan and Kay Whitlock, "Rituals of Glory and Degradation: The Life of Anna E. Dickinson," unpublished paper, New York Lesbian Herstory Archives.

35. Almeda Sperry to Emma Goldman quoted in Cook, p. 57, and Candace Falk, *Love, Anarchy, and Emma Goldman* (New York: Holt, Rinehart and Winston, 1984), pp. 174–75.

36. Quoted in Richard and Anna Maria Drinnon, eds., *Nowhere at Home: Letters from Exile of Emma Goldman and Alexander Berkman* (New York: Schocken Books, 1975), pp. 132–33.

37. Wanda Fraiken Neff, *We Sing Diana* (Boston: Houghton Mifflin, 1928). M. Carey Thomas quoted in Leila J. Rupp, " 'Imagine My Surprise': Women's Relationships in Historical Perspective," *Frontiers* (1981), 5(3):62.

38. For examples of recent historians who deny their subjects' homosexuality see Wells; Doris Faber, *The Life of Lorena Hickok: E. R.'s Friend* (New York: William Morrow, 1981); Dobkin; Fowler; Alice Wexler, *Emma Goldman: An Intimate Life* (New York: Pantheon Books, 1984), pp. 182–83. See also Blanche Cook, "The Historical Denial of Lesbianism," *Radical History Review* (1979), 20:60–65.

2. A Worm in the Bud

1. Marion S. Goldman, *Gold Diggers and Silver Miners: Prostitution and Social Life on the Comstock Lode* (Ann Arbor: University of Michigan Press, 1981), pp. 120–21. Michelle Zimbalist Rosaldo, "Women, Culture and Society: A Theoretical Overview," in Michelle Zimbalist Rosaldo and Louise Lamphere, eds., *Women, Culture and Society* (Palo Alto: Stanford University Press, 1974), pp. 17–42.

2. Margaret Otis, "A Perversion Not Commonly Noted," *Journal of Abnormal Psychology* (June/July 1913), 8(2):113–16. In an article written fifteen years later, Charles Ford observed similar relations between black and white women in prison: "Homosexual Practices of Institutionalized Females," *Journal of Abnormal and Social Psychiatry* (January/March 1929), 23:442–48.

3. Figures cited in Joanne Meyerowitz, *Holding Their Own: Working Women Apart from Family in Chicago, 1880–1930* (Ph.D. diss., Stanford University, 1983), p. 1.

4. Daniel Scott Smith, "The Dating of the American Sexual Revolution: Evidence and Interpretation," in Michael Gordon, ed., *The American Family in Social-Historical Perspective* (New York: St. Martin's Press, 1973); Meyerowitz, p. 149.

5. Kathy Peiss, *Cheap Amusements: Working Women and Leisure in Turn-of-the-Century New York* (Philadelphia: Temple Univesity Press, 1986), esp. pp. 62, 103–14, 163–68. See also the discussion of working class sexuality in John D'Emilio and Estelle B. Freedman, *Intimate Matters: A History of Sexuality in America* (New York: Harper and Row, 1988), especially parts 2 and 3.

6. William Lee Howard, "Effeminate Men and Masculine Women," *New York Medical Journal* (1900), 71:686–87.

7. Karl Friedrich Otto Westphal, "Die Kontrare Sexualempfindung: Symptom eines neuropathologischen (psycopathischen) Zustandes," *Archiv für Psychiatrie und Nervenkrankheiten* (1869), 2:73–108. George Chauncey, in an often-quoted article, was the first to suggest a shift from inversion to homosexuality in medical discourse, which he claimed occurred around the turn of the century. In a recent reprint of the article, however, he added a postscript revising his orginial observation: "Inversion continued for decades to be a major medical concern and to be linked to homosexuality; the shift, as I may not have indicated clearly enough, was hardly decisive or unanimous by the 1920s"; "From Sexual Inversion to Homosexuality: The Changing Medical Conceptualization of Female 'Deviance'," *Salmagundi* (Fall/Winter 1983), 58/59:114–146, reprinted in Kathy Peiss and Christina Simmons, eds., *Passion and Power: Sexuality in History* (Philadelphia: Temple University Press, 1989), pp. 87–117.

8. Estimate of female transvestites in the Civil War in George Washington Adams, *Doctors in Blue: The Medical History of the Union Army* (New York: 1952). "Harry Gorman" discussed in Xavier Mayne (Edward I. Prime Stevenson), *The Intersexes: A History of Psychosexualism as a Problem in Social Life* (1908; reprint, New York: Arno Press, 1975), pp. 149–50. Numerous passing women are presented in Jonathan Katz, *Gay American History: Lesbians and Gay Men in the U.S.A.* (New York: Thomas Crowell, 1976) and *Gay/Lesbian Almanac: A New Documentary* (New York: Harper and Row, 1983). It was Katz who first popularized the term "passing women." See also Allan Berube, "Lesbian Masquerade," *Gay Community News*, November 17, 1979, pp. 8–9, and slide show (with the San Francisco Gay and Lesbian Historical Society), *She Drank, She Swore, She Courted Girls, She Even Chewed Tobacco*; also my earlier work, *Surpassing the Love of Men: Romantic Friendship and Love Between Women from the Renaissance to the Present* (New York: William Morrow, 1981), passim; Kore Archer, "The One-Eyed Amazon of Santa Cruz County," *Lavender Reader*, Summer 1987, pp. 14–15; and Babe Bean file, New York Lesbian Herstory Archives.

9. Lucy Ann Lobdell, *The Narrative of Lucy Ann Lobdell, the Female Deer Hunter of Delaware and Sullivan Counties* (1885), presented in Katz, *Gay American History*, pp. 214–21. Warner is quoted in Berube, "Lesbian Masquerade." Babe Bean newpaper accounts in New York Lesbian Herstory Archives. A few women continued to pass even into our era for similar reasons. Billy Tipton, for example, a jazz musician, began passing in order to play with the all-male swing bands of the '30s. She was not discovered to be a woman until her death in 1989: Radio interview, Lynn Niery and Lillian Faderman, *All Things Considered*, National Public Radio, February 5, 1989. Although most passing women appear to have been working-class, there are several recorded exceptions such as Babe Bean, who claimed to have come from a distinguished family. Another notable exception was Alberta Lucille Hart, who received a medical degree from Stanford in the second decade of the twentieth century and spent most of her career as a physician in male guise; see Katz, *Gay American History*, pp. 258–79 and *Gay/Lesbian Almanac*, pp. 516–22.

10. Mary Fields is discussed in William Katz, *The Black West* (New York: Doubleday, 1973). Kerwinieo is quoted in Jonathan Katz, *Gay American History*, pp. 254–57.

11. Richard von Krafft-Ebing, "Perversion of the Sexual Instinct—Report of Cases," *Alienist and Neurologist*, October 1888.

12. Havelock Ellis, *Studies in the Psychology of Sex* (1897; reprint, New York: Random House, 1936, rev. ed.), pp. 261–62.

13. Julien Chevalier, *Inversion sexuelle* (Paris: Masson, 1893), pp. 219–25.

14. James Weir, Jr., "The Effects of Female Suffrage on Posterity," *American Naturalist* (September 1895), 24(345):815–25.

15. William Lee Howard, *The Perverts* (New York: 1901) and "Effeminate Men and Masculine Women," p. 687.

16. For a discussion of that literature see *Surpassing the Love of Men*, op. cit., parts 1B, 2A (chs. 2, 4, 5), 3A (ch. l).

17. Figures cited in William G. Shade, "A Mental Passion: Female Sexuality in Victorian America," *International Journal of Women's Studies* (1978), 1(1):16. Albert H. Hayes, *Physiology of Women* (Boston: Peabody Medical Institute, 1869), p. 226.

18. *Index Catalogue of the Library of the Surgeon General's Office, U.S. Army* (1896–1916), second series, quoted in Nancy Salhi, "Changing Patterns of Sexuality and Female Interaction in Nineteenth Century America," paper delivered at Berkshire Women's History Conference, June 11, 1976, pp. 12–13, in Schlesinger Library, Radcliffe College.

19. R. N. Shufeldt, "Dr. Havelock Ellis on Sexual Inversion," *Pacific Medical Journal* (1902), 45:199–207. Carroll Smith-Rosenberg points out that it was in the 1890s that physicians and social critics began to initiate a new wave of attacks on the New Woman, the focus of whose deviance in their view shifted from her rejection of motherhood to her rejection of men. "From being 'unnaturally' barren, the autonomous woman . . . emerged as 'unnaturally' sexual"; "The New Woman as Androgyne: Social Disorder and

the Gender Crisis, 1870–1936," *Disorderly Conduct: Visions of Gender in Victorian America* (New York: Alfred Knopf, 1985), p. 265. Girls discussed in Denslow Lewis, *The Gynecological Considerations for the Sexual Act* (1900; reprint, Weston, Mass.: M&S Press, 1970), p. 13. "Numerous phases of inversion" in Joseph Richardson Parke, *Human Sexuality: A Medico-Literary Treatise on the Laws, Anomalies, and Relations of Sex with Especial Reference to Contrary Sexual Feelings* (Philadelphia: Professional Publishing Company, 1906), p. 272.

20. Bernard Talmey, *Woman: A Treatise on the Normal and Pathological Emotions of Feminine Love* (1904; reprint, New York: Practioners Publishing Company, 1910), p. 123. Regarding popular magazine fiction see my article, "Lesbian Magazine Fiction in the Early Twentieth Century," *Journal of Popular Culture* (Spring 1978), 11(4):800–17.

21. A. A. Brill, *Psychoanalysis: It Theories and Practical Application*, 2nd rev. ed. (Philadelphia: W. B. Saunders, 1914), p. 55, and Douglas Mc-Murtrie, "Manifestations of Sexual Inversion in the Female," *Urologic and Cutaneous Review* (1914), 18:425. Such "self-ignorance" continued even into the 1920s in England, as an article by British psychologist Stella Browne suggests: "Studies in Feminine Inversion," *Journal of Sexology and Psychoanalysis* (1923), 1:51–58.

22. William Alger, *The Friendships of Women* (Boston: Roberts, 1868), p. 364. Isabelle Mallon (Ruth Ashmore), *Side Talks with Girls* (New York: Charles Scribner, 1895), pp. 122–23. Irving D. Steinhardt, *Ten Sex Talks with Girls* (Philadelphia: Lippincott, 1914), pp. 57–62. A College Graduate, "Your Daughter: What Are Her Friendships?" *Harper's Bazaar,* October 1913, p. 16+.

23. Irving C. Rosse, "Sexual Hypochondraisis," *Journal of Nervous and Mental Disease* (November 1892), 17(1):807. August Forel, *The Sexual Question: A Scientific, Psychological, Hygenic, and Sociological Study* (1906; reprint, New York: Physicians and Surgeons Book Company, 1924), pp. 251–52.

24. Marion Joyce, "Flight from Slander," *Forum,* August 1938, reprinted in Jonathan Katz, *Gay/Lesbian Almanac,* pp. 539–45.

25. Yearbook pictures in New York Lesbian Herstory Archives, file: "History, the 1920s." Elizabeth Goodwin and Katharine Woodward, "My Heart Leaps Up," Bryn Mawr Yearbook, 1921, quoted in Catharine R. Stimpson, "The Mind, The Body, and Gertrude Stein," *Critical Inquiry* (1977), 3:491–506.

26. Cather's masculine dress in college is described in James Woodress, *Willa Cather: Her Life and Art* (New York: Pegasus, 1970), p. 33. Cather's "unentangled" image is discussed in Elizabeth Sergeant, *Willa Cather: A Memoir* (Lincoln: University of Nebraska Press, 1963), pp. 115–16. Her relationships with women, particularly Isabelle McClung, are discussed more openly in Sharon O'Brien, *Willa Cather: The Emerging Voice* (New York: Oxford University Press, 1987).

27. Jeannette Marks' papers, "Unwise College Friendships," Williston Memorial Library, Mount Holyoke College. See also Jeannette Marks, *A Girl's School Days and After* (New York: Fleming H. Revell, 1911), pp. 36–37. Discussion of projected book on homosexuality occurs in unpublished correspondence with Dr. Arthur Jacobson, 1923–1924, Williston Memorial Library, Mount Holyoke College. See also Alice Stone Blackwell, who enjoyed numerous passionate relationships with females yet denounced them when she served on a committee of the Association of Collegiate Alumnae (forerunner of the AAUW), which investigated the effects of smashing on college women's health, discussed in Peter Filene, *Him/Her/Self: Sex Roles in Modern America* (New York: Mentor Books, 1976), pp. 45–46, 252, and Nancy Salhi, "Smashing: Women's Relationships Before the Fall," *Chrysalis* (1979), 8:17–27.

28. Mary Casal, *The Stone Wall: An Autobiography* (Chicago: Eyncourt Press, 1930), pp. 165, 185.

29. My article, "Lesbian Magazine Fiction in the Early Twentieth Century," discusses through literary examples in American and English magazines the persistence in the first two decades of our century of the view of love between women as socially sanctioned romantic friendship. Constance Fenimore Woolson, "Felipa," (*Lippincott's Magazine,* 1876; reprint, *Rodman the Keeper,* New York: D. Appleton, 1880).

30. Jonathan Katz includes lengthy excerpts about the Alice Mitchell case from both popular and medical periodicals: *Gay American History,* pp. 53–58, 136; *Gay/Lesbian Almanac,* pp. 223–27 and passim.

31. Mary C. Wilkins Freeman, "The Long Arm," (1895; reprinted in Carolyn Wells, ed., *American Detective Stories* [New York: Oxford University Press, 1927], pp. 134–78. Mary R. P. Hatch, *The Strange Disappearance of Eugene Comstock* (New York: G. W. Dillingham, 1895).

32. John Wesley Carhart, *Norma Trist; or Pure Carbon: A Story of the Inversion of the Sexes* (Austin, Tex.: Eugene von Boeckmann, 1895). Carhart also refers specifically in this novel to his knowledge of Krafft-Ebing (p. 56). Carhart apparently believed that few other Americans were familiar with the phenomenon of lesbianism. He observed, looking back over the nineteenth century: "It is true, French and German literature abounded with fiction to which sexual abnormalities have given rise; but it was almost universally of so gross a nature as to render it unfit for translation into English for the American reader; and since the subject at that time had awakened no scientific interest, few American readers, from curiosity or pleasure, would seek such literature in the German or French language" (p. 57). For a similar view by a nineteenth-century medical man regarding American innocence about lesbianism see Dr. Allan McLane Hamilton, "The Civil Responsibility of Sexual Perverts," *American Journal of Insanity* (April 1896), 52:503–9. The Mitchell case may also have influenced a later work, Gertrude Atherton's *Mrs. Balfame* (New York: Frederick A. Stokes, 1916), in which Anna Steuer, a respected

doctor, has a lifelong attachment to Enid Balfame. Unlike Alice Mitchell, however, Dr. Steuer kills not the woman she loves, but rather Enid's obnoxious husband who has made his wife's life unhappy. It is not clear if Atherton believed she was depicting lesbianism or a more spiritual romantic friendship, but as one of the characters in the novel observes, Enid was definitely "the romance of poor Anna's life" (p. 332).

33. Forel, p. 244.

34. Natalie Barney quoted in Jean Chalon, *Portrait of a Seductress: The World of Natalie Barney,* trans. Carol Baker (New York: Crown, 1976), p. 47.

35. Esther Newton, "The Mythic Mannish Lesbian," in Estelle Freedman et al., eds., *The Lesbian Issue: Essays from Signs* (University of Chicago Press, 1985), pp. 7–25. Frances Wilder to Edward Carpenter, 1915, in Ruth F. Claus, "Confronting Homosexuality: A Letter from Frances Wilder," *Signs* (Summer 1977), 2(4):928–33.

36. I discuss the rare historical instances of lesbian persecution in *Surpassing the Love of Men,* pp. 47–54. See also Louis Crompton, "The Myth of Lesbian Impunity: Capital Punishment from 1270 to 1791," *Journal of Homosexuality* (Fall/Winter 1980/81), 6(1/2):11–25.

37. Joseph Richardson Parke, *Human Sexuality: A Medico-Literary Treatise on the Laws, Anomalies and Relations of Sex, with Especial Reference to Contrary Sexual Feelings* (Philadelphia: Professional Publishing Company, 1906), p. 245.

38. Walhalla (Valhalla?) Hall dance described by Dr. Charles Nesbitt, quoted in Jonathan Katz, *Gay/Lesbian Almanac,* pp. 218–20. Mary Casal, a lesbian who was born in 1864, also alludes to a small lesbian subculture in New York around the turn of the century: *The Stone Wall,* pp. 180–85. An unpublished story by Harriet Levy (an early friend of Alice B. Toklas), written around the turn of the century, suggests that the new awareness even sometimes promoted "cruising" between women and attempts to pick each other up: "A Beautiful Girl," in ms. collection of Harriet Levy, chapter 20, unpublished stories, Bancroft Library, University of California, Berkeley, pp. 54–65. See also my dicussion in *Surpassing the Love of Men,* pp. 188–89. In a 1914 article Douglas McMurtrie wrote of "lesbian assembilies," but in the light of his antifeminist source his reference is most likely to feminist societies for career women such as Heterodoxy (see p.83 here); "Notes on the Psychology of Sex," *American Journal of Urology and Sexology* (Sept. 1914), 10(9):432. See also William Lee Howard, "Sexual Perversion in America," *American Journal of Dermatology and Genito-Urinary Diseases* (1904), 8:9–14. Chauncey, pp. 105–6.

39. Personal interview with Barbara Gittings, age 55, Philadelphia, October 7, 1987.

40. Personal interview with LuAnna, age 35, Austin, Tex., April 1, 1988. On the uses of essentialism see Paul Horowitz, "Beyond the Gay Nation: Where Are We Marching?," *Out/Look,* Spring 1988, pp. 7–21.

3. Lesbian Chic

1. Quoted in Nathan G. Hale, Jr., *Freud and the Americans: The Beginnings of Psychoanalysis in the United States, 1876–1917* (New York, 1971), p. 405.

2. Susan Glaspell, quoted in Albert Parry, *Garrets and Pretenders: A History of Bohemianism in America* (1933; reprint, New York: Dover, 1960), p. 278.

3. Lesbian communities in Salt Lake City and San Francisco are discussed in Vern Bullough and Bonnie Bullough, "Lesbianism in the 1920s and 1930s: A New Found Study," *Signs* (Summer 1977), 2(4):895–904. Discussion of small town homosexuality in the 1920s is in Bob Skiba, "Pansies, Perverts, and Pegged Pants," *Gay and Lesbian Community Guide to New England,* 1982, p. 3, in New York Lesbian Herstory Archives, file: 1920s.

4. Katharine Bement Davis, *Factors in the Sex Life of Twenty-Two Hundred Women* (New York: Harper and Row, 1929), p. 247. See also my analysis of Davis' data in *Surpassing the Love of Men: Romantic Friendship and Love Between Women from the Renaissance to the Present* (New York: William Morrow, 1981), pp. 326–27.

5. George Hannah, "Boy in the Boat," *AC-DC Blues: Gay Jazz Reissues,* side B, Stash Records, ST-106.

6. Hemingway's most recent biographer, Kenneth Lynn, observes "a larger drama of sexual confusion" in Hemingway's life: a mother who was a lesbian, sisters who wished to be boys, obsession with women's short hair, cross dressing. He was intrigued by Gertrude Stein's lesbianism and was also close friends with other expatriate lesbians such as Djuna Barnes and Natalie Barney. Lynn suggests that Hemingway derived the name of his impotent hero in *The Sun Also Rises* from them: "Jacob" from Natalie's famous address, 20 rue Jacob, and "Barnes" from Djuna's last name. Jake is in love with Brett who is sexually aggressive and mannish, and Lynn states that his "dilemma is that, like a lesbian, he cannot penetrate his loved one's body"; Kenneth S. Lynn, *Hemingway* (New York: Simon and Schuster, 1987). But Hemingway's interest in lesbians may be explained as easily in the context of his times as in the context of his personal life. Sherwood Anderson, *Dark Laughter* (New York: Boni and Liveright, 1925), pp. 150–55.

7. Kaier Curtin discusses the flurry over *God of Vengeance, Sin of Sins,* and *The Captive* in *"We Can Always Call Them Bulgarians": Lesbians and Gay Men on the American Stage* (Boston: Alyson, 1987). When Thomas Dickinson's *Winter Bound,* a play that seems to be influenced by D. H. Lawrence's novella of lesbian defeat, *The Fox,* appeared on Broadway at the end of the decade it caused little stir, perhaps because by then the public had become more used to the subject of lesbianism, particularly through *The Well of Loneliness,* which was published in America shortly before the production of *Winter Bound* (1929) and quickly became a best-seller.

8. Quoted in "That Was New York," *New Yorker,* Feb. 1940, pp. 35–38.

9. Gertrude Stein, "Miss Furr and Miss Skeene," (1922; reprinted in *The Selected Writings of Gertrude Stein,* ed. Carl Van Vechten [New York: Random House, 1962], pp. 561–68).

10. "Synonym" quoted in John B. Kennedy, "So This Is Harlem," *Colliers,* October 28, 1933, p. 27+. Straight/gay Harlem in the '20s described in George Chauncey, Jr., "The Way We Were," *Village Voice,* July 1, 1986, pp. 29–30+; Blair Niles, *Strange Brother* (1931; reprint, New York: Arno, 1975), p. 210; Milt Machlin, *Libby* (New York: Tower, 1980), p. 59.

11. Niles, p. 151–52.

12. On Harlem Renassiance homosexuality see Eric Garber, " 'Tain't Nobody's Business: Homosexuality in Harlem in the 1920s," *Advocate,* May 13, 1982, pp. 39–43+. On McKay's homosexuality see Wayne F. Cooper, *Claude McKay: Rebel Sojourner in the Harlem Renaissance* (Baton Rouge: Louisiana State University Press, 1987), passim. Claude McKay, *Home to Harlem* (1928; reprint, Chatham, New Jersey: Chatham 1973), pp. 128–29, 91–92. Bessie Smith recorded a slightly different version of the song called "Foolish Man Blues":

> "There's two things got me puzzled,
> There's two things I don't understand,
> That's a mannish-acting woman,
> And a skippin', twistin,' woman-acting man."

In Chris Albertson, *Bessie* (New York: Stein and Day, 1972), p. 125. In Smith's version its razzing nature is mitigated through the title, which laughs at the speaker, and through the fact of the singer's own bisexuality.

13. Wallace Thurman, *The Blacker the Berry* (1929; reprint, New York: Arno, 1969), pp. 211, 135–36.

14. Niles, pp. 47, 56, 155–56.

15. John Dos Passos, *The Big Money* (New York: Harcourt Brace, 1936), pp. 514–17.

16. Machlin, pp. 69–71. See also Mercedes de Acosta, *Here Lies the Heart* (1960; reprint, New York: Arno Press, 1975), p. 128, and Lee Israel, *Miss Tallulah Bankhead* (New York: Dell, 1973), pp. 68–70.

17. Jervis Anderson, *This Was Harlem: A Cultural Portrait, 1900–1950* (New York: Farrar, Straus and Giroux, 1982), p. 169; Roi Ottley and William Weatherby, eds., *The Negro in New York: An Informal Social History* (Dobbs Ferry, N.Y.: Oceana, 1967), p. 249; Gladys Bentley, "I Am a Woman Again," *Ebony,* (August 1952), pp. 92–98; personal interview with Mabel Hampton, cohort of Bentley, age 85, New York, October 4, 1987.

18. Margaret Otis discussed early twentieth-century black and white lesbian behavior in jails in "A Perversion Not Commonly Noted," *Journal of Abnormal Psychology* (June-July 1913), 8(2): 113–16.

19. Luvenia Pinson, "The Black Lesbian—Times Past, Times Present," *Womanews,* May 1980. See also Niles, for Harlemites' knowledge of black lesbian marriages.

20. Gloria Hull, in "Under the Days: The Buried Life and Poetry of Angelina Weld Grimke," *Conditions: Five, The Black Women's Issue* (Autumn 1979), 2(2):23, suggests that Grimke was not more prolific because she felt she had to hide her lesbianism. But it is actually unclear to what extent Grimke felt it necessary to be secretive about her affectional preference. Some ostensibly lesbian poems by Grimke did appear during her lifetime, such as "Mona Lisa," in Countee Cullen, ed., *Caroling Dusk: An Anthology of Verse by Negro Poets* (New York: Harper and Row, 1927), p. 42. See also the poems of May V. Cowdery, who published frequently in *Crisis* during the 1920s. Cowdery's book of collected verse, *We Lift Our Voices and Other Poems* (Philadelphia: Alpress, 1936), contains several poems that appear to be lesbian, such as "Insatiate," a sardonic poem about how only jealousy can keep the speaker faithful to her woman lover (pp. 57–58). Information about clubs from Bentley; Machlin, pp. 69–70; Garber, p. 41; and personal interview with Mabel Hampton, Carl Van Vechten, *Nigger Heaven* (rpt. New York: Harper and Row, 1971), pp. 12, 137.

21. Interview with Ruby Smith by Chris Albertson, 1971, *AC-DC Blues,* side A. See also Albertson, *Bessie,* p. 123. History of buffet flats in Garber, p. 41; McKay, p. 103; Machlin, p. 71.

22. Elaine Feinstein, *Bessie Smith* (New York: Viking, 1985), p. 38. Albertson, *Bessie,* chapter 5.

23. Sarah Lieb, *Mother of the Blues: A Study of Ma Rainey* (Amherst: University of Massachusetts Press, 1981), pp. 17, 18.

24. Ad for "Prove It on Me Blues," *Chicago Defender,* September 22, 1928, 1:27. Hazel V. Carby briefly discusses "Prove It on Me Blues" and Ma Rainey's lesbian relationship with Bessie Smith in "It Jus Be's Dat Way Sometimes: The Sexual Politics of Women's Blues," *Radical America* (1986), 20(4):9–22.

25. Frank C. Taylor with Gerald Cook, *Alberta Hunter: A Celebration in Blues* (New York: McGraw Hill, 1987), passim.

26. Personal interview with Mabel Hampton, cited above.

27. A'Lelia P. Bundles, "Madame C. J. Walker to Her Daughter, A'Lelia —The Last Letter," *Sage: A Scholarly Journal on Black Women* (Fall 1984), 1(2):34–35. Personal interview with Mabel Hampton, cited above. David Levering Lewis, *When Harlem Was in Vogue* (New York: Alfred Knopf, 1981), pp. 165–68.

28. Ma Rainey, "Prove It on Me Blues," on *AC-DC Blues: Gay Jazz Reissues,* side A, Stash Records, St-106.

29. Bessie Jackson, "B.D. Women's Blues," *AC-DC Blues.* Transcribed in a slightly different version in Paul Oliver, *The Meaning of the Blues* (1960; reprint, New York: Collier Books, 1972), pp. 137–38. See also references in Leib, p. 123, to "BD Women" and "BD Dream," which confirm that the "bulldyker" was a recurrent figure in the blues.

30. "It's Dirty But Good," in Jonathan Katz, *Gay American History: Lesbians and Gay Men in the U.S.A.* (New York: Harper and Row, 1976), p. 77.

31. W. T. Kirkeby and Sinclair Traill, *Ain't Misbehavin'* (New York: Peter Davies, 1966), p. 41. Paul Oliver, *Aspects of the Blues Tradition* (New York: Oak, 1970), p. 203. An earlier version called "The Bull Diker's Dream" had been written by Jesse Pickett and was circulated by the beginning of the 1920s. It is described as starting out at a fast tempo and moving into a slow drag style "where it got mean and dirty. It was one of those 'put out the lights and call the law' things that went over big just before dawn"; in Willie Smith and George Hoefer, *Music on My Mind* (New York: MacGibbon and Kee, 1965), pp. 55–56. These blues songs with homosexual references were not limited to the 1920s. Perhaps motivated by male anxiety about going off to another war, Memphis Willie B complained in the early '40s:

Women loving each other, they don't think about no man. (twice)
They ain't playing it secret no more. These women playing a wide
    open hand

I buzzed a girl the other day,
I wanted a little thrill,
She said, "I'm so sorry,
My missus is putting out the same thing you is. "

Quoted in Samuel Charters, *The Poetry of the Blues* (New York: Oak, 1963), pp. 82–83.

32. Lewis Erenberg, *Steppin' Out: New York Nightlife and the Transformation of American Culture* (Westport, Conn.: Greenwood Press, 1981); Joanne Meyerowitz, *Holding Their Own: Working Women Apart from the Family in Chicago, 1880–1930* (Ph.D. diss., Stanford University, 1983); Kathy Peiss, *Cheap Amusements: Working Women and Leisure in Turn-of-the-Century New York* (Philadelphia: Temple University Press, 1986).

33. Lyrics quoted in Oliver, 207, 225–26.

34. Harvey Warren Zorbaugh, *The Gold Coast and the Slum: A Sociological Study of Chicago's Near North Side* (Chicago: University of Chicago Press, 1929). Chicago lesbian bars discussed in newspaper article about a police raid: "Shut Two Night Clubs With Girls Garbed as Men," in New York Lesbian Herstory Archives, file: 1930s.

35. Frances Donovan, *The Woman Who Waits* (1920; reprint, New York: Arno Press, 1974), pp. 143–44.

36. Quoted in Meyerowitz, p. 175.

37. Millay quotation in Max Eastman, *Great Companions* (1942; reprint, New York: Farrar, Straus, Cudahy, 1959), p. 83.

38. The Village in 1860 is discussed in Allen Churchill, *The Improper Bohemians: A Recreation of Greenwich Village in Its Heyday* (New York: E. P. Dutton, 1959), p. 25.

39. Dodge's salons are discussed in Carl Van Vechten, *Peter Whiffle* (New York: Alfred Knopf, 1922); Robert E. Humphrey, *Children of Fantasy: The*

First Rebels of Greenwich Village (New York: John Wiley, 1978), pp. 26–27; Churchill, pp. 54–55; Albert Parry, *Garrets and Pretenders: A History of Bohemianism in America* (1933; reprint, New York: Dover, 1960), p. 273. In addition to Mabel Dodge's own discussion in her memoirs of her various lesbian experiences they are also discussed in more recent biographies of her, e.g., Emily Hahn, *Mabel: A Biography of Mabel Dodge Luhan* (Boston: Houghton Mifflin, 1977); Winifred L. Frazer, *Mabel Dodge Luhan* (Boston: Twayne, 1984). Dodge lived closely to male ambivalence over lesbianism. Her third husband bragged to Djuna Barnes that he succeeded in destroying a lesbian relationship by making love to both women: quoted in Andrew Field, *Djuna: The Formidable Miss Barnes* (Austin: University of Texas Press, 1985), p. 48.

40. Invitation in New York Lesbian Herstory Archives, file: 1920s. Retreats mentioned in Caroline F. Ware, *Greenwich Village, 1920–30: A Comment on American Civilization in the Post War Years* (Boston: Houghton Mifflin, 1935), pp. 96, 238. Brothel reference in Field, p. 79. Parry also refers to "Lesbian harems that were open to the knowing," again, unfortunately, without documentation (p. 327).

41. Judith Schwarz, *Radical Feminists of Heterodoxy: Greenwich Village, 1912–1914* (Norwich, Vt.: New Victorian, 1986).

42. Chauncey. Personal interview with Mabel Hampton, cited above.

43. Ware, pp. 55, 237, 252–53.

44. Ann Cheney, *Millay in Greenwich Village* (University, Alabama: University of Alabama Press, 1975), p. 16; Elizabeth Atkins, *Edna St. Vincent Millay and Her Times* (Chicago: University of Chicago Press, 1936), pp. 37–38. Atkins was the first to suggest that while *The Lamp and the Bell* purports to be set in the ancient kingdom of Fiori, it is really Poughkeepsie-on-the-Hudson that Millay is describing. *Letters of Edna St. Vincent Millay,* ed. Allan Ross Macdougall (New York: Harper and Brothers, 1952), pp. 92, 84–85.

45. "Virgin" quoted in Humphrey, p. 224. "Fonder of women" quoted in Emily Hahn, *Romantic Rebels: An Informal History of Bohemians in America* (Boston: Houghton Mifflin, 1967), p. 241.

46. Millay on psychoanalysis in Cheyney, p. 65. Millay on Eugen Boissevain, her husband, in Jean Gould, *The Poet and Her Book: A Biography of Edna St. Vincent Millay* (New York: Dodd, Mead, 1969), p. 189.

47. See, e.g., "The Button" and "The Tigress" in Floyd Dell, *Love in Greenwich Village* (New York: George H. Duran, 1926). Ellen Kay Trimberger points out that Dell was not alone among Greenwich Village men who in practice fell considerably short of their ideals concerning women's freedom. Trimberger discusses Max Eastman and Hutchins Hapgood, who were leaders of Greenwich Village Bohemia, along with Dell, in "Feminism, Men, and Modern Love: Greenwich Village, 1901–1925," in Ann Snitow et al., eds., *Powers of Desire: The Politics of Sexuality* (New York: Monthly Review Press, 1983), pp. 131–52. Hutchins Hapgood, *A Victorian in the Modern World* (New York: Harcourt, 1939), p. 320.

48. Village gay areas cited in Churchill, p. 320; Ware, p. 237.

49. Clarence P. Oberndorf, "Diverse Forms of Homosexuality," *Urologic and Cutaneous Review* (1929), 33:518–23. A. A. Brill, "The Psychiatric Approach to Homosexuality," *The Journal-Lancet* (April 15, 1935), 55:249–52.

50. The 1925 team is Irene Case Sherman and Mandel Sherman ("The Factor of Parental Attachment in Homosexuality," *Psychoanalytic Review* [1925] 13:34; other warnings in George W. Henry, M.D., *Sex Variants: A Study of Homosexual Patterns* (1941; reprint, New York: Paul B. Hoeber, 1960), p. 1025; Winifred Richmond, *The Adolescent Girl: A Book for Parents and Teachers* (New York: Macmillan, 1926), pp. 124–25.

51. On the campaign for intercourse see Morton M. Hunt, *The Natural History of Love* (New York: Alfred A. Knopf, 1959), pp. 344–45; William J. Fielding, *Sex and the Love Life* (1927; reprint, New York: Ribbon Books, 1930), pp. 120–21; Walter M. Gallican, *The Poison of Prudery: A Historical Survey* (Boston: Stratford, 1929), p. 135. "Flaming bright red" quotation in Lorine Pruette, "The Flapper," in V. F. Calverton and Samuel D. Schmalhausen, eds., *The New Generation: The Intimate Problems of Modern Parents and Their Children* (1930; reprint, New York: Arno Press, 1971), p. 581. "Excess" quotation in Samuel D. Schmalhausen, "The Sexual Revolution," in V. F. Calverton and Samuel D. Schmalhausen, eds., *Sex in Civilization* (Garden City, N.Y.: Garden City Publishers, 1929), p. 416.

52. "Outworn traditions" statement by Stella Browne, quoted in Sheila Jeffreys, *The Spinster and Her Enemies: Feminism and Sexuality, 1880–1930* (London: Pandora Press, 1985), p. 117; see also Floyd Dell, *Love in the Machine Age: A Psychological Study of the Transition from Non-Patriarchal Society* (1930; reprint, New York: Farrar, Straus and Giroux, 1973), p. 238. William Alger, *The Friendships of Women* (Boston: Roberts, 1868), p. 364.

53. For a discussion of the effects of companionate marriage on views of lesbianism see Christina Simmons, "Companionate Marriage and the Lesbian Threat," *Frontiers: A Journal of Women's Studies* (Fall 1979), 4(3):54–59. For examples of marriage manuals that promoted performance see Maria Stopes, *Married Love* (London: A. C. Fifield, 1918); Theodore H. van de Velde, *Ideal Marriage* (1926; reprint, New York: Covici Friede, 1930); Gilbert van Tassel Hamilton, *A Research in Marriage* (1929; reprint, New York: M. D. Lear, 1948); G. V. Hamilton and Kenneth Macgowan, "Physical Disabilities in Wives," in Calverton and Schmalhausen, eds., *Sex in Civilization;* Wilhelm Reich, *The Function of the Orgasm* (1926; reprint, New York: Orgone Institute Press, 1942). Women's "failure" is discussed in Dell, *Love in the Machine Age,* p. 239.

4. Wastelands and Oases

1. Thomas Minehan, *Boy and Girl Tramps in America* (New York: Farrar, 1934); Callman Rawley, "A Glimpse of the Unattached Woman Transient in New Orleans," *Family* (May 1934), 15:118; Susan Ware, *Holding Their Own:*

American Women in the 1930s (Boston: Twayne, 1982), pp. 33–34; Box-Car Bertha, As Told to Dr. Ben L. Reitman, *Sister of the Road: An Autobiography of Box-Car Bertha* (1937; reprint, New York: Harper and Row, 1975), pp. 65–67.

2. Bureau of the Census, *Historical Statistics of the United States: Colonial Times to 1970* (Washington, D.C.: 1975), pp. 126 ff. Alice Kessler-Harris, *Out to Work: A History of Wage Earning Women in the United States* (New York: Oxford, 1982), pp. 259–60, 263, 270–71. The number of women librarians, nurses, and social workers decreased only slightly or held steady during the decade of the depression, but there was a dramatic decrease in the number of women teachers, administrators, professors, clergywomen, etc. Women also made considerably less than men in identical professions. For example, in 1939 male teachers averaged $1,953, female teacher $1,394; Male social workers averaged $1,718, female social workers $1,442. According to an AAUW survey during the depression, 80 percent of the female respondents said they received less pay than men for equal work. A 1931 study also found that the percentage of female unemployment was highest in the higher income professions, with a considerable drop between 1929 and 1931. American Women's Association, *The Trained Woman and the Economic Crisis: Employment and Unemployment Among a Selected Group of Business and Professional Women in New York City* (New York: American Women's Association, 1931); Cynthia Fuchs Epstein, *Woman's Place: Options and Limits in Professional Careers* (Berkeley: University of California Press, 1971), p. 7; Ware, op. cit., pp. 69, 71–73.

3. Robert Latou Dickinson, "The Gynecology of Homosexuality," in George W. Henry, *Sex Variants: A Study of Homosexual Patterns* (1941; reprint, New York: Paul B. Hoeber, 1960), p. 1070. Dorothy Bromley and Florence Britten (*Youth and Sex: A Study of 1300 College Students* [New York: Harper, 1938], p. 118) also conclude, rather simplistically, that lesbianism in the 1930s was less prevalent among college women than it had been in the 1920s, "when a few campus leaders in several of the larger women's colleges made it something of a fad."

4. For late 1920s objections to working women see Henry R. Carey, "This Two-Headed Monster—The Family," *Harpers* (January 1928), 15:162–71, and Anon. "A Case of Two Careers," *Harpers* (January 1929), 17: 194–201. Quotations from the 1930s: Frank L. Hopkins, "Should Wives Work?," *American Mercury* (December. 1936), 39:409–16; Norman Cousins, "Will Women Lose Their Jobs?," *Current History and Forum* (September 1939), 41:14.

5. Barnard dean quoted in Edna McKnight, "Jobs—For Men Only? Shall We Send Women Workers Home?," *Outlook and Independent,* September 2, 1931, p. 18+. Sarah Comstock, "Marriage or Career?," *Good Housekeeping* (June 1932), 94:32–33+.

6. "What Do the Women of America Think About Careers?" *Ladies Home Journal* (Nov. 1939), 56:12; Claire Howe, "Return of the Lady," *New Outlook*

(Oct. 1934), 164:34–37; Jane Allen, "You May Have My Job: A Feminist Discovers Her Home," *Forum* (April 1932), 87:228–31.

7. Henry, *Sex Variants,* and George Henry, "Psychogenic Factors in Overt Homosexuality," *American Journal of Psychiatry* (January 1937), 93(4):889–908.

8. Personal interview with M.K., age 79, San Francisco, October 22, 1988.

9. Gloria T. Hull, *Color, Sex and Poetry: Three Women Writers of the Harlem Renaissance* (Bloomington: Indiana University Press, 1987), pp. 95–96, and *Give Us This Day: The Diary of Alice Dunbar-Nelson,* ed. Gloria T. Hull (New York: W. W. Norton, 1984), pp. 25, 249–50, 359–63, 421–22.

10. Sheila Donisthorpe, *Loveliest of Friends* (New York: Charles Kendall, 1931); William Carlos Williams, "The Knife of the Times," in *Knife of the Times* (Ithaca, N.Y.: Dragon Press, 1932); Dorothy Parker, "Glory in the Daytime," in *After Such Pleasure* (New York: Viking, 1934); Ernest Hemingway, "The Sea Change," in *The Fifth Column and the First Forty-Nine Stories* (New York: Collier, 1938). Barbara Goldsmith, *Little Gloria—Happy at Last* (New York: Knopf, 1980).

11. Quoted in Doris Faber, *The Life of Lorena Hickok: E.R.'s Friend* (New York: William Morrow, 1980), March 4, 1933 (p. 110); December 5, 1933 (p. 152), January 27, 1934 (p. 161), September 1, 1934 (p. 176).

12. Victor Robinson, introduction to Diana Frederics, *Diana: A Strange Autobiography* (New York: Dial, 1939), p. ix.

13. Henry, *Sex Variants,* pp. 1023–27. "Surgery May Save Human Race from Extinction: Evolutionary Trend Toward Neuter Race May Be Checked by Gland Operation," *Science News Letter,* May 19, 1934; "Women's Personalities Changed by Adrenal Gland Operation," *New York Times,* October 28, 1935, pp. 1+.

14. For an extensive bibliographic study of lesbian novels of the 1930s see Jeannette Foster, *Sex Variant Women in Literature* (1956; reprint, Baltimore, MD.: Diana Press, 1975), pp. 290–324. Donisthorpe, p. 234. For my discussion of nineteenth-century French decadent novels see *Surpassing the Love of Men: Romantic Friendship and Love Between Women from the Renaissance to the Present* (New York: William Morrow, 1981), pp. 254–94. There were a few early twentieth-century novels published outside of France in which lesbians were depicted as monsters, but such characterizations were relatively rare at that time, e.g., Clemence Dane, *Regiment of Women* (New York: Macmillan, 1917). Nineteen-thirties novels: Idabell Williams, *Hellcat* (1934; reprint, Dell 1952); Lois Lodge, *Love Like a Shadow* (New York: Phoenix, 1935); Lilyan Brock, *Queer Patterns* (New York: Greenberg, 1935); Helen Anderson, *Pity for Women* (New York: Doubleday, 1937).

15. Elisabeth Craigin, *Either Is Love* (New York: Harcourt, 1937), pp. 45, 146. Diana Frederics, p. 119.

16. Djuna Barnes, *Nightwood* (New York: Harcourt, 1937); Gale Wilhelm, *We Too Are Drifting* (1935; reprint, New York: Triangle Books, 1940), pp. 11, 14.

17. Publisher's ad for *The Scorpion* in *New York Herald Tribune*, April 2, 1933.

18. Discussion of expurgation of *Club de Femmes* in *Time* (October 25, 1937, pp. 26–28.

19. Theater censorship attempts discussed in Kaier Curtin, *"We Can Always Call Them Bulgarians": The Emergence of Lesbians and Gay Men on the American Stage* (Boston: Alyson, 1987), pp. 210–11. George Jean Nathan, "Design for Loving," *American Spectator* (April 1933), pp. 2–3. Review of *Girls in Uniform* in *New York Morning Telegraph,* January 1, 1933.

20. Robert Coleman, "Love of Women," *New York Daily Mirror,* December 14, 1937. *The Children's Hour* received a much friendlier critical reception than other lesbian plays of the decade, perhaps because Martha fulfills the maxim through her suicide that "the only good lesbian is a dead lesbian." See Kaier Curtin's review of the critical reception of *The Children's Hour* in *"We Can Always Call Them Bulgarians"*.

21. Interview with Anne Revere in Curtin, p. 201.

22. Early studies of lesbianism in correctional institutions include Margaret Otis, "A Perversion Not Commonly Noted," *Journal of Abnormal Psychology* (June/ July 1913), 8(2):113–16; Charles A. Ford, "Homosexual Practices of Institutionalized Females," *Journal of Abnormal and Social Psychiatry* (March 1929), 23:442– 48; Samuel Kahn, *Mentality and Homosexuality* (Boston: Meador, 1937). Study of slang: Gershon Legman, "The Language of Homosexuality" (1941), appendix in Henry, *Sex Variants*. Books such as *Imitation of Sappho* (1930) and *Diana* (1939) were tellingly bound in lavender. Lavender may have come to be associated with lesbianism through the play *The Captive* in which one woman sends violets to another, which resulted in a long popular association of violets and lesbianism. But in Mary Casal, *The Stone Wall* (Chicago: Eyncourt Press, 1930), p. 155, Mary sends Juno violets when she courts her in the early twentieth century, so such a gift may have been customary between women lovers even before *The Captive* brought it to public attention. Frederics, p. 123.

23. Box-Car Bertha, pp. 65–67.

24. Paul Yawitz, "Greenwich Village Sin Dives Lay Trap for Innocent Girls," *New York Evening Graphic,* 1931, in Lesbian Herstory Archives, files: 1920s and 1930s. Arno Karlen refers to lesbian bars in New York in the 1930s in *Sexuality and Homosexuality: A New View* (New York: W. W. Norton, 1971), p. 311. Other information about lesbian bar life in the 1930s comes from *Lesbian Herstory Archives News* (December 1981), 7:16; the newsletter of the West Coast Lesbian Collections: *In the Life* (Fall 1982), 1:5; Vern Bullough and Bonnie Bullough, "Lesbianism in the 1920s and 1930s: A New Found Study," *Signs* (Summer 1977), 2(4):902; Box-Car Bertha, p. 65.

25. Personal interview with Win, age 74, San Francisco, August 15, 1987. Lesbian bars were sometimes raided by police in the 1930s. A mid-'30s Chicago newspaper article headlined "Shut Two Nightclubs with Girls Garbed as Men" reported that women in masculine attire were nightly patrons. The article quoted the police major as saying, "Such places are a disgrace to the

city, and they will not be tolerated in Chicago. Every place of such character will be closed": New York Lesbian Herstory Archives, file: 1930s. On lesbian nightclubs in Berlin before 1933 see Adele Meyer, *Lila Nächte: Die Damenklubs der Zwanziger Jahre* (Cologne: Zitronenpresse, 1981). See also "Sixty Places to Talk, Dance and Play," *Connexions* (Jan 1982), 3:16–18. For a discussion of lesbian bars in 1930s Paris see Brassai (Gyula Halasz), "Sodom and Gomorrah," *The Secret Paris of the '30's* (New York: Pantheon, 1976).

26. Nucleus Club information in letter from Gean Harwood and Bruhs Mero, SAGE (New York), February 1989.

27. Personal interview with Mary, age 68, Marin, Calif., August 12, 1987. Personal interview with Olivia, San Antonio, Tex., August 17, 1990. See Foster, ch. 10, for a bibliographic discussion of women's institutions as a meeting place for lesbians during the 1930s.

28. Personal interview with Mary, cited above.

29. Personal interview with Sandra, age 77, San Francisco, August 9, 1987.

30. Personal interview with May, age 82, Los Angeles, August 2, 1987.

31. Craigin, p. 145.

32. Richard Lockridge, "The New Play," *New York Sun,* November 21 1934).

33. For a discussion of middle-class lesbians' rejection of the popular view of lesbianism see Bullough and Bullough. Henry, *Sex Variants.* pp. 771, 825, 839, 864, 867, 916.

34. In *Surpassing the Love of Men* I explore male pornographic images of lesbians in fiction from the sixteenth through the nineteenth centuries, as well as the nineteenth-century sexologists' discussions of lesbian sexuality. I also deal with Renee Vivien and her predecessors in that book. Mary MacLane, *The Story of Mary MacLane by Herself* (Chicago: Herbert S. Stone, 1902), p. 182. Radclyffe Hall, *The Well of Loneliness* (Garden City, NY: Blue Ribbon Books, 1928), p. 458.

35. Casal, p. 185.

36. Vida Dutton Scudder, *On Journey* (New York: Dutton and Company, 1937), pp. 224, 226, 211-12.

37. Frederics, pp. 168–69, 210.

38. Elisabeth Craigin, pp. 11, 15, 117. For earlier lesbian writing that dealt with the emotional aspects of love between women see my discussion in *Surpassing the Love of Men,* pp. 197– 230, 297–313.

5. *Naked Amazons and Queer Damozels*

1. Fleischmann's ad reprinted in Allan Bérubé, *Coming Out Under Fire: The History of Gay Men and Women in World War II* (New York: Free Press, 1990).

2. Public impression discussed in Mattie Treadwell, *The Women's Army Corps* (Washington, D.C.: 1954), pp. 625–26, 767.

3. For the effects of World War I on lesbianism see Compton Mackenzie, *Extraordinary Women* (1928; reprint, London: Secker, 1932); for the effects of World War II, Frank S. Caprio, *Female Homosexuality: A Psychodynamic Study of Lesbianism* (New York: Grove Press, 1954), pp. 134–35. Women comprised the bulk of the civilians who migrated to large cities in order to work during World War II. See William Chafe, *The American Woman: Her Changing Social, Economic, and Political Roles, 1920–1970* (New York: Oxford University Press, 1972), chs. 6–8. Allan Bérubé points out that World War II was as crucial to the creation of a homosexual culture at that time as the 1969 Stonewall Rebellion was to a later generation, but its impact was lost in the tragedy of the war, and no gay movement or gay press could be developed in those years to record its history: "Marching to a Different Drummer," in Ann Snitow et al., eds., *Powers of Desire: The Politics of Sexuality* (New York: Monthly Review Press, 1983), pp. 88–99.

4. Personal interview with Mildred, age 58, Berkeley, August 10, 1987.

5. *Miami News*, May 20, 1942, quoted in John Costello, *Virtue Under Fire: How World War II Changed Our Social and Sexual Attitudes* (Boston: Little, Brown, 1985), p. 43.

6. For a history of women in the American military see Martin Binkin and Shirley T. Bach, *Women and the Military* (Washington, D.C.: Brookings Institute, 1977), and Jeanne Holm, *Women in the Military: An Unfinished Revolution* (Novato, Calif.: Presidio Press, 1982). For military policy toward homosexuals see *Newsweek* (July 9, 1947), 29:54, which notes the Army's change of policy in instituting the "undesirable" discharge in 1947. See also Allan Bérubé and John D'Emilio, "The Military and Lesbians During the McCarthy Years," Estelle Freedman et al., eds., in *The Lesbian Issue: Essays from Signs* (Chicago: University of Chicago Press, 1985), pp. 279–95.

7. Information on WAC psychological examination from written communication, H.P., age 68, accepted for WAC officer training in 1943 (Los Angeles, May 28, 1988). At the end of 1942 the adjutant general issued a confidential letter ordering recruiters to investigate women applicants' "local reputations" to determine whether they had undesirable traits such as "homosexual tendencies," but nothing came of this order since by that point women were desperately needed in the military. In fact, only a few months later the adjutant general ordered looser screening standards for women in order to meet unfilled quotas. Although other directives against lesbians were halfheartedly issued now and again during the war, they continued to have little or no effect on lesbians being accepted or retained in the armed forces. Finally only a minute number of women were discharged for lesbianism. The Army and Navy kept no record of such discharges; Marine records indicate that twenty women were discharged. Bérubé, *Coming Out Under Fire*, pp. 30–32, 147.

8. Sex Hygiene Course (for Officers and Officer Candidates, WAAC), War Department, Pamphlet no. 35-l (Washington, D.C.: Government Printing Office, 1943), see especially "Lecture V: Homosexuality."

9. Personal interview with Mary, age 68, Marin County, Calif., August 12, 1987.

10. Rita Laporte, "Living Propaganda," *The Ladder,* June 1965, pp. 21–22.

11. Bérubé, "Marching to a Different Drummer." Although the investigative team could find no real "homosexual addicts" the brutal psychological techniques used by their psychiatrists to determine whether a woman was lesbian caused three women to be hospitalized by emotional stress. Bérubé, *Coming Out Under Fire,* p. 345.

12. Personal interview with Elizabeth, age 66, Marin County, Calif., August 12, 1987.

13. Pat Bond, quoted in Bérubé, "Coming Out Under Fire," *Mother Jones,* February/March 1983, pp. 23–29 +.

14. Harrison Carrol, "Miss Dietrich Defends Use of Pants," *World Telegram,* January 17, 1932. Garbo headline quoted in Mercedes de Acosta, *Here Lies the Heart* (1968; reprint, New York: Arno Press, 1975), p. 229.

15. Rusty Brown, "Always Me," in Marcie Adelman, ed., *Long Time Passing: Lives of Older Lesbians* (Boston: Alyson, 1986), pp. 146–47.

16. "Past Times: Unearthing the History of Gay G.I.s," *Chicago Reader* (June 18, 1982) 11:36.

17. Personal interview with Mac, age 63, San Francisco, August 11, 1987.

18. Pat Gozemba and Janet Kahn, presentation given at the session, "Love and Friendship in the Lesbian Bar Communities of the 1940s, 1950s, and 1960s," Berkshire History of Women Conference, Wellesley College, Mass., June 19–21, 1987, and Bérubé, "Coming Out Under Fire," p. 20.

19. Information on Lucky's in "Harlem's Strangest Night Club," *Ebony* (Dec. 1951), 7:80–85. Information on the 181 Club from personal interview with Lyn, age 64, now living in San Diego, July 28, 1987. Information on the Music Hall from personal interview with Elizabeth, cited above. See also description of Boston bars during this period in Bob Skiba, "Pansies, Perverts, and Pegged Pants," *Gay and Lesbian Guide to New England* (n.p., 1982), pp. 2–5, in New York Lesbian Herstory Archives, file: 1950s.

20. *Yank,* November 16, 1945, p. 18, quoted in Bérubé, *Coming Out Under Fire,* p. 253.

21. Personal interview with Betty, age 66, Omaha, Neb., October 11, 1988.

22. Lisa Ben, *Vice Versa,* September 1947, pp. 4–5.

23. Freud's antifeminist attitudes have been frequently discussed in feminist writing since the publication of Kate Millett's *Sexual Politics* (New York: Doubleday, 1970). Hannah Lerman's *A Mote in Freud's Eye: From Psychoanalysis to the Psychology of Women* (New York: Springer, 1986) is a book length study of Freud's blind spots with regard to feminism. Sigmund Freud, "The Psychogenesis of a Case of Homosexuality in a Woman" (1920), in *The Standard Edition of the Complete Psychological Works of Sigmund Freud,* ed. James Strachey, vol. 18 (London: Hogarth Press, 1955), pp. 147–72.

24. Clara Thompson, "Changing Concepts of Homosexuality," in Patrick Mullahy, ed., *A Study of Interpersonal Relations* (New York: Hermitage Press, 1949), pp. 249–61.

25. Caprio, p. 143.

26. Charles Berg and Clifford Allen, *The Problem of Homosexuality* (New York: Citadel Press, 1958), p. 53. Edmund Bergler, *Homosexuality: Disease or Way of Life?* (1956; reprint, New York: Collier Books, 1962), p. 9.

27. Thompson. Albert Ellis, introduction to Donald Webster Cory, *The Lesbian in America* (New York: Tower, 1964), p. 13. Charles W. Socarides, *Homosexuality* (New York: Free Press, 1978), p. 60.

28. Sigmund Freud, "The Sexual Aberrations," *Standard Edition,* 18:556. Prison populations have also been used to help establish a picture of the homosexual, e.g., Samuel Kahn, *Mentality and Homosexuality* (Boston: Meador, 1937). Kahn based his discussion of homosexuality on his examination of homosexuals in prison without attempting to discover whether homosexual prisoners were different from heterosexual prisoners or whether they were similar in any way other than their sexual orientation to homosexuals outside of prison.

29. Cornelia Wilbur, "Clinical Aspects of Female Homosexuality," in Judd Marmor, ed., *Sexual Inversion: The Multiple Roots of Homosexuality* (New York: Basic Books, 1965), pp. 268–81.

30. Vicki Owen, "A Story of Punishment," in Margaret Cruikshank, ed., *The Lesbian Path* (Tallahassee, Fla.: Naiad Press, 1981).

31. Ferdinand Lundberg and Marynia Farnham, *Modern Woman: The Lost Sex* (New York: Harper and Row, 1947), pp. 143, 296. Caprio, p. 133. The popular press shared these ideas and promulgated them to the masses. See, e.g., William G. Niederland, "'Masculine' Women Are Cheating Love," *Coronet,* May 1953, pp. 41–44.

32. Freud, "The Psychogensis of a Case of Homosexuality in a Woman," and "Historical Notes: A Letter from Freud" [to an American mother about her homosexual son, written 1935, uncovered by Alfred Kinsey], *American Journal of Psychiatry* (April 1955), 108:787–89. Cf. letter from William J. Fielding to Mr. James Cissel, December 21, 1923, in New York Lesbian Herstory Archives, file: 1920s; Aaron J. Rosanoff, "Human Sexuality, Normal and Abnormal, from a Psychiatric Standpoint," *Urologic and Cutaneous Review* (1929), 33:505–18; and Helene Deutsch, "On Female Homosexuality," *Psychiatric Quarterly,* (October 1932), 1:484–88 + .

33. Albert Ellis, "The Effectiveness of Psychotherapy with Individuals Who Have Severe Homosexual Problems," *Journal of Consulting Psychology* (1956), 20(3):191–94. Bergler, *Homosexuality,* p. 178.

34. Richard C. Robertiello, *Voyage from Lesbos: The Psychoanalysis of a Female Homosexual* (New York: Citadel Press, 1959), pp. 27, 76, 234–35, 239, 246.

35. Caprio's *Female Homosexuality* is also a particularly good compendium of myths about lesbian murder, suicide, etc. See, e.g., pp. viii, 146, 148.

Cannibalism statement by Paula Heimann and Susan Isaacs (1952), following the 1948 theory of Edmund Bergler that homosexuality was a defense against the acute anxieties connected with oral and cannabilistic fantasies, quoted in Berg and Allen, pp. 145, 149. This insane idea was taken literally in 1977 in Anita Bryant's hate-filled antihomosexual campaign. Bryant wrote: "Oral sex, where the tongue is used to stimulate the clitoris producing an orgasm, is a form of vampirism or eating of blood. Such degeneracy produces a taste and craving for the effects, as does liquor and narcotics." Quoted in Sarah Schulman, "The History of the Commie-Pinko-Faggot," *Womanews* (New York), July/August 1980, p. 1+. "Curable Disease?" *Time* (Dec. 10, 1956), 68:74–76.

36. Allison in Marcy Adelman, ed., *Long Time Passing: Lives of Older Lesbians* (Boston: Alyson, 1986), pp. 60–61.

37. Thomas Szasz, "Legal and Moral Aspects of Homosexuality," in Marmor, pp. 124–39. Bergler, p. 271. For a similar position see Caprio, *Female Homosexuality*, pp. 285–86.

38. Written communication from Harriet, age 68, Los Angeles, May 28, 1988.

6. The Love That Dares Not Speak Its Name

1. Alfred Kinsey et al., *Sexual Behavior in the Human Female* (Philadelphia: W. B. Saunders, 1953), pp. 474–75; also, Alfred Kinsey, *Sexual Behavior in the Human Male* (Philadelphia: W. B. Saunders, 1948), p. 623. Kinsey also found that 37 percent of all males and 13 percent of all females had had homosexual experiences to orgasm. Edmund Bergler, "Homosexuality and the Kinsey Report" (1948; reprinted in Aron M. Krich, ed., *The Homosexuals As Seen by Themselves and Thirty Authorities* [New York: Citadel Press, 1954], pp. 226–50. Kinsey pointed out what many Americans did not want to recognize—e.g., "Such a high proportion of the females and males in our population is involved in sexual activities which are prohibited by the law of most of the states of the union, that it is inconceivable that the present laws could be administered in any fashion that even remotely approached systematic and complete enforcement," *Sexual Behavior in the Human Female*, p. 20. M. S. Guttmacher, *Sex Offenses* (New York: Norton, 1957).

2. Dismissal figures quoted in "Report on Homosexuality, with Particular Emphasis on this Problem in Governmental Agencies, Formulated by the Committee on Cooperation with Governmental (Federal) Agencies of the Group for the Advancement of Psychiatry," report no. 30 January 1955, p. 5. McCarthy's charge of the State Department reported in *New York Times*, March 9, 1950, p. 1. Regarding the homosexuality of McCarthy's aides see Nicholas von Hoffman, *Citizen Cohn: The Life and Times of Roy Cohn* (New York: Doubleday, 1988).

3. *New York Times*, April 19, 1950, p. 25. *New York Times*, May 5, 1950, p. 15. *New York Times*, May 20, 1950, p. 8.

4. "Employment of Homosexuals and Other Sex Perverts in Government: A Report Submitted to the Senate Committee on Expenditures in the Executive Departments by its Subcmmittee on Investigations, December 15, 1950," reprinted in *Government vs. Homosexuals* (New York: Arno Press, 1975). John D'Emilio estimates that by the mid-1950s 20 percent of the labor force faced security investigations, "The McCarthy Era," *The Advocate,* December 3, 1982, pp. 25–27.

5. E. M., "To Be Accused Is to Be Guilty," *One* (April 1953), 1(4):3–4.

6. *New York Times,* December 20, 1951, p. 1. All the cliches to be found in psychiatric writing of the period were reiterated in government writing on all levels: e.g., Judge Morris Ploscowe argued that homosexuals must not be employed by government: "There is no real permanence to homosexual relationships. The quality of emotional instability encountered in homosexuals, both male and female, makes them continually dissatisfied with their lot. Many of them are continually on the prowl, looking for sexual partners": "Homosexuality, Sodomy, and Crimes Against Nature," (1951); reprinted in Donald Webster Cory, ed., *Homosexuality: A Cross Cultural Approach* (New York: Julian Press, 1956), pp. 394–406.

7. *New York Times,* December 16, 1950, p. 3. Wherry discussed in Max Lerner, *The Unfinished Country: A Book of American Symbols* (New York: Simon and Schuster, 1959), pp. 311–19. See also Max Lerner, interviews with Kenneth Wherry, *New York Post,* July 11, 17, 18, 1950.

8. Personal interview with M.K., age 79, San Francisco, October 22, 1988.

9. The text of this Executive Order was reprinted in the *New York Times,* April 28, 1953, p. 20+. For an example of state harassment see the Florida report, "Homosexuality and Citizenship in Florida," which was begun by an interim committee established in 1955 to investigate homosexuals in government employment. Homosexual teachers were especially singled out for attack. Reprinted in *Government vs. Homosexuals.*

10. Audre Lorde, *Zami: A New Spelling of My Name* (Watertown, Mass.: Persephone Press, 1982), pp. 149, 198.

11. "The ACLU Takes a Stand on Homosexuality," *The Ladder* March 1957, pp. 8–9. The ACLU did, however, protest when two San Francisco State College coeds were arrested that year in a gay bar and charged with wearing men's clothes. See "ACLU Clashes with San Francisco Police on Vagrancy Arrests," *The Ladder,* March 1957, p. 19. In the early 1950s the ACLU refused to help lesbians who were discharged from the military because "the ACLU held that homosexuality was relevant to an individual's military service." In responding to a discharged Air Force woman who asked for help in 1951, the ACLU staff counsel advised her to submit herself to medical treatment that would enable her to "abandon homosexual relations"; quoted in Allan Berube and John D'Emilio, "The Military and Lesbians During the McCarthy Years," in Estelle Freedman et al., *The Lesbian Issue: Essays from Signs* (Chicago: University of Chicago Press, 1985), pp. 290–95.

More recently the ACLU has been very active in gay rights and has even published a gay rights manual, Thomas B. Stoddard et al., *The Rights of Gay People* (1975; rev. ed. New York: Bantam, 1983).

12. Milton E. Hahn and Byron H. Atkinson, "The Sexually Deviant Student," *School and Society* (September 17, 1955), 82: 85–87. Personal interview with Betty, age 66, Omaha, Neb., October 11, 1988.

13. Jack Lait and Lee Mortimer, *Washington Confidential* (New York: Crown Press, 1951), p. 94.

14. Ralph H. Major, Jr., "New Moral Menace to Our Youth," *Coronet*, September 1950, pp. 101–108. "Women Who Fall for Lesbians," *Jet* (February 1954), 5:20–22.

15. Rosie G. Waldeck, "Homosexual International," *Human Events*, in New York Lesbian Herstory Archives, file: 1950s.

16. Court decison quoted in *One*, March 1957, pp. 5–20. See also "*One* Takes a Stand," *The Ladder*, June 1957, pp.3–6. *One* appealed to the Supreme Court which reversed the ruling of the lower court in 1958. See *One*, March 1958, p. 6, and *Homophile Studies* (1958), 1:60–64.

17. "Sword of self-revulsion" from Edwin West, *Young and Innocent* (New York: Monarch, 1960), p. 43.

18. Publishers' demands discussed by 1950s novelist Vin Packer, quoted in Roberta Yusba, "Twilight Tales: Lesbian Pulps, 1950–1960," *On Our Backs*, Summer 1985, pp. 30–31 +. Paula Christian, another prolific lesbian paperback writer of the 1950s, similarly observed: "Through my own experience at Fawcett, it should be understood that a publisher (with the moral character of a nation in mind) cannot allow this theme to be promoted as something to be admired or desired. Nor can a publisher in the paperback field expect the general public to accept a truly sophisticated treatment where there is no justification for the 'deviation' with a great deal of why's, wherefore's, and 'we hate ourselves, but what can we do?' " *The Ladder* (February 1961), 5(5):19. For discussions of lesbians' reading of the pulps as the only literature in which lesbian love was portrayed see Kate Millett, *Flying* (New York: Ballantine Books, 1974), p. 202; Dorothy Allison, "A Personal History of Lesbian Porn," *New York Native,* June 16, 1982, p. 22; Fran Koski and Maida Tilchen, "Some Pulp Sappho," in Karla Jay and Allen Young, eds., *Lavender Culture* (New York: Jove, 1979), pp. 262–74.

19. Helen Hull papers, Columbia University, photocopy in New York Lesbian Herstory Archives, Hull biographical file.

20. In the '50s, as in earlier decades, front marriages were not uncommon among black lesbians as well as white. See Virginia Harris' story about middle-class black lesbians in the 1950s, "A Pearl of Great Price," *Common Lives/ Lesbian Lives*(Spring 1987), 2:3–10. Regarding parents having children committed see interview with Whitey in Nancy Adair and Casey Adair, *Word Is Out: Stories of Some of Our Lives* (San Francisco: New Glide Publications), pp. 6–7. Personal interview with Terry, age 58, in Kansas City, Kans., October 16, 1988.

21. Personal interview with Del Martin and Phyllis Lyon, San Francisco, August 14, 1987.

22. DOB greeter in Sidney Abbott and Barbara Love, *Sappho Was a Right-On Woman: A Liberated View of Lesbianism* (New York: Stein and Day, 1972), p. 100. "Attorney Stresses Nothing to Fear in Joining DOB," *The Ladder,* April 1957, pp. 15–16; "Your Name is Safe," *The Ladder,* Novemeber 1956, pp. 10–12. The latter article was reprinted in *The Ladder,* February 1958, pp. 4–6.

23. FBI File 94–843, 8/6/59.

24. Allan Bérubé, "Behind the Spectre of San Francisco," *The Body Politic,* April 1981, pp. 25–27, and personal interview with Martin and Lyon, cited above. Homosexuality was never illegal under California state law, although certain acts such as oral sex were until the mid-'70s: Sarah Senefield et al., *Sex Code of California: A Compendium* (Sausalito, Calif.: Graphic Arts of Marin, 1973), pp. 164–65.

25. "Instructions for Committee on Indoctrination and Education," quoted in Bérubé and D'Emilio.

26. "Discharge of Homosexuals," Air Force Regulation 35–66, Department of Air Force, Washington, D.C., May 31, 1956.

27. Personal interview with Annie, age 65, San Francisco, August 11, 1987. Official treatment of suspected lesbians in "Report on Homosexuality with Particular Emphasis on this Problem in Governmental Agencies," p. 4, and Louis Jolyon West et al., "An Approach to the Problem of Homosexuality in the Military Service," *American Journal of Psychiatry* (1958), 115:392–401.

28. Personal interview with Dina, age 56, Fresno, Calif., November 1, 1987.

29. Personal interview with Sandy, age 57, Lincoln, Neb., October 12, 1988.

30. Interview with Pat Bond in Adair and Adair, pp. 57–61.

31. Maida Tilchen and Helen Weinstock, "Letters from My Aunt," *Gay Community News,* July 12, 1980, pp. 8–9.

32. Jackie Cursi, "Leaping Lesbians," *Lesbian Ethics* (Fall 1986), 2(2):81–83.

33. Personal interview with Marie, age 58, Fresno, Calif., April 26, 1988.

34. Investigative board quoted in Bérubé and D'Emilio, p. 280. Personal interview with Elizabeth, age 66, Marin County, Calif., Aug. 12, 1988. Personal interview with Marie, cited above.

35. Vito Russo, "Pat Bond: The Word Is Out WAC," *Christopher Street* (May 1978), 2:11.

36. Case summarized in Jonathan Katz, *Gay American History: Lesbians and Gay Men in the U.S.A.* (New York: Thomas Crowell, 1976), pp. 119–23.

37. Personal interview with Wilma, age 54, Los Angeles, May 14, 1988.

38. Janet S. Chafetz et al., "A Study of Homosexual Women," *Social Work* (November 1974), 19(6):714–23, and Virginia R. Brooks, *Minority Stress and Lesbian Women* (Lexington, Mass.: Lexington Books, 1981), p. 63. Other studies show that even higher percentages of lesbians believe they must be closeted at work. For example, Martin Levine and Robin Leonard studied 203 middle-class, white collar, highly educated lesbians in New York City. Three-fifths expected discrimination at work if their sexual orientation became known. Those who did not either worked in fields accepting gays or their employers were gay: "Discrimination Against Lesbians in the Work Force," in Freedman, pp. 187–97.

39. Written communication with H.P. cited above. Such trepidation and suspicions are not limited to women who survived the 1950s. In the mid-1970s much younger lesbians, who were members of the middle-class feminist organization NOW, insisted that the FBI, which had just infiltrated radical lesbian communities in the East and South looking for Weathermen Susan Saxe and Katherine Ann Powers, had begun to harass the middle-class lesbian commuity in an attempt to destroy lesbian-feminist progress. In a flyer titled What to Do When the Man Comes to Your Door, lesbian NOW members complained that the FBI had already visited some of them and were beginning a campaign that was comparable to the Salem witch trials. See Sarah Schulman, "The History of the Commie-Pinko-Faggot," *Womanews* (New York), July/August 1980, p. 1+.

7. Butches, Femmes, and Kikis

1. Early German homophile activism discussed in Lillian Faderman and Brigitte Eriksson, *Lesbians in Germany: 1890–1920,* (Tallahasee, Fla.: Naiad Press, 1990), introduction. Lesbian society in France discussed in Catherine van Casselaer, *Lot's Wife: Lesbian Paris, 1890–1914,* (Liverpool: Janus Press, 1986).

2. Personal interview with Pat, age 51, former member of the Orange County Lionettes, the Huntington Park Blues, and the Fresno Rockettes, Fresno, March 5, 1988, and personal interview with Cleo, age 61, Omaha, Neb., October 11, 1988. Softball continues to be a major activity among young lesbians in areas such as the midwest. As Rhonda, age 26, observed, "Softball is the only consistent thing in this community. Political groups and social groups come and go, but softball will always be around"; Omaha, Neb., October 11, 1988. On the continuing importance of softball in the lesbian community see also Yvonne Zipter, *Diamonds Are a Dyke's Best Friend: Reflections, Reminiscences, and Reports from the Field on the Lesbian National Pastime* (Ithaca, NY: Firebrand Books, 1989).

3. Personal interview with Donna, age 54, Carson City, Nev., June 10, 1987.

4. A 1973 study of lesbians indicated that both sexually and socially, homosexual women tend to behave by and large like heterosexual women,

rather than like gay or straight men. Only in their interest in sports and abuse of alcohol were lesbians more like men than like other women: Marcel T. Saghir and Eli Robins, "Clinical Aspects of Female Homosexuality," in Judd Marmor, ed., *Homosexual Behavior: A Clinical Reappraisal* (New York: Basic Books, 1980), pp. 280–95. Esther Newton observes in "A Place in the Sun," a study of middle- and upper-middle class lesbians of Cherry Grove, that those women too had a drinking problem, perhaps acquired at their cocktail parties, where the excitement of alcohol may have been associated with the rebellion of the speakeasies, where modern women could drink in public for the first time (paper given at the Berkshire History of Women Conference, Wellesley College, Mass., June 20, 1987).

5. Reported in "The Gay Bar—Whose Problem Is It?" *The Ladder,* 4: 3 (Dec. 1959), pp. 4–13 +.

6. Ohio woman quoted in Margaret Hunt, "A Fem's Own Story: Interview With Joan Nestle," *Gay Community News* (October 4–10, 1987), 15(12):16–17 +. Personal interview with L.J., age 57, Los Angeles, April 5, 1987.

7. Reported in "The Gay Bar . . . ," and "Sequel to the 'Gay' Bar Problem," *The Ladder* (February 1960), 4(5):5–9 +.

8. Personal interview with Marlene, age 60, San Francisco, August 9, 1987. Interview with Rikki Streicher, 1981, New York Lesbian Herstory Archives, file: 1950s. Kelley's raid reported in *The Ladder,* (November 1956), 1(2):5. Personal interview with D.F., age 55, Los Angeles, April 5, 1987. Sea Colony information from Joan Nestle interview in *Neighborhood Voices,* producer Amber Hollibaugh, 1985.

9. Quoted in Bob Skiba, "Pansies, Perverts, and Pegged Pants," *Gay and Lesbian Community Guide to New England* (n.p., 1982), p. 4.

10. Oral interview with Peg. B. by Joan Nestle, New York Lesbian Herstory Archives, file: 1950s.

11. Merril Mushroom, "Confessions of a Butch Dyke," *Common Lives/ Lesbian Lives* (Fall 1983), 9:39–45.

12. Personal interview with Shirley, age 60, San Francisco, January 31, 1987. Although many black women were, according to Lorde, "into heavy roles," others like Lorde rejected them and felt especially resentful that white America's "racist distortions of beauty" meant that in an interracial couple it was usually only the white woman who could be femme, *Zami: A New Spelling of My Name* (Watertown, Mass.: Persephone Press, 1982), p. 224.

13. New England lesbians discussed in Skiba, pp. 2–5 and in paper presentation by Mirtha Quintanales et al., Berkshire History of Women Conference, Wellesley College, Mass., June 20, 1987. Bluff discussed in Julia Penelope, "Whose Past Are We Reclaiming?," *Common Lives/Lesbian Lives* (Autumn 1984), 13:16. Greenwich Village discussed in Maida Tilchen and Helen Weinstock, "Letters from My Aunt," *Gay Community News* (July 12, 1980), 7(5):8.

14. Personal interview with Toni, age 59, Kansas City, Mo., October 16, 1988.

15. Joan Nestle, "Butch/Fem Relationships: Sexual Courage in the 1950s," *Heresies: Sex Issue* (1981), 12(3):21–24, and personal interview with Joan Nestle, New York, October 6, 1987. Judy Grahn, *Another Mother Tongue: Gay Words, Gay Worlds* (Boston: Beacon Press, 1984), pp. 30–31, 47. See also Madeline Davis and Elizabeth Kennedy, "Oral History and the Study of Sexuality in the Lesbian Community: Buffalo, NY, 1940–1960," in Martin Duberman et al., eds., *Hidden From History: Reclaiming the Gay and Lesbian Past* (New York: New American Library, 1989), pp. 426–40.

16. On being flipped among white lesbians: Mushroom, p. 42. Penelope, p. 26; personal interview with Suzanne, age 39, Boston, Mass., June 16, 1987. Being flipped among black lesbians discussed in Lorde, p. 140 and Ethel Sawyer, "A Study of a Public Lesbian Community," unpublished M.A. thesis, Washington University, St. Louis, Mo, 1965. In women's prisons during the 1950s various other terms were used to describe being flipped. At the Federal Reformatory for women at Alderson, West Virginia, a butch who became a femme was said to have "dropped the belt." At Frontera it was said she "gave up the works." See Rose Giallombardo, *Society of Women* (New York: John Wiley and Sons, 1966).

17. Laurajean Ermayne, "My Friend the Night" *Vice Versa,* October 1947, pp. 11–12. Joan Nestle, "The Fem Question, or We Will Not Go Away," lecture notes for conference, "The Scholar and the Feminist: Toward a Politics of Sexuality," Barnard College, New York, April 24, 1982.

18. Personal interview with J. C., Houston, Tex., March 26, 1988. Personal interview with Ann, cited above. Judy Grahn also remembers that in Washington, D.C., some women in the bars would be femme one night and butch the next: Grahn, p. 156.

19. Personal interview with Lucia, age 42, San Francisco, August 2, 1988.

20. Penelope, 23.

21. Laurajean Ermayne, "Radclyffe Hall," *Vice Versa,* November 1947. In her own life the strict role division between Hall and her primary partner, Una Troubridge, seems to have faded as their years together passed. While Troubridge appeared traditionally feminine at the beginning of their relationship, later photographs show her to be increasingly less so. The two women appeared often in public in men's jackets and ties. After Hall's death, Troubridge wore exclusively men's clothes. See Richard Ormrod, *Una Troubridge: The Friend of Radclyffe Hall* (New York: Carroll and Graf, 1985). With regard to the influence of *The Well of Loneliness* see Blanche Weissen Cook, "Women Alone Stir My Imagination," *Signs* (1979), 4:718–39. See also Rebecca O'Rourke, *Reflecting on the Well of Loneliness* (London: Routledge, 1989).

22. John D'Emilio as respondent on panel, "Love and Friendship in Lesbian Bar Communities of the 1940s, '50s, and '60s," Berkshire History of Women Conference, Wellesley College, Mass., June 19, 1987.

23. Newton.

24. Jon Bradshaw, *Dreams That Money Can Buy: The Tragic Life of Libby Holman* (New York: William Morrow, 1985).

25. Bradshaw; Milt Machlin, *Libby* (New York: Tower, 1980).

26. Denis Brian, *Tallulah, Darling* (New York: Macmillan, 1980), pp. 34, 67–68; Bradshaw, p. 84.

27. Bradshaw, pp. 260–61, 310.

28. George Wickes, *The Amazon of Letters: The Life and Loves of Natalie Barney* (New York: G. P. Putnam's Sons, 1976), p. 44.

29. Elisabeth Craigin, *Either Is Love* (New York: Harcourt, 1937), pp. 68–70. Diana Fredricks, *Diana: A Strange Autobiography* (New York: Dial, 1939), pp. 72–73.

30. Lisa Ben, "Protest," *Vice Versa*, January 1948, p. 14. In later writings Lisa Ben acknowledged the importance of butch/femme in her own social group. For example, she wrote a "gay parody" of "Hello, Young Lovers" with the line: "All you cute butches lined up at the bar,/ I've had a love like you," Leland Moss, "Interview with Lisa Ben," *Gaysweek*, January 23, 1978, pp. 14–16.

31. "The President's Message," *The Ladder* (November 1956), 1(2): 3. A 1958 DOB questionnaire indicated that the lesbian readership of *The Ladder* was solidly middle- to upper-middle class in terms of education, occupation, property ownership, and civic activities such as voting: *The Ladder* (September 1959), 3(12):4–32. The appeal to homosexuals to blend in had some resurgence at the end of the 1980s, which may be a harbinger of more conservative times: see Marshall Kirk and Hunter Madsen, *After the Ball* (New York: Doubleday, 1989).

32. "Readers Respond," *The Ladder* (October 1958), 3(1):30.

33. Suzanne Prosin, "The Concept of the Lesbian: A Minority in Reverse," *The Ladder* (July 1962), 6(10):5–22.

34. Dinner parties described in personal interview with Mildred, age 58, Berkeley, Calif., August 10, 1987.

35. Personal interview with Jane, age 54, Los Angeles, April 7, 1987.

36. Interview with two women who lived through the McCarthy era, in Sasha Gregory Lewis, *Sunday's Women: A Report on Lesbian Life Today* (Boston: Beacon Press, 1979), pp. 58–59 and written communication from Nora, age 67, Los Angeles, March 6, 1988.

37. Personal interview with Jeanette, age 63, San Francisco, August 11, 1987.

38. Personal interview with Betty, age 66, Omaha, Neb., October 11, 1988.

39. Sten Russell in *One*, Febuary 1954, pp. 18–19. Personal interview with Jane, age 54, Los Angeles, April 7, 1987. Barbara Gittings interview, in Kay Tobin and Randy Wicker, eds., *The Gay Crusaders* (1972; reprint, New York: Arno Press, 1975), p. 209.

40. Regarding violence against lesbians see interviews with Greenwich Village lesbians from the 1950s in video, *Neighborhood Voices,* producer Amber Hollibaugh, 1985. Typescript of interview with Sandy K., New York Lesbian Herstory Archives, file: 1950s. William Fitzgerald, "Psuedo-Hetero-

sexuality in Prison and Out: A Study of the Lower Lower Class Black Lesbian," doctoral diss., City University of New York, 1977, p. 121.

41. Personal interview with Jackie, age 60, San Francisco, August 11, 1987.

42. Marlin Prentiss, "The Feminine Viewpoint," *One* (April 1955), 3(4): 37–40.

43. Julie Smith, "The Lesbian's Story: How Does Girl Meet Girl?," *San Francisco Chronicle,* July 1, 1969, p. 17.

8. "Not a Public Relations Movement"

1. History of the Scientific Humanitarian Committee in John Lauritsen and David Thorstad, *The Early Homosexual Rights Movement, 1864–1935* (New York: Times Change Press, 1974), and Lillian Faderman and Brigitte Eriksson, *Lesbians in Germany: 1890–1920* (Tallahassee, Fla: Naiad Press, 1990).

2. Editorial, "The Homosexual Vote," *The Ladder* (July 1960), 4(10):4–5.

3. Mattachine's early years are discussed in John D'Emilio, *Sexual Politics, Sexual Communities: The Making of a Homosexual Minority in the U.S., 1940–1970* (Chicago: University of Chicago Press, 1983). Personal interview with Del Martin and Phyllis Lyon, San Francisco, August 14, 1987. DOB's early years are also recorded in the organization's magazine, *The Ladder.*

4. Personal interview with Barbara Gittings, Philadelphia, October 7, 1987. Convention discussed by Del Martin, panel: "Daughters of Bilitis: The First National Lesbian Organization," Berkshire History of Women Conference, Wellesley College, Mass., June 19, 1987.

5. Picket signs in Andrea Weiss and Greta Schiller, *Before Stonewall: The Making of a Gay and Lesbian Community* (Tallahassee, Fla: Naiad Press, 1988). Personal interview with Barbara Gittings, cited above.

6. *New York Times* (Western Edition), December 27, 1963. Although media coverage on homosexuality increased greatly during the mid-1960s, it was not always positive or neutral. For example, *Time* Magazine ran an essay on homosexuality calling for more tolerance but admonishing that homosexuality deserves "no fake status as minority martyrdom . . . and, above all, no pretense that it is anything but a pernicious sickness": "The Homosexuals," *Time,* June 21, 1966, pp. 40–41. DOB convention discussed in Del Martin and Phyllis Lyon, *Lesbian/ Woman* (New York: Bantam, 1972), p. 224. Statistics from Edwin M. Schur, *Crimes Without Victims: Deviant Behavior and Public Policy* (Englewood Cliffs, N. J.: Prentice-Hall, 1965), p. 97.

7. Personal interview with Del Martin and Phyllis Lyon, cited above. See also "The Church and the Homosexual: A New Rapport," *The Ladder,* September 1964, pp. 9–13.

8. New York City Civil Service Commission action reported in *New York Times,* January 7, 1967, p. 1. NACHO discussed in D'Emilio, pp. 197–99. Rita Mae Brown, *Plain Brown Rapper* (Oakland, Calif: Diana Press,

1976). Police discussed in Roxanne Thayer Sweet, "Political and Social Action in Homophile Organziations," doctoral diss. University of California, Berkeley, 1968.

9. See, e.g., Lee Ebreo, "A Homosexual Ghetto?," *The Ladder* (Dec. 1965), 10(3):8; "U.S. Homophile Movement Gains National Strength," *The Ladder* (April 1966), 10(7):4–5; Barbara Grier (Marilyn Barrow), "The Least of These," *The Ladder,* October/November 1968, pp. 30–33; and Martha Shelley, "Readers Respond," *The Ladder,* April/ May 1969, pp. 42–3.

10. Editorial, "A Suggested Policy: Confrontation and Implementation," *Homophile Action League Newletter,* 1:4 (Feb. 1969), pp. 1–2.

11. *New York Times,* June 29, 1969, p. 33. The second night of riots received similarly unexcited coverage in the *New York Times:* "Police Again Rout 'Village' Youths," June 30, 1969, p. 22. Papers such as the *Village Voice* were more perceptive: see July 3, 1969, p. 1. See also New York Mattachine *Newsletter,* July 1969, pp. 21–25 and August 1969, pp. 1–6. The newsletter decribed the riots, in which many gay male transvestites participated, in camp terms such as "the hairpin drop heard round the world."

12. Gay liberation speaker quoted in Sidney Abbott and Barbara Love, *Sappho Was a Right-On Woman: A Liberated View of Lesbianism* (New York: Stein and Day, 1970), p. 160.

13. 1966 and 1969 *Time* articles cited above. NIMH report discussed in the 1969 article. Despite such liberalization, the view of homosexuality as deleterious still continued among many professionals: see, e.g., Linda Norris, "A Comparison of Two Groups in a Southern State Women's Prison: Homosexual Behavior vs. Non-Homosexual Behavior," *Psychological Reports* (1974), 34:75–78.

14. Julie Smith, "The Lesbian's Story: How Does Girl Meet Girl?" *San Francisco Chronicle,* July 1, 1969, p. 17.

15. Ann Lisa, "Boycott Leonardo's," *Gay Sunshine,* October 1970, pp. 1–2.

16. New York DOB demonstration reported in *Lesbian Tide,* December 1971, p. 12.

17. Minneapolis and Milwaukee events reported in *Proud Woman* (March/ April 1972), 2(12):3, 8. Boise case reported in *Gaysweek* (Dec. 25, 1978), 96:1.

18. School board accomplishments discussed in "School Is Not a Gay Place to Be, but It's Getting Better in San Francisco," in *Growing Up Gay: A Youth Liberation Pamphlet* (Ann Arbor, Mich.: 1978), p. 23. O'Leary victory reported in *The Advocate* (May 5, 1976), 189:6.

19. Anita Bryant, *The Anita Bryant Story: The Survival of Our Nation's Families and the Threat of Militant Homosexuality* (Old Tappan, N.J.: Fleming H. Revell, 1977). Editorial, "The Pink Triangle Ranch," *Lesbian Tide* (July/ August 1978), 8(5):27.

20. News of the anti-Briggs campaign in *Lesbian Tide,* from July to December 1978. "Gay movement came of age" from personal interview with Susie Bright, age 29, San Francisco, August 11, 1987. Seattle battle reported

in *Off Our Backs* (December 1978), 8(11). The aftermath of the slaying of supervisor Harvey Milk and Mayor George Moscone in San Francisco also helped to unite the lesbian and gay community. After thousands rioted over the lenient sentence given to the killer, Dan White, the protestors came together in a peaceful memorial birthday party for Harvey Milk. A speaker told the gathering, "Last night gay men and lesbian women showed the world we're angry and are on the move. . . . Tonight we are going to show them that we are building a strong community." A large crowd of lesbians and gay men also gathered in Greenwich Village on the day of the rioting, carrying signs declaring "Lesbians and Gay Men Fight Back" and proclaiming solidarity with male and female homosexuals everywhere: *San Francisco Chronicle,* May 22, 1979, p. 1, and May 23, 1979, pp. 1, 4, 5.

21. Helen Gurley Brown, *Sex and the Single Girl* (New York: Pocket Books, 1962), p. 240. New attitudes toward sex discussed in Barbara Ehrenreich et al., *Re-Making Love: The Feminization of Sex* (Garden City, N.Y.: Anchor, 1986), pp. 80–81. Institute for Sex Research quoted in Martin and Lyon, *Lesbian/Woman,* p. 85.

22. Ann Roiphe, "Who's Afraid of Lesbian Sex?," *Vogue,* August 1977, pp. 150+.

23. "The Homosexual: Newly Visible, Newly Understood," *Time,* October 3, 1969, pp. 56–57.

24. Personal interview with Clare, age 35, San Francisco, August 5, 1987.

25. Feminists and the Left discussed in Sara Evans, *Personal Politics: The Roots of Women's Liberation in the Civil Rights Movement and the Left* (New York, 1979); Martha Shelley, "Notes of a Radical Lesbian," in Robin Morgan, ed., *Sisterhood Is Powerful: An Anthology of Writings from the Women's Liberation Movement* (New York: Random House, 1970), pp. 306–11; Barbara Leon, "Separate to Integrate," *Redstockings: Feminist Revolution* (n.p., 1975), pp. 139–44; Ginny Berson, "Only by Association," *The Furies* (June/ July 1972), 1(5):5–6. The Left of the early '70s was generally homophobic, although there were some exceptions. The Workers World Party was represented in a 1970 Gay Pride parade with members carrying signs that read "Say No To Racism and Anti-Gay Bigotry": see photographic retrospective in "Lesbians and Gay Men Fight Back," *Workers World* (October 15, 1987), 29(41): supplement. By 1971 the Socialist Workers Party, impressed by the serious struggle of gay militants, came out for "total unconditional support for the gay liberation movement," but most leftist groups did not share their position: see e.g. Holly Near incident reported in *Big Mama Rag* (September 1978), 6(8):8. For lesbian rejection of the Left see also Charlotte Bunch, "Out Now!" *The Furies* (June/ July 1972), 1(5):12–13.

26. Ti-Grace Atkinson, "Lesbianism and Feminism," in Phyllis Birkby et al., eds, *Amazon Expedition: A Lesbian-Feminist Anthologym* (Albion, Calif.: Times Change Press, 1973), pp. 11–14.

27. For similarities between lesbian and feminist goals and interests see editorial (comments by staff members on how women's liberation has changed

their lives), *Women: A Journal of Liberation* (1972), 2(4): inside front cover. New York Radicalesbians, "Woman-Identified-Woman" (1970; reprinted in *Lesbians Speak Out* [Oakland, Calif.: Women's Press Collective]), pp. 87–89.

28. The ability of all women to be lesbian is discussed in Jane B., "Me, a Lesbian?," *The Ladder* (1972), 16:31–32; Loretta Ulmschneider, "Bisexuality," in Nancy Myron and Charlotte Bunch, eds., *Lesbians and the Women's Movement* (Baltimore: Diana Press, 1975); J. Antonelli, "What Is a Lesbian?," *Sinister Wisdom,* Fall 1977, pp. 57–59. Adrienne Rich expanded on these ideas in *Compulsory Heterosexuality and the Lesbian Threat* (Only Women Press, 1981), suggesting that the term "lesbian" should embrace many more forms of relating between women, including sharing a rich inner life, bonding against male tyranny, giving and receiving practical and political support, etc. Terms "primary" and "elective" lesbians used in Barbara Ponse, *Identities in the Lesbian World: The Social Construction of Self* (Westport, Conn.: Greenwood Press, 1978). Rita Mae Brown, "Take a Lesbian to Lunch," in *Plain Brown Rapper* (Oakland, Calif.: Diana Press, 1976), and "The Shape of Things to Come," *Women: A Journal of Liberation* (1972), 2(4):44–46.

29. Personal interview with Lisa, age 49, New York, October 12, 1987.

30. Elizabeth Wilson, "I'll Climb the Stairway to Heaven: Lesbians in the 1970s," in Sue Cartledge and Joanna Ryan, eds., *Sex and Love* (London: Woman's Press, 1983), pp. 180–95. Wilson suggests that many of the young women who elected to become lesbians through radical feminist dogma were doomed to disillusionment and eventually returned to heterosexuality. See also Zira Defries, "Political Lesbianism and Sexual Politics," *American Academy of Psychoanalysts Journal* (January 1978), 6(1): 71–78. and Zira Defries, "Pseudohomosexuality in Feminist Students," *American Journal of Psychiatry* (April 1976), 133(4):400–404. Two-thirds of the lesbian-feminist students Defries treated returned, more or less, to heterosexuality. But it must be noted that those students were self-selected, having felt conflicts about their lesbian relationships to begin with.

31. Personal interview with Z. Budapest, age 48, Oakland, Cal., August 1,1988. For popular affirmations in the 1960s and 1970s of sex between women see Ann Koedt, "The Myth of the Vaginal Orgasm" (1969; reprinted in *Notes from the Second Year,* p. 41) and Jill Johnston, *Lesbian Nation: The Feminist Solution* (New York: Simon and Schuster, 1973), p. 165.

32. For discussions of CR and lesbianism in the early 1970s see Coletta Reid, "Ideology: Guide to Action," *Furies,* (March/April 1972), 1(3): 6, and Christine Mimichilld, "Gay and Straight in the Movement," *Women: A Journal of Liberation,* (1972), 2(4): 41–42. Personal interview with Lois, age 55, San Antonio, March 29, 1988.

33. Personal interview with Sandy, age 57, Lincoln, Neb., October 12, 1988.

34. Bernice Goodman, "Notes on Creating a Lesbian Community," paper given at the Berkshire History of Women Conference, Mount Holyoke

College, August 23–25, 1978. Personal interview with Barbara Gittings, cited above.

35. Some articles appeared in the *Ladder* even as early as the 1950s outlining the need for a lesbian movement separate from men, e.g., October 1958, p. 5. The speech of Shirley Weller, national president of DOB, at the North American Conference of Homophile Organizations is an example of an angry pre-lesbian-feminist split that was emerging between gay men and lesbians: reported in Martin and Lyon, p. 280. Del Martin also called for lesbians to work outside the gay movement in "If That's All There Is," *Motive: Lesbian/ Feminist Issue,* (1972), 1(32): 45–46. "Ladies' auxiliary" comment in Sharon Zecha on NOW Panel on Life Styles, March 25, 1971, reported in *Everywoman* (July 9, 1971), 2(10). See also Rose Jordan et al., "Forum: Can Men and Women Work Together?," in Karla Jay and Allen Young, eds., *After You're Out: Personal Experiences of Gay Men and Lesbian Women,* (1975; reprint, New York: Pyramid Books, 1977), p. 174.

36. Ginny Berson, "Reformism: The Politics of Ostriches," *Motive,* (1972), 32(1):4–8.

37. Adrienne Rich, "The Meaning of Our Love for Women Is What We Have Constantly to Expand," speech at the New York Lesbian Pride Rally, June 26, 1977 (Brooklyn, N.Y.: Out and Out Books, 1977).

38. Betty Friedan quoted in Robin Morgan, *Going Too Far* (New York: Random House, 1976), p. 176.

39. Gloria Steinem, "The Politics of Supporting Lesbianism," in Ginny Vida, ed., *Our Right to Love: A Lesbian Resource Book,* (Englewood Cliffs, NJ: Prentice-Hall, 1978), pp. 266–69.

40. Anonymous letter, "Right to Closets," *Off Our Backs,* (December 1978), 8(11):16.

9. Lesbian Nation

1. Jane Rule, *Contract with the World* (Tallahassee, Fla: Naiad Press, 1980), p. 154.

2. Barbara Ponse discusses "destigmatization" and "aristocraticization" of lesbianism in *Identities in the Lesbian World: The Social Construction of Self* (Westport, Conn.: Greenwood, 1978), pp. 99–100.

3. Quoted in Ponse, pp. 84–85.

4. For discussions of terms see Letters to the Editor, *Focus: A Journal for Lesbians,* February 1978; Sharon Crase, *Sisters* (June 1973), 4(6): pp. 18–19; and Laurel Galana, "Distinctions: The Circle Game," in Gina Covina and Laurel Galana, eds., *The Lesbian Reader* (Guerneville, Calif.: Amazon Press, 1975), p. 159. According to a nineteenth-century lexicon, the word "dike" meant a man in a full dress suit or a full set of men's clothes: see Maximillian Schele De Vere, *Americanisms: The English of the New World* (New York: 1871), p. 597. But lesbian scholars have attempted to give the word more

heroic meaning. Judy Grahn speculates that the word came from the goddess Dike of Greece, who was Gaia's granddaughter. Grahn says the name meant "the way, the path," and the goddess' social function was keeping the balance of forces, *Another Mother Tongue: Gay Words, Gay Worlds* (Boston: Beacon, 1984), p. 47. See also pp. 139–40.

5. List of groups, journals, and bookstores published in *Amazon Quarterly* (1973), 1(4) 61–67.

6. Nancy Groschwitz, "Practical Economics for a Women's Community," in Karla Jay and Allen Young, eds., *Lavender Culture* (New York: Harcourt Brace, 1978), pp. 477–83.

7. Charlotte Bunch and Rita Mae Brown, "What Every Lesbian Should Know," *Motive* (1972), 32(1) 4–8. Lee Schwing and Helaine Harris, "Building Feminist Institutions," *Furies* (May/ June 1973), 2(3) 2–3: 7.

8. Willie Tyson, "Lima Bean: Take One," *Off Our Backs* (August/ September 1974), 4(9): 4–5.

9. Alix Dobkin, "Talking Lesbian," *Lavender Jane Loves Women* (New York: Women's Music Network, 1974).

10. Meg Christian quoted in "The Muse of Olivia: Our Own Economy, Our Own Song," *Off Our Backs* (August/ September 1974), 4(9). Cris Williamson complained that she had received little response from the festival audience in Champagne: "Perhaps they thought I was too 'slick.' I got the feeling if I had made more mistakes, put myself down more, been more tentative, maybe I would have gotten more feedback. Maybe women aren't ready yet to identify with a strong woman image": Interview, *Lesbian Tide* July 1974, p. 19. Professionalism discussed in editorial statement, *The Rock* (Northampton, Mass.: Magaera Press, 1977).

11. Many of the women's music companies could not survive long financially, but others cropped up to take their places when they went under. Companies such as Icebergg, Rosetta, Labyris, and Windham Hill were started in the 1980s. Ladyslipper, Pleiades, and Holly Near's Redwood Records have held on since the mid- 1970s. For discussions of financial difficulties in women's music see "Financial Letter from the Women of the 'We Want the Music' Collective," *Pearl Diver*, Fall 1977, and Lynn D. Shapiro, "The Growing Business Behind Women's Music," in Jay and Young, p. 197. Women's music audience responses described in Astrib Bergle, "Women Concerts Reviewed," *So's Your Old Lady: A Lesbian Feminist Journal* May 1977, pp. 16–17. Personal interview with Deb, age 36, Fresno, April 29, 1987.

12. History of Olivia from Judy Dlugacz, "If It Weren't for the Music: Fifteen Years of Olivia Records," *Hot Wire* (July 1988), 4(3): p. 28–35; Grahn, pp. 190–91; Shapiro, pp. 195–200; Judy Nixon and Ginny Berson, "Women's Music," in *Our Right to Love: A Lesbian Resource Book* (Englewood Cliffs, N.J.: Prentice-Hall, 1978), pp. 252–55; "The Muse of Olivia," pp. 2–3 +. Ginny Berson quoted in "The Muse of Olivia."

13. "A Man is a Man," *Pearl Diver,* May 1977, p. 19; Dlugacz.

14. Bonnie Zimmerman, "Exiting from the Patriarchy: The Lesbian Novel of Development," in Elizabeth Abel et al., eds., *The Voyage In: Fictions of Female Development* (Hanover, N.H.: University Press of New England, 1983), pp. 244–57. Elana Nachman, *Riverfinger Woman* (Plainfield, VT.: Daughters, 1975). See also my discussion in *Surpassing the Love of Men: Romantic Friendship and Love Between Women from the Renaissance to the Present* (New York: William Morrow, 1981), pp. 405–10.

15. "Creating a Women's World," *New York Times,* January 2, 1977.

16. Lesbian Food Conspiracy in *Furies* (March/ April 1972), 1(3). Women's credit unions discussed in *Pearl Diver,* May 1977. Lesbian Clinic reference in *Lesbian Tide,* June 1974, p. 18. Workshop on what lesbians should do to protect personal and property rights, Women in the Law Conference, Wisconsin, 1977, discussed in *Pearl Diver,* May 1977.

17. Riki, "Aging," in Karla Jay and Allen Young, eds., *After You're Out: Personal Experiences of Gay Men and Lesbian Women* (1975; reprint, New York: Pyramid Books, 1977), pp. 216–17.

18. Barbara Love and Elizabeth Shanklin, "The Answer Is Matriarchy," *Our Right To Love,* pp. 183–87. Toni McNaron, "Political and Palliative Implications of Women's Spirituality," *So's Your Old Lady* (May 1977), 17:7–8. Shannon, "A Non-Linear Conversation on Spirituality and Politics," *WomanSpirit* (Summer 1978), 4(16):5–9. Not all lesbian-feminists accepted such views. See, e.g., Sally Binford's attempt to explode what she regarded as "the New Feminist Fundamentalism" and the myth of matriarchy in "Myths and Matriarchies," *WomanSpirit* (Fall 1979), 6(21). "Building the Lesbian Nation," Bloomington, Ind. conference discussed in *Lesbian Connections* (March 1976), 2(1).

19. Elizabeth Gould Davis, *The First Sex* (New York: G.P. Putnam's Sons, 1971).

20. Max Xarai, "A Witch Dream Presentation," *Matriarchal Comix* (Oakland, Calif.: Women's Press Collective, 1974). The Matriarchists are discussed in Charovla, "Matriarchists, Queens and the Star System," *Tribad: A Lesbian Separatist Newsjournal* (September/ October 1978), 2(3):1–4. Merlin Stone, *When God Was a Woman* (London: Virago, 1976). Stone's proposal for a new system of time reckoning was made at the Great Goddess Re-Emerging conference, University of California, Santa Cruz, 1978.

21. Personal interview with Z. Budapest, age 48, Oakland, Calif., August 1, 1988.

22. Jane Chambers, *Burning* (New York: JH Press, 1978). Z. Budapest, *The Feminist Book of Lights and Shadows* (Venice, Calif.: Susan B. Anthony Coven #1, 1975). Personal interview with Z. Budapest, cited above. Oak, "The Vision of a Coven," *Womanspirit* (Fall 1976), 3(9).

23. Personal interview with Nan, age 36, Syracuse, N.Y., June 2, 1987 (in Fresno). Women's spirituality remained a vital topic in the 1980s: see Charlene Spretnak, ed., *The Politics of Women's Spirituality: Essays on the Rise*

of Spiritual Power Within the Feminist Movement (Garden City, N.Y.: Double-day, 1982) and women's spirituality magazines (often implicitly or explicitly lesbian), e.g., *Sage Woman: A Quarterly Magazine of Women's Spirituality* (Santa Cruz, Calif.); *Of a Like Mind: An International Newspaper and Network for Spiritual Women* (Madison, Wis.); *Spiritual Women Times: Women Learning from Women* (Seattle, Wash.); *Women of Power* (Cambridge, Mass.).

24. Rita Mae Brown complained about the phenomenon in her speech "The Crab that Got Away," quoted in *Lesbian Tide* (September/ October 1976), 6(2). Charoula, "Matriarchies, Queens, and the Star System," op. cit.

25. Laurel Galana, "Distinctions: The Circle Game," *Amazon Quarterly* (February 1973), 1(2): 26–33.

26. Personal interview with Nan, cited above.

27. Barbara Lipschutz, "Nobody Needs to Get Fucked," *Lesbian Voices* (September 1975), 1(4): 57. See also Nina Sabaroff, "Lesbian Sexuality: An Unfinished Saga," in Karla Jay and Allen Young, eds., *After You're Out: Personal Experiences of Gay Men and Lesbian Women* (1975; reprint, New York: Pyramid Books, 1977). Boston Women's Health Course Collective, *Our Bodies, Ourselves: A Course by and for Women* (Boston: New England Free Press, 1971), p. 20.

28. Susan Helenius, "Returning the Dykes to the Dutch," *Everywoman* (July 9, 1971), 2(10). But see also Evan Paxton, "Notes on Lesbianism, Individualism, and Other Forbidden Practices." Paxton presents the butch as a culture hero—a critical forerunner to Stonewall and lesbian-feminism. "Shit games" quotation in interview with Charlene and Linda, *Sisters* (January 1972), 3(1): 6–11.

29. Rosalie Nichols, letter to the editor, *Albatross*, Spring 1976, p. 34.

30. Julie Lee, "Some Thoughts on Monogamy," in Jay and Young, *After You're Out*, pp. 46–47; Ginny Berson, "Freest Fancy," *Furies* (June/July 1972), 1(5): 9; Martha Shelley, "On Marriage," in *The Lavender Herring: Essays from the Ladder*, Barbara Grier and Coletta Reid, eds. (Baltimore: Diana Press, 1976); Donna Martin, "The Lesbian Love Ethic," in Covina and Garland, pp. 41– 42. In smaller cities the fashion for non-monogamy seldom caught on. One lesbian-feminist who had been in women's communities in Oklahoma, North Texas, and Missouri throughout the 1970s claims never to have seen a "smash monogamy" button: "Monogamy remained the culture of those geographical areas even then," she says. "Even the radical women couldn't escape it if they stayed here. It was a goal to find one person and settle down;" personal interview with Frederika, age 37, Kansas City, Mo., Oct. 14, 1988.

31. Sheila's lover quoted in Jeri Dilno, "Monogamy and Alternate Life-Styles," *Our Right to Love*, p. 59. Personal interview with Beverly, age 36, San Francisco, August 14, 1987. See also poem by Jean Fowler, "Outside the One to One," *The Rock,* and song by Marilyn Gayle on the complications of non-monogamy, "Let's Do a Three Way," *Dyke Music* (Portland, Ore.: Godiva Records, 1977).

32. Jill Johnston, *Lesbian Nation: The Feminist Solution* (New York: Simon and Schuster, 1973), p. 179. Loretta Ulmschneider, "Bisexuality," in Nancy Myron and Charlotte Bunch, eds., *Lesbianism and the Women's Movement* (Baltimore: Diana Press, 1975), pp. 85–88. Debbie Willis, "Bisexuality: A Personal View," *Women: A Journal of Liberation* (Winter 1974), 14(1):10–11. Sally Gearhart, "A Kiss Does Not a Revolution Make," *Lesbian Tide,* July 1974, pp. 10–ll +.

33. Rita Mae Brown, *A Plain Brown Rapper* (Oakland, Calif.: Diana Press, 1976), pp. 16–17.

34. For examples of minority complaints and factions within the community see *Sinister Wisdom* (issue on aging) (1979) 10; on fat oppression, Letter from Marisa, *WomanSpirit* (March 1975) 1(3): 62, and "Fat as a Lesbian-Feminist Issue," *Albatross,* Fall 1978; on teenage lesbian oppression, Shelley Ettinger, "The Bottom Rung: Ageism in the Gay Movement," *Growing Up Gay: A Youth Liberation Pamphlet* (Ann Arbor, Michigan, 1978) and Lee Schwing and Helaine Harris, "I Was a Teenage Lesbian," *Furies* (August 1972), 1(6):2–4; on the socialist versus nonsocialist issue see Marilyn Gayle, "Sacred Bull," *Pearl Diver,* Fall 1977, pp. 34–39, and Beth Elliott, Book Review essay, *Sisters* (November 1971), 2(11): 20; for complaints from working-class lesbians, lesbians of color, and lesbian separatists see notes below. Los Angeles Gay Women's Intergroup Council discussed in *Lesbian Tide,* December 1971.

35. Class issues discussed in Rita Mae Brown, "The Last Straw," *Motive* (1972) 32(1); Charlotte Bunch and Coletta Reid, "Revolution Begins at Home," *Furies* (May 1972), 1(4): 2–4; Dolores Bargowski and Coletta Reid, "Garbage Among the Trash," *Furies* (August 1972), 1(6): 8–9; Ginny Berson, "Class Revisited: One Step Forward, Two Steps Back," *Furies* (May/June 1973), 2(3): 8–9.

36. Nancy Myron, "Class Beginnings," *Furies* (March/April 1972), 1(3): 2–3. Laurel Galana, "Conversation," in Gina Covina and Laurel Galana, eds., *The Lesbian Reader* (Guerneville, Calif.: Amazon Press, 1975), p. 86. All studies I am familiar with that consider the question have shown that statistically lesbians tend to be far better educated than heterosexual women, but there is evidence to suggest that among lesbian-feminists the educational levels were extremely high, perhaps because the movement had considerable intellectual appeal: e.g., an *Amazon Quarterly* (1973), 1(4/2): 30–34, statistical analysis of lesbian-feminists included in a nationwide series of interviews showed that 88 per cent had at least some college education. The study also showed that over 60 per cent had fathers who were in business or the professions. Upper class women who became radical lesbian feminists had an easier time with regard to the class problem than middle-class women, perhaps partly because of their generosity in many cases, influenced by their socialist idealism, and partly because they were perceived as invulnerable. An Austin woman who inherited money from her grandfather, who had been one of the ten wealthiest oil men in Texas, declassed herself in terms of dress and lifestyle in the community but made no secret of her wealth: "I didn't

really get a hard time from people," she remembers about the 1970s. "There were a group of us who had inherited money. If some person or some organization needed something they would come talk to us. We would always sponsor things. We would be billed as 'your host committee' "; personal interview with Carla, age 41, Austin, Tex., March 31, 1988.

37. "Separatist Symposium," *Dyke: A Quarterly* (Summer 1978), 6: 31–41. Gearhart, "A Kiss Does Not a Revolution Make." "Dyke/Amazon" quoted in Laurel Galana, "Distinctions: The Circle Game." Galana, like many other women in the lesbian-feminist community of the 1970s, was at odds with such militancy. She scoffs in this article: "As of this writing it is no longer enough to be a feminist, lower class, and funkily male dressed in order to be a dyke. It is necessary to hate men with a passion and to want above all else to kill them."

38. Charlotte Bunch, "Learning from Lesbian Separatism," *Ms.* (November 1976), 5. A. J. Loeson, "America and Women," *Sisters* (November 1971), 2(11):1–7. Red Dykes, "To Revolutionary Dykes," *Lesbian Connections* (March 1976), 2(1): 14. Personal interview with Naomi, member of a Northampton, Mass. separatist community in the 1970s (interview in Berkeley), July 30, 1988.

39. Sally Gearhart, *The Wanderground* (Watertown, Mass.F: Persephone Press, 1978); Rochelle Singer, *The Demeter Flower* (New York: St. Martin's, 1980).

40. Country separatism discussed in Flying Thunderwoman, "Notes of a Native Woman," *WomanSpirit* (Spring 1976), 2(7): 24–26; Womanshare Collective, *Country Lesbians: The Story of the Womanshare Collective* (Grants Pass, Ore.: Womanshare, 1977); Womanshare Collective, "Communal Living," *Our Right to Love*, pp. 66–69; advertisement for Oregon Women's Land Trust, *Albatross*, Summer 1976, p. 10; personal interview with Carla, cited above. Joyce Cheney, ed., *Lesbian Land* (Minneapolis, Minn.: Word Weavers, 1985), looks at many of the communes that were flourishing during the 1970s and reveals an assortment of reasons for their demise by the 1980s.

41. Personal interview with Suzanne, age 39, Boston, July 3, 1987.

42. Bunch. Personal interview with Paula, age 34, member of Woman-Space Collective in the 1970s, Omaha, Neb., October 10, 1988.

43. Ann Allen Shockley, "The Black Lesbian in American Literature: An Overview," *Conditions: Five, The Black Women's Issue* (Autumn 1979), 2(2):133–42.

44. Zulma Rivera, "Written Testimony," *Our Right to Love*, pp. 225–27. The Combahee River Collective, "A Black Feminist Statement," in Zillah Eisenstein, ed., *Capitalist Patriarchy and the Case for Socialist Feminism* (New York: Monthly Review Press, 1978).

45. Personal interview with Leslie, age 41, San Diego, July 31, 1987.

46. Pat Parker, *Pit Stop* (Oakland, Calif.: Women's Press Collective, 1973).

47. Eleanor Hunter, "Double Indemnity: The Negro Lesbian in the Straight White World," quoted in Del Martin and Phyllis Lyon, *Lesbian/Woman* (New

York: Bantam, 1972), pp. 123–25. Gente discussed in "We Have to be Our Own Spark: An Interview with Gente," *Lesbian Tide,* July 1974. See also "Open Letter from a Filipina/ Indian Dyke," *Off Our Backs* (December 1978), 8(11): and Flying Cloud's response to "Racism in the Women's Movement," *Tribad* (July/August 1978), 2(2): 5–6: Flying Cloud calls for lesbians of color to unite, complaining that at that time, "a fight for feminism is really a fight for white women's supremacy." Few Asian lesbians had developed bonds within either the Asian community or the lesbians of color community during the 1970s. Those who were lesbian-feminists tended to agree with writers such as Liza May Chan ("A Lesbian-Feminist Assesses Her Heritage," *Albatross,* Summer 1976, pp. 24–25), who observes: "The entire Chinese culture has denied me my human rights, specifically, my right to choose 'the kind of woman' I want to be. . . . I identify myself with sisters of every race who are being 'fucked over' in the male dominated world with male dominated issues. . . . In dealing with our true foe—sexism, our real suppressors —we may be able to reconcile with and accept each other disregarding race, class background, and cults." See also Willyce Kim, *Eating Artichokes* (Oakland, Calif.: Women's Press Collective, 1972), and Yee Lin, "Written Testimony," *Our Right to Love,* pp. 227–29. Barbara Cameron, a Native American lesbian, organized a Gay American Indian group in 1974 in the conviction that Third World gay people's needs and struggles were different from those of the gay white community; personal interview with Barbara Cameron, San Francisco, August 12, 1988. Formation of Latin American Lesbians of Los Angeles discussed in *Lesbian Tide,* July 1974. See also discussion of formation of the San Francisco Latina Lesbian Alliance in *Lesbian Tide,* July/August 1978, and the New York La Luz de la Lucha in *Tribad* (New York) (July/ August 1978), 2(2): 8.

48. Cherrie Moraga Lawrence, "La Guera," in Susan J. Wolf and Julie Penelope Stanley, eds., *Coming Out Stories* (Watertown, Mass.: Persephone Press, 1980), pp. 187–94. Moraga dropped the patronymic Lawrence shortly after the publication of this essay. Editorial on the need to broaden the base of the movement in *Women: A Journal of Liberation* (1972), 2(4): inside front cover. See also "National Lesbian Feminist Organization Spotlights Civil Rights," *Lesbian Tide,* July/ August 1978, p. 23, regarding NLFO's plan for a campaign to "increase the participation of women of color as planners, members and endorsers" of the organization. Personal interview with Suzanne cited above.

49. Written communication from Eliza, age 44, San Francisco, May 11, 1988.

10. *Lesbian Sex Wars in the 1980s*

1. Colette, *The Pure and the Impure,* trans. Herman Briffault (1930; reprint. New York: Farrar, Straus and Giroux, 1967), p. 111.

2. Alex Comfort, *The Joy of Sex* (New York: Simon and Schuster, 1972). Helen Singer Kaplan, *The New Sex Therapy: Active Treatment of Sexual*

Dysfunctions (New York: Brunner/Mazel, 1974). How-To books on lesbian sexuality such as Emily Sisley and Bertha Harris, *The Joy of Lesbian Sex* (New York: Simon and Schuster, 1977), created little stir among lesbians. John D'Emilio and Estelle B. Freedman, *Intimate Matters: A History of Sexualtiy in America* (New York: Harper and Row, 1988), ch. 14, "The Sexualized Society."

3. Philip Blumstein and Pepper Schwartz, *American Couples: Money, Work, Sex* (New York: William Morrow, 1983), p. 196.

4. Letitia Anne Peplau, "Research on Homosexual Couples: An Overview," *Journal of Homosexuality* (Winter 1982), 8; Beverly Burch, "Barriers to Intimacy: Conflicts over Power, Dependency, and Nurturing in Lesbian Relationships," in Boston Lesbian Psychologies Collective, eds., *Lesbian Psychologies: Explorations and Challenges,* (Chicago: University of Chicago Press, 1987), pp. 126–41. Regarding the sexual barrier theory see C. A. Tripp, *The Homosexual Matrix* (New York: McGraw Hill, 1975). On fusion and bed death see JoAnn Loulan, *Lesbian Sex* (San Francisco: Spinster's Ink, 1985); Jo-Ann Krestan and Claudia Bepko, "The Problem of Fusion in Lesbian Relationships," *Family Process,* (September 1980), 19:277–89; and Margaret Nichols, "Lesbian Sexuality: Issues and Developing Therapy," in Boston Lesbian Psychologies Collective, pp. 97–125.

5. Personal interview with Pam, age 51, Fresno, March 5, 1988.

6. Robin Morgan, "Goodbye to All That," (1970; reprinted in Wendy Martin, ed., *The American Sisterhood* (New York: Harper and Row), p. 361. Robin Morgan, *Going Too Far* (New York: Random House, 1976), p. 169. Susan Brownmiller, *Against Our Will: Men, Women and Rape* (New York: Simon and Schuster, 1975). For works arguing that the Court ignored available evidence regarding the link between pornography and sexual violence see Irene Diamond, "Pornography and Repression: A Reconsideration of 'Who' and 'What,' " in Laura Lederer, ed., *Take Back the Night: Women on Pornography* (New York: William Morrow, 1980), pp. 187–203, and Neil M. Malamuth and Edward Donnerstein, eds., *Pornography and Sexual Aggression* (Orlando, Fla.: Academic Press, 1984), passim. While these works show a significant correlation between pornography and violence, others show that the evidence is still unclear: e.g., a 1983 study that concludes that pornography "stimulates sexual activity and sexual fantasy but does not alter established sexual practices," cited in Thelma McCormak, "Making Sense of the Research on Pornography," in Varda Burstyn, ed., *Women Against Censorship* (Vancouver: Douglas and McIntyre, 1985), pp. 181–205.

7. Sally Roesch Wagner, "Pornography and the Sexual Revolution: The Backlash of Sadomasochism," in *Against Sadomasochism: A Radical Feminist Analysis* (Palo Alto, Calif.: Frog in the Well Press, 1987), pp. 23–44.

8. Sheila Jeffreys, "Sado-Masochism: The Erotic Cult of Fascism," *Lesbian Ethics* (Spring 1986), 2(1): 64–82. Kris Drumm, in "Sex: A Readers' Forum," *Lesbian Ethics* (Summer 1987), 2(3): 58–60.

9. Jesse Meredith, "A Response to Samois," *Plexus,* November 1980, p. 8. Jeanette Nichols et al., "Is Sadomasochism Feminist?," in *Against Sadoma-*

sochism, pp. 137–46. Julia Penelope, "Whose Past Are We Reclaiming?" *Common Lives/Lesbian Lives* (Autumn 1984), 13: 16– 36.

10. Leaflet, "We Protest," distributed by the Coalition for a Feminist Sexuality at Barnard College Conference "The Scholar and the Feminist."

11. Sharon Page, "The Festival Sex Debates," *On Our Backs* (Spring 1985), 1(4): 13 +. Jeanne F. Neath, "Let's Discuss Dyke S/M and Quit the Name Calling: A Response to Sheila Jeffreys," *Lesbian Ethics* (Summer 1987), 2(3): 95–99. Personal interview with Monarch, age 54, Kansas City, Mo., October 15, 1988.

12. J. Lee Lehman, "Lust is Just a Four-Letter Word," *Heresies: The Sex Issue* (1981), 12:80–81.

13. JoAnn Loulan, "Good News About Lesbian Sex," *Out/Look: National Lesbian and Gay Quarterly*, Spring 1988, pp. 90–93. Statistics on lesbians' similarity to heterosexual women in Blumstein and Schwartz pp. 272–73. Survey among Boulder, Col. lesbians, *On Our Backs* (Summer 1987), 4(1):12–13.

14. Samois, ed., *What Color Is Your Handkerchief: A Lesbian S/M Sexuality Reader* (Berkeley: Samois, 1979). Personal interview with Kathy Andrew of Stormy Leather, San Francisco, August 10, 1987.

15. For discussion of a brief 1970s attempt to open a gay bathhouse to lesbians see Arthur Bell, "The Bath Life Gets Respectability," in Karla Jay and Allen Young, eds., *Lavender Culture* (New York: Harcourt Brace, 1978). Rita Mae Brown, "Queen for a Day: A Stranger in Paradise," *The Real Paper*, October 8, 1975.

16. Personal interview with JoAnna, age 38, San Francisco, September 12, 1987. Personal interview with Clare, age 35, San Francisco, August 5, 1987.

17. Personal interview with Rainbeau, age 29, San Francisco, August 7, 1987. Tatoo Blue, interview in *On Our Backs* (Spring 1986), 2(4): 22–26 +.

18. Personal interview with Susie Bright, San Francisco, August 11, 1987. For fantasy fiction that reflects the influence of gay male sexual patterns see, for example, Vera Goeglein, "Sunday Strangers," *On Our Backs*, Winter 1986, p. 21 +; Leatherwing Bat, "Out for the Evening," *Bad Attitude*, Summer 1987, pp. 20–23. A melange of sexual adventurism and traditional female values of concern, gentleness, and romance similar to that prevalent in the porno magazines may be found in recent pornographic novels written by and for lesbians. See, for example, the volumes produced by the Denver-based Lace Publications in the mid-1980s, such as Artemis Oakgrove's trilogy *The Raging Peace* (1984), *Dreams of Vengeance* (1985), and *Throne of Council* (1986), as well as Lady Winston, ed., *The Leading Edge: An Anthology of Lesbian Sexual Fiction* (Denver: Lace Publications, 1987).

19. Mary Riege Laner, " 'Personals' Advertisements of Lesbian Women," *Journal of Homosexuality* (Fall 1978), 4(1):41–61. Sex ads quoted are from *On Our Backs* (Spring 1986), 2(4).

20. Kinsey statistics cited in *The Report of the Commission on Obscenity and Pornography* (Washington, D.C.: United States Government Printing Office, September 1970). Julia R. Heiman, "The Physiology of Erotica: Women's Sexual Arousal," *Psychology Today* (November 1975), 8: 90–94.

21. Personal interview with Kathy, age 36, San Francisco, August 10, 1987.

22. For descriptions of the procedures of lesbian s/m see Samois, ed., *Coming to Power: Writings and Graphics on Lesbian S/M*, 2d rev. ed. (Boston: Alyson, 1982) and Pat Califia, *Sapphistry: The Book of Lesbian Sexuality*, 2d rev. ed. (Tallahassee, Fla.: Naiad Press, 1983). Karen Winter, "Lesbian Limerick," *Commmon Lives/ Lesbian Lives* (Summer 1986), 20: 85.

23. "Samois: Who We Are," in *Coming to Power*, p. 288. Gayle Rubin quoted in Carole S. Vance, "Gender Systems, Ideology, and Sex Research," in Ann Sitow et al. eds., *Powers of Desire* (New York: Monthly Review Press, 1983), p. 372. Sarah Zoftig, "Coming Out," in *Coming to Power*, pp. 86–94. I am grateful to Gayle Rubin for sharing with me the history of the lesbian s/m movement, in a personal interview, San Francisco, August 14, 1987. For a concise discussion of the lesbian s/m movement in San Francisco, which has been a leader in the lesbian sexual revolution, see Pat Califia, "A Personal View of the History of the Lesbian S/M Community and Movement in San Francisco," in Samois, *Coming to Power*, pp. 243–81.

24. Personal interview with Corona, age 41, San Francisco, August 17, 1987. Gayle Rubin, "The Leather Menace," *Body Politic* (April 1982), 82: 33–35.

25. For lesbian therapists as proponents of s/m see, e.g., Carol Stack, "Lesbian Sexual Problems," *Bad Attitudes* (Spring 1985), 1(4): 20–21; Nichols; River Malcolm, "Passing Through," *Thursday's Child* (San Diego), September 1979.

26. Personal interview with Karen, age 37, and LuAnna, age 35, Austin, Tex., April 1, 1988.

27. Personal interview with Karyn, age 32, Fresno, December 12, 1987. Personal interview with Dr. Sharon Young, San Diego, July 31, 1987.

28. The poignant essays of Joan Nestle, which created cultural heroes out of 1950s butches and femmes, were central to the reexamination of butch/ femme roles for the 1980s. See, for example, "Butch/Fem Relationships: Sexual Courage in the 1950s," *Heresies: The Sex Issue* (1981), 12(3): 21–24. Several of the essays are reprinted in Joan Nestle, *A Restricted Country* (Ithaca, N.Y.: Firebrand Books, 1987). Donna Allegra, "Butch on the Streets," in *Fight Back: Feminist Resistence to Male Violence* (Cleis Press, 1981), pp. 44–45. Paula Mariedaughter, "Too Butch for Straights, Too Femme for Dykes," *Lesbian Ethics,* (Spring 1986), 2(1): 96–100. Norma, "Butch/Fem Relationships Revisited," *Hartford Women's Center Newletter* (Dec. 1982), 5(12): 1-2.

29. Joan Nestle, "The Fem Question," in Carol Vance, ed., *Pleasure and Danger: Exploring Female Sexuality* (Boston: Routledge and Kegan Paul, 1984), pp. 232–41. Personal interview with Neva, age 46, Lincoln, Neb., October

12, 1988. *Random House Dictionary of the English Language* (New York: Random House, 1966).

30. Jean Lynch and Mary Ellen Reilly, "Role Relationships: Lesbian Perspectives," *Journal of Homosexuality* (Winter 1985/86), 12(2): 53–69. See also the attempt by Esther Newton and Shirley Walton to refine our understanding of concepts such as butch/femme through a more precise sexual vocabulary that distinguishes between sexual preference, erotic identity, erotic role, and erotic acts: "The Misunderstanding: Towards a More Precise Sexual Vocabulary," in Vance, pp. 242–50.

31. Personal interview with Sally, age 29, San Francisco, September 12, 1987.

32. Ellen Frye, *Look Under the Hawthorne* (Norwich, Vt.: New Victoria, 1987), p. 108. Lee Lynch, *The Swashbuckler* (Tallahassee, Fla.: Naiad Press, 1985), p. 66. Bonnie Zimmerman, in *The Safe Sea of Women: Lesbian Fiction, 1969–1989* (Boston: Beacon Press, 1990), pp. 113–14, discusses the metamorphosis if the butch figure.

33. Amber Hollibaugh and Cherrie Moraga, "What We're Rollin' Around in Bed With: Sexual Silences in Feminism," (1981; reprinted in Ann Snitow et al., eds., *Powers of Desire: The Politics of Sexuality* (New York: Monthly Review Press, 1983), pp. 396, 400.

34. Hollibaughand Moraga, p. 398.

35. Jess Wells, "The Dress," *Common Lives/ Lesbian Lives,* (Summer 1983), 8.

36. Personal interview with Phyllis Lyon, San Francisco, August 14, 1987. Karen Cameron in "Femme and Butch: A Readers' Forum," *Lesbian Ethics* (Fall 1986), 2(2): 96–99. Norma, "Butch/Fem Relationships Revisited."

37. Personal interview with Susie Bright, cited above.

38. Michael Bronski, *Culture Clash: The Making of Gay Sensibility* (Boston: South End Press, 1984), p. 214.

11. From Tower of Babel to Community

1. *New York Times,* August 18, 1984, p. 2.

2. Jean Swallow, *Leave a Light On for Me* (San Francisco: Spinters/Aunt Lute, 1986).

3. K. D. Lang quoted in Burt Kearns, "Canadian Cowpie," *Spin Magazine,* September 1988.

4. Lori Ryan, "The Razor Edge of Truth—A Conversation with Robin Tyler," *Visibilities,* November/ December 1988, pp. 8–11.

5. Personal interview with Frederika, age 37, Kansas City, Mo., October 14, 1988.

6. Personal interview with Lois, age 48, Omaha, Neb., October 11, 1988.

7. Personal interview with Nora, age 36, San Diego, July 30, 1987.

8. "Politics of accommodation"phrase in paper by Marilee Lindemann, panel: "Changing (Re)Presentations of Lesbian Sexuality in the Lesbian Novel

Since 1945," Berkshire History of Women Conference, Wellesley College, Mass., June 22, 1987. Personal interview with Sandy, age 39, Fresno, May 7, 1987.

9. Personal interview with Nicole Shapiro, founder of Bay Area Career Women, San Francisco, August 12, 1988.

10. Personal interview with Phyllis Lyon, San Francisco, August 14, 1987. List of luxuries culled from Georgia Cotrell, *Shoulders* (Ithaca, N.Y.: Firebrand Books, 1987); Ann Allen Shockley, *Say Jesus and Come to Me* (1982; reprint, Tallahassee, Fla: Naiad Press, 1987); Mary Wings, *She Came Too Late* (Freedom, Calif.: Crossing Press, 1987); Artemis Oakgrove, *The Raging Peace* (Denver: Lace Publications, 1984).

11. Personal interview with Matile, San Francisco, September 26, 1988.

12. Personal interview with Kasey, age 42, Austin, Tex., April 1, 1988.

13. Noretta Koertge, *Valley of the Amazons* (New York: St. Martin's Press, 1984), p. 58. See also Bonnie Zimmerman's discussion of this work in *The Safe Sea of Women: Lesbian Fiction, 1969–1989* (Boston: Beacon Press, 1990), p. 136.

14. Maureen Brady, *Folly* (Trumansburg, N.Y.: Crossing Press, 1982); Barbara Wilson, *Ambitious Women* (Seattle: Seal Press, 1982); Chris South, *Clenched Fists, Burning Crosses* (Trumansburg, N.Y.: Crossing Press, 1984).

15. Paula Culbreth, "A Personal Reading of *This Bridge Called My Back*," *Sinister Wisdom* (1982), 21:15–28. Barbara Epstein, "Direct Action: Lesbians Lead the Movement," *Out/Look* (Summer 1988), 1(2):27–32.

16. Ellen Herman, "Getting to Serenity: Do Addiction Programs Sap Our Political Vitality?" *Out/Look* (Summer 1988), 1(2):10–21. Personal interview with Nancy, age 38, San Diego, July 30, 1987. Peg Byron, "Say It Ain't So: Is the Lesbian Sex Revolt Dead?," *On Our Backs*, Winter 1986, pp. 10–11. Eleanor Lord, "The Heart Connection," unpublished study of 100 lesbians, Berkshire County, 1986. Panel on lesbian lifestyles, Sociology of Women in Contemporary Society class, University of Nebraska, Lincoln, October 12, 1988.

17. Jean Swallow, *Out from Under: Sober Dykes and Our Friends* (San Francisco: Spinsters Ink, 1983), introduction. A national lesbian health care survey, reported in the *Journal of the American Medical Association*, recorded far different statistics: while 25 percent of the respondents reported drinking several times a week, only 6 percent said they drank daily. *JAMA*, January 1, 1988, p. 19. Personal interview with Diane, age 41, Boston, June 18, 1987.

18. Personal interview with Stacy Raye, age 23, Berkeley, July 27, 1988. Boston meetings reported in Herman. San Francisco meetings reported in "Living Sober, 1988)," *Coming Up!* (August 1988), 9(11):11. In San Francisco the 1987 gay and lesbian Living Sober regional conference drew 4,000; the 1988 conference drew 5,000. Pride Institute discussed in *Journal of the American Medical Association* (January 1, 1988), 259(1):19.

19. Personal interview with Janet, age 36, San Francisco, August 3, 1987.

20. Personal interview with Maureen, age 36, Fresno, February 27, 1988.

21. Personal interview with Jody, age 47, San Antonio, March 27, 1988. Barbara Sang, "Some Existential Issues of Middle Aged Lesbians," unpublished paper, 1987.

22. Joy Schulenberg, "Parade Update," *Coming Up!* (August 1987), 8(11):16.

23. Regarding suspicions by lesbians of color of tokenism among "progressive" white lesbians see, e.g., Cathy Cockrell, "NOW Lesbian Conference Sparks Internal Dissent," *San Francisco Sentinel,* October 21, 1988, p. 3. Information also from personal interview (by telephone) with Camille Barber, age 34, and Loni, age 25, discussion leaders of Lesbians of Color rap group, Berkeley, August 11, 1988. In San Francisco during the late 1980s, a Native American woman, Barbara Cameron, was the co-chair for the Lesbian Agenda for Action and the vice president of the Alice B. Toklas Lesbian-Gay Democratic Club; Carmen Vasquez, a Chicana, was the coordinator of the Lesbian and Gay Health Organization and the president of the San Francisco Women's Building Board; Pat Norman, a black, was the co-chair of the Gay and Lesbian National March on Washington; Melinda Paras, a Filipina, was a coordinator of the lesbian and gay Community United Against Violence.

24. Personal interview with Abby Abinanti, age 40, San Francisco, August 12, 1987. Cf. Anu, a South Asian woman, who writes of going back to Calcutta for a visit and feeling both happy to be with Indians again and alienated because she could not talk about her lesbianism, yet she observes that the lesbian community in the States does the reverse: "denies the 'Indianess' that is so essential to who I am, but affirms the equally essential 'lesbian' in me," "Notes from an Indian Diary," *Anamika* (March 1986), 1(2):7–8. Personal interview with Mariana Romo-Carmona, age 35, New York, October 9, 1987. Gwendolyn Weindling, a black lesbian, also talks of the frustration of realizing that one's feelings and perceptions cannot be validated by the white community. She complains that whenever she got emotional, white women found it intimidating and accused her of being angry: "I've come to understand emotionalism as being taboo in white 'cultures'," "Righteous Anger in Three Parts: Racism in the Lesbian Community—One Black Lesbian Perspective," in Joan Gibbs and Sarah Bennett, eds., *Top Ranking: A Collection of Articles on Racism and Classism in the Lesbian Community* (Brooklyn: February 3rd Press, 1980), pp. 76–77.

25. June Chan, "Asian Lesbians of the East Coast," panel presentation, Berkshire Women's History Conference, Wellesley College, June 21, 1987.

26. *Phoenix Rising* (December/January 1987/88), 20:1. See also the *Asian Lesbians of the East Coast Newsletter,* which reiterates the group's conviction that Asian lesbians must achieve visibility (no. 3, Summer 1986).

27. Personal interview with Tobie, age 36, Kansas City, Mo., October 15, 1988. Private Eyes incident reported in *Womanews,* December/January 1986, pp. 9, 14; February 1987, p. 1; March 1987, p.6; June 1987, p. 8; May 1987, p. 6.

28. Valley Fat Dykes, "Miss Fat Manners' Rules of Etiquette," *Common Lives/ Lesbian Lives* (1986), 20:83. Firing and appeal to lesbian community reported in *Lesbian News* (Santa Cruz), February 1988.

29. Buffy Dunker with Jennifer Abod, "From the First Old Lesbians Conference," *Sojourner,* July 1987. Shevy Healey, Welcome address; Jeanne Adleman, "We're Here, We Won't Go Away," speech; Barbara McDonald, "A Movement of Old Lesbians," speech: West Coast Conference and Celebration by and for Old Lesbians, April 24, 1987. Personal interview with Sally Binford, age 63, San Francisco, August 6, 1987.

30. Barbara McDonald with Cynthia Rich, *Look Me in the Eye: Old Women, Aging, and Ageism* (San Francisco: Spinsters Ink, 1983); Baba Copper, *Over the Hill: Reflections on Ageism Between Women* (Freedom, Calif.: Crossing Press, 1988); also, Baba Copper, *Ageism in the Lesbian Community* (Freedom, Calif.: Crossing Press, 1987).

31. Susan R. Johnson et al., "Factors Influencing Lesbian Gynecological Care: A Preliminary Study," *American Journal of Obstetrics and Gynecology* (May 1981), 140(1):23. Examples of books on lesbian pregnancy and parenting: Cheri Pies, *Considering Parenthood: A Workbook for Lesbians* (San Francisco: Spinsters/ Aunt Lute, 1985); Susan Robinson and H. F. Pizer, *How to Have a Baby Without a Man* (New York: Simon and Schuster, 1985). Examples of films: *We Are Family* (directed by Aimee Sands); *Choosing Children* (directed by Debra Chasnoff and Kim Kavsner).

32. Custody cases discussed in Karla Dobinski, "Lesbians and the Law," in Karla Jay and Allen Young, eds., *After You're Out: Personal Experiences of Gay Men and Lesbians* (New York: Pyramid Books, 1977), pp. 156–57; film, *Sandy and Madeline's Family* (1971); Judy Gerber and Leslie Mullin, "Lesbian Mothers: Rozzie and Harriet Raise a Family," *Breakthrough* (Summer 1988), 12(1):27–32. Further information about lesbian mother battles for custody from personal interviews with Mariana Romo-Carmona, cited above; Tobie, age 36, Kansas City, Mo., October 15, 1988; Monarch, age 54, Kansas City, Mo., October 15, 1988. Lindsy Van Gelder, "Gay Gothic," *Ms.,* July/August 1987, pp. 5–12. Courts have approved joint adoptions by lesbian couples in San Francisco and Alameda Counties. Baby boom: In 1986, in San Francisco alone at least 500 babies were known to have been born to lesbian mothers through donor insemination.

33. Lesbian mothers' groups listed in *Coming Up!* (August 1987) 8(11). Play group reported in Becky Dixon, "Lesbian Parenting," *Bay Area Career Women Newsletter* (August/ September 1988), 8(4):1+. Exhortation in Cheryl Jones, "Motherliness," *Coming Up!* (August 1987), 8(11):14.

34. Julie V. Iovine, "'Lipsticks' and Lords: Yale's New Look," *Wall Street Journal,* August 4, 1987, p. 24.

35. For lesbian separatist communes still in existence in the 1980s see Joyce Cheney, ed., *Lesbian Land* (Minneapolis: Word Weavers, 1985) and *Maize: A Lesbian Country Magazine.* Many of the women who write for the

more radical lesbian periodicals such as *Common Lives/Lesbian Lives* still call
themselves separatists. Personal interview with lesbian separatists Madeline,
age 37, and Naomi, age 33, Berkeley, July 30, 1988. See also contemporary
defenses of separatism, especially Sarah Hoagland, "Lesbian Separatism: An
Empowering Reality," *Sinister Wisdom* (Spring 1988), 34:23–33. Hoagland
continued to maintain that separatism is an excellent strategy for challenging
the system of patriarchy by "rendering it nonsense," refusing to act according
to the system's rules and framework. Lesbian attachments discussed in Rima
Shore, "Sisterhood—and My Brothers," *Conditions: Eight* (Spring 1982),
3(2).

36. Advertisement, *Coming Up!* (August 1987), 8(11):8.

37. Quoted in Dennis Altman, *AIDS in the Mind of America: The Social,
Political, and Psychological Impact of a New Epidemic* (Garden City, N.Y.:
Doubleday, 1987), p. 94.

38. Ryan, p. 11.

39. Cindy Patton, *Sex and Germs: The Politics of AIDS* (Boston: South
End Press, 1985), pp. 3–4. Patton quotes at length antigay literature from
right wing hate groups that claim AIDS is God's punishment for homosexuality: passim. Those few recorded instances of lesbian transmission of AIDS
usually involve intravenous drug use coupled with sexual activity during
menstruation or traumatic enough to cause bleeding: see, e.g., Michael Marmor et al., *Annals of Internal Medicine* (December 1986), 105(6):969.

40. Videotape of the march, *Part of the USA,* October 11, 1987, Girard
Video Productions. See also Paul Horowitz, "Beyond the Gay Nation: Where
Are We Marching?," *Out/Look,* Spring 1988, pp. 7–21. Washington, D.C.,
police ultimately estimated the size of the march at 650,000: *Lesbian Connections* (July/August 1988), 11(1):4. Expectations and demands of the marchers
discussed in Lori Ryan, "For Love and for Life, We're Not Going Back,"
Visibilities (Fall 1987), 1(2):17.

41. Vicki P. McConnell, *The Burnton Widows* (Tallahasse, Fla.: Naiad Press,
1984), p. 181. See Bonnie Zimmerman's discussion of *The Burnton Widows* in
The Safe Sea of Women, pp. 160–61.

42. Personal interview with Lee Hudson, the mayor's liaison to the lesbian and gay community, New York, December 19. 1988.

43. Personal interview with Joanna, age 38, San Francisco, September 12,
1987. Sharon Ullman, "History and Current Concerns, or Making History
Bigger," Berkshire History of Women Conference, Wellesley College, Mass.,
June 21, 1987.

44. Personal interview with Cynthia, age 49, Austin, Tex., April 1, 1988.
More recently such "bisexual openness" has led some women who identified
as lesbian to opt for heterosexuality and marriage, which by 1990 is beginning
to create a sense of betrayal and anger among committed lesbians. See, e.g.,
Jan Clausen, "My Interesting Condition," *Out/Look* (Winter 1990), 7:10–24
and the controversy that followed in the Letters section, *Out/Look* (Spring

1990), 8:4–5. Lesbians have now begun to call women who switch to heterosexuality "has-be-ans."

45. See Hannah Doress, "Maggie Rubenstein: Bisexual Rights Activist," *Plexus* (Aug. 1987), 14(2):6–7. Also, space devoted to bisexual ads, etc., in *Coming Up!* (San Francisco). Mary Wings, *She Came Too Late* (Freedom, Calif.: Crossing Press, 1987), p. 39.

46. Personal interview with Kriss, age 21, San Francisco, September 11, 1987.

47. Sharon Raphael and Mina Robinson, "Love Relationships and Friendship Patterns," *Alternate Lifestyles* (May 1980), 3(2): 207– 209.

48. Personal interview with Janet, age 36, San Francisco, August 3, 1987.

49. ACT-UP demonstration reported in *Outweek,* August 8, 1990, p. 24.

50. Laura Briggs, "Birth of a Queer Nation," *Gay Community News,* August 5–11, 1990, pp. 3 +.

51. Quoted in Guy Trebay, "In Your Face," *Village Voice,* August 14, 1990, pp. 34–39.

Index

Valley of the Amazons (Koertge), 280
Vanderbilt, Gloria, 98
Vanilla sex, 253, 260
Van Vetchen, Carl, 73
Vassar, 13, 20, 30, 35, 85
Vice Versa, 171, 179
Victorian era, middle-class women in, 15
Violence, literature about, 55-56
Violent protest tactics, 194-195
Viraginity, 46-47
Vivien, Renee, 113

Wagner, Jane, 273
Walker, A'Lelia, 76
Walton, Shirley, 356*n*39
Wanderground, The (Gearhart), 239
Ward, Freda, 46, 56
Warner, Charles, 44
Waters, Ethel, 75
WAVEs, 1950s policy on homosexuals, 151
We Sing Diana (Neff), 35, 65
We Too Are Drifting (Wilhelm), 102, 178
Webb, Clifton, 175
Weir, James, 46-47
Weirauch, Anna, 102-103
Well of Loneliness, The (Hall), 34, 57, 63, 65, 83, 93, 101, 113, 173
Wellesley, 13
Westphal, Karl, 41
When God Was A Woman, 228
Wherry, Kenneth, 143, 146
White, Dan, 344*n*20
Whites, 1920s Harlem experimentation and, 67-72
Wilder, Frances, 58
Wilhelm, Gale, 102
Willard, Frances, 11, 16
Williams, Ethel, 75
Williams, William Carlos, 98
Williamson, Cris, 223, 279, 347*n*10
Wilson, Barbara, 280
Winesburg, Ohio (Anderson), 73
Winsloe, Christa, 104
Winter Bound, 65, 321*n*7
Wishing Well, 259
Witches, as spiritual-political models, 229
Witherspoon, Frances, 24
Wolden, Russell, 149, 150
Wolff, Charlotte, 31

Womanspirit, 229
Women's Army Corps (WAC), 122-124, 153
Women's colleges, 13-21, 306, 311*n*5, 313*n*14
Women's culture, 218-220, 244
Women's culture books, 219
Women-identified women community, 1970s, 215-245
Women's Land Army, 121
Women's movement: 1920s, 97 late nineteenth-century, 205 lesbian-feminists and, 212-213
Women's music, 210, 220-224, 279
Women's music festivals, 221-222, 251, 275
Women's Pentagon Action, 281
Women's presses, 1970s, 224-226
Women's Trade Union League, 23
Women With Inherited Wealth, 278
Wood, Thelma, 86-87
Woolf, Virginia, 173
Woolley, Mary, 53
Woolson, Constance Fenimore, 55
Working-class lesbians: butch/femme roles, 41-44, 126, 167-174; communities and, 79-81; Depression and, 94-97; gay bars and, 161-167; gay movement and, 200; lesbian-feminists and, 236-237; military witch-hunts and, 150; 1930s bar scene, 107; 1930s slang and, 106; passing as men, 42-45; radical movement and, 191; romantic friendship and, 37-39; sexologists and, 39-44; turn-of-the-century, 12-13, 37-39
Working-class women, heterosexual practices, 38
Working women: Depression and, 94; family structure and, 96
World War I: women's participation in, 63-64, 122; women's sexual experimentation during, 64
World War II, women's participation in, 64, 119-125

X-rated movie houses, 246

Yale University, 292
Young lesbians: butch/femme roles, 167-174; gay bars and, 161-167